USING TECHNOLOGY
IN THE CLASSROOM

FIFTH EDITION

USING TECHNOLOGY
IN THE CLASSROOM

GARY G. BITTER

Arizona State University

MELISSA E. PIERSON

University of Houston

ALLYN AND BACON

Boston ▪ London ▪ Toronto ▪ Sydney ▪ Tokyo ▪ Singapore

Series Editor: *Arnis E. Burvikovs*
Editorial Assistant: *Matthew Forster*
Marketing Manager: *Kathleen Morgan*
Production Coordinator: *Mary Beth Finch*
Editorial-Production Service: *Omegatype Typography, Inc.*
Manufacturing Buyer: *Julie McNeill*
Cover Administrator: *Linda Knowles*
Electronic Composition: *Omegatype Typography, Inc.*

Previous editions appeared under the title *Using a Microcomputer in the Classroom.*

Internet: www.ablongman.com

Between the time Website information is gathered and published, some sites may have closed. Also, the transcription of URLs can result in typographical errors. The publisher would appreciate notification where these occur so that they may be corrected in subsequent editions.

Library of Congress Cataloging-in-Publication Data

Bitter, Gary G
    Using technology in the classroom/Gary G. Bitter, Melissa E. Pierson.—5th ed.
      p. cm.
    Includes bibliographical references and index.
    ISBN 0-205-33247-1
    1. Computer-assisted instruction. 2. Microcomputers. 3. Educational technology. I.
Pierson, Melissa. II. Title.

LB1028.5 .B47   2002
371.33'4—dc21

                                           2001022377

Printed in the United States of America

10 9 8 7 6 5 4 3 2   06 05 04 03 02 01

CONTENTS

CHAPTER TWO

Basic Productivity Operations   46

CHAPTER THREE

Electronic Messaging   59

CHAPTER FOUR

Feeling at Home on the Internet   73

CHAPTER FIVE

Emerging Technologies   88

SECTION II   Planning and Designing Learning Environments   109

CHAPTER SIX

Research on Technology in Teaching and Learning   109

CHAPTER NINE

Integrating World Wide Web Resources   161

CHAPTER TEN

Designing Online Instruction   178

SECTION IV   Assessment and Evaluation   280

CHAPTER SEVENTEEN

Assessing and Evaluating   280

PREFACE

Using Technology in the Classroom was written to help classroom teachers, school personnel, and parents understand the role of technology in PreK–12 education. Based on the authors' experiences with teaching children and adults in schools at all levels, an attempt is made to explain clearly the most important information about computers and their applications in the educational environment, with technical jargon avoided as much as possible. The book may be read from cover to cover for a total perspective, or topics may be selected and returned to as needed.

This fifth edition has been completely reorganized to reflect the new International Society for Technology in Education (ISTE) National Educational Technology Standards for Teachers (NETS–T). It is especially designed for the introductory undergraduate or graduate education student who needs an overview of the role and use of technology in education. Specific education examples and applications at all levels are provided throughout the book. Readers are encouraged to keep their own teaching goals in mind as they read. Learner activities have been designed for students to further explore specific educational understanding and applications.

Section I, Technology Operations and Concepts, introduces readers to technology issues. The first chapter gives an overview of technological literacy and its effect on education. A discussion of computer applications in society as a whole is included, as is a discussion of the computer's potential contributions to the school and home. Chapter 1 concludes with a brief historical discussion of early computing devices and an overview of hardware components. Chapter 2 serves as an introduction and resource for basic operations of the most common productivity software: word processors, spreadsheets, and databases. Educational uses are discussed, and a glossary of terms is presented for each application. Electronic communication already plays a significant role in all levels of education. Chapter 3 introduces the basic concepts of electronic mail, focusing on email procedures, etiquette, and educational applications. Listservs are introduced and their relevance for education is detailed. Chapter 4 continues the discussion of online applications in education by defining the structure of the Internet. Strategies and tips are given for finding specific information through various search strategies, and security issues with regard to students' exploring the online world are presented. Chapter 5 rounds out Section I by tipping educators off to emerging trends, with a look at new technologies and what these advancements might mean for students of the future.

Section II, Planning and Designing Learning Environments, deals with the planning and designing processes of using technology in the classroom. At the outset of the planning process, it is vital that new teachers understand what research has shown regarding the use of technology in education; Chapter 6 summarizes recent findings. Chapter 7 advises the reader about the choices involved with selecting quality educational resources, including both software and websites. Criteria are presented so educators can make well-informed buying decisions, and a detailed evaluation instrument is included. Educational software is one of the first technologies that teachers new to technology attempt to use, and Chapter 8 presents an index of the unique features of each educational software type. The list includes descriptions of each category, along with tips for practical classroom integration and illustrative classroom vignettes. The resources available on the World Wide Web hold much promise for educators at all levels; Chapter 9 highlights a selection of exemplary web resources, presented according to a helpful organizing framework. Following the discussion of using web resources in Chapter 9, Chapter 10 focuses on creating original web-based instruction. Helpful considerations are suggested for planning an effective website, and specific instructions are given for creating a web page using a variety of web editing software solutions.

Section III, Teaching, Learning, and the Curriculum, discusses the various uses of technology. Chapters 11 and 12 explore strategies for technology integration in the content areas and across disciplines in multidisciplinary units. The lesson plans given as examples should be used as a springboard to develop your own lessons that meet the unique needs of your students. Chapter 13 takes a closer look at using technology to support data analysis and simulations, and Chapter 14 extends the discussion to the use of computers for mathematical modeling. Chapter 15 highlights multimedia projects and computer-based presentation techniques. Its aim is both teachers and learners, reflecting the blurring of the leadership roles in new educational philosophy. Finally, Chapter 16 aims to supply very practical procedures for keeping the technologically enhanced class organized. Specific emphasis is on using computers both in computer labs and classroom settings.

Assessment and evaluation have an expanded focus in this edition. Section IV, Assessment and Evaluation, demonstrates how technology can make the assessment process more efficient, either as the focus of assessment or as an instructional tool. In Chapter 17 ways that technology can impact alternative assessment methods as well as more traditional test-taking uses are given, as are practical tips on using productivity tools to record both quantitative and qualitative assessment, including portfolios.

The teacher's roles beyond teaching form the basis for Section V, Productivity and Professional Practice. Chapter 18 suggests ways to use basic productivity software, as well as newer specific-purpose software, to perform a myriad of daily administrative tasks, such as keeping records and producing materials. Chapter 19 on the professional educator is a new discussion for this edition. The online world brings teachers increased opportunities for communication, collaboration, and professional growth that they have not traditionally had in previously isolated classrooms.

Section VI, Social, Ethical, Legal, and Human Issues, discusses the social, ethical, legal, and human issues facing the educational field in Chapter 20. Along with all of the ways that technology makes certain tasks easier and brings people closer, come new questions of the ways its presence impacts people both in classrooms and in society at large. Teachers need to be aware of the challenges and mixed messages that students in today's classrooms will face in their information-saturated lives.

The appendix provides supplemental contact information for software manufacturers. A new companion website <http://www.ablongman.com/bitter5e> developed by Melissa E. Pierson will assist students and faculty with additional help in understanding text content, link to additional resources, provide course objectives, and offer sample test items.

We would like to express our appreciation to the persons and organizations that have contributed in some way to this publication. Specifically, we thank the preservice teachers of the University of Houston and Arizona State University for challenging us to constantly examine the ways in which technology can be included in their education. We are also grateful to John and Nancy Searle for the extensive time and photographic skill they donated to this book, and to Alexander, Brittany, Hannah, Matthew, and Zach for their modeling talents. Thanks to Russ Gilmore for his assistance with editing the appendix. Finally, a heartfelt thank you to Deborah Stirling for all of her contributions to the book.

For reviewing the fifth edition of *Using Technology in the Classroom,* we would like to thank Mac Adkins, Troy State University; Ivana Batarelo, Arizona State University; Sharon McNeely, Northeastern Illinois University; and Sylvester Robertson, California State University–San Bernardino.

We hope you will find ways to make technology a meaningful and authentic part of your teaching and your students' learning. The possibilities technology presents for bringing the world into the classroom are endless.

CHAPTER 1

GETTING STARTED WITH TECHNOLOGY

FOCUS QUESTIONS

1. How have societal trends during the Information Age been influenced by technological advances?

2. In what ways can basic technology standards and profiles be used to plan for technology integration at all levels of education?

3. What terminology is necessary for successful operation of current computer hardware components?

Technology is an agent of change, spurring our redefinition of time and space. In 1998, for the first time in 50 years, young people's television viewing time declined. Television viewing gave way to the Internet, video games, palm pilots, pagers, cell phones, and personal digital assistants (PDA). With emerging technologies rapidly become commonplace, how do we keep pace? Moore's Law provides at least one method of forecasting the future by predicting computing power advances.

In 1965, Gordon Moore was preparing a speech and made a memorable observation. When he graphed data on the growth in memory chip performance, he realized there was a striking trend. Each new chip contained roughly twice as much capacity as its predecessor, and each chip was released within 18 to 24 months of the previous chip. If this trend continued, he reasoned, computing power would rise exponentially over relatively brief periods of time. Moore's observation, now known as Moore's Law, predicted a trend that has continued and is still remarkably accurate. It is the basis for many planners' performance forecasts. In 26 years, as Moore's Law predicted, the number of transistors on a chip has increased more than 3,200 times, from 2,300 on the 4004 in 1971 to 9.5 million on the Pentium III processor. Intel's cofounder predicted transistor density on microprocessors would double every 2 years. This prediction, so far, has proven amazingly accurate. The website at <http://www.audionet.com/events/intel/idf97/0930/ra28.html> has a webcast of Moore's 1997 CEO Intel Forum speech, and the website at <http://www.intel.com/intel/museum/25anniv/hof/moore.htm> has a graph of Moore's Law and related information.

LITERACY

During the 1980s, society grappled with the issue of defining literacy. The definition of literacy as a process developed cognitively and organizationally through verbal and visual thinking was expanded to include oral literacy (listening and speaking), textual literacy (reading and writing), visual literacy (producing, creating, composing, and understanding images), and computer literacy. The capabilities that a literate person possessed and demonstrated were elevated due to the widening chasm between skilled and unskilled laborers in the workplace. An X or a personal signature once was the marker of literacy. Now the ability to read and write at a sixth-grade level is required. To read a ballot, a driver's license test, or the IRS tax forms are three experiences used to determine literacy. Reading, writing, thinking, formulating opinions, and the ability to continue one's learning are essential literacy skills needed for all Information Age workers. Illiteracy is associated with industrial accidents, prison costs, and public assistance. Nearly 50 percent of adult illiterates are under the age of 50 and are key to the rate of unemployment and poor job performance. Estimates of economic losses stemming from illiteracy range from $20 billion to $225 billion and affect the United States' ability to compete in the global marketplace.

Parallel to the expansion of oral and written literacy concepts, the notion of computer literacy now includes measures of graphic and visual literacy. Expanded definitions suggest that students should acquire basic computer skills between fourth and sixth grade. The ability to create, compose, communicate, and conduct critical analyses using the computer with other interfacing technologies is a rising expectation as people examine the nature and trends of the Information Age.

TRENDS OF THE INFORMATION AGE

The formative years of the Information Age, 1956 and 1957, were marked by the launching of *Sputnik* and the increased numbers of white-collar workers in relationship to blue-collar workers. The *Sputnik* launch marked the beginnings of satellite communications applications, other opportunities to develop global perspectives, and the space industry. The number and capability of workers are indicative of a change in the nature of the kind of commodity being produced. As we moved from the Industrial Age into the Information Age, more workers became involved in the creation, management, and transfer of information than in the manufacturing of products. An economy built on information rather than goods and services began to emerge. Knowledge (cognition) and knowing how to learn (meta cognition) increased in global importance, significance, and value.

Three significant trends with implications for education mark the Information Age: a shift in demographics, an acceleration of technology, and an ever-expanding base of available data through which to search, sift, sort, and select. It is estimated the amount of information in the world doubles every 900 days. Therefore, by the time a first-grader progresses through the traditional public educational system and is preparing for high school graduation, the information base will have quadrupled.

The shift in demographics is startling, somewhat frightening, and potentially overwhelming. The number of children in nontraditional familial structures, children with special educational, developmental, and social needs, and children engulfed in poverty continues to rise. Most of these children have never lived in a noncomputerized society.

Great portions of their leisure time are spent viewing television and playing electronic interactive adventure games within imagined, fanciful environments. The number of children raised by single parents with limited income potential due to court-established child support and only one adult fully contributing to the household account is rising. Therefore, the opportunity to have sophisticated, later-model computers and other technological peripherals and devices will be lessened. This means schools will become even more responsible for providing access to (including economic access) and the opportunity to learn and use technology. These children present new, formidable challenges to educators.

The acceleration of technology increases the pace of change. Within the Agrarian Society, the pace of change was established by the seasons; each season had specific activities, events, and purposes. The yearly calendar and the almanac were used to mark time. Time orientation moved to the present within the Industrial Age. The 40-hour workweek and time clocks were used to measure productivity and profit. In the Information Age, the orientation has become the future. Satellite communications now allow information to travel across time, space, and distance as the information float collapses.

RACING TOWARD THE BIOTECHNOLOGY AGE: THE THIRD MILLENNIUM

The third millennium is being viewed as a time to close the door on the past and begin anew. The acceleration of technology has allowed the communication and application of information, especially within the fields of science and mathematics, to be rapidly disseminated. Scientists are able to share knowledge and to build cooperative projects wherein information explodes as problems are addressed, breakthroughs are made, and problems are solved. Electronic information networks shuttle data and discoveries that have increased life expectancy, designed artificial organ implants, formulated chemicals that alter the genetic makeup of plants, and manage organ-transplant operations.

Within the Biotechnology Age, the valued resources will be mind and life. The mind as a resource of value demands that people be not only literate but also competent, critical, and creative thinkers. People must become independent, lifelong learners, constantly updating their skills, knowledge, and experiences. The ability to participate fully in a technologically rich society will require people to scan entire landscapes of information; to select that which is pertinent, meaningful, and applicable to the task and their thinking; to construct problems and simulations that test hypotheses; to analyze and integrate information; to evaluate results; and to compose and communicate their thoughts to form new knowledge.

WHAT IS OF SUCH INTRINSIC VALUE?

Knowing that information will quadruple within a student's traditional school experience has teachers asking what skills, concepts, and information students will need as participants within such a society. What knowledge is of such intrinsic value that each child from every culture must have and share it within the "global village"? What skills will teachers need? What responsibility must teachers share? What will be the role of the teacher? How will educators effect responsiveness in such an expansive, ever-changing environment?

Imagine receiving a one-way ticket to a far-off land to which you must travel. You are limited in the amount of provisions you may take with you. However, you will have communication access to the information, people, and culture you leave behind. What would you take with you into your future to use for your survival and prosperity? What would you want safely deposited for future electronic access? Many educators believe the traditional, basic three R's will no longer be the end products students possess, but will become means to create the qualities of independence, integrity, image, and invention within each student. The development of students as thinkers, problem solvers, and creators requires teachers to create projects in which students work with ideas, symbols, and abstractions. Student work will require them to do something with the information they access and acquire.

HOW IS THIS AFFECTING EDUCATION AND EDUCATORS?

The publication of *A Nation at Risk* (1983) served as a harbinger of an educational reform movement. Arguments still rage as to the depth and degree of restructuring needed to bring about the levels of educational equity and excellence desired. Much of the reform movement's impetus is being fueled by corporate, industry, and business interests. The shrinking of the U.S. middle class due to the change in demographics and family structures and the emergence of a global economy divided into "information haves" and "information have-nots" are creating a situation in which, for the United States to continue to lead, compete, or cooperate within a global marketplace, the outlook must change. We must move from an oil-powered and human-powered labor force to a brain-powered force that creates, maintains, and dominates the technology-driven industry and society. In some ways, the end of the twentieth century was reminiscent of its beginning. Today's students are also ethnically diverse and impoverished, with tenuous familial roots as were the immigrants to the United States at the turn of the twentieth century. Literacy was an issue then and is an issue now. Education was seen to be the means to achievement and success. It was also seen to be the handmaiden of industry. Today, industry and education are becoming fast allies as they realize that they are now in the same business.

The educational system is regarded as the force that, when functioning properly, promotes literacy or, when failing, allows illiteracy. Many U.S. corporations have undergone a transformation to respond to the changes in the world marketplace and have installed state-of-the art technology to make the workplace more efficient, economical, and safe. They have retooled the workplace and are presently retraining their workers. With the installation of new technology, the training of employees needs to be at a compatible level. There are very few places within the workplace now for the unskilled and the high school dropout. Many of those jobs are now exported to Third World nations in which the labor laws are few and the costs are minimal. Business has accepted the double financial burden of both retooling and retraining. However, the enormous retraining costs cannot be incurred indefinitely solely by industry. Education must share the responsibility of developing technologically literate people, not only to help people maintain a standard of living but also to help people create a balanced lifestyle.

Fear of the unknown, of trying something new, has caused some educators to avoid the computer's presence in society, let alone in the classroom. Steve Jobs, cofounder of Apple Computer, has suggested that people can be classified in two categories: b.c. or a.c.

(before computers or after computers). Since the inception of the microcomputer in 1977, two "generations" (two 12-year cycles) of students have progressed through the school system. Their experiences with computers depended on the visions and financial priorities of their teachers, administrators, and state and community leadership. In many cases, they left high school less prepared than their parents for the demands of the workplace and the decisions of the lifestyle they dream of enjoying.

Business and government interests are forming new coalitions for the purposes of raising the educational standards for determining proficiency. Professional organizations for educators have issued position statements regarding the desired availability and use of computers in the classroom. One of the most prominent groups that has developed standards for teachers and students is the International Society for Technology in Education (ISTE).

ISTE National Educational Technology Standards for Teachers (NETS–T)

The ISTE National Educational Technology Standards for Teachers (NETS–T) provide guidelines for applying information technology in educational settings. All candidates seeking initial certification or endorsements in teacher preparation programs should have opportunities to meet these standards. NETS for Teachers are organized into six broad categories with 23 performance indicators.*

Technology Operations and Concepts.   Teachers demonstrate a sound understanding of technology operations and concepts. Teachers:

1. Demonstrate introductory knowledge, skills, and understanding of concepts related to technology (as described in the ISTE National Educational Technology Standards for Students).
2. Demonstrate continual growth in technology knowledge and skills to stay abreast of current and emerging technologies.

Planning and Designing Learning Environments and Experiences.   Teachers plan and design effective learning environments and experiences supported by technology. Teachers:

1. Design developmentally appropriate learning opportunities that apply technology-enhanced instructional strategies to support the diverse needs of learners.
2. Apply current research on teaching and learning with technology when planning learning environments and experiences.
3. Identify and locate technology resources and evaluate them for accuracy and suitability.
4. Plan for the management of technology resources within the context of learning activities.
5. Plan strategies to manage student learning in a technology-enhanced environment.

*Reprinted with permission from *National Educational Technology Standards for Teachers,* copyright © 2000, ISTE (the International Society for Technology in Education), 800.336.5191 (U.S. & Canada) or 541.302.3777 (Int'l), iste@iste.org, www.iste.org. All rights reserved. Permission does not constitute an endorsement by ISTE. For more information about the NETS Project, contact Lajeane Thomas, Director, NETS Project, 318.257.3923, lthomas@latech.edu.

Teaching, Learning, and the Curriculum.   Teachers implement curriculum plans that include methods and strategies for applying technology to maximize student learning. Teachers:

1. Facilitate technology-enhanced experiences that address content standards and student technology standards.
2. Use technology to support learner-centered strategies that address the diverse needs of students.
3. Apply technology to develop students' higher-order skills and creativity.
4. Manage student learning activities in a technology-enhanced environment.

Assessment and Evaluation.   Teachers apply technology to facilitate a variety of effective assessment and evaluation strategies. Teachers:

1. Apply technology in assessing student learning of subject matter using a variety of assessment techniques.
2. Use technology resources to collect and analyze data, interpret results, and communicate findings to improve instructional practice and maximize student learning.
3. Apply multiple methods of evaluation to determine students' appropriate use of technology resources for learning, communication, and productivity.

Productivity and Professional Practice.   Teachers use technology to enhance their productivity and professional practice. Teachers:

1. Use technology resources to engage in ongoing professional development and life-long learning.
2. Continually evaluate and reflect on professional practice to make informed decisions regarding the use of technology in support of student learning.
3. Apply technology to increase productivity.
4. Use technology to communicate and collaborate with peers, parents, and the larger community in order to nurture student learning.

Social, Ethical, Legal, and Human Issues.   Teachers understand the social, ethical, legal, and human issues surrounding the use of technology in PreK–12 schools and apply that understanding in practice. Teachers:

1. Model and teach legal and ethical practice related to technology use.
2. Apply technology resources to enable and empower learners with diverse backgrounds, characteristics, and abilities.
3. Identify and use technology resources that affirm diversity.
4. Promote safe and healthy use of technology resources.
5. Facilitate equitable access to technology resources for all students.

Teacher education should emphasize these standards in technology courses, integrated technology-content methods courses, and classroom experiences. To facilitate this emphasis, the chapters in this book are organized by the ISTE categories just presented. Merchuria Chase Williams (2000, 2), vice president, NEA Georgia Affiliate, stated, "The best predictor of technology's effectiveness in the classroom is the degree to which teachers are prepared to use it." <http://www.iste.org/news/NETS_T_Release.pdf> Tom Carroll

(2000, 2), director of the U.S. Department of Education's Preparing Tomorrow's Teachers to Use Technology (PT3), said, "The power of technology for student learning doesn't come from the presence of classroom computers or the Internet. The real power of technology in education will come when teachers have been trained well and have captured the potential of technology themselves." <http://www.iste.org/news/NETS_T_Release.pdf>

NETS PROFILES OF TECHNOLOGY-LITERATE TEACHERS

A major component of the ISTE NETS–T project is the creation of performance profiles at key developmental points in teacher preparation programs to determine if candidates are meeting the standards.

Technology Performance Profiles for Teacher Preparation

Note: Numbers in parentheses listed after each performance indicator in the following profiles refer to the standards category to which the performance is linked. The categories are:

1. Technology operations and concepts
2. Planning and designing learning environments and experiences
3. Teaching, learning, and the curriculum
4. Assessment and evaluation
5. Productivity and professional practice
6. Social, ethical, legal, and human issues

GENERAL PREPARATION PERFORMANCE PROFILE

Performance Indicators. Upon completion of the general preparation component of their program, prospective teachers:

1. Demonstrate a sound understanding of the nature and operation of technology systems. (1)*
2. Demonstrate proficiency in the use of common input and output devices; solve routine hardware and software problems; and make informed choices about technology systems, resources, and services. (1)*
3. Use technology tools and information resources to increase productivity, promote creativity, and facilitate academic learning. (1, 3, 4, 5)
4. Use content-specific tools (e.g., software, simulation, environmental probes, graphing calculators, exploratory environments, web tools) to support learning and research. (1, 3, 5)*

*Adapted from the ISTE National Educational Technology Standards for Students.

5. Use technology resources to facilitate higher-order and complex thinking skills, including problem solving, critical thinking, informed decision making, knowledge construction, and creativity. (1, 3, 5)*
6. Collaborate in constructing technology-enhanced models, preparing publications, and producing other creative works using productivity tools. (1, 5)*
7. Use technology to locate, evaluate, and collect information from a variety of sources. (1, 4, 5)*
8. Use technology tools to process data and report results. (1, 3, 4, 5)*
9. Use technology in the development of strategies for solving problems in the real world. (1, 3, 5)*
10. Observe and experience the use of technology in their major field of study. (3, 5)
11. Use technology tools and resources for managing and communicating information (e.g., finances, schedules, addresses, purchases, correspondence). (1, 5)
12. Evaluate and select new information resources and technological innovations based on their appropriateness to specific tasks. (1, 3, 4, 5)*
13. Use a variety of media and formats, including telecommunications, to collaborate, publish, and interact with peers, experts, and other audiences. (1, 5)*
14. Demonstrate an understanding of the legal, ethical, cultural, and societal issues related to technology. (6)*
15. Exhibit positive attitudes toward technology uses that support lifelong learning, collaboration, personal pursuits, and productivity. (5, 6)*
16. Discuss diversity issues related to electronic media. (1, 6)
17. Discuss the health and safety issues related to technology use. (6)

PROFESSIONAL PREPARATION PERFORMANCE PROFILE

Performance Indicators.   Prior to the culminating student teaching or internship experience, prospective teachers:

1. Identify the benefits of technology to maximize student learning and facilitate higher-order thinking skills. (1, 3)
2. Differentiate between appropriate and inappropriate uses of technology for teaching and learning while using electronic resources to design and implement learning activities. (2, 3, 5, 6)
3. Identify technology resources available in schools and analyze how accessibility to those resources affects planning for instruction. (1, 2)
4. Identify, select, and use hardware and software technology resources specially designed for use by PreK–12 students to meet specific teaching and learning objectives. (1, 2)
5. Plan for the management of electronic instructional resources within a lesson design by identifying potential problems and planning for solutions. (2)
6. Identify specific technology applications and resources that maximize student learning, address learner needs, and affirm diversity. (3, 6)
7. Design and teach technology-enriched learning activities that connect content standards with student technology standards and meet the diverse needs of students. (2, 3, 4, 6)
8. Design and peer teach a lesson that meets content area standards and reflects the current best practices in teaching and learning with technology. (2, 3)
9. Plan and teach student-centered learning activities and lessons in which students apply technology tools and resources. (2, 3)
10. Research and evaluate the accuracy, relevance, appropriateness, comprehensiveness, and bias of electronic information resources to be used by students. (2, 4, 5, 6)

11. Discuss technology-based assessment and evaluation strategies. (4)
12. Examine multiple strategies for evaluating technology-based student products and the processes used to create those products. (4)
13. Examine technology tools used to collect, analyze, interpret, represent, and communicate student performance data. (1, 4)
14. Integrate technology-based assessment strategies and tools into plans for evaluating specific learning activities. (4)
15. Develop a portfolio of technology-based products from coursework, including the related assessment tools. (4, 5)
16. Identify and engage in technology-based opportunities for professional education and lifelong learning, including the use of distance education. (5)
17. Apply online and other technology resources to support problem solving and related decision making for maximizing student learning. (3, 5)
18. Participate in online professional collaborations with peers and experts. (3, 5)
19. Use technology productivity tools to complete required professional tasks. (5)
20. Identify technology-related legal and ethical issues, including copyright, privacy, and security of technology systems, data, and information. (6)
21. Examine acceptable use policies for the use of technology in schools, including strategies for addressing threats to security of technology systems, data, and information. (6)
22. Identify issues related to equitable access to technology in school, community, and home environments. (6)
23. Identify safety and health issues related to technology use in schools. (6)
24. Identify and use assistive technologies to meet the special physical needs of students. (6)

STUDENT TEACHING/INTERNSHIP PERFORMANCE PROFILE

Performance Indicators.   Upon completion of the culminating student teaching or internship experience, and at the point of initial licensure, teachers:

1. Apply troubleshooting strategies for solving routine hardware and software problems that occur in the classroom. (1)
2. Identify, evaluate, and select specific technology resources available at the school site and district level to support a coherent lesson sequence. (2, 3)
3. Design, manage, and facilitate learning experiences using technology that affirm diversity and provide equitable access to resources. (2, 6)
4. Create and implement a well-organized plan to manage available technology resources, provide equitable access for all students, and enhance learning outcomes. (2, 3)
5. Design and facilitate learning experiences that use assistive technologies to meet the special physical needs of students. (2, 3)
6. Design and teach a coherent sequence of learning activities that integrates appropriate use of technology resources to enhance student academic achievement and technology proficiency by connecting district, state, and national curriculum standards with student technology standards (as defined in the ISTE National Educational Technology Standards for Students). (2, 3)
7. Design, implement, and assess learner-centered lessons that are based on the current best practices on teaching and learning with technology and that engage, motivate, and encourage self-directed student learning. (2, 3, 4, 5)
8. Guide collaborative learning activities in which students use technology resources to solve authentic problems in the subject area(s). (3)

9. Develop and use criteria for ongoing assessment of technology-based student products and the processes used to create those products. (4)
10. Design an evaluation plan that applies multiple measures and flexible assessment strategies to determine students' technology proficiency and content area learning. (4)
11. Use multiple measures to analyze instructional practices that employ technology to improve planning, instruction, and management. (2, 3, 4)
12. Apply technology productivity tools and resources to collect, analyze, and interpret data and to report results to parents and students. (3, 4)
13. Select and apply suitable productivity tools to complete educational and professional tasks. (2, 3, 5)
14. Model safe and responsible use of technology and develop classroom procedures to implement school and district technology acceptable use policies and data security plans. (5, 6)
15. Participate in online professional collaboration with peers and experts as part of a personally designed plan, based on self-assessment, for professional growth in technology. (5)

FIRST-YEAR TEACHING PERFORMANCE PROFILE

Performance Indicators.   Upon completion of the first year of teaching, teachers:

1. Assess the availability of technology resources at the school site, plan activities that integrate available resources, and develop a method for obtaining the additional necessary software and hardware to support the specific learning needs of students in the classroom. (1, 2, 4)
2. Make appropriate choices about technology systems, resources, and services that are aligned with district and state standards. (1, 2)
3. Arrange equitable access to appropriate technology resources that enable students to engage successfully in learning activities across subject/content areas and grade levels. (2, 3, 6)
4. Engage in ongoing planning of lesson sequences that effectively integrate technology resources and are consistent with current best practices for integrating the learning of subject matter and student technology standards (as defined in the ISTE National Educational Technology Standards for Students). (2, 3)
5. Plan and implement technology-based learning activities that promote student engagement in analysis, synthesis, interpretation, and creation of original products. (2, 3)
6. Plan for, implement, and evaluate the management of student use of technology resources as part of classroom operations and in specialized instructional situations. (1, 2, 3, 4)
7. Implement a variety of instructional technology strategies and grouping strategies (e.g., whole group, collaborative, individualized, and learner centered) that include appropriate embedded assessment for meeting the diverse needs of learners. (3, 4)
8. Facilitate student access to school and community resources that provide technological and discipline-specific expertise. (3)
9. Teach students methods and strategies to assess the validity and reliability information gathered through technological means. (2, 4)
10. Recognize students' talents in the use of technology and provide them with opportunities to share their expertise with their teachers, peers, and others. (2, 3, 5)
11. Guide students in applying self- and peer-assessment tools to critique student-created technology products and the process used to create those products. (4)

12. Facilitate students' use of technology that addresses their social needs and cultural identity and promotes their interaction with the global community. (3, 6)
13. Use results from assessment measures (e.g., learner profiles, computer-based testing, electronic portfolios) to improve instructional planning, management, and implementation of learning strategies. (2, 4)
14. Use technology tools to collect, analyze, interpret, represent, and communicate data (student performance and other information) for the purposes of instructional planning and school improvement. (4)
15. Use technology resources to facilitate communications with parents or guardians of students. (5)
16. Identify capabilities and limitations of current and emerging technology resources and assess the potential of these systems and services to address personal, lifelong learning, and workplace needs. (1, 4, 5)
17. Participate in technology-based collaboration as part of continual and comprehensive professional growth to stay abreast of new and emerging technology resources that support enhanced learning for PreK–12 students. (5)
18. Demonstrate and advocate for legal and ethical behaviors among students, colleagues, and community members regarding the use of technology and information. (5, 6)
19. Enforce classroom procedures that guide students' safe and healthy use of technology and that comply with legal and professional responsibilities for students needing assistive technologies. (6)
20. Advocate for equal access to technology for all students in their schools, communities, and homes. (6)
21. Implement procedures consistent with district and school policies that protect the privacy and security of student data and information. (6)

The National Educational Technology Standards (NETS) Project also has been developing technology performance standards for PreK–12 students, establishing specific applications of technology through the curriculum, providing standards for support of technology in schools and addressing student assessment and evaluation of technology used to improve learning (Bitter et al., 1997; Thomas & Bitter, 2000).

The following are recommended standards and profiles for students in grades PreK–12.*

ISTE National Educational Technology Standards for Students (NETS–S)

The technology standards for students are divided into six broad categories. Standards within each category are to be introduced, reinforced, and mastered by students. These categories provide a framework for linking performance indicators found within the Profiles for Technology-Literate Students to the standards. Teachers can use these standards and profiles as guidelines for planning technology-based activities in which students achieve success in learning, communication, and life skills.

TECHNOLOGY STANDARDS FOR STUDENTS

1. Basic operations and concepts
   - Students demonstrate a sound understanding of the nature and operation of technology systems.
   - Students are proficient in the use of technology.
2. Social, ethical, and human issues
   - Students understand the ethical, cultural, and societal issues related to technology.
   - Students practice responsible use of technology systems, information, and software.
   - Students develop positive attitudes toward technology uses that support lifelong learning, collaboration, personal pursuits, and productivity.
3. Technology productivity tools
   - Students use technology tools to enhance learning, increase productivity, and promote creativity.
   - Students use productivity tools to collaborate in constructing technology-enhanced models, preparing publications, and producing other creative works.
4. Technology communications tools
   - Students use telecommunications to collaborate, publish, and interact with peers, experts, and other audiences.
   - Students use a variety of media and formats to communicate information and ideas effectively to multiple audiences.
5. Technology research tools
   - Students use technology to locate, evaluate, and collect information from a variety of sources.
   - Students use technology tools to process data and report results.
   - Students evaluate and select new information resources and technological innovations based on the appropriateness to specific tasks.
6. Technology problem-solving and decision-making tools
   - Students use technology resources for solving problems and making informed decisions.
   - Students employ technology in the development of strategies for solving problems in the real world.

NETS PROFILES OF TECHNOLOGY-LITERATE PREK–12 STUDENTS

A major component of the NETS standards project for students grades PreK–12 is the creation of general profiles of technology-literate students at key developmental points in their precollege education. These profiles provide rather broad descriptions of technology competencies that students should have developed by the time that they exit the target grades.

These profiles reflect the underlying assumption that all students should have the opportunity to develop technology skills that support learning, personal productivity, ethical behaviors, decision making, and daily life. They prepare students to be lifelong learners and make informed decisions about the role of technology in their lives.

These profiles are indicators of achievement at certain points in PreK–12 education. Technology skills are to be developed by coordinated activities that support learning throughout a child's education. They must be introduced, reinforced, and finally mastered and integrated into an individual's personal learning and social framework.

The profiles reflect the following basic principles and assumptions:

1. Students acquire steadily increasing skills and knowledge related to the use of technology for enhancing personal and collaborative abilities.
2. Students acquire steadily increasing ability to make quality decisions related to managing their own learning.
3. Students acquire steadily increasing skills to work in collaboration with others, with hardware and software and information resources, and to some problems with the support technology tools.
4. Students become responsible citizens and users of technology and information.
5. Students have access to current technology resources, including telecommunications and multimedia enhancements.
6. Students acquire skills that prepare them to learn new software and hardware technology to adapt to the complex technology environments that emerge in their lifetime.

Profiles for Technology-Literate Students

> *Note:* Numbers in parentheses listed after each performance indicator in the following profiles refer to the standards category to which the performance is linked. The categories are:
>
> 1. Basic operations and concepts
> 2. Social, ethical, and human issues
> 3. Technology productivity tools
> 4. Technology communication tools
> 5. Technology research tools
> 6. Technology problem-solving and decision-making tools

GRADES PREK–2

Performance Indicators.   All students should have opportunities to demonstrate the following performances. Prior to completion of Grade 2, students will:

1. Use input devices (e.g., mouse, keyboard, remote control) and output devices (e.g., monitor, printer) to successfully operate computers, VCRs, audiotapes, and other technologies. (1)

2. Use a variety of media and technology resources for directed and independent learning activities. (1, 3)
3. Communicate about technology using developmentally appropriate and accurate terminology. (1)
4. Use developmentally appropriate multimedia resources (e.g., interactive books, educational software, elementary multimedia encyclopedias) to support learning. (1)
5. Work cooperatively and collaboratively with peers, family members, and others when using technology in the classroom. (2)
6. Demonstrate positive social and ethical behaviors when using technology. (2)
7. Practice responsible use of technology systems and software. (2)
8. Create developmentally appropriate multimedia products with support from teachers, family members, or student partners. (3)
9. Use technology resources (e.g., puzzles, logical thinking programs, writing tools, digital cameras, drawing tools) for problem solving, communication, and illustration of thoughts, ideas, and stories. (3, 4, 5, 6)
10. Gather information and communicate with others using telecommunications, with support from teachers, family members, or student partners. (4)

GRADES 3–5

Performance Indicators.   All students should have opportunities to demonstrate the following performances. Prior to completion of Grade 5, students will:

1. Use keyboards and other common input and output devices (including adaptive devices when necessary) efficiently and effectively. (1)
2. Discuss common uses of technology in daily life and the advantages and disadvantages those uses provide. (1, 2)
3. Discuss basic issues related to responsible use of technology and information and describe personal consequences of inappropriate use. (2)
4. Use general-purpose productivity tools and peripherals to support personal productivity, remediate skill deficits, and facilitate learning throughout the curriculum. (3)
5. Use technology tools (e.g., multimedia authoring, presentation, web tools, digital cameras, scanners) for individual and collaborative writing, communication, and publishing activities to create knowledge products for audiences inside and outside the classroom. (3, 4)
6. Use telecommunications efficiently and effectively to access remote information, communicate with others in support of direct and independent learning, and pursue personal interests. (4)
7. Use telecommunications and online resources (e.g., email, online discussions, web environments) to participate in collaborative problem-solving activities for the purpose of developing solutions or products for audiences inside and outside the classroom. (4, 5)
8. Use technology resources (e.g., calculators, data collection probes, videos, educational software) for problem-solving, self-directed learning, and extended learning activities. (5, 6)
9. Determine when technology is useful and select the appropriate tool(s) and technology resources to address a variety of tasks and problems. (5, 6)
10. Evaluate the accuracy, relevance, appropriateness, comprehensiveness, and bias of electronic information sources. (6)

GRADES 6–8

Performance Indicators.   All students should have opportunities to demonstrate the following performances. Prior to completion of Grade 8, students will:

1. Apply strategies for identifying and solving routine hardware and software problems that occur during everyday use. (1)
2. Demonstrate knowledge of current changes in information technologies and the effect those changes have on the workplace and society. (2)
3. Exhibit legal and ethical behaviors when using information and technology, and discuss consequences of misuse. (2)
4. Use content-specific tools, software, and simulations (e.g., environmental probes, graphing calculators, exploratory environments, web tools) to support learning and research. (3, 5)
5. Apply productivity/multimedia tools and peripherals to support personal productivity, group collaboration, and learning throughout the curriculum. (3, 6)
6. Design, develop, publish, and present products (e.g., web pages, videotapes) using technology resources that demonstrate and communicate curriculum concepts to audiences inside and outside the classroom. (4, 5, 6)
7. Collaborate with peers, experts, and others using telecommunications and collaborative tools to investigate curriculum-related problems, issues, and information, and to develop solutions or products for audiences inside and outside the classroom. (4, 5)
8. Select and use appropriate tools and technology resources to accomplish a variety of tasks and solve problems. (5, 6)
9. Demonstrate an understanding of concepts underlying hardware, software, and connectivity, and of practical applications to learning and problem solving. (1, 6)
10. Research and evaluate the accuracy, relevance, appropriateness, comprehensiveness, and bias of electronic information sources concerning real-world problems. (2, 5, 6)

GRADES 9–12

Performance Indicators.   All students should have opportunities to demonstrate the following performances. Prior to completion of Grade 12, students will:

1. Identify capabilities and limitations of contemporary and emerging technology resources and assess the potential of these systems and services to address personal, lifelong learning, and workplace needs. (2)
2. Make informed choices among technology systems, resources, and services. (1, 2)
3. Analyze advantages and disadvantages of widespread use and reliance on technology in the workplace and in society as a whole. (2)
4. Demonstrate and advocate for legal and ethical behaviors among peers, family, and community regarding the use of technology and information. (2)
5. Use technology tools and resources for managing and communicating personal/ professional information (e.g., finances, schedules, addresses, purchases, correspondence). (3, 4)
6. Evaluate technology-based options, including distance and distributed education, for lifelong learning. (5)
7. Routinely and efficiently use online information resources to meet needs for collaboration, research, publications, communications, and productivity. (4, 5, 6)

8. Select and apply technology tools for research, information analysis, problem solving, and decision making in content learning. (4, 5)
9. Investigate and apply expert systems, intelligent agents, and simulations in real-world situations. (3, 5, 6)
10. Collaborate with peers, experts, and others to contribute to a content-related knowledge base by using technology to compile, synthesize, produce, and disseminate information, models, and other creative works. (4, 5, 6)

This NETS project is ongoing and will continue to be updated as technology continues to change, which causes basic skills to change. The ISTE NETS project represents this movement as well as an articulated clear vision through its development of the following standards:

- NETS for Students (1998) describes what students should know about technology and be able to do with technology.
- NETS for Students—Connecting Curriculum and Technology (2000) describes how technology can be used throughout the curriculum for teaching, learning, and instruction management using the student standards with subject matter standards.
- NETS for Teachers (2000) describes what teacher candidates should know about technology and be able to do with technology.
- NETS for Teachers—Preparing Teachers to Use Technology (2001) describes how technology can be used throughout teacher education programs.
- Educational Technology Support Standards (2002) describes systems, access, staff development and support services essential to support the effective use of technology.
- Standards for Student Assessment and Evaluation of Technology (2002) describes various means of assessing student progress and evaluating the use of technology in learning and teaching.

Now is the time for schools to be retooled and educators retrained. For some time, education may face the same double financial burden that business has been shouldering: tools and training. Financial constraints have spurred educational systems to set priorities and develop strategies that encourage the acquisition of new technological skills and information. Some school systems are finding that some of the ideas of the 1960s and 1970s, such as open-space classrooms, peer tutoring, modular scheduling, and individualized instruction, are now more likely to succeed because instructional strategies such as cooperative learning and state-of-the-art technology can meet the logistical, managerial, and instructional needs of large numbers of students, sources, and faculty. Outside funding, business partnerships, and foundation grants are being promoted as sound investments in the development of a cooperative, interdependent system of human enterprise based on Francis Bacon's premise: Knowledge is power.

COMPUTER USAGE IN SOCIETY

In today's business world, computers have become standard equipment. The most familiar application of computers in business is data processing. Businesses are faced with an extensive number of accounting and bookkeeping procedures that must be performed routinely, quickly, and accurately. The computer's ability to perform mathematical calculations with lightning speed and virtual infallibility accounts for its immediate and widespread acceptance in the world of business.

Computers control the ability to expedite and reduce the plethora of paperwork necessary to keep a business running. Computers perform inventory, record keeping, billing, payroll, and a seemingly infinite number of other functions. Word processing technology has changed the nature of secretarial work and freed many secretaries to perform other tasks, which has resulted in many positions being upgraded to administrative assistantships.

Another attractive feature of computers is that they can be programmed to make accurate predictions that help managers make sound decisions. The computer can consider a wide variety of contingencies and predict what conditions will arise in the event of such contingencies. Such predictions may save businesses vast amounts of money by anticipating adverse conditions and, in many cases, can increase businesses' profits by forecasting favorable conditions.

Not only is the computer an invaluable tool in the business office, but it is also a vital part of industry. The use of robotic technology in manufacturing is one example. Robots perform work that is boring, repetitious, difficult, or dangerous for human workers to do; indeed, they can function around the clock without tiring or requiring breaks.

Another application of robots is quality control. First, a robot is programmed with information about a product of acceptable quality. Then it can perform routine tests to determine if the items being manufactured meet acceptable standards. The robot is capable of checking minute details that may not be visible to the human eye.

The use of nanotechnology is another example. Nanotechnology is manufacturing at the molecular level using programmed nanoscopic robot arms. A nanometer is one billionth of a meter (three to four atoms wide). This technological advance impacts miniaturization processes as well as the quality of manufactured products. In the future, nanotechnology will scale up current successes to molecular computers.

Computers are used widely in the field of engineering. Computer-aided design (CAD) refers to the use of computers in designing and testing new products. The computer can speculate about various design ideas to determine which will work and which will not. It can simulate conditions for testing new products to determine their feasibility. In the past, design and research was an expensive and time-consuming process because engineers relied on actual physical models of designs to perform such tests. CAD helps eliminate costly mistakes in research and development.

The business world is not the only place where computers are found. Computer technology makes work faster and more efficient on the farm, where computers help farmers evaluate climatic conditions, control inventory, feed and care for livestock, and keep up with many accounting and bookkeeping procedures. Although computers may seem out of place among chickens and silos, they are helping to make agriculture more productive and cost-effective. The use of biotechnology in agriculture to produce useful products is one example. Since the mid-1990s genetically engineered crops have been available. Biotechnology manipulates living organisms at the molecular genetic level. Developments in food biotechnology will help address world hunger. In addition, the application of biotechnology in medicine creates more effective drugs and vaccines.

Another facet of society in which computers have become an integral part is the arts. In music, for example, electronic and digital sound synthesizers are producing a popular sound often referred to as "New Age." Computers are being used in music composition, and they are also useful in designing and choreographing marching band performances.

An exciting development of computers in the arts has resulted from increasingly sophisticated computer graphics technology. Stunning visual displays can be created by computers with graphics capabilities. Animation created by human artists is time-consuming and astronomically expensive, but computers can create equally striking effects in a fraction of the time required for an artist to produce similar effects. Computers with graphics capabilities allow textile artists and weavers to design fabrics and then interface their looms with computers to execute their computer-created designs.

Computers expedite the complicated process of filmmaking in other ways as well. They are useful in film editing, calculating the number of frames of film per scene, and controlling property inventory. The applications of computers to the entertainment industry are numerous and many are applicable to multimedia and hypermedia concepts.

Among the largest users of computers are federal, state, and local governments. Governmental agencies collect vast amounts of data that must be processed and stored in various ways. Consider, for example, the amount of data generated by a national census. Computers expedite the process of handling these data so that they can be used for research and allocation of funds and grants that improve the quality of the lives of many citizens.

The annual task of assessing and collecting taxes is one more job that has been simplified by the use of computers. Computers record vast amounts of information submitted by taxpayers and employers, calculate and verify tax returns, and generate refund checks.

Governments also use computers for processes such as license renewal and vote tabulations. Using computers to tabulate election results has made for much faster and more accurate reports of election results. Computers are used to predict election results even while votes are still being cast and tabulated.

Yet, perhaps the fastest growing area of computer application in our society is occurring in our own homes. Declining costs of owning and operating personal computer systems have put computer power in the hands of the average person. A popular use of personal computers is computer games, which are fun, challenging, entertaining, and often educational. They provide an enjoyable and nonthreatening means of interacting with the computer system. Advances in computer graphics constantly heighten the appeal of these games.

Personal computer users perform accounting and record-keeping functions on their systems, much as large corporations do. Personal computers can also monitor checking accounts, maintain household inventory, generate budgets, store important records, and perform many other tasks that keep a household running smoothly.

Another application of the home computer is education. Educational software enables parents to participate in, enrich, reinforce, and supplement the education of their children. The computer is a versatile tutor; it can help to teach reading skills to a small child or sophisticated, graduate-level university courses to a well-educated adult. It can be a useful tool in learning many subjects included in conventional academic curricula.

For example, in mathematics, students can use numerical and symbolic computation and scientific visualization. In the Mathematica program, students begin with interactive calculations, quickly create publication-quality two- and three-dimensional graphics, apply hundreds of built-in functions to problems, and use them as building blocks to extend the system and develop Mathematica programs. Mathematica notebooks are ideal for documenting work and creating technical reports and presentations that mix text, active formulas, and graphics. Mathematica notebooks are transferable among more than 20 different platforms (see Figures 1.1, 1.2, and 1.3).

FIGURE 1.1   Modeling in mathematics using Mathematica.

FIGURE 1.2   Mathematica showing a crystal structure of a high-temperature superconductor.

FIGURE 1.3   Mathematica lets users display data or functions in specialized formats, such as bar charts, pie charts, or log–log plots.

Personal computers keep their users aware and informed in an information-rich society. The personal computer user can gain access to nationwide databases that provide the latest information about current news, issues, sports updates, and leisure interests. Many online services provide newspapers, stock reports, weather information, shopping and ravel services, reference encyclopedias, and movie and TV reviews. Message boards and electronic mail are also available.

A BRIEF HISTORY OF COMPUTERS

A logical first step in becoming computer literate is to appreciate the origins of computers. Computers are the result of a long history of mathematical explorations and innovations. They have their earliest roots in primitive systems of counting that relied on fingers and toes or stones to objects.

Eventually, these primitive systems gave way to mechanical devices aimed at making complex calculations quickly and accurately. One of the earliest of such devices was Babbage's Analytic Engine. Charles Babbage was a nineteenth-century mathematician who designed the Difference Engine. He saw a need for such a device because, in an era of increasing use of mathematics, people were making large numbers of errors in building logarithm tables. Babbage sought to eliminate the repetitive and time-consuming creation of these tables.

The Difference Engine was the first result of his efforts. It was a combination of rods, gears, and ratchets that jammed constantly and made the Difference Engine impractical to use. Undaunted, Babbage set to work on a more ambitious project: the Analytic Engine. A forerunner of the computer, Babbage's device had an input section that read data from holes punched in cards. It also had provisions for printing results. More importantly, Babbage provided a "control" unit for operating the computer, a "mill" unit for performing calculations, and a "store" unit for holding up to 1,000 fifty-digit numbers.

The Analytic Engine was, in many ways, analogous to computers of today in that it could store, execute, and change instructions. The machine was doomed to failure. The state of technology in Babbage's day was such that the 50,000 parts necessary to manufacture a single Analytic Engine could not be produced to build it (see Figure 1.4).

Fortunately for us, Babbage had an excellent assistant in his efforts. Ada Augusta Byron worked closely with Babbage in his research. Formally titled Lady Lovelace, Ada Augusta Byron was the only daughter of the poet Lord Byron (George Gordon) and his wife Annabelle. Following in her mother's footsteps, Byron was an accomplished mathematician.

(a)

(b)

(c)

FIGURE 1.4   (a) Pascal's mechanical calculator. (b) Charles Babbage's Difference Engine. (c) Scheutz's Printing Calculating Machine.

Upon meeting Babbage, Byron took an immediate interest in his work. For many years, Byron kept meticulous records of Babbage's work so that we are able to retrace his efforts today. Personal correspondence between the two indicates that Byron was much more than a passive observer of Babbage's work. In fact, she sometimes suggested alternative hypotheses and methods to Babbage as well as encouraging him to persevere when his efforts seemed to be fruitless.

In recognition of her contributions to the development of computer technology, Byron was honored by having a computer programming language, ADA, named for her.

Although designed in 1847, Babbage's Engine No. 2 was not built until 1891. His calculator delivers more precise answers because it can extend an answer to 31 digits. Modern-day calculators are faster due to their electronic design. Babbage's calculator is operated by turning a crank or handle. To get an answer carried out to 31 digits, the operator must turn the handle 27,000 times!

The next influential invention was the census machine of Herman Hollerith. In the late nineteenth century, census taking had become a major task; tabulation of such a vast amount of data was slow and problematical. In an effort to find a faster way to compile raw statistical data, the Census Bureau sponsored a contest. Herman Hollerith's device was chosen as the most effective and practical.

Hollerith had designed a device that read data from punched cards and kept track of the count. The keypunch system of data processing was popular for many years, although recently it has succumbed to faster and less cumbersome methods (see Figure 1.5). Hollerith was so successful, in fact, that he left the Census Bureau in 1896 to form International Business Machines Corporation (IBM), a recognized leader in the field of data-processing technology even today.

Then, in 1939, the first digital-computing device was constructed by John V. Atanasoff. As the cost of producing electronic components decreased, a group of Harvard scientists

(a)   (b)

FIGURE 1.5   (a) Mechanical keypunch machine. (b) Card tabulating machine.

headed by Howard Aiken and working in conjunction with IBM developed the Mark I. This computer is considered to be the forerunner of the first generation of computers.

The First Generation of Computers

Developed in 1944, the Mark I was primarily electromechanical; that is, it was made up of mechanical switches that opened and closed by electrical current. It was 51 feet long, 8 feet high, and contained 1 million components and over 500 miles of electric wire. It was capable of adding three 8-digit numbers per second. The Mark I was noisy, slow, and cumbersome compared to computers in use today.

At approximately the same time, Grace Hopper and others were beginning to develop the computer languages that were necessary to program these new electronic computers.

Hopper was responsible for the development of the first compiler in 1952. Five years later, in 1957, Hopper designed the first English-language compiler, which was a major breakthrough in the human–computer interface. She is also considered to be the "grandmother" of the programming language COBOL (Common Business Oriented Language).

The next major development in computer technology culminated in the Electronic Numerical Integrator and Computer (ENIAC). Designed by John W. Mauchly and J. Prespert Eckert, Jr., ENIAC was intended to be used by the military. It was programmed by means of switches and connections. ENIAC was more than 1,000 times faster than the Mark I, performing 5,000 calculations per second. Weighing 60,000 pounds and containing nearly 2,000 vacuum tubes, ENIAC required tremendous amounts of electricity and gave off large amounts of heat (see Figure 1.6).

The most significant feature of ENIAC was that it introduced vacuum-tube technology, and no longer were calculations and operations performed by moving mechanical parts. This gesture allowed for greatly increased speed of performance.

The next computer was developed by Mauchly, Eckert, and others and was called the Electronic Discrete Variable Automatic Computer (EDVAC). It was smaller and more powerful than its predecessors. It also had two other important features: It used the binary numbering system and it could store internally instructions in numeric form. Today, all data and programs are stored in binary form. This method of storing instructions inside the computer is far more efficient than paper-tape storage used with earlier devices.

(a)   (b)

FIGURE 1.6   (a) The Electronic Numerical Integrator and Computer (ENIAC), designed by John W. Mauchly and J. Prespert Eckert, Jr. (b) The ENIAC contained nearly 2,000 vacuum tubes.

Another member of the first generation of computers was the Electronic Delayed Storage Automatic Computer (EDSAC) built at Cambridge University in England. This computer introduced the concept of stored programs. Before this, computers often had to be used for specific applications. Their memories were incapable of storing more than one program at a time. EDSAC helped eliminate time-consuming and costly rewiring procedures.

At this point, computers were built primarily for scientific applications. In 1946, however, Mauchly and Eckert formed a corporation to build computers for commercial use; in 1951, the UNIVAC (Universal Automatic Computer) was the first electronic computer used by large business firms. This launched the major growth of computers into the business field.

As computer technology expanded from military and scientific applications into the world of business, it became necessary to develop a programming language particularly suited to business applications. Thus, the COBOL language was developed by Jean Sammet and others in 1959. Working with her colleagues at IBM, Sammet also participated in the development of another language, FORMAC (Formula Manipulation Compiler), which was the first programming language used on a practical basis to solve mathematical problems.

The first generation of computers, which thrived from 1951 until 1959, is characterized by vacuum-tube technology. Although they were amazing devices in their time, they were large, were expensive to operate, and required almost constant maintenance to function properly. The next generation of computers attempted to resolve some of these problems.

The Second Generation of Computers

The second generation of computers extended from 1959 until 1964 and was characterized by transistor technology. The transistor was developed in 1947 by John Bardeen at Bell Laboratories in New Jersey. Bardeen studied substances that permitted a limited flow of electricity through semiconductors. Transistors that used semiconductor material could perform the work of vacuum tubes and took up much less space.

Because transistors were smaller, the distance between operating parts was reduced and speed of performance was increased significantly. Transistors were also much cooler than vacuum tubes, reducing the need for expensive air conditioning in areas where computers were housed (see Figure 1.7).

Transistors did present several problems, though. They were relatively expensive because each transistor and its related parts had to be inserted individually into holes in a plastic board. Also, wires had to be fastened by floating boards in a pool of molten solder. The number of parts required for even the simplest transistors was staggering. Even though

FIGURE 1.7   Electronic panel containing transistors. Invention of the transistor made possible a decrease in the size and an increase in the power of computers.

the distance between individual parts was reduced, it was still great enough to limit the speed of computer operations. The next generation of computers helped to alleviate some of these problems.

The Third Generation of Computers

The development of integrated circuits in 1963 spawned the third generation of computers, lasting from 1964 until 1975. Integrated circuits developed from a need to mass produce in a few simple production steps.

The production process begins when tubes of silicon are sliced into wafer-thin disks that are chemically pure and cannot hold electrical charge. Then a preconceived design is etched onto the surface of the wafer with the use of light rays. Once the entire surface of the wafer has been processed, the wafer is placed in an acid bath to eliminate all unexposed areas. To enable the wafer to carry an electrical impulse, slight traces of impurities must be added in a specified pattern. Finally, a fine diamond saw slices through the wafer and divides it into dozens of blocks, like postage stamps in a large sheet. Each tiny piece is now a chip. After discarding unusable chips, the manufacturer encases the wafer and connects it to the outside of the case with gold wires. This is the integrated circuit—a sandwich of carefully treated silicon that now forms the transistor, a device that acts as an electrical switch (see Figure 1.8).

The integrated circuit continued the trend toward miniaturization that has resulted in the popularity of the microcomputer and the personal computer system. Because the chips are tiny, the pathways through which electrical current must pass are short. Therefore, the number of calculations that can be performed each second is increased tremendously. Also the chip is manufactured in such a way that its performance is virtually guaranteed for a practically unlimited life span.

Integrated-circuit technology spawned a generation of computers that had greater storage capacity and tremendously increased speeds of performance. Also during this period, many accessory devices were developed and marketed, such as magnetic-tape drives and disk drives. Popular programming languages were developed and refined, many of which are still in use today. Time-sharing was introduced as a way of maximizing the efficiency of systems that performed calculations at incredible speeds.

Third-generation computers were not aimed at specific applications such as business or scientific use. Rather, they were designed as general-purpose computers. They represented a giant leap forward in the data-processing field. Not only were speed and reliability enhanced, but power consumption was decreased markedly. Computers became smaller and less expensive, putting computer power into the hands of a greater number of users than ever before. Computer technology began to accelerate.

The Fourth Generation of Computers

Engineers were not satisfied with the degree of miniaturization that resulted from the integrated circuit. Also, the integrated circuits of the third generation were designed primarily with chips having only one function. For example, a chip might perform calculations or amplify weak currents in a television or radio. As engineers learned how to manufacture chips more easily, they conceived the idea of grouping an assortment of functions on a

(a)

(b)   (c)

**FIGURE 1.8   (a) One step in the manufacture of integrated circuits. (b) The
integrated circuit led to smaller computers. (c) Magnified view of an
integrated circuit.**

single chip, creating a microelectronic "system" capable of performing various tasks required for a single job. This technology became known as large-scale integration (LSI).
Thus, the fourth generation of computers was born in the mid-1970s.

LSI has many applications other than large-scale computers. One such application is
the pocket calculator so common today. This calculator has a single "block" that contains
6,000 transistors capable of adding, subtracting, dividing, and multiplying. Another device
made possible by LSI technology is the digital watch. It contains 2,000 transistors on a
single chip. Today's video games also rely on LSI technology.

Still another innovation of LSI technology is the computer-on-a-chip. Its manufacturers compress nearly all the subsystems of a computer into 1/20 square inch. Over 15,000
transistors combine to form a brain that stores, processes, and retrieves data with a capacity
that rivals room-sized computers of a decade earlier.

LSI technology is responsible for the popularity of the microcomputer. These "little
giants" fit easily on a desktop and put computer power in the hands of an increased number
of people (see Figures 1.9, 1.10 and 1.11). Declining prices of powerful computer systems
have encouraged development of the electronics field in general. LSI turned computer
technology into big business (see Table 1.1).

FIGURE 1.9   Original Apple I.

FIGURE 1.10   Apple I board.

FIGURE 1.11   Steve Jobs's garage, where the original Apple computer was produced.

Another benefit of LSI technology is the production of computers that are easier to maintain and upgrade. The early computers required almost constant attention by highly trained computer technicians. Microcomputers, on the other hand, are relatively easy to own and maintain. This is one reason why so many people, adults and children alike, are exploring the many advantages of computers without needing to have a thorough knowledge of electronics.

TABLE 1.1   Decreasing Cost of Computer Operations

GENERATIONS	TECHNOLOGY	COST PER 100,000 COMPUTATIONS
First	Vacuum tubes	$1.25
Second	Transistors	0.25
Third	Integrated circuits	0.10
Fourth	LSI	Less than 0.01

Computer technology continues to advance at a tremendous rate. Today, we are living with fourth-generation computers, but already new developments are surfacing that give us some idea of what future generations of computers will be like (see Figure 1.12).

Future Generations of Computers

A hint of tomorrow's computer capability can be found in very large-scale integrated (VLSI) circuitry, a concept that was essentially a refinement of LSI technology. VLSI circuitry further increased the speed at which computers were able to function.

Multiprocessing, the simultaneous running of several programs by one computer, is being developed further in fifth-generation computers. Multiprocessing makes computerized data processing even more cost-effective.

Today, the microcomputer has become an important interactive tool for teaching and learning. Multimedia peripherals, CD-ROM (compact disc read-only memory), CD-RW (compact disc rewritable), and DVD (digital versatile disc) can be interfaced with the microcomputer and the World Wide Web, which greatly expanded its utilization. Microcomputers with their multimedia capabilities are continually being integrated into the classroom curriculum. Using microcomputers and the World Wide Web, educators are creating new learning environments. Within these environments, teachers become facilitators and students become constructors of knowledge. Together, teachers and students become *knowledge navigators,* a term coined by John Sculley, past CEO of Apple Computers.

Certainly, the trend of miniaturization witnessed throughout the past several generations of computers will also continue in the next generations, concentrating greater amounts of computer capacity in ever smaller spaces (Moore's Law). Not only are computers becoming smaller, but their prices are lower. Advanced manufacturing technology will lead to much more affordable computer systems within the near future. An excellent source of information for classroom ideas and hardware information is located on Intel's website <http://www.intel.com/education/index.htm>.

Analog and Digital Computers

Computers fall into two categories, depending on the system by which they operate, *analog* and *digital. Analog computers* represent numbers internally by measuring quantities and then converting electrical energy into impulses that run mechanical devices. They

FIGURE 1.12   Supercomputer Cray X-MP/48.

perform work that is tiring, boring, or dangerous for human workers. Examples of instruments with analog readouts include a mercury thermometer, older-style radios with dials, televisions, a conventional typewriter, spring-wound wristwatches, and an odometer.

In contrast, *digital computers* convert information in the form of numbers, letters, and special characters into digital form. The digital system is binary; that is, it depends on the system of numeration that includes only 0 and 1. Information is converted into electrical impulses during which a switch is either off (0) or on (1). The digital computer accepts input, converts input into electrical impulses, processes and manipulates data and information, and produces output.

Whether analog or digital, computers depend entirely on the humans who design, build, program, operate, and maintain them. Used properly, the computer is a tool that can help humans accomplish the work necessary to participate in an increasingly complex society.

Analog-to-Digital Conversion.   Modern science labs in industry, research, and universities now use computers for the collection of scientific data. At the heart of scientific applications of computer power are hardware components that allow analog measurements (such as temperature, pressure, and movement) to be converted to the digital form (or signal) understood by computers. Most microprocessors deal with 8-bit or 16-bit binary numbers, called bytes, most ranging from 0 to 255. Therefore, the analog-to-digital converter accepts physical measurements (input), which are processed by a transducer and support circuits; a computer program collects the measurements and they are converted to digital form. The computer displays the results of the calculations based on the measurements.

Researchers have developed hardware and software of this particular type, but it is not useful for all applications. Other special interfaces have been designed and are available.

Almost daily, newspapers and news broadcasts report new advances in computer technology. It is vital that people become technologically literate with computers and their capabilities because computers are becoming standard appliances in homes, and play an integral part in businesses and industrial occupations. Used widely, computers can and do enhance the quality of our lives.

THE LANGUAGE OF COMPUTERS

There are a number of terms that are basic to an understanding of computer operations. One term is *software.* Software, also called computer programs, refers to the commands that instruct the computer to perform tasks in a specific logical sequence. People who write these instructions are called *computer programmers.*

There are two types of software. *Systems software* instructs the computer to carry out its basic operations. *Language interpreters,* which allow a person to program in various computer languages, are examples of systems software. The second type, *applications software,* instructs the computer to carry out specific tasks, such as writing payroll checks.

Software may originate from one of several sources. Large computer installations usually hire computer programmers on a full-time basis to write software to meet the installation's particular needs. Smaller computer users may purchase prepackaged programs from commercial software developers. Many personal computer users learn computer languages that enable them to write software for use on their own systems, allowing them to tailor software to their own individual needs.

In contrast to software, *computer hardware* is the physical machinery that makes up the computer system. Hardware is the equipment that you see when you visit a computer room or computer retail store. Computer hardware is sophisticated electronic equipment that must be handled and used appropriately and safely, and maintained properly in order for the computer system to operate with optimal efficiency.

The heart of the computer system is the *central processing unit (CPU)*. The CPU controls all the computer's functions because it is made up of circuitry that interprets and carries out instructions written into software. The CPU also retrieves software instructions before decoding and executing them. The components of the CPU are the *arithmetic/logic unit (ALU),* the *memory,* and the *control unit* (see Figures 1.13 and 1.14).

The ALU is that part of the CPU capable of performing mathematical calculations required for many data-processing applications. The ALU performs these calculations with greater speed and accuracy than humans do. Imagine, for example, how the mathematical capabilities of the computer's ALU have revolutionized the work of the Internal Revenue Service in calculating tax returns.

FIGURE 1.13   **The central processing unit (CPU).**

(a)   (b)

FIGURE 1.14   **(a) Sharp Ultralite Notebook PC. (b) Compaq's PC Companion.**

The memory of the CPU is made up of integrated circuitry in which information can be stored. Software instructions are retained in memory that is directly accessible to the CPU.

When the computer requires these instructions for operations, the CPU retrieves them from memory, decodes them, and then carries them out.

The control unit of the CPU controls the flow of the computer's operations, including data transfer, acceptance of input, functioning of the ALU, and other related functions. The control unit is a vital part of the operation of the computer system.

PRIMARY COMPONENTS OF A MICROCOMPUTER

Microcomputers are big business primarily because they put computer power in the hands of individual users. They are being used to automate households; maintain household budgets and accounts; provide hours of challenging entertainment, and supplement and enrich learning; edit textual material; and expedite the business procedures of owners of large and small businesses. The list of microcomputer applications seems limitless, indeed.

What is this powerful "little giant" that is making daily life simpler and more enjoyable? The microcomputer is made up of several hardware devices that function similarly to very large computer systems (see Figure 1.15).

The Microphone/Keyboard/CPU

The brain of the microcomputer system resides in the CPU. Through microphones and keyboards, instructions and data are entered into the computer system. Advances in speech technology have made hands-free control of systems, applications software, and web

FIGURE 1.15   Primary components of a microcomputer system.

searching possible. The microcomputer keyboard is similar to a standard typewriter keyboard. It is made up of keys that represent letters of the alphabet and numbers, as well as special symbols such as @, $, %, and *. In addition to these familiar characters, the microcomputer keyboard usually includes special-function keys that instruct the computer to perform specific tasks. The microcomputer keyboard is simple and comfortable to use (see Figures 1.16 and 1.17). Wireless technologies now provide untethered keyboard communication with other computers, printers, notebooks, and peripherals.

In some microcomputer systems, the keyboard is included in the same housing as the CPU. As in larger systems, the CPU is made up of the control unit, the ALU, and memory. The size of a microcomputer system's memory is vital to the speed and efficiency with

FIGURE 1.16   Wireless keyboard.

FIGURE 1.17   LCD touchscreen monitor when a keyboard is not practical.

which the system will operate. Some of the most impressive advances in microcomputers during the last several years have been substantial increases in memory and, thus, in speed.

Microcomputer Memory

The advent of the microcomputer era began with silicon chip technology. The technical properties of silicon chips will be discussed later, but it is important to note here that the silicon chip has brought about the miniaturization of electronic equipment. Consequently, a greater amount of memory capacity can be included in the CPU than was previously possible. This has significantly increased the power of microcomputer systems.

The typical microcomputer system includes *boards* onto which chips with memory capability have been fastened. At the time of purchase, a microcomputer will possess a certain amount of memory capacity; this amount can be increased according to the user's needs by inserting additional components. Memory components have become more affordable to the average microcomputer owner. Adding memory to a microcomputer is a simple process that most users can perform themselves (see Figure 1.18).

To determine the memory size of a microcomputer system, it is necessary to understand several quantitative terms that apply to computer capability. A digital computer operates using a binary system of 0's and 1's. A *bi*nary digi*t* is called a *bit* and is the smallest unit of digital information. A *byte* is the number of bits necessary to store one character of text. A byte is usually 8 or 16 bits. These bits represent combinations of 0's and 1's, according to the binary system.

Computer memory capacity is generally measured in *kilobytes, megabytes,* and *gigabytes.* In the binary system, a kilo refers to 1,024, or 2 raised to the tenth power. The amount of memory capacity required to store 1,024 bytes of information is referred to as 1K.

Microcomputers have *hard* or *fixed* disk memory, which enables them to store far greater amounts of data. Memory is usually measured in *megabytes* and *gigabytes.* A megabyte is approximately 1 million bytes of information. One gigabyte is equal to 1,024 megabytes.

A major advantage of microcomputer systems is that extra memory space can be added simply and quickly as the needs of the user expand. Extra memory space allows the system to operate with greater speed and efficiency. More complex programs with lengthier instructions can be stored and run on a system to which extra memory space has been added.

There are two major types of semiconductor memory: *random-access memory (RAM)* and *read-only memory (ROM).* RAM is designed to store new data and programs. Data and program instructions are entered into the memory of the central processing unit and then accessed, or retrieved from memory, in random fashion. RAM is not permanent memory. For

FIGURE 1.18   Motherboard of an IBM personal computer. Computer chips inserted on board contain RAM (random-access memory) and ROM (read-only memory).

example, if the computer system loses power during operation, the information stored in RAM is lost forever. This requires that the lost information be reloaded into memory.

To maintain program instructions and data in the assigned RAM locations, the system must "refresh" its memory. The system does this by supplying small amounts of electricity to memory locations at the rapid speed of several hundreds or even thousands of times per second. There are two variations of RAM: *Static RAM (SRAM)* and *Dynamic RAM (DRAM)*. SRAM maintains its data while power to the memory chips is on. No periodic rewriting of data is needed. SRAM is faster, but more expensive than DRAM. SRAM is used for cache memory. Dynamic RAM (DRAM), to maintain data, must rewrite program instructions. DRAM is used for system memory because it is small and inexpensive.

In contrast to RAM, ROM (read-only memory) is comprised of computer chips that have had program instructions manufactured into them permanently. Information stored on ROM chips cannot be lost in the event of a power failure. ROM chips contain programs that are used repeatedly for various applications; programs that control the video terminal and programs that control the mechanical operations of devices such as disk drives are two examples of programs stored on ROM chips.

ROM can be built into computers at the time they are manufactured, or it can be purchased in modules to be inserted into special receptacles built into a computer. Some ROM chips contain programs that make the task of programming easier or more enjoyable. For instance, some ROM chips include a shape table, much like a dictionary, that holds a set of shapes already done so that the programmer can reuse these shapes numerous times without having to recreate them for each use. The primary difference between RAM and ROM is that RAM is programmed by the user and ROM is programmed by the manufacturer. There is one variation of ROM, however, that cuts across the distinctions between RAM and ROM. This variation is *erasable programmable memory (EPROM)* or *programmable read-only memory (PROM)*. EPROM chips come with program instructions stored on the chips by the manufacturer. If the purchaser wishes to alter these program instructions, it is possible to erase them and then store new instructions on the chips.

Memory Storage Devices

Another essential part of computer hardware is the memory storage device. Storage devices retain data and instructions outside of the computer's central processing unit so that information is not lost when the computer is turned off. This allows the data and instructions stored to be used repeatedly or kept for future reference. Several popular storage devices are available for use with microcomputer systems.

The most popular storage device in use for computers in general is the *magnetic disk drive*. The disk drive reads and records information stored on *magnetic disks*. These *hard disks* look like small CDs and are stored inside the computer (see Figure 1.19). Each disk has two recording surfaces: top and bottom. On the recording surfaces are concentric circles moving outward from the center of the disk to its edge. Inside the disk drive are mounted several *read/write heads* that record and retrieve information on magnetic disks.

Information stored on magnetic disks is relatively safe from loss. Loss of stored material may result from writing too much information onto a disk. Disks may also be erased by a computer-controlled device called a *bulk eraser*. Accidental loss of information stored on magnetic disks is unusual, though, and this factor adds to the popularity of magnetic disk storage.

(a)   **(b)**

FIGURE 1.19   (a) Hard disk. (b) 5¼-inch diskette with disk drive.

The *floppy disk* functions similarly to the hard disk. Floppy disks (or diskettes) come in a variety of sizes. Early microcomputers used flexible (hence "floppy") disks that were 5¼ inches in diameter. One or both surfaces were used for recording. Floppy disks today have a diameter of 3½ inches and are enclosed within a hard plastic container. The storage capacity of floppy disks increased tremendously in recent years, and capacities continue to grow. Floppy disks can now hold over one hundred times the information once stored on a 5¼-inch disk. Many other types of memory devices exist with even greater storage capacities. They include CD-ROMs with rewrite capabilities, DVD-ROMs, various types of data cards, and the use of network capabilities (see Figures 1.20 to 1.24).

As we have already seen, ROM chips are another way of retaining program instructions externally to the microcomputer system. The instructions on ROM chips are manufactured into the chips and are, therefore, permanently stored there. Hence, ROM chips are generally safe from loss of information.

Magnetic tapes are a common method of storage in large computer systems, but advances in CD and DVD technology have made CD and DVD storage safe, very cheap, and easy to use. Backup storage for computer systems and networks is migrating from magnetic tape to CDs and DVDs. Magnetic tape, CDs, and DVDs provide inexpensive and convenient means for storing great quantities of data.

Scanners are another method of entering information into the computer. *Text scanners* can "read" textual information printed on a page from any source. *Image scanners* "read" black-and-white and color images. These scanners convert the analog information to digital information. Some scanners also convert text to speech.

A scanner may be configured as a flatbed, operating similar to a copy machine in which the user lifts the lid and places the material to be scanned flat on the bed of the scanner. Scanners may also be sheet-fed, hand-held, or attached to a printer (see Figure 1.25).

Still other methods of inputting information are *optical character readers (OCRs), optical mark readers (OMRs),* and bar-code readers. For example, OCRs "read" the characters on the bottom of personal checks as well as all mail sent to a post office. Some uses of OMRs are to score objective tests where the answers have been blacked in, to control the inventory of library books, and to monitor classroom attendance.

FIGURE 1.20   Portable CD-ROM drive with built-in speakers.

FIGURE 1.21   52X CD-ROM drive.

FIGURE 1.23   CD-rewritable recorder.

FIGURE 1.22   (left) 100-disk CD changer. (right) 50-disk CD changer.

FIGURE 1.24   DVD-ROM drive.

Display Devices

For the computer to work efficiently with the humans who use it, it must include some means of communicating. Display devices enable humans to see what instructions are being given to the computer; to respond to erroneous information; to enter data and verify

FIGURE 1.25   Page scanner.

data for correctness; and to see the output, or final product, of the computer's operation. Several hardware devices for display are available.

Microcomputer systems rely on a variety of *video screens* for display purposes. Many computers can be adapted for use with ordinary television screens, the most common video screen in our society. Video games that plug into the family television set are popular examples. As computer graphics technology advances, the visual displays on video screens are becoming more sophisticated (see Figures 1.26 and 1.27).

Other terms for video screens are *monitors* or *cathode-ray tubes (CRTs)*. CRTs rely on the same cathode-ray tube technology that television is based on, but are designed strictly for use with computers. Images are generated on the screen when a series of points

FIGURE 1.26   SVGA monitors.

FIGURE 1.27   Flat panel multimedia monitor.

are lighted to create a pattern of images. Simple CRTs display characters in green or white on a black background; more complex monitors can generate characters in a range of colors. With improvements in flat panel technology and lower-cost versions, liquid-crystal displays (LCDs) will continue to replace CRTs. LCDs are often used to project for presentations and classroom lessons (see Figure 1.28).

The next generation of displays for television and computers is HDTV (high-definition television). This display provides much clearer displays. The advent of HDTV will mean the demise of one of the last vacuum tubes—the television picture tube.

Printing Devices

Once the computer has completed its data-processing function, it is necessary to generate some human-readable, permanent copy of the resulting output. A record of computer transactions printed onto paper is referred to as hard copy. Hard copies are often necessary for filing purposes or for reporting the results of data processing to many departments within an organization.

The printer usually cannot be used as an input device; it functions as an output device. Data are read from the computer, processed according to instructions, and the results written out by the printer. Printers operate within a wide range of speeds from very slow to extremely fast, from 10 characters per second to many thousands of characters per second.

Several factors determine the rate at which a printer operates. The type of printer is one factor. Some printers print material one character at a time, a relatively slow method of printing. A faster method is to set up a line of text at a time and then print the entire line. Another enhancement is to print in two directions, from left to right and then from right to left. This saves the time spent in returning to the left margin of the page to print each subsequent line.

One method of printing is *thermal printing,* which generates characters on heat-sensitive paper. These printers have the advantage of functioning very quietly, whereas other printers may cause a distracting level of noise in their immediate vicinity. However, thermal printing usually does not produce high-quality copies and requires the purchase of special paper.

(a)   **(b)**

FIGURE 1.28   (a) LCD projector. (b) LCD panel.

A second method of printing is *impact printing*. In impact printing, characters are formed when the printing element, the part that includes the pattern or mold for characters, strikes or contacts the paper. This process is quite similar to the process of a typewriter key striking a ribbon against a sheet of typing paper to produce the image of a character.

A common type of impact printer is the *dot-matrix printer*. The writing head of the dot-matrix printer is made up of wires that represent each letter, number, or symbol. Because each character is printed by a combination of separate wires, the resulting copy generally has a dotty appearance that may be unacceptable when high-quality copies are required. Dot-matrix printers that print a high density of dots per inch produce the best-quality copies.

Inexpensive dot-matrix printers with near-letter-quality printing have helped to blur the distinctions between dot-matrix and letter-quality printers. These near-letter-quality or correspondence-quality printers have become a common choice for schools, homes, and businesses because they serve a dual role: letter quality and graphics printing. Pictures, graphs, maps, charts, and various typefaces can be printed out on paper, as can professionally typed documents.

Special graphics plotters are also available; they allow the user to print detailed drawings and blueprints on paper. Some models include color capabilities to make the output even more attractive (see Figure 1.29).

The printing of web pages sparked the growth of two types of color printers, the inkjet and laser. Inkjet printers electrostatically spray small ink droplets from a nozzle onto the paper. Although inkjet printers are the least expensive to buy, they are the most expensive to run. Replacement ink cartridges and the need to use special paper to achieve photo quality results account for the expense.

The other method of color printing is *laser printing*. Based on laser technology, this method employs some design concepts that have been used in photocopying machines. Laser printing is much quieter than impact printing. A laser printer has much more flexible and sophisticated printing capabilities than a matrix printer. Laser printers are capable of printing copy of nearly *typeset* quality. The initial purchase of a laser printer is more expensive than the matrix and inkjet printer. However, the durability of the laser copy and the avoidance of smudging and fading problems give laser printers the advantage over inkjet printers (see Figure 1.30).

FIGURE 1.29   Color printer.

FIGURE 1.30   Laser printer.

An emerging color printing technology is High Fidelity or Hi-Fi. Although still expensive, Hi-Fi color technology provides an alternative to traditional four-color offset printing methods. By increasing the number of standard colors from four (cyan, magenta, yellow, and black) to six, seven, or even eight colors, the accuracy of reproducing screen images increases.

USING YOUR MICROCOMPUTER

Now that you have a moderate vocabulary of computer terminology and can recognize the function of various kinds of computer hardware, you are probably eager to try working with the microcomputer. Microcomputers have an amazing amount of capability and using the technology correctly will help to unleash its potential power.

The microcomputer is user-oriented. It is said to be "user-friendly"; that is, using a microcomputer does not require an extensive background in computer science or an orientation toward electronics. Many owners of microcomputers begin slowly and find themselves learning more with continued use and experimentation.

There is, of course, a significant difference between *operating* a microcomputer and *programming* one. Operating the computer refers to the process of controlling the functions of the system, selecting software, and manipulating the equipment to cause it to perform given tasks. Programming, on the other hand, refers to the process of writing instructions that tell the computer how to perform its operations. Programming requires a more extensive knowledge of the computer and of computer languages than does merely operating the computer.

Often microcomputer users begin by learning to operate their systems using prepackaged software. Software publishing is a fast-growing industry with newer and better software available all the time. This software can perform many types of applications so that the microcomputer user need not know how to program the computer in order to use it.

Educational programs are available for use in homes and schools. More educational institutions are installing microcomputers in their classrooms for a number of reasons. Not only does the computer execute programs that cover topics that teachers may not be familiar with, but it can also present those topics in interesting and colorful ways. In addition, the computer is a patient teacher, offering feedback, reinforcement, repetition, flexibility, and remediation whenever appropriate.

Educational software is available to teach mathematics, science, reading, foreign languages, and practically any other subject typically covered in traditional curricula. Whether students use such programs at home or in the classroom, they are learning several important lessons simultaneously. Not only are students tutored and challenged in academic subject areas, but they are also given an opportunity to become familiar and comfortable with microcomputer systems. This is important for children who will live in an increasingly computerized world.

Along with educational software, programs that help the microcomputer user manage personal business are also popular. Some programs are written to keep track of household accounts and budgets. Others help the user to determine whether a hypothetical purchase is a wise investment. Still others store records of financial transactions for future reference and help the homeowner with physical tasks such as turning lights on or off, setting clocks accurately, and monitoring locked doors for security.

Software is available that maintains household inventories, computes income taxes, and analyzes the stock exchange. Many microcomputer users find that computerizing their personal business makes such chores easier and faster to accomplish, and the results more accurate.

Perhaps the single most popular type of prepackaged software is software that entertains the user. These programs usually involve games of strategy, skill, or chance and are very popular. Some computer games can be played either with other people or with the computer itself as competitor. The computer keeps track of the score as well as recording each player's moves.

Many computer games can be adjusted for players at different ability levels and may be enjoyed by players of all ages. Games that include graphics are visually exciting to play. Computer games are currently the fastest selling type of prepackaged software on the personal computer market.

The variety and availability of prepackaged software for use on microcomputer systems makes operating a personal computer simple and enjoyable for the novice. Of course, the new microcomputer owner should follow instruction manuals and materials carefully in setting up the system properly. Most microcomputer retailers are happy to assist the novice in setting up and learning to operate a microcomputer system. Many personal computer owners find that once they have become familiar with the operations of their systems, they want to learn more about computers and about programming languages so that they can write software suitable for their own needs.

PROGRAMMING YOUR MICROCOMPUTER

A novice computer programmer can begin to learn by using programs published in computer-oriented periodicals or available on the World Wide Web (WWW). While keying in the program instructions (or code, as it is called by programmers), the user can begin to learn about the structure of computer programs. Programs may be written (i.e., web pages using hypertext markup language [HTML] code) specifically for use on a system other than the one the user owns.

In the beginning, adapting such programs may be largely a trial-and-error endeavor. As in all new experiences, though, the user can learn as much from failures as from successes. The range of possibilities of writing and adapting microcomputer software is limited only by the user's imagination. Writing and altering programs also has the advantage of making the user's involvement with the microcomputer system more active and creative so that eventually the user becomes more computer literate.

Some microcomputer users will wish to study programming languages in a more structured way. A number of books are available on the subject of computer programming. As personal computers become more popular, numerous courses are being offered by universities, community colleges, and technical schools. Any of these will provide an adequate background to the user who wishes to program. Many communities now have clubs and organizations of personal computer hobbyists in which the novice can interact with others having similar experiences and problems with their computers.

Microcomputer users who learn to write their own software will need to purchase hardware devices for storing and printing program instructions (see Figure 1.31).

FIGURE 1.31   On-screen interaction to object-oriented computing.

Besides needing to store the programs they write, microcomputer users will also want to generate hard copies of their software for their own use and so that they may share their software with other personal computer users. To do this, they must purchase a printing device. Computer retailers are trained to assess the user's needs and to recommend appropriate hardware.

THE PERSONAL COMPUTER AND THE WWW

The fastest-growing use of personal computers in homes and schools is as a communication tool. Homes and schools are connecting at a very rapid pace to the Internet (see Figures 1.32 and 1.33). With the advent of Internet connectivity, access and web accessibility become important concerns for educators and learners with disabilities. Assistive technologies make it possible for learners with disabilities to use computers and web-based technologies. Electronic mail and the World Wide Web (WWW) provide many opportunities in education. Later chapters will detail these concerns, technologies, and applications.

FIGURE 1.32   Modem PC card.

FIGURE 1.33   Intranet media server.

SUMMARY

Because computers are pervasive in our society, there is a great need for people, young and old, to become computer literate. Computer awareness refers to the ability to recognize computers and work comfortably with them. Computer literacy, often referred to as technology literacy, refers to a fundamental understanding of computer operations and terms, applications of computers in society, and uses and limitations of technology. Educational technology standards and profiles are essential for all students. Technology literacy is a given in our society.

One reasonable place to begin with computer and technology literacy is to gain an understanding of the history of the machines themselves. Although many primitive mathematical devices contributed to the development of computer technology, the first generation of computers was considered to have begun with the introduction of vacuum-tube technology. The second generation of computers incorporated transistor technology in an attempt to resolve some of the problems presented by vacuum tubes. The third generation of computers was based on integrated-circuit technology, which was enhanced in the large-scale integrated (LSI) circuits of the fourth generation of computers.

We can speculate about the future generations of computers based on the trends that are currently emerging. Very large-scale integration (VLSI) technology has continued the trend toward miniaturization, making computer systems smaller, more powerful, and more affordable. As this occurs, computers will gain even more popularity. The logical consequence of this trend will be an increased need for computer literacy for people of all ages and occupations.

Computers are a vital part of our society today. The personal computer industry with the advent of electronic mail and the WWW is booming, indicating that a great number of people are discovering the benefits of computing and technology. This will require that technology users acquire a greater degree of technological literacy.

Software refers to the written instructions that tell a computer how to operate. Hardware refers to the electronic equipment that carries out the software instructions. The central processing unit, the brains of the computer system, is made up of the arithmetic/logic unit, the control unit, and memory. Other hardware devices include storage devices such as magnetic disk drives and display devices such as the video screen, input devices such as keyboards, and output devices such as thermal printers, inkjet printers, and laser printers.

Microcomputers are said to be user-oriented because their operation does not require an extensive knowledge of computers. They are designed to be used by the average person. Many personal computer users choose to learn more about computers and about programming languages. This enables them to tailor software to their own individual needs and to become more actively involved with their computer systems.

LEARNER ACTIVITIES

1. Interview a local businessperson and write a report about how his or her company uses computers.

2. List at least five major advantages of using computers in business, in school, and in the home.

3. Determine the technology teacher foundations required in your state. How do they compare to the ISTE requirements?

4. Research the contributions of women (other than those discussed in this chapter) to the development of computers.

5. Design a sequence of lessons for one ISTE Technology Foundation standard for students.

6. Develop a portfolio assessment plan for one of the Technology-Literate student profiles.

7. Select one of the performance indicators and provide student activities to determine a student's understanding of the content listed.

8. Outline the need for computer literacy education in the public schools. At what age should students be introduced to computers?

9. Design a lesson plan that introduces one major application of computers in our society.

10. Research and prepare a report on how extensively computers are used in your local school district for administrative functions and curriculum enhancement.

11. Research and prepare a report on the extent to which the International Society for Technology in Education (ISTE) National Educational Technology Standards for Teachers have been implemented in college and university teacher preparation programs.

12. Research and prepare a report on how computers are used in the musical and/or visual arts. In what ways are computers being used in the composition of music? How are computers used in teaching piano keyboarding skills? How are textile artists and weavers using computers to design their handwoven pieces?

13. Visit a retail store that sells primarily electronic equipment. Observe and prepare a report on how the use of the computer-on-a-chip has influenced the size and capability of electronic "gadgets."

14. Outline a plan for implementing the NETS PreK–12 student profiles into education in the United States. Include factors of cost, availability, and education implications.

15. Visit a local computer retail store and prepare a list of computer hardware currently on the market.

16. Write a brief report on the different devices used with computers. Discuss how these devices could enhance the use of the computer in the curriculum.

17. Research current developments in computer memory technology. Identify major trends.

18. Write a brief report that discusses the similarities and differences of various printers. Include in your report a discussion of the variety of applications for each type of printer.

19. Design a lesson plan to demonstrate the flow of information into and out of the computer: INPUT—PROCESSING—OUTPUT.

20. Prepare a report including a time line of the evolution of the computer.

21. List the most common analog devices.

22. Prepare a set of transparencies to present a brief lesson on the components of a computer.

23. Describe the difference between the Dvorak and Qwerty keyboards.

24. Prepare a list of common input and output methods for computers.

BIBLIOGRAPHY

Bitter, G. G. (1991). Vision: Technologically enriched school of tomorrow (TEST) communicator. *Journal of the California Association for the Gifted, 21*(1), 20–21.

Bitter, G. G. (1992). *Macmillan encyclopedia of computers.* New York: Macmillan.

Bitter, G. G., Thomas, L., Knezek, D. G., Friske, J., Taylor, H., Wiebe, J., & Kelly, M. G. (1997). National educational technology standards: Developing new learning environments for today's 1998 classrooms. *Bulletin of the National Association of Secondary Principals, 81*(592), 52–58.

Brady, M. L. (1991). Keeping current with technology. *Mathematics Teacher, 84,* 92–96.

Brush, T., & Bitter, G. G. (2000). An innovative approach to high-tech learning. *Learning and Leading with Technology, 28*(1), 22–30.

Bush, G. (1991). *America 2000—source book.* Washington, DC: U.S. Department of Education.

Carter, C. N., Childress, N. A., Mullican, S. L., & Sheubrooks, L. D. (1996). Computers in the classroom of the future. *TECHNOS, 5*(2), 28–32.

CEO Forum on Education and Technology. (2000, June). *The power of digital learning: Integrating digital content.* Washington, DC: Author.

Chung, J. (1991). Collaborative learning systems: The design of instructional environments for the emerging new school. *Educational Technology, 31*(12), 15–22.

Clements, D. H. (1991). Enhancement of creativity in computer environments. *American Educational Research Journal, 28,* 173–187.

Collins, A. (1991). The role of technology in restructuring schools. *Phi Delta Kappan, 73,* 28–36.

Collins, A., Hawkins, J., & Frederickson, J. R. (1991). *Three different views of students: The role of technology in assessing student performance.* New York: Center for Children and Technology, Bank Street College of Education.

David, J. L. (1991). Restructuring and technology: Partners in change. *Phi Delta Kappan, 73,* 37–40.

Flagg, B. N. (1990). *Formative evaluation for educational technologies.* Hillsdale, NJ: Lawrence Erlbaum.

Frand, J. L. (2000). The information age mindset: Changes in students and implications for higher education. *Educause Review, 35*(5), 15–24.

Fuller, H. L. (2000). First teach their teachers: Technology support and computer use in academic subjects. *Journal of Research on Computing in Education, 32*(4), 511–537.

Fulton, K. (1997). *Learning in a digital age: Insights into the issues.* Santa Monica, CA: Milken Exchange on Educational Technology.

Integrating technology into teaching. (1997, November). Alexandria, VA. *Educational Leadership, 55*(3), Association for Supervision and Curriculum Development.

International Society for Technology in Education. (1998, June). *National educational technology standards for students.* Eugene, OR: Author.

International Society for Technology in Education. (2000, June). *National educational technology standards for teachers.* Eugene, OR: Author.

ISTE develops technology standards for teacher preparation: New ISTE standards guide university programs in preparing new teachers for technology-rich teaching and learning. (2000, June). Eugene, OR: International Society for Technology in Education. Retrieved from the World Wide Web: <http://www.iste.org/news/NETS_T_Release.pdf>

Johnson, D. L., & Maddux, C. D. (Eds.). (1997). *Using technology in the classroom.* New York: The Haworth Press.

Kinnaman, D. E. (1990). What's the research telling us? *Classroom Computer Learning, 10*(6), 31–39.

McCarthy, R. (1990). The hardware dilemma. *Electronic Learning, 9*(5), 20–24.

A nation at risk: The imperative for educational reform. (1983, April). The National Commission on Excellence in Education. U.S. Department of Education.

Papert, S. (1980). *Mindstorms: Children, computers, and powerful ideas.* New York: Basic Books.

Software and Information Industry Association. (2000). *2000 report on the effectiveness of technology in schools: Executive summary.* Washington, DC: Author.

Solomon, C. (1986). *Computer environments for children.* Cambridge, MA: The MIT Press.

Sutton, R. E. (1991). Equity and computers in the schools: A decade of research. *Review of Educational Research, 61*(4), 475–503.

Taylor, R. (1980). *The computer in the school: Tutor, tool, tutee.* New York: Teachers College Press.

Thomas, L., & Bitter, G. G. (2000). (Eds.). *National Educational Technology Standards for Students: Connecting curriculum and technology.* Eugene, OR: International Society for Technology in Education.

Tomas Rivera Center. (1986). *The new information technology and the education of Hispanics.* Claremont, CA: Author.

U.S. Congress, Office of Technology Assessment. (1988). *Power on! New tools for teaching and learning,* OTA-SET-379. Washington, DC: U.S. Government Printing Office.

Vockell, E. L. (1990). Instruction principles behind computer use. *The Computing Teacher, 18*(1), 10–15.

WEBSITES

Intel Corporation <http://www.intel.com>

International Society for Technology in Education <http://www.iste.org>

National Educational Technology Standards for Teachers and Students <http://cnets.iste.org>

NCATE Technology Report <http://www.ncate.org>

Technology Based Learning and Research <http://tblr.ed.asu.edu>

CHAPTER 2

BASIC PRODUCTIVITY OPERATIONS

FOCUS QUESTIONS

1. What are the commonalities and differences among word processors, spreadsheets, and databases?
2. How can productivity software be used by teachers and students?
3. What are basic productivity tool operations?

Productivity software is readily available on new computers and relatively easy to learn for new computer users. Fortunately, these tools are also some of the most versatile ways to put computers to work making your personal and professional life more efficient. The authors believe that learning disconnected software procedures out of context is not the most effective way to become a technologically proficient teacher. Students will remember what they learn longer if they learn it for a real purpose. This chapter, therefore, is not intended as a step-by-step tutorial. For such detailed direction, students are encouraged to consult the Help features of the specific software they are using or other software procedure manuals. Instead, this chapter serves as an overview of possibilities of the most common productivity applications: word processing, spreadsheet, and database applications. Students are advised to scan this information briefly and then return to it periodically as a reference as the occasion for learning new procedures arises.

COMMON PRODUCTIVITY FEATURES

Most productivity software is now available as an integrated suite of software from one publisher, designed to function together to provide the user the most effective options and compatibility. All of the tools in the suite share some features in common so that the user can move easily among the suite components. The following terms describe functions common to most productivity software tools. These commands are generally available from pull-down menus, buttons on a toolbar, and keyboard shortcuts.

Bold. An individual character, a word, or a block of text may be printed in bold type for emphasis.

Center. Centering means automatically placing titles and other text evenly between the left and right margins.

Comment. Users can insert comments about selected areas of text to make notes for later editing or to communicate with others in collaborative work. Comments are not part of the printed text, but rather "pop up" when the cursor is paused over the highlight comment marker.

Copy. The user can highlight and copy text already entered in one part of a document to be pasted into another part of the document automatically without having to retype it.

Find. Given the Find command, the software will locate and pause at every occurrence of a particular character, word, phrase, or number in a text.

Footer. The footer is the text at the bottom of a page, such as a page number or section title. Footers may be programmed to appear on all or any number of specified pages.

Header. The header is the text at the top of a page; this space can consist of a heading, image, page numbers, or any other text that the user wishes to have appear on every page or specified pages of a document.

Macro. A macro is a shortcut for entering frequently used commands by recording and saving a sequence of keystrokes in a file that can be recalled for future use. Each macro is assigned a name that the user types to implement the series of keystrokes or data that it represents.

Margins. The space around the text at the edge of the paper may be specified, left and right, as well as top and bottom.

Paste. The user can insert text that has been copied or cut from another part of a document without having to retype it.

Print. The Print command directs the computer to print an entire document, or a portion of it, in multiple copies and various formats.

Replace. This command will find every occurrence of a particular character, word, phrase, or number in a document and replace it with another character, word, phrase, or number.

Save. The Save command copies the document to a disk for storage. Documents can generally be saved in a variety of formats to be accessible in other software programs. Recent versions of productivity software allow files to be saved in web format to be displayed on the World Wide Web.

Scroll. Scrolling is moving quickly through a document vertically or horizontally.

Template. Templates allow users to save formatted styles and layouts and attach those styles to other documents.

Type Style. Type style refers to the font, the design of the characters, and the size of the text.

Underline. Characters, words, or blocks of text may be underlined, either continuously (words and spaces) or separately (words only).

Wizards. Wizards guide a user through a procedure by asking for information and then placing that information into a preformatted document.

Word Wrap. At the end of each line of text, word wrap automatically returns the text insertion point to the left margin of new line so the user can continue typing without interruption.

WORD PROCESSING

Word processing is the writing, manipulating, and storing of textual material in a computerized medium, and it is a tool that has become a vital everyday function in classrooms, offices, and homes. Advanced software features now allow users to move beyond these simple operations to interact with other software, to embed multimedia elements into documents, and to easily save files in web-ready format.

Word Processing in Education

Word processing is often the first use of computers in classrooms because its capabilities can quickly improve efficiency of PreK–12 students and teachers alike. Word processors in the classroom can expand the horizons of learning in ways not possible before this technology was available. Users can produce professional-quality documents with the limitless ability to edit, change layouts, and reformat. As students and teachers create documents, the word processor prompts them to consider how the material will appear on the printed page, including choices about margins, spacing, and font.

Spelling and vocabulary are other areas in which students are provided with instant feedback. By using the *spell check* feature, students can tell if a word is spelled incorrectly and often can select the correct spelling. The *thesaurus* feature provides a list of words with similar meanings, allowing students to vary word choice and to augment their written vocabulary. *Grammar check* features highlight any problematic sentence structure, encouraging students to consider options for rewording. The immediacy of these individualized help options promotes continuous learning, prevents students from repeating errors, and extends the teacher's capabilities by offering another dimension of assistance to students.

By using a word processor's many functions, students can produce better first drafts that are eye-pleasing and easy for the teacher to read and grade. Students are able to see their work as valued and are more able and likely to make revisions, retrieving the original and making the necessary changes, without having to reproduce the whole text.

Composing text on the screen is a new skill made possible by word processors (see Figure 2.1). Depending on the age and abilities of students and the type of work being done, the steps of handwriting a rough draft and then typing a final version can be bypassed. On-screen composition requires different organizational and mental skills, which likely will be necessary for future employment. Teachers also might prefer to evaluate text on screen rather than from a printed copy. Editing and Comment features enable collaborative writing processes between teachers and students as well as among peer teams. One

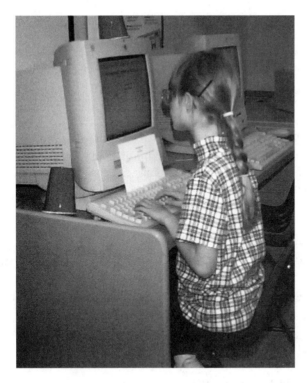

FIGURE 2.1   A student composes a story using a word processor.

piece of writing can be edited by multiple people, thereby encompassing a variety of expertise and viewpoints. The time saved for both student and teacher is one of the positive aspects of word processing.

Content areas such as history, social studies, English, foreign languages, science, and the arts also benefit from the use of word processing. On any level, teachers can prepare lesson plans, examinations, and other classroom materials using a word processor (see Chapters 11–14). The material can be updated from year to year as necessary without having to recreate the whole body of information. In addition, teachers can administer and grade exams and quizzes using a word processor (see Chapter 17). Word processing can assist educators to meet professional and administrative needs, including writing manuscripts, research reports, grant proposals, and public relations materials (see Chapter 19).

Word Processing Fundamentals

Whatever the software and whoever the user, certain characteristics are common to most word processing software, so that once learned, users can typically transfer similar skills among different programs. Generally, the user enters text on a keyboard and sees each character displayed on a monitor as it is typed. An *insertion point,* a small marker of space, moves along the line of type, indicating the position at which the next character will be entered. In addition to common typewriter symbols, the keyboard includes directional arrows that, when pressed, move the cursor up and down, and to the left or right, at the discretion of the user. Other keys allow the user to insert or delete characters, spaces, or lines.

Further adjustments to a text are possible by giving different commands to the system. Although all software does not use identical terminology, users will soon become familiar with the terminology of the particular piece of software they have available. This alphabetized glossary defines common terms found in most word processing packages.

Break. A break is a mark inserted to manually separate pages, columns, or sections so that text can be segmented or formatting can be customized.

Bullet. An individual character that marks the items in a list is a bullet.

Columns. It is often desirable to present text in multiple vertical sections on one page, similar to newspaper text. Text in columns can continue from one column to another on the same page and onto subsequent pages, with the word wrap function keeping the text within the defined column width.

Grammar Check. The Grammar Check command identifies grammatical mistakes in the document and suggests alternate wording.

Insert. The insert feature allows the user to add items to the text of a document, such as pictures, other files, objects, comments, and symbols.

Justify. The word processor can easily produce text with even, or justified, right and left margins.

Merge. The merge function allows information from two or more documents to be combined. The classroom teacher can use the merge function to combine a form letter with a document containing student and parent names and addresses so that the letters appear to be individualized for each family.

Spacing. Spacing refers to how many blank line spaces there are between lines of text. The usual defaults are single spacing and double spacing, although there are capabilities for half-line spacing options as well.

Spell Check. Spell checking features use a preloaded dictionary of common words. The spell checker will highlight words that are spelled incorrectly or that are not recognized, either when manually activated or automatically as words are typed. The user may then select the correct word from a list of choices or type the correct spelling. Some common words can be automatically corrected as they are typed.

Tab. Similar to a typewriter tab, the cursor moves a predetermined number of spaces to the right each time the tab key is pressed.

Tables. Tables consist of individual cells arranged in any configuration of rows and columns, limited only by the width of the document itself. Table columns and rows can be manipulated in much the same way as other text, such as inserted, deleted, moved, and copied. When revising a document, each column is treated as a separate block of text or media elements and can be changed without affecting other columns.

Thesaurus. The thesaurus will, upon command, produce a list of words of similar meaning that may be substituted for a given word. If the list contains a more appropriate word, the user may then instruct the computer to exchange a word for the given word.

Track Changes. This feature allows multiple writers to edit a single document, marking insertions and deletions in different colors for each user.

SPREADSHEETS

Perhaps the best way to describe an electronic *spreadsheet* is to visualize on the computer screen an accountant's ledger sheet with its array of horizontal rows and vertical columns. Each row and column contains information, either letters or numbers, which may be organized in such a way as to be meaningful to the user. Although the electronic spreadsheet performs exactly such a function, that is only the beginning of its capabilities. Each piece of data entered into the spreadsheet is considered as it relates to all the other data contained therein. In this way, any change made in one cell can affect the whole spreadsheet, with the spreadsheet automatically able to recompute and update any data affected by an entry. It takes little imagination to recognize the time saved and errors avoided over doing the same task on a ledger sheet, with an eraser and calculator at hand.

Spreadsheets in Education

One of the most obvious uses for spreadsheets in education is for numerical applications, such as for manipulating math and science information and understanding mathematical formulas. By entering instructions in the form of formulas, students reinforce the learning of mathematical symbols and the standard order of precedence. Decimals, percentages, and the computation of simple and compound interest are other mathematical areas expedited and explained more fully when displayed in spreadsheet format.

In addition to math, other subjects may also be better explained, as well as made more interesting, with the use of spreadsheets. The analysis of social studies data (such as population growth, income distribution, census information) and the results of scientific studies are only a few of the potential uses for spreadsheets in classroom teaching. Another educational function for spreadsheets is the management of research data. Large amounts of demographic and statistical information can be gathered through survey questionnaires and entered into a computer's database. The spreadsheet can be used to compile and analyze the data in whatever way fits the purpose of the research project (see Figure 2.2).

Students will be working in the real world—in business and industry, in education, or in government or nonprofit agencies. Because spreadsheets will inevitably be a part of their world, students will benefit from hands-on classroom experience with spreadsheet software.

Teachers can use spreadsheets to maintain student records and grade reports. To use the computer's power to manipulate data most effectively, grades can be combined to compute average, mean, median, and various ranges in a class or group of classes. Specific data can also be isolated from the rest, for example, to view an individual student's records. Virtually any piece of information desired is at the user's fingertips.

Spreadsheet Fundamentals

The spreadsheet has three modes of operation: *ready, entry,* and *command.* The user always begins in the ready mode, in which the directional, or arrow, keys can be used to move around within the spreadsheet. When the user begins to enter data into the spreadsheet, the entry mode is activated automatically. The command mode is used to manipulate or perform calculations on data for various purposes that we will explore later.

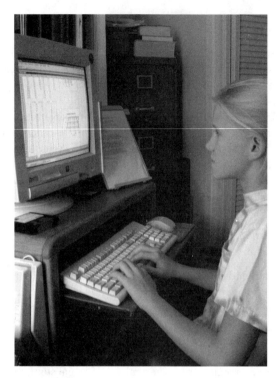

FIGURE 2.2   Spreadsheets can be used to compile and analyze research data.

The following alphabetized glossary defines common commands and operations associated with most spreadsheet programs.

Analysis. Analysis is the examination and evaluation of data. By defining a range of cells, rows, or columns, any part of a spreadsheet may be retrieved and displayed for comparison.

Cell. A cell is the point on the spreadsheet at which a row and column intersect. Most programs provide letter designations for columns, for example, A, B, C,...on to Z, then AA to AZ, BA to BZ, and so on for as many columns as the spreadsheet contains. Rows are numbered beginning with 1. Thus, the cell location D3, can be found at the intersection of column D and row 3.

Chart. A graphics option allows the user to create visual aids, such as pie charts, based on the figures represented in the spreadsheet so that the data can be compared and evaluated at a glance.

Copy. Copying in spreadsheets is done in two ways: *duplicating* (or exact copying of data) and *replicating* (sometimes called relative copying). Duplicating is the copying of a block of data—defined by a cell, row, column, or a range of these—exactly as it appears. Replicating is the copying of formulas and functions, so that once pasted, the calculation will be performed on the data contained in a new column or row.

Cursor Movement. The directional arrows move the cursor to the left or right and up or down. Some programs allow the cursor to move more rapidly when the Home,

End, Page Up, or Page Down keys are pressed. In addition, most programs allow the user to move directly to any specific cell location with a Go To command.

Fill. Clicking a *fill handle,* a mark usually on the corner of a cell, and dragging to adjacent cells allows formulas to be copied and series of predictable information, such as a number, date, or time series, to be extended automatically.

Format. The Format command is used to define the arrangement and placement of a selection of data. One way to arrange data is to adjust the width of columns to accommodate the data that the cells will contain. Data can also be aligned within a cell, for instance, justified or centered. Most importantly for spreadsheet data, the user can define the way the data will be interpreted by the spreadsheet. Numerical data, for instance, can contain commas to make long numbers more readable or can begin with a dollar sign ($) to indicate currency. Dates, percentages, times, and scientific data can also be displayed in a variety of formats.

Formulas. Once data are entered into cells, the user must tell the computer what is to be done with the data, through the use of formulas. The formulas used in spreadsheets are much like the mathematical formulas used elsewhere. The standard mathematical order of precedence is used, whereby the higher orders of precedence are performed before the lower orders (e.g., multiplication and division are calculated before addition and subtraction, and formulas enclosed in parentheses are always calculated first). Usually, the plus (+) sign is used for addition, the minus (–) sign for subtraction, the asterisk (*) for multiplication, and the forward slash (/) for division. Formulas are entered into the cell where the result is to be displayed. Although the cell actually contains the formula, the user does not see it but rather sees its numeric result on the screen. Because the formula remains in the cell, whenever a value is changed in any of the cells that the formula uses, the resulting numerical value changes automatically (see Formula Example).

Functions. Functions are preprogrammed formulas that are most commonly used in spreadsheets. For instance, the function *SUM* adds numbers in a designated group of cells, whereas *AVG* totals the numbers in a group of cells and calculates the average.

Graph. A graphics option allows the user to create visual aids, such as line graphs and vertical and horizontal bar graphs, based on the figures represented in the spreadsheet so that the data can be compared at a glance.

Insert. The insert feature allows the user to insert an entire row or column without disturbing data that have already been entered.

Headings. Headings appear at the top of the spreadsheet and can be titles, names, or any identifying information that describes the contents of the spreadsheet.

Labels. Labels are titles, names, or other identifying information that describe the contents of rows or columns.

Modeling. Users can employ "what-if" statements to create a model of what might occur if certain conditions existed. Modeling may be likened to the actual building of a physical model, such as architects do when designing a building. A spreadsheet model is created and its figures displayed; the user then asks the computer "what if" a specific value were to be changed. The value can be a change in actual numbers or an increase or decrease by a specified percentage rate.

■ ■ ■ ■ ■

FORMULA EXAMPLE

Let's consider a formula for simple addition.

Column B contains 10 numbers in cells B2 through B11. It is always a good idea to leave a blank row between the total and the column being added. A blank row separates the total from the other numbers and makes it more visible. Therefore, leave cell B12 blank, place the cursor on cell B13, and enter a formula. The formula tells the computer to add the numbers and display the total in cell B13. This may be done as follows:

SUM (B2+B3+B4+B5+B6+B7+B8+B9+B10+B11)

However, as in this instance, there may be lots of numbers to add and this method would be cumbersome. For that reason, the formula may be written in an easier and quicker way by defining a range of cells as follows:

SUM (B2...B11)

Many programs use ellipses (...) to separate the first and last cell designations. The colon (:) or period (.) is also commonly used for this purpose. After the formula is entered into the cell, the computer adds the numbers in cells B2 and B11 plus all the cells in between. It will then display the total in the cell containing the formula. As long as the formula remains in cell B13, if the value of any cell between B2 and B11 is changed, the total in cell B13 will automatically be changed and displayed.

Projection. Projection is the use of spreadsheet calculations to predict what may be logically expected to occur in the future based on data that has been collected. For example, educational institutions must predict potential changes in student population and project funding needs based on tuition and fees.

Size. The software program being used determines the total size of a spreadsheet, but the number of rows and columns needed to perform a specific task determines the size of the formatted spreadsheet. Only a small portion of the entire spreadsheet is visible on the screen at one time. However, the user can view any other portion of the spreadsheet by using the directional keys to bring other areas into view.

Status Line. An aid for entering data correctly is the status line, telling the user where the cursor is located and what that cell contains.

Values. Values are numbers entered into any cell. The computer always interprets numeric entries as values, unless indicated otherwise.

Window. Occasionally, the user wants to view two separate portions of a spreadsheet at the same time for purposes of comparison. A window is a portion of the spreadsheet that is displayed on the screen at the top or bottom, or side-by-side, at the same time that another portion appears.

Worksheet. Spreadsheets allow one open file to contain a number of different worksheets, or the documents used to store and manipulate data. Calculations can be performed on multiple worksheets simultaneously.

DATABASES

Before the advent of computers, information files had to be maintained manually, with paper-based files kept on index cards stored alphabetically in boxes or drawers or file cabinets. With the creation of *database* software, files can now be manipulated by the computer, thus saving hours of physical labor in handling, updating, and moving information when changes are made.

Databases in Education

The educational community has been a beneficiary of the database's ability to compile, store, and manipulate huge amounts of demographic and statistical information. For example, once student records are entered into a database, they can be accessed by any criteria the user wishes and compiled to generate specific and individually designed reports. School districts and universities have built databases to handle student files, which can include currently enrolled students, classes, financial accounts, grades, and schedules.

Databases are also an invaluable new tool for the classroom teacher. A database can be created for members of an individual class and used to arrange information, as the teacher requires. Curriculum enhancements are available through library databases and other sources of reference materials. By implementing a database search for content-relevant information, a teacher can locate multiple sources of material in much less time than that required for a physical library search. Educators and students should be aware of the use of databases in other sectors of society; information from online databases frequently can be accessed for educational purposes. Government agencies, nonprofit organizations, businesses, and private individuals all store information in databases.

Database Fundamentals

Database software enables users to create new files; add, delete, or change entries in files; perform limited calculations using data; sort records according to varying criteria; and merge two or more files into one. A file is created when information such as identification numbers, names, social security numbers, grades, and other pieces of data are gathered. As with manual files, the file must be revised constantly to remain useful.

To create, test, and manage a successful database, it is necessary to have a thorough understanding of the data to be stored, the reason for their existence, and how they can be managed to provide the desired end product. Only then will the user have the full advantage of the many benefits provided by a database. Based on the type of information to be stored, three types of database structures are available: *hierarchical, network,* and *relational.*

Hierarchical Databases.   The simplest database is the hierarchical, or tree-structured, model. By the nature of its organization, information is accessed from the top down. For example, a social security number may be used to identify a record and would therefore be the first data item entered at the top of the treelike structure. Following it might be a student's name and address, which would be placed on lower branches of the tree. If the user wants to search the records and knows only a student's name, the system must follow the hierarchical path, starting from the top, to reach that particular field. This method is said to be a parent–child relationship; that is, each item relates only to the one above and below it in the hierarchy. This necessity to follow the hierarchical structure can be cumbersome and ill suited to some needs. For this reason, network models were developed.

Network Databases.   To meet the needs of users who wanted more flexibility of access, the network model was devised. Network databases allow multiple, explicit relationships to exist, rather than only top-to-bottom relationships. The network model also differs from the hierarchical because the search structure is less rigid. Through pointers, or links, set up within the system, the shortest distance to the required information is followed, rather than a top-to-bottom route, which is unchangeable. The complexity of this system makes modification a more involved procedure, demanding that great care be taken to maintain all of the pointers that join the relationships so that none of the links in a chain is lost. Because relationships are explicit, the route from one relationship to another must be consistently maintained.

This model works well for standardized operations where transactions predictably follow a preconceived path for each occurrence, such as banking transactions, airline reservations systems, and inventory control. With these examples, defining an explicit relationship with pointers from one step to the next is a practical application. When transactions are not so predictable, a less explicit path from one record to another is necessary. For that purpose, the relational model was developed.

Relational Databases.   A relational model allows multiple associations among common fields in more than one database. Relational databases are arranged in table format, two-dimensionally, with rows and columns. What was referred to in the previous two models as a file is now a *relation*. A record is now termed a *row;* a field is now a *column*. In order to avoid confusion, we will continue to refer to files, records, and fields throughout this description. The relational database performs three basic functions:

> **Joining.**   Two files are merged into one.
>
> **Projection.**   Fields are extracted from various files to form a new file.
>
> **Selection.**   Various records may be chosen according to the user's own criteria; this is called selection.

A relational database is useful for data such as school records. Student information, course information, class information, and instructor information, can all be stored in a database, and then managed according to the desired results. Schedules can be created and modified for a student, for an instructor, for a department, or for the whole institution. Grades can be maintained, averaged, compared, printed, and mailed to students. Libraries are another area in which relational databases are used with extreme effectiveness. Huge volumes of text, as well as scientific data, can be stored in a database and accessed according to the interest of the user.

One disadvantage of the relational model is that there is no practical way to link one field with many others that may relate to it. Its very flexibility in mixing and managing fields limits its ability to establish explicit links. Files can be created by the user using any number of fields, limited only by the contents of the database. However, the user must define and implement the creation of the files; it is not done by the system. For this reason, most database systems are not strictly relational.

The following alphabetized glossary defines common commands and operations associated with most database programs.

Edit. The Edit command is used to change or modify data that are already part of a file. The system displays the entire record and fields can be altered as necessary. Entered changes replace the earlier entries.

Enter. When the user chooses the Enter command, a new record is created and stored in the file.

Field. A field is a category of information. Multiple fields make up a single record.

File. A group of related records is called a file.

Form. Forms can be created to assist entry and viewing of data. Forms contain input areas based on the database fields.

Query. Running a query allows the user to select only certain records within a file based on a set of criteria. For example, a principal may want to generate a mailing list of parents of a specified segment of the student population; however, the database files contain addresses of parents of all the students. A query can be used to search for only the specified parents.

Record. A record is the basic unit of database organization. The information for each person in a contact database, for example, would be a separate record.

Report. Once a query has been run, the selected data can be displayed and printed in a formatted report.

Sort. The user can reorder records by performing a sort based on any one field of a record. For example, student records might be arranged alphabetically according to students' names or numerically according to zip codes for mailing purposes. Sorting can be done in ascending or descending order according to the chosen field.

SUMMARY

This chapter provides an overview of possibilities of the most common productivity applications: word processing, spreadsheet, and database applications. Productivity software is readily available and easy-to-use for new computers users. It is also a versatile way to use computers for personal and professional effectiveness. Most productivity software is available as an integrated suite designed to function together, with all of the tools in the suite sharing common features so the user can move easily among the suite components. Writing, editing, storing, and copying text can all be done efficiently by computer. Advanced software features move users beyond these simple operations to interacting with other software, embedding multimedia elements, and saving as web-ready documents.

Word processing is often the first use of computers in classrooms because its capabilities can so quickly improve work for students and teachers. Word processing features can give students instant feedback on spelling and vocabulary, and other functions allow students to produce eye-pleasing and easy-to-read drafts. Depending on student age and ability, as well as the type of work being done, the steps of handwriting a rough draft and then typing a final version might be bypassed in favor of on-screen composition.

Electronic spreadsheets are electronic versions of an accountant's ledger sheet. One of the most obvious education uses for spreadsheets is for numerical applications, such as for manipulating math and science information.

Database files can be manipulated electronically, thus saving time in handling, updating, and moving files. The educational community has been one of the primary beneficiaries of the database's ability to compile, store, and manipulate huge amounts of demographic and statistical information. Educators should also be aware of the use of databases in other sectors of society, as information from online databases frequently can be accessed for educational purposes.

LEARNER ACTIVITIES

1. Open a word processing program and type some sample text. Practice formatting the text with the Bold, Italic, and Underline Commands. Use the pull-down menu commands, the toolbar icons, and the keyboard shortcuts for these formatting features.

2. Type a block of text. Try formatting the text as aligned left, centered, aligned right, and justified. In what situations would each style be appropriate?

3. Practice inserting a comment. Highlight the text about which you would like to make a comment, locate the software's comment feature, and type your comment. Once you get the hang of the process, try to edit a document with a colleague communicating only through the electronic comments.

4. Using a long document, use the Replace feature to substitute another word for a word you suspect you use too frequently. How many instances of that word were replaced?

5. Run a Spell and Grammar Check on a document you have completed. How many incorrect items were identified?

6. Open a new database document to practice. Insert at least five fields to hold information about yourself or your students. Now, enter this information for at least five individual records. Once entered, attempt to sort the information according to at least two different fields.

7. Enter student grade information into the cells of a spreadsheet. Use column headings to organize the data. Now, insert simple sum and average formulas. Try to copy exact numerical and relative formula information.

8. Insert a chart to illustrate the relationships among data in a spreadsheet document. Format the chart, and insert it into a word processing document.

9. To represent related lists of information, such as days and times of classes, insert a table into a word processed document. Adjust the column widths, and format the column and row headings for readability.

10. After you have created a database of student contact information, type a form letter in the word processing program. Insert the merge fields for the fields of information you would like, and run the merge. Did the merge successfully create unique letters for each contact in your database?

CHAPTER 3

ELECTRONIC MESSAGING

FOCUS QUESTIONS

1. What basic email skills are transferable among various software programs?
2. How can email be used to enhance communication in educational communities?
3. What privacy issues must be considered when communicating electronically?

Professional isolation is an unfortunate hallmark of teaching. Traditional school practices require teachers to work alone with their own students, inside the four walls of their classrooms, with little contact among colleagues on any given day. The technology that has the most potential to bridge physical distances between teachers and learners and to provide a method for collegial collaboration is electronic messaging. As easy as it is to learn to use, email can quickly be mastered even by novice computer users. With a little awareness of the privacy issues that could affect its use, email can successfully be used for planning and instruction among teachers, students, and experts worldwide.

ELECTRONIC MAIL FUNDAMENTALS

Electronic mail, commonly known as *email*, is a way of sending paperless "letters" from one computer user to another. With a few keystrokes and a few seconds, messages can be sent and received, allowing for nearly immediate written communication. The concept of email is often compared to the familiar traditional mail to better understand its similarities and differences. For instance, an email message must be sent to a unique address, and the recipient "opens" his or her mail once it has arrived in a "mailbox." The similarities end there, however. The speed and ease with which messages can be sent and organized using email software truly separate this communication medium from anything seen previously. A number of email software packages are currently available, but once the basic procedures of sending, replying, forwarding, and organizing messages are mastered, they can be easily transferred for use in any email program.

Sending a Message

To mail someone a regular message, you must first write the message on a piece of paper, put it in an envelope labeled with the person's full address, add a stamp, and drop the letter into a mailbox for the Postal Service to deliver. To send a message electronically, you must follow very similar steps.

Using an email software program, you first choose to compose a message. Messages are written in the form of a business memo. The *header,* a collection of pertinent information at the beginning of a message, opens with the recipient's address.

Everyone who has an email account has a unique email address that allows mail to be sent directly to that address, either to a desktop computer or to a server account that the recipient may access remotely. An email address has two parts that are separated by the @ sign and essentially represents a particular person at a particular location. An address begins with a person's name or user ID, often a shortened version of a name, such as the first initial and the last name (see Figure 3.1). Following the @ sign is the domain name, which identifies the server (a computer connected to a network) that houses the person's email account and may consist of a number of subdomain, or third-level domain, names.

Finally, the address ends with an extension identifying the domain type. Domain types within the United States are identified by the nature of their business: *.com* for commercial companies, *.edu* for educational and research institutions, *.gov* for government facilities, *.int* for international intergovernmental, *.mil* for military agencies, *.net* for gateway or host, and *.org* for other miscellaneous and nonprofit organizations. Outside the United States, domain type names are identified by two-letter codes: *.ca* for Canada, *.es* for Spain, *.tw* for Taiwan, *.uk* for the United Kingdom, and so forth. However, the use of *.us* for the United States is becoming more common especially for educational email addresses.

All components of the domain name of an email address are separated by periods, and there are no spaces in the entire address. Some email systems use addresses that are case-sensitive, meaning that a capital letter in an address means something very different than a lowercase letter, whereas case makes no difference at all with other systems. With

FIGURE 3.1
Components of an email address.

traditional mail, if one of the parts of an address is left off the envelope, it is possible that some diligent postal employee might track down the recipient. Unfortunately, electronic messages require all of the components of an address to be present. A message sent to an incorrect or incomplete address almost surely will not reach the person for whom it was intended, but instead will be returned to the sender as "undeliverable mail" or lost forever in cyberspace.

Because accuracy is so critical, it is helpful to use an email program's capability of saving addresses to an *address book*. Generally, you can save the email address of a person to whom you frequently write under a simpler nickname, so that instead of remembering a long, multidomained address, you can type a nickname, and the address of the person will automatically be inserted.

Completing the header information, the sender can list other addresses of people to whom copies of the message should be sent, usually marked *Cc* for "carbon copy" or *Bcc* for "blind carbon copy." Use the Bcc option when you want a recipient not to be identified to the other recipients, including those in the Cc list. Other files, such as word processing documents or spreadsheet worksheets, can be sent along with an email message. In the *attachment* line, the desired file is identified or linked to the message according to the procedures of the email program. Finally, a brief *subject* is listed, giving the recipient some idea of what the message contains. The subject is not required to be completed in order for the message to be sent, but it is a courtesy to the person reading the message not to have to guess at a message's content.

Composing is essentially the same as using a word processor, as errors can be easily corrected and text can be manipulated to some degree. Most programs come with spell checkers to proofread messages for accuracy, and some allow text to be formatted, such as boldfacing or changing the font. Email conventions do not demand strict adherence to formal letter writing rules.

One distinct advantage that email holds over traditional mail is the ability to easily send identical messages to more than one person. By simply adding the additional addresses to the header, the message is sent out to all parties listed. If you find that you frequently send messages to the same group of people, you can make a *distribution list* of the addressees so they will not need to be input each time. The distribution list can be given a name, and from then on, only the name has to be entered into the address line in the header to send the message to the entire list.

Responding to a Message

When you access your email account, the first thing you will want to do is check your *mailbox,* also called an *inbox,* to see if you have any messages. Although the procedures vary slightly with each program, the messages can generally be viewed in a list form with the date the message was sent, the name or email address of the sender, and the subject line. New messages that have not yet been "opened" are marked as such so they can be easily distinguished from messages you have already read. Clicking on the message line will bring up the complete text of the message. After reading the message, a decision can be made as to what to do next.

If after the message is read it is determined that it requires an answer, you can send a *reply.* When you choose to reply, you can usually choose whether to include a copy of the original message along with your response, to remind the sender what was said, or you can simply send the answer by itself. The header is supplied automatically with the recipient's return address already listed, and the subject line usually includes a prefix of *RE:* indicating to the recipient that this message is a reply to the earlier message.

Sometimes a message you receive might be of interest to another party. In this case, you can *forward* an exact copy of the message to that other person. When you choose to forward a message, a new header appears with a blank address line. You supply the address of the person to whom the message will be forwarded. The subject line contains the original subject with the addition of a *fwd* affix, indicating to the recipient that this message has been forwarded.

Whether a message has been replied to or forwarded, two more options remain. If the message is important, it can be saved. Saved messages can be organized into folders, like other computer files, so that they will be easy to retrieve at a later date. A message can also be saved by just leaving it where it is in the inbox, where it can stay until it is removed. If a message is no longer needed, the inbox can be cleaned out by *deleting* the message. When you choose to delete, the program prompts you to confirm this is the action you want to take. If it is, the message is removed to a "trash can." Of course, as with a real letter that is thrown away in a trash can, if you change your mind, you can usually rescue a deleted message by taking it out of the trash can, provided you have not changed the default settings.

ADVANCED FEATURES OF EMAIL
SOFTWARE APPLICATIONS

The email software packages available today range from the very basic to those with the "bells and whistles" found in high-end software tools, although the end product, an electronic message, is virtually the same. New programs rapidly appear on the market, each bringing new and improved features to email users. Streaming technologies make it possible to send audio and video email messages just as easily as text email. The best advice is to investigate the program to which you will have access to make yourself familiar with the options available to you.

Most Internet browser programs (see Chapter 4) offer an email component to give their users a more complete communications package. Netscape Communicator, for instance, contains Messenger, which presents a graphical interface to the user (see Figure 3.2). Icons, or pictures, show whether messages are new or have already been read and give navigational clues to perform standard email functions. High-priority messages can be marked with a *flag* as they are sent, so that the recipient is aware of messages that should be answered right away. The text of a message is easier to manipulate in the graphical programs such as Netscape, because you can highlight and drag text just like in a word processor. The advantage to using an email program that is part of your Internet browser is that you can check for new messages while you are already online using the Internet. URLs (Uniform Resource Locator), or Internet addresses, sent within an email message are hotlinked to take the user directly to that website with just a click. Netscape's AOL Instant Messenger feature (also available with other mail programs) lets you chat with people. Chat is synchronous, meaning that the messages are answered the moment they are received.

FIGURE 3.2   Composing a message in Netscape Communicator's Messenger Mailbox.

Microsoft Outlook, the email component of Internet Explorer (see Figure 3.3), allows the user to customize the interface, or what the user sees on the screen, to fit the individual's purposes. An "inbox assistant" lets you organize your messages even before you receive them. For instance, if you get quite a few messages from a listserv to which you subscribe, you may want to have those messages automatically sorted into a separate folder so you can go through them at your leisure without having them get in the way of your other messages. Outlook has a diary/scheduling system, which is extremely helpful when trying to arrange a meeting with colleagues. Other programs, such as Lotus cc:Mail, allow the sender to easily attach files, such as spreadsheets or graphic files. You can find numerous free email programs on the Internet, such as Eudora Light, Pegasus Mail, and Phoenix Mail. As programs continue to evolve, new models for the navigation and organization of

FIGURE 3.3   Composing a message in Microsoft's Outlook Mailbox.

mail will appear, as well as multimedia capabilities including audio and video email options. Fancy features aside, though, whichever email program you have access to will always be able to perform the basic functions of sending, replying, forwarding, and saving.

Email sent between people using the same software application often works with the least problems, but most programs are now able to cooperate with each other through electronic gateways, or bridges, between systems. Occasionally, you may notice some cryptic lines at the beginning of an incoming message from another system, identifying the minor alterations that were necessary to make the message readable under your email software. These alterations generally do not change the body of the message in any way and so can be ignored.

As you become more familiar with email programs and more comfortable communicating through this medium, you will start to pick up on some of the standard practices and conventions of email discourse. Table 3.1 offers a number of good tips to get you started.

LISTSERVS

Once you have an email account and are comfortable with the basic email procedures, you might want to try participating in a *listserv*. A listserv is like a giant conversation among many people with a common interest. The ongoing dialogue that listservs facilitate keep

TABLE 3.1   Good Email Habits

- Check your email regularly. Once people know you have email, they will start using it and expect you to do the same.

- Include a subject line so the person who is receiving your message can quickly prioritize the messages in his or her inbox.

- Use all capital letters sparingly, only when what you are saying is extremely important. When an email message written in all capital letters is read, it appears as though the sender is "SHOUTING!"

- Read your messages before you send them. Spelling and grammatical errors make a message seem poorly written and can reflect on your intelligence.

- Give yourself time to calm down before responding to a controversial or inflammatory message. Sometimes the written message does not appear on-screen the way it sounded in your head. Virginia Shea, author of *Netiquette* (1994), suggests asking yourself whether you would say to the person's face what you have written in the message. If not, you should rewrite it until you are sure it is acceptable. Once you send a message, it cannot be retrieved, and once it arrives at another person's inbox, it is out of your control and can be easily forwarded on to others you may not have intended to see it.

- Use sarcasm with caution and preferably with people who have personally met you or are familiar with your sense of humor. Facial gestures that help give meaning to a sarcastic remark made in person do not transmit through email, and sarcastic words alone could easily be misinterpreted.

- Remove the previous headings from messages that have been forwarded several times so your recipient does not have to scroll through a lot of useless text trying to find the message.

- If you are replying to just the sender of a message from a listserv or distribution list, be sure to choose the option to reply to the sender only. Others on the list will appreciate the courtesy of not cluttering their inbox with personal messages intended for other people.

teachers in touch with the most current educational issues. When you subscribe to a list-serv, your email address is added to the list of members. Any time a message is sent to the list address, a copy of the message is sent to every email address on the list.

Joining a Listserv

Subscribing procedures vary slightly with each list, but generally you send a regular email message to the address of the list manager, who may be a person who moderates the list screening messages to see if they are relevant to the list topic, or may be a computer that automatically distributes an identical copy of every sent message to every member. In your request, leave the subject line blank and in the body of the message, type:

subscribe listname firstname lastname

Because you are most likely "talking" to a computer, your instructions must be exact or they might not be interpreted correctly and you will not be subscribed. Most listservs will send you a confirmation message asking you to reply within a certain time frame confirm-ing that you do want to be a member of that list. Once you have subscribed, expect to start receiving messages, sometimes quite a few messages, every day. The level of participation in the discussions will vary depending on the topic of the list and the individuals involved. Listserv members have the option to be active participants, contributing opinions and advice to the list regularly, or to remain passive observers, or "lurkers," who read all messages without actually sending a message. Any level of participation with which a person is com-fortable is acceptable on a listserv. Keep in mind, however, that the information and view-points presented on the listserv come from other members of the list. These people are not necessarily experts in the field and may or may not be relaying accurate information.

Many lists have rules, both formal and informal, for participating. As a courtesy to those who have already subscribed, participate in the list at first in a silent mode. Watch for the "code of conduct" that is accepted and for the type of information and comments that are typical. Pay attention to the tone of the messages. Regular listserv members are often intoler-ant of newcomers who do not play by the rules, and they may *flame* you, or send you a mes-sage that in no uncertain terms lets you know what part of your message was not welcome.

When you are ready to participate in the list, just send a message to the list address. This address should have been given to you in the information sent when you subscribed. Note that it is not the same address as the list manager's address to whom you subscribed. Try subscribing to a listserv for a while. If you find the topic or tone of the discussion is not quite what you had expected, you can take yourself off the list at any time. Again, the pro-cedures for unsubscribing vary by list, but for most lists, you send a message to the list manager with the word *unsubscribe* substituted into the body of the original subscribe message. Be very sure not to send this message to your list address or everyone on the list will receive it. There is not anything the list members can do to take your name off the list, although they may want to by that time!

Conversations for Everyone

Lists are available for every conceivable interest area, from professional to personal. Public lists cover topics from medicine and politics to religion and recreation and allow anyone with an email address to subscribe. Private lists restrict membership to just certain groups, such as particular college graduating classes or groups that use the list to stay in touch between annual meetings. Performing an Internet search (see Chapter 4) on "listservs" will yield a staggering array of lists that might be of interest. A more defined search can be done at websites such as the Liszt site <http://www.liszt.com> (see Figure 3.4). Table 3.2 provides a selection of general education and subject-specific listservs that might be of professional interest to educators.

THE ISSUE OF PRIVACY

Mail tampering is a federal offense. Barring any unforeseen natural disasters or lawbreakers, we feel safe that our mail will reach its intended receiver unmolested. Once that letter is in the hands of that person, he or she owns it and can throw it away or save it, thus ending the story of the letter. Not so with an electronic message. An email message is not the sole property of the person who sent it or the person who received it. In fact, if it is sent from a school, which is a public institution, it may even be considered to be public information (Descy, 1997). Just because you send your message to one person's email address, it is possible for any of a number of people to read your supposedly confidential message. Building administrators, district network supervisors, even people operating computers through which your message passes on its way to its final destination, all may have access to your message. Unlike the laws that govern tampering with traditional mail, it is perfectly legal to monitor the content of your email messages. Even messages that have been deleted from the receiver's account can be recovered if necessary because the files on server computers are regularly saved on backup files. The advice email users should heed is to be very cautious about writing anything in an email message that you would not want other people to

FIGURE 3.4   Liszt's search website on available listservs.

TABLE 3.2 General Education and Subject-Specific Listservs

Under each list description is the listname in capital letters followed by the email address of the list manager.

GENERAL EDUCATION	SUBJECT AREA
Educational Administration Discussion ADMIN listproc@bgu.edu	**Discussion of Middle School-Aged Children** MIDDLE-L listserv@postoffice.cso.uiuc.edu
Early Childhood Education (8–9 years) ECENET-L listserv@postoffice.cso.uiuc.edu	**Multicultural Education Discussion** MULTC-ED listserv@umdd.umd.edu
Updates from the U.S. Department of Education EDINFO listproc@inet.ed.gov	**Teaching Whole Language Discussion** TAWL listserv@listserv.arizona.edu
Legal Issues in Education EDLAW listserv@ukcc.uky.edu	**Ideas, Research, and Questions about Teaching** TEACHNET listserv@byu.edu
Integrating Technology in the Schools ITS listserv@unm.edu	**Talented and Gifted Education Discussion** TAG-L listserv@vm1.nodak.edu
NETFUTURE: Technology and Human Responsibility NETFUTURE listserv@maelstrom.stjohns.edu	**Geography Education List** GEOGED listserv@lsv.uky.edu
Biology and Education Discussion BIOPI-L listserv@ksuvm.ksu.edu	**National Forum on Information Literacy** INFOLIT listproc@ala1.ala.org
Foreign Language Teaching Forum FLTEACH listserv@ubvm.cc.buffalo.edu	**The Reading Teacher** RTEACHER listserv@bookmark.reading.org
Teaching Social Studies in Secondary Schools H-HIGH-S listserv@h-net.msu.edu	**Using the Internet for Teaching Mathematics** UIME listproc2@ecnet.net
The World Wide Web and Education WWWEDU listserv@lists.lightspan.com	**Special Education Discussion List** SPECED-L listserv@listserv.uga.edu
Music Education Discussion MUSIC-ED listserv@artsedge.kennedy-center.org	**Educational Technology** EDTECH listserv@h-net.msu.edu
Language Learning and Technology International LLTI listserv@listserv.dartmouth.edu	**History of Science, Medicine & Tech** H-SCI-MED-TECH listserv@h-net.msu.edu
Teachers of ESL to Children TESLK-12 listserv@cunyvm.cuny.edu	**Math and Science Education Alerts** MATH-SCI-ALERTS listserv@lists.rbs.org

see. If you hear a rumor that your principal is peeking into people's messages, believe that it is indeed possible! When instructing even young students how to use email, the issue of privacy must be discussed. Once they click on *send,* the message is out of their control.

IMPLICATIONS FOR EDUCATION

With access to email in their classrooms, teachers have the opportunity to communicate with colleagues at their school, educators at other schools, parents, administrators, and educational contacts worldwide. The ease and immediacy of email can have an enormous impact on the sharing of ideas, the making of requests, and the completion of other daily communication, both educational and managerial. Email allows teachers to be more productive and time-efficient, leaving more time that can be spent working for and with students. It cuts down on the stacks of papers teachers find in their box at the end of the day. Meetings can now be organized through email, mailing out the plans to several people at once. Consensus on decisions between groups of teachers can be made without even dragging the plastic school chairs together to sit down. The opinions and contributions of even shy participants can be given equal weight in the final decision. Some schools are now sending attendance in via email, making it possible to very quickly identify students who are absent. Parents with email access can contact a teacher with a question without having to wait until after school to call. Because email is asynchronous, meaning that the messages do not have to be answered the moment they are received, teachers can respond at their convenience.

Students, too, can make use of email (see Figure 3.5). Some schools have set up accounts for each of their students, and others allow students to email using their teachers' accounts. Before giving out email accounts, schools require students to sign an *Acceptable Use Policy (AUP).* The school- or district-developed AUP defines acceptable behaviors by students and states the rules for email and Internet use. Parents are also required to sign the AUP granting permission for their sons or daughters to access their email account and use the Internet. (See Chapter 20 for details.) The possibilities for email to support and inspire educational inquiry are virtually endless. Activities such as the following demonstrate the authentic uses of technology in the classroom.

Classes can participate in telementoring projects that connect experts in every conceivable field of knowledge to students in classrooms everywhere, all through email. The Electronic Emissary Project <http://emissary.ots.utexas.edu/emissary/index.html> out of the University of Texas at Austin was begun in 1993 (Harris, O'Bryan & Rotenberg, 1996) and acts as matchmaker between students and experts. The teachers, students, and experts work as a team to design projects that are goal-oriented and curriculum-based, with the teachers and students sharing their work with and looking for guidance from the experts. This program utilizes online facilitators who serve as liaisons between the classes and the experts, bridging the gaps between the ages of participants and the different environments. Students in such relationships with real-life mentors gain not only content-oriented knowledge, but also authentic communication skills, career encouragement, and motivation to learn.

Much of the collaboration needed for projects with students in other classes can be accomplished via email messages. Students can interact with other students from other grades without having to leave their classrooms and walk around campus by themselves. Writing can be sent through email by one student, modified by a student at the other end, and sent

FIGURE 3.5   Students communicating through e-mail.

back for a continuous cooperative effort. Older students might even submit complete assignments and receive teacher feedback entirely electronically, all without using a single sheet of paper (Dowden & Humphries, 1997). Teachers having assignments submitted in this way have less paperwork and an accurate documentation of when assignments were received.

Videoconferencing and Internet Relay Chat are alternative collaboration tools. *Videoconferencing* is a live, two-way, interactive electronic means of message exchange. Global and national videoconferencing exchanges can be set up through lists available through the Lightspan.com website located at <http://www.lightspan.com/common/pages/linkout5.asp? loc=gsh.lightspan.com/cu/&setInternal=true&_prod=GSH>. *Internet Relay Chat (IRC)* is a synchronous or real-time conferencing conversation tool that lets multiple discussions go on at the same time. The Global News Challenge located at <http://www1.minn.net/~shubert/GNplan.html#anchorcon> engages students in a current event game activity using IRC.

Students in classes across the country and around the world can be "key pals," the electronic version of pen pals. Even young students are able to work on writing skills in a fun, meaningful activity, without the problems of deciphering developing handwriting or even paying for postage. Students learn that they have to use conventional spelling in order for their key pals to be able to understand their messages. Key pals can serve as cultural guides to their part of the state or country or world, exchanging pictures and brochures, and making faceless parts on the globe come alive. Because electronic messages are communicated through text, students with different racial, ethnic, or religious backgrounds can learn to meet the person inside rather than perpetuating any stereotypes about outside appearances. Thinking critically about the circumstances of lives in other places or cultures helps

CLASSROOM VIGNETTE

The classroom door is pushed open and the hot, sweaty fifth-graders pile inside after lunch recess. Ms. Gomez calls out to the class as she stands at the door talking to a student, "Let's continue where we left off before lunch. If you need to check your email, you may wait at the computers." One or two still-chattering students have already plopped down at each of the four computers in the room.

"I probably won't have an answer yet from Mr. Carter because I just sent my message this morning," Ming says to Lindsay as she confidently clicks her way into the email program and her own inbox. "Sometimes he doesn't check his mail until the afternoons because he has so many meetings."

As she says this, she sees the lone message sitting in her mailbox, the envelope icon still unopened. "He did write!" she exclaims and quickly opens the message from Mr. Carter, their class Emissary match. Mr. Carter is a state senator and he is working with students in Ms. Gomez's class to understand the election process and to help them to plan their own mock campaigns. Ming had asked him just that morning whether he got nervous during speeches, because she has one scheduled in front of another class for the next day, and she is starting to get butterflies in her stomach.

In his brief email reply, Mr. Carter says that he does, in fact, still feel nervous right before he has to speak in public, but that it usually goes away after he sees the audience become interested in what he has to say. He gives her a couple of ideas that always work for him so she can rehearse that night. Ming immediately clicks on the reply button and thanks him for the advice, promising to let him know how it goes after the speech the next day.

On the next computer, Antonio and Blake have just read the latest installment of their cooperative email story and are discussing what twist the plot should take next. The two take turns with students in four other classes, two of which are not even at their school, adding a paragraph or two each time to a continuing story. When they are finished with each installment, they forward the updated story on to the next group. So far, the two fictional boys in the story entitled "Escape from the Jungle" have made their way down a mountain, dodging gold smugglers and enemy aircraft in the process, only to find out that they forgot their walkie-talkies back by the bridge.

Antonio's eyes light up. "I know! They could hike back up the mountain, but come up to the bridge by a different trail, just in time to see some gorillas trying to eat their walkie-talkies!"

"Yeah!" agrees Blake. "But maybe the gorillas are really spies undercover!" The boys type in what they have come up with, make a few minor modifications, and send the story on its way to the next authors.

As they finish, Ms. Gomez looks up from the groups of students she is working with. "Boys, could you send an email to Mrs. Dillon to ask if we can schedule a time to use the art room to paint our campaign signs? I didn't see her at lunch today."

students to identify and better understand what they believe to be important in their own lives (Rice, 1996). Key-pal programs can be set up privately between two teachers, or teachers can apply for key pals for their students through teaching magazines, the ePALS website at <http://www.epals.com/>, listservs such as KIDINTRO (subscribe to <listserv @sjuvm.stjohns.edu>), or the Intercultural E-Mail Classroom Connections website located at <http://www.iecc.org/>. (See http://www.connectingstudents.com/interact.htm#E-mail for a listing of email activities.)

SUMMARY

Email has the potential to provide for regular and quick communication among all members of the educational community. Those new to using email will quickly notice some similarities to the concept of traditional mail, such as the need to address a message with a person's unique location, but the speed and ease of sending electronic messages soon becomes apparent. All software programs allow for the basic operations necessary to compose, open, respond to, and save electronic messages. Higher-end software allows for more control over a user's mail management, such as graphical icons, direct links to the World Wide Web for URLs included as part of a message, and automatic mail sorting according to categories.

By joining a listserv, you can use email to participate in ongoing conversations with people on an unlimited array of topics. Once you have subscribed by sending an appropriate message to the list manager, you will begin receiving copies of all messages sent to the list. You can either sit back and read passively or actively participate by sending your own contributions. Attention to the implicit and explicit rules of the list community will make the experience productive and pleasant for you and for other list members.

Educators should remain aware of and make sure their students are aware of the privacy issues related to the use of electronic messages. With thoughtful use, email can provide a forum for quality collaborative work among students, teachers, colleagues, and the resource-rich community outside the walls of the school.

LEARNER ACTIVITIES

1. Experiment with two different email packages. Compare features and evaluate the effectiveness of each.

2. Address an email message *incorrectly* and send it. What happens?

3. Find a listserv of either a professional or personal interest. Join and watch the messages passively for several weeks, or until you feel comfortable to contribute a message of your own.

4. Research contacts for student key pals. Are there many organizations or individuals that exist to set up such relationships? Are there key pals available for all ages of students?

5. Begin an address book of professional colleagues, student family members, and community contacts.

6. Brainstorm a list of all the ways electronic communication can facilitate quality learning.

7. Research current privacy laws governing electronic communications. How often does your school or university back up email files?

8. Develop a learning activity that incorporates the use of email for the level student you plan to teach. What special help might they need to be successful? To what extent will email be a part of your comprehensive educational plan?

9. Organize a virtual meeting between professional colleagues entirely through email. Include sending out an agenda, encouraging discussion on the topics, summarizing key points, and providing a summary of conclusions reached. Then solicit reaction from those involved as to how email might contribute to or detract from decision-making processes.

10. Find addresses of educational experts or community leaders in newspapers or journals. Send an email message with a comment or a concern to several people and compare the response rates between different professions of people. Do those in the educational community tend to respond more readily? Are there any similarities among those from whom you never heard back?

BIBLIOGRAPHY

Abilock, D. (1996). Integrating email into the curriculum. *Technology Connection, 3*(5), 23–25.

Besnard, C. (1996). Students' empowerment: Email exchange and the development of writing skills. *Mosaic, 3*(2), 8–12.

Coulter, B., Konold, C., & Feldman, A. (2000). Promoting reflective discussions. *Learning and Leading with Technology, 28*(2), 44–49, 61.

Descy, D. E. (1997). The Internet and education: Some lessons on privacy and pitfalls. *Educational Technology, 37*(3), 48–52.

Dowden, R., & Humphries, S. (1997). Using email in computer assisted freshman composition and rhetoric. *T.H.E. Journal, 24,* 74–75.

Ekhaml, L. (1996). Making the most of email: How to be concise, courteous, and correct online. *Technology Connection, 2*(10), 18–19.

Fargen, T. (1996). Surfing the Internet in gym class: Physical education email keypals. *Teaching and Change, 3,* 272–280.

Hackett, L. (1996). The Internet and email: Useful tools for foreign language teaching and learning. *On-Call, 10*(1), 15–20.

Hamilton, M. C. (1996). The trouble with email. *CUPA Journal, 47*(2), 1–5.

Harris, J., O'Bryan, E., & Rotenberg, L. (1996). It's a simple idea, but it's not easy to do! Practical lessons in telementoring. *Learning and Leading with Technology, 24*(2), 53–57.

Rice, C. D. (1996). Bring intercultural encounters into classrooms: IECC electronic mailing lists. *T.H.E. Journal, 23*(6), 60–63.

Rogers, F. (1996). Email to the neighborhood. *TECHNOS, 5*(4), 33–36.

Scott, J. (1996). Creating your own Internet projects with email. *School Library Media Activities Monthly, 12*(9), 43–48.

Shea, V. (1994). *Netiquette.* San Francisco: Albion.

■ ■ ■ ■ ■

CHAPTER 4

FEELING AT HOME
ON THE INTERNET

FOCUS QUESTIONS

1. How does the hypertext structure of the World Wide Web facilitate nonlinear, dynamic access to information?
2. What search strategies make it easier to find exactly what you are looking for on the World Wide Web?
3. How can you keep your students safe while they explore the Internet?

From its humble beginnings as a government experiment to provide strong, transparent connections among military and research institutions, yet impenetrable enough to withstand a nuclear attack, the Internet has grown to be an incomprehensibly strong and far-reaching information network that bonds computers virtually everywhere. Someone sitting at one computer screen can travel to any computer that is connected to the Internet in mere seconds. The dynamic nature of the Internet, however, implies a future of continual growth beyond even what can be imagined today. Even with the understanding that the Internet may yet be in its developmental infancy, educators cannot ignore the limitless resources available from the worldwide community. They must become familiar with its basic operation in order to make the most of its benefit to students. This chapter gives an introduction to what the Internet is and how it is structured, and later chapters in this book invite educators to explore resources available online and to participate in designing their own web-based instruction.

In its most simplistic form, the Internet can be seen as a network of networks. Two or more computers linked together by wires and having the capability of communicating, or sharing information, form the base unit of a network. Most offices and many schools have found that by linking all of their computers together to form a *local-area network* (*LAN*), they can increase communication and thus increase efficiency. These LANs connected to other LANs connected to yet other LANs make up the basic structure of the Internet. But the Internet is more than just the physical wires and machines. It is also composed of the resources available through these connections. Information on any topic, no matter how specialized or obscure, can be found somewhere on some computer connected to the Internet, and clearly these pieces of information are made possible by the people who create them. It is people who choose to make connections to others. It is people who place information online for others to access. Finally, it is people who make decisions on how to use the resources available to them. The Internet, then, can be really seen as a partnership among physical, informational, and human elements.

In the true spirit of this partnership, and as a key feature of the original military design, there exists no central Internet entity. There is no "home" computer at which all of the wires ultimately converge; instead, each host computer shares equally the authority and the responsibility for successful connections. Because of this, the network is perpetually strong, able to bypass any wires or machines that are not functioning by routing information in other directions. The Internet also lacks a main receptacle of knowledge and information. Its users both provide and draw from the vast selection of resources that make the Internet dynamic and rich with substance. Finally, there is no presiding human authority in charge of maintaining the Internet. It is a cooperative environment, with its participants governing themselves for the most part. The Internet Society (ISOC) is a nonprofit organization of volunteers that assumes responsibility for guiding the technical and practical growth of the Internet. Members of the ISOC make recommendations regarding what protocols will be necessary to support communication with new technology and also organize and assign unique addresses to Internet host computers. Other than these "housekeeping" functions, the ISOC does nothing to regulate, rate, or otherwise rule on the kinds of information that bounce throughout the world connections. The absence of a central overseer leads to quite an excess of duplicated, poor-quality, and even objectionable material that can be accessed online, but it also has created a democratic environment, for the people and by the people, the likes of which the world has never seen.

Unfortunately, for simplicity's sake, computers around the world are not all manufactured by the same company or with the same speed and capabilities, so there exists a need for a consistent way that they all can communicate. The Internet allows for standard communication by operating according to standard rules, or *protocols*. Every bit of information that is sent through the Internet must be broken down into manageable pieces, or *packets,* that can fit through the phone lines that are used to connect. These packets must conform to the *Transmission Control Protocol/Internet Protocol,* or *TCP/IP.* By formatting messages according to this protocol, any computer with the ability to connect to the Internet will have the ability to receive and reassemble the packets, resulting in a complete message. It is in this way that the Internet is able to be platform-independent.

THE WORLD WIDE WEB

There are a number of "entrances" onto the mighty network of networks known as the Internet. One is through email, as was discussed in Chapter 3. Another, which is quickly becoming the most popular way to locate many types of information, is through the *World Wide Web* (WWW).

Hypertext

The web is an attractive, graphically arranged, nonlinear way to access information available on the Internet. The key to navigating through the World Wide Web is *hypertext.* The prefix *hyper* means "above" or "beyond" and *text* refers to words on a web *page,* which is the basic unit of the web structure. Hypertext, then, is the word or words that when clicked on, present some information beyond the word itself. In today's increasingly multimedia-enhanced web environment, that information might be audio or video, but the most frequent use of hypertext is to *link* one web page with another. By clicking on a word identified as hypertext, usually underlined and of a different color than other text, you can jump to another page of information. You might even be taken to a completely different *website.* A website is a collection of a number of web pages at one address location introduced or organized by a *homepage.* The *hyperlinks,* or hypertext that links to other pages, allow you to immediately see additional information on just exactly what you choose, rather than having to page through irrelevant information as you might need to in a reference book. It is exactly this freedom to explore documents in a three-dimensional way that gives the web its appeal.

The Purpose of Web Browsers

In keeping with the goal of consistent accessibility of the Internet, documents on the World Wide Web are accessible to any computer that has *browser* software. Browsers do two things that allow you to see World Wide Web documents. First, the software seeks out and retrieves a document requested by clicking on a hyperlink or by entering a web address, called a *Uniform Resource Locator (URL).* A URL is similar to an email address in that it identifies the specific location of the requested document by computer-domain designations separated by periods. The address does not include a person's log-on name followed by the @ sign, as in an email address, but instead may identify a particular document name at the end of the address (see Figure 4.1). Additionally, a URL must begin with *http://,* which shows that this document follows the *hypertext transfer protocol,* or the specific rules that are set up for transferring documents in the World Wide Web environment.

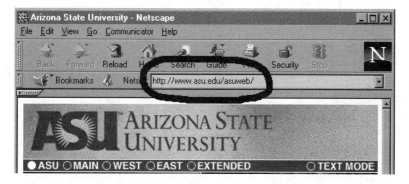

FIGURE 4.1   The hypertext transfer protocol prefix and URL displayed in Netscape.

The second thing a browser does is allow you to see the document you have requested. Documents on the web must be written in *hypertext mark-up language* (*HTML*), which is a coded language that gives the directions necessary for documents to have specific layouts, including graphics and formatted text (see Chapter 10 for more information on creating HTML documents). HTML allows any document on the web to be viewed by any computer that has a browser. The browser interprets the HTML code in which the page has been tagged and displays the page on your computer screen as the person who wrote the page intended (see Figures 4.2 and 4.3).

How to Use a Web Browser

When the browser software is launched, it first shows the website that has been identified as its homepage, or starting point. This starting page can be changed to be any website, but often is the homepage of the school where the computer is located or can even be someone's personal homepage. From here, there are two main ways a browser helps you to see World Wide Web documents: simple browsing, or "surfing," and going directly to a website.

Surfing is quite simple and intuitive. From that very first website you see, you can begin surfing by simply clicking with the mouse on any of the hyperlinks. You will notice that when your pointer is poised over a hyperlink, the arrow changes into a pointing hand, indicating that this is indeed an active link. Clicking on that link points your browser to the location of the requested document, and once found, the document is loaded so that you can see it. When you "arrive" at that next site, you can read the information there, click on another link, or go back to the page you just left by clicking on the **Back** button. The browser remembers where you have been, so that even when you have wandered from site to site, you can always step back until you arrive back to where you started. If you want to go back to a particular site you have seen, rather than stepping back page by page, select the name of the site from the **Go** pull-down menu. If you would like to start again from the beginning, click on the **Home** button to take you back to your home site. Browsing is best when you are not exactly sure what you are looking for because you can take the time to slowly investigate all of the related links. If you do know where you want to be, you will probably want to go directly there.

If you have the URL for the site you wish to visit, type it directly into the **Location** text box and then press **Enter.** If the address is correct and the site is still current, you will

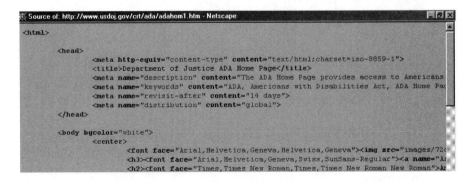

FIGURE 4.2   A portion of the source document for a web page.

FIGURE 4.3   The same document as rendered in a browser.

be taken directly to it. If you have mistyped the URL, or if the site is no longer being maintained by its operator, you will be taken to a page that says that you have requested an invalid address. If this happens, check the address you typed to see if you made a mistake.

To avoid having to continually input the long address to a favorite site you visit frequently, you can click on **Bookmarks** and **Add** to add a bookmark at that site, thus saving the URL. The next time you want to go to that site, click on **Bookmarks** again, and just choose the name of the desired site to go there automatically.

SEARCHING THE WORLD WIDE WEB

Sometimes you do not have the URL for the website you need, and surfing from link to link would be too time-consuming and haphazard of a way to find it. In this case, you will want to perform a web search. In addition to searching for textual information, you can also search for graphics, sounds, and other kinds of files. There are essentially two approaches to searching for information on the Internet (Pierson, 1997). The first is to use a hierarchical subject directory, such as Yahoo! or LookSmart, which first shows a list of very general subjects. Choosing from these subjects will narrow the search until actual web-page links are given. Be prepared to spend some time looking through the threads of topics to find what you want because the directory designers may have a different idea of the organization of information than you do. A subject directory is handy if you want quick, general information.

The other, more directed, approach to finding information on the Internet is to use a *search engine* or a *meta-search engine*, such as the currently popular Google, Excite, Lycos, AltaVista, or Dogpile. In a meta-search engine like Dogpile, you submit keywords and the search spiders send your search simultaneously to several individual search engines such as Google and AltaVista. Almost instantaneously, you view the results from all the search engines. Clicking on the **Search** button in your web browser should take you to a site with links to all of the largest engines, or look at Table 4.1 for the URLs to take you directly to the engine websites.

Search engines and meta-search engines are actually enormous indices of information locations that have been amassed by computer programs designed to go out and find these sources automatically. Lawrence and Giles (1999) estimated the size of indexed information at 800 million pages in 1999. Search engine sites allow you to input keywords, or *search strings*, to guide the search of the indexes. All of the available search engines vary according to size, speed, options, and how documents are actually indexed. Some engines, for example, search for terms only on the headers or page titles, whereas others thoroughly inspect the entire page text for the requested keywords. Many of the major search engines are also becoming known as "Internet Portals" because they provide a number of popular services on a centralized website. (See <http://fer.scdsb.on.ca/simcoe/search.htm> for a comprehensive listing.)

Searching Strategies

Once you have located a search engine site, the best thing to do is to check the help section available on all sites for search tips specific to that engine. Being aware of an engine's features will help you to perform more efficient searches. With the constant updates and improvements being made to each engine, however, it is nearly impossible to be an expert on every feature of every engine. It makes good sense, then, to become familiar with general properties and basic search strategies common to most search engines. Table 4.2 describes

TABLE 4.1   World Wide Web Search Engines

SEARCH ENGINES			
AltaVista	<www.altavista.com>	Hotbot	<www.hotbot.com>
Excite	<www.excite.com>	Lycos	<www.lycos.com>
Google	<www.google.com>	Netscape Search	<search.netscape.com>
GoTo	<www.goto.com>	Northern Light	<www.northernlight.com>
META-SEARCH ENGINES			
Metacrawler	<www.metacrawler.com>	Dogpile	< www.dogpile.com>
SUBJECT DIRECTORIES			
LookSmart	<www.looksmart.com>	Yahoo!	<www.yahoo.com>

TABLE 4.2   World Wide Web Search Strategies

Search for the singular form of a term. This search will give you both *convertible* and *convertibles.*	**convertible**
Enter all of the spellings you think might apply for a given term, separating each by a space.	**Hanukkah Hanukah Chanukah**
Enclose a phrase in double quotes, otherwise the engine will find every occurrence of each individual word.	**"Grand Canyon"**
Be as precise as possible. Entering a common word, such as *book,* would give you far too many useless sites. Include the word in a specific phrase to help narrow the search.	**"antique book dealer"**
Require that a term must be contained in every document by preceding it directly with a + sign.	**+ mineral**
Prohibit a term, meaning that no documents found will contain it, by preceding it with a – sign.	**– music**
Require some terms and prohibit others within one search string. This example will give you documents about rocks that are minerals, but will not include anything about rock music or rock bands.	**"rock" +mineral –music –band**
Use wildcard characters at the end of a phrase to substitute for several missing letters. AltaVista, for example, uses the asterisk (*) as a wildcard character. This search will give you *vegetable, vegetarian, vegetation,* etc.	**vege***
Use Boolean operators AND, OR, AND NOT, and NEAR to narrow searches.	
■ Use AND to find documents containing more than one term occurring together.	**scholarship AND loan**
■ Use OR to specify one term or the other found separately.	**Kansas OR Illinois**
■ Use AND NOT to exclude a term from the search.	**farming AND NOT wheat**
■ Use NEAR to find documents that contain two terms in close proximity to each other, usually within 10 words.	**"United Nations" NEAR Bosnia**
Combine Boolean operators and phrases into logical groupings with parentheses.	**(African OR Asian) AND elephant**

some helpful search tips and gives examples of the search strings you would enter into the search engine. Figure 4.4 shows the results of a simple query using one popular search engine. There is no one best search engine that will serve your needs every time. For the best results, enter the term you want into several different search engines to ensure a complete and well-rounded search. Visit the University of Berkeley Library site at <http://www.lib.berkeley.edu/Help/search.html> for additional help.

In the ever-evolving search engine market, there are now available specialized search engines that allow you to focus your search on documents related to very specific topics (Vaughan-Nichols, 1997). A list of the most current specialized engines, such as ones that

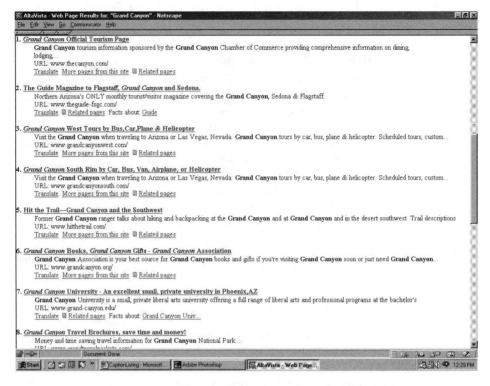

FIGURE 4.4   Results from using the AltaVista search engine to search for the string "Grand Canyon."

locate health-related sites or information on computer-related searching, to name a couple, can be found by clicking on the search button on your browser or the website at <http://www.searchenginewatch.com/links/Specialty_Search_Engines/>. In addition, searchable databases such as Ask Jeeves provide answers to natural language questions. For instance, if you wanted to know about portals, you would enter the question "What is a portal?" Your inquiry will result in a listing of related links.

OTHER INTERNET SERVICES

In addition to presenting hypertext web documents, browsers also offer easy access to resources available through the older, text-based services. Access to services such as transferring files, logging on to systems remotely, and reading news are so seamless that you might not even realize you have left the World Wide Web.

File Transfer Protocol (FTP)

If you want to send or receive an entire file, such as a database or graphics file, you will want to use *file transfer protocol (FTP)*. FTP is the set of Internet rules governing the sending of files from one computer to another. You can use FTP through the World Wide Web to *download files,* or copy them to your system from another remote system. You can also use an FTP program, such as WS-FTP for Windows and Fetch for Macintosh (see Figures 4.5 and 4.6). FTP programs are available for download from the Tucows website at <http://www.tucows.com/>.

The software window on either program prompts you to log in and give your password to gain access to files on the remote system. Some systems allow you to use FTP anonymously by giving the word *anonymous* for your login name and your email address as your password, if you do not have an account on that system. This will give you access to the archives of files that the institution has made available to the public. FTP also lets you *upload* files from your computer to a computer on another system.

Telnet

Another way of accessing remote systems is through *Telnet,* which is yet another Internet protocol. Rather than just letting you download files such as FTP, Telnet actually lets you log-in to other systems, using programs they have, searching databases, such as library holdings, or even checking email from remote locations. Some versions of Telnet come preloaded as part of Windows or Macintosh operating systems, and others are available for free download at numerous websites. Telnet can also be accessed through most web browsers by typing in **telnet://** followed by the host computer name in the location text box. As with other communication applications, an online connection must already be established in order to use Telnet to connect to remote locations.

Newsgroups

Newsgroups, like listservs (see Chapter 3), are a way to discuss timely issues related to a topic of your choice with other people who share similar interests. The difference with newsgroups is that the messages are not automatically distributed to each member's email account, but rather "posted" on something like an electronic bulletin board for others to see at their leisure. You can look at messages only or choose to post a reply for all to see. Most browser software also includes a newsreader component that allows you to choose which newsgroups you wish to peruse on a regular basis. When you enter a newsgroup, you will see the messages listed by subject, the name of the author, and the length of the message in lines. These messages are arranged in threads, with replies to particular messages listed underneath the originals so you can follow the line of dialogue. You can click through the messages, reading only the ones that interest you and skipping the others.

PRIVACY AND SECURITY

Because the Internet has become a true community of people, it faces some of the same serious issues that plague real communities. Just as people put up fences around their yards and alarm their cars to protect their families from outside harm, so will they also need to take care to protect themselves from potential privacy invasions and other dangers lurking within the Internet society.

Privacy

Even though you may be sitting by yourself at your home computer, if you are exploring the Internet, many people may know exactly who you are and what you are doing. Some of

FIGURE 4.5   WS-FTP.

FIGURE 4.6   Fetch.

the information they find out about you is given by you voluntarily, when you fill out an online registration form, such as to receive complimentary software. This personal information is often sold to marketing companies, who will probably begin sending you piles of junk email. To keep your information from being sold, inspect online registration forms carefully to see if they have a policy of not selling the information that they receive. If you do not see any type of disclaimer, you might want to resist divulging your personal data.

Other information can be collected from you without you even knowing about it. Websites are able to detect what type of computer you are using, what browser software you have, and what other sites you have recently visited, all from your browser (Mann, 1997). After some sites get this information, they are happy to leave your computer with a little treat, called a *cookie*. Cookies are pieces of text that a website you visit actually stores on your computer. The next time you visit that location, the site requests the cookie from your hard drive, getting the information on who you are and the specifics on the business you might have done with it in the past. In certain instances it is helpful to have particular sites know who you are, such as when a frequently visited site can customize the path it presents to you to fit your particular interests. It may be a little unsettling, however, that this information exchange is being done right under your nose without you even knowing it. All of these privacy issues can be dealt with by using a variety of software tools, available online or commercially. The first step to understanding the potential privacy invasions is being aware that you are not alone out there.

In 1997, over 4 million children accessed the Internet from school and 5.7 million from home (FTC, 1998). Between 1997 and 1999 the availability of classroom computers and connectivity had increased more than 12 percent and will continue to increase (Williams, 2000). With growing numbers of children online, safety and privacy issues become serious concerns for educators and parents. The Federal Trade Commission voiced its concern in its historic 1998 report to Congress. Congress responded by passing the Children's Online Privacy Protection Act (COPPA). This act of legislation, effective April 2000, established rules to safeguard children's privacy online. Websites catering to children 12 and under must get "verifiable parental consent" before obtaining any personal information from a child. To help educators and parents better understand privacy issues, Classroom Connect and TRUSTe published *Parents' and Teachers' Guide to Online Privacy* <http://connectedteacher.classroom.com/privacy/privacyguide.asp>.

Security

Because the Internet operates in an essentially unregulated arena, material that is objectionable to or inappropriate for students can be stumbled upon. Parents and educators alike will need to make proactive choices to ensure that the computer world is a protected place to explore. Although supervision is unquestionably the best way to know what students are coming across on the Internet, an Acceptable Use Policy (AUP) clearly defines appropriate and inappropriate use of classroom computers. Additionally, Internet "filtering" software gives varying amounts of control over the sites students can access. The software can be programmed to keep students from venturing to sites with certain objectionable words in their titles, and some can keep track of what sites have been visited. Even as these programs progress in their sophistication, none of them is designed to be a substitute for watchful, responsible adult supervision while children are using the computer. The frequency with

■ ■ ■ ■ ■

CLASSROOM VIGNETTE

Mike Chang has faced the unique challenges of teaching the middle school grades for over 22 years. He is an expert in his content area. He knows how to keep students motivated and inspired. He even makes an effort to keep informed of current trends and practices of today's young adult culture. All in all, he feels that he does a good job in his teaching responsibilities.

He learned today that one of his top students, Terrell, has been diagnosed with a rare brain disorder. It is operable, but the surgery is going to be postponed until the winter break so that Terrell can finish the semester. Mike recalls the worried look on the face of Terrell's mother as she explained the situation to him this afternoon. It would be a struggle for her to keep her spirits up, as well as those of her son.

This disease was unknown to Mike, and Terrell's mother had very little information from the doctor. The teacher wanted to be sure he was doing what he could to help Terrell get through these last few weeks successfully. On his way back to his classroom after the last hour's class, he had stopped by the school media center to see if it had any information on the disease. The media specialist, Sue Jaffries, could find nothing that they had actually on campus; it was apparently a little known and fairly recently discovered ailment. She recommended that he do a search on the Internet to see if he could find some recent information.

As he walked through the door of his classroom, he glanced at the "computer corner," boasting of one dust-covered Macintosh computer. He had used it a few times, and he had some basic computer skills from his machine at home, on which he kept his personal finances. Students typed reports on the word processor occasionally, but other than that, he had not incorporated computer technology into either his teaching or his planning. Within the last year, he vaguely remembered some technicians coming in after school hours to install some wires, and he heard that every classroom was now connected to the Internet. There had been a couple of in-service training sessions on computer integration, but he had skipped them in favor of getting other work finished. A colleague had chided him for missing the training and had said, "Hey, if you ever decide to join the Information Age, just click on Netscape and you'll figure it out!" Well, no time like the present, thought Mike, and he flipped on the power strip and wiped the dust off the screen.

When he had logged on to his account, he found the Netscape icon and hesitantly double-clicked on it. An unfamiliar screen opened up, and he took a few minutes to study it. He saw a selection of buttons, such as **Back** and **Home,** as well as a menu bar at the top that looked pretty much like the one he had seen in word processing programs: **File, Edit, Help,** and so on. In the center part of the screen, he saw a white background with his district's familiar logo, as well as a list of topics, such as "District Mission Statement" and "List of Schools." He poked around experimentally for several minutes, learning that clicking on the blue words took him to other pages, and that the **Back** button at the top brought him back to the first page.

Intrigued, and actually finding out things he didn't even know about his own district, he remembered what his goal was today. Sue had mentioned that he needed to do a "search," and he took a chance on clicking the button labeled "Search." After several seconds, he was shown a screen that said "AltaVista," and after a few minutes of examining the screen, he tentatively typed the name of the disease into the text box and began his first Internet search.

By the time he looked at his watch, it was 6:30 p.m., and he had been surfing the Internet for almost three hours! He had discovered a couple of references to the disease from which Terrell suffered, as well as a whole host of other topics that had attempted to distract him from his mission. From what he had seen so far, there indeed appeared to be plenty of information available on the Internet, but he was not sure he was going about finding it in the right way. He came across countless pages that had nothing to do with what he was looking for, even though he had typed in the right term. He made a mental note to ask Sue tomorrow for some advice on searching. He hoped to find some information to share with Terrell's mother, and he also had his curiosity piqued as to what kind of educational resources he might be able to locate. He closed out of Netscape, logged off the computer, and stood up and stretched, inspired after having survived this first trip into the online world.

which new and potentially dangerous sites are added to the Internet makes that goal a practical impossibility. Instead, this software is meant to provide some convenient safeguards to keep students safe in their pursuit of information on the Internet.

SUMMARY

The Internet is essentially a large network linking together all of the smaller networks that connect computers around the world. The physical wires that form the Internet carry information composed by and for people. There is no central authority that governs Internet activity or operation, nor is there a central information repository. The spirit of the Internet requires its users to monitor the quality of their own contributions to the collective information whole.

The World Wide Web offers nonlinear access to information through hypertext links. Web browsers allow you to travel to other sites either by clicking on a hyperlink or by inputting a Uniform Resource Locator. The browser then displays the requested document as the page designer intended it to look.

You can search for sites on specific information by using a search engine, a web application that indexes websites and allows you to search for information by inputting keywords. A number of strategies let you narrow your search to more efficiently find what you are looking for.

Other Internet applications let you transfer files (FTP), access other computers remotely (Telnet), and discuss topical issues with others (newsgroups). All online activity should be undertaken with the understanding that it is not entirely secure or private. With the open community inspired by the Internet, some available material may be inappropriate for some audiences. Being aware of such issues will help educators constantly seek ways in which to allow students to safely explore the Internet.

LEARNER ACTIVITIES

1. Open a web browser application, such as Netscape, and familiarize yourself with its components. Where can a URL be inputted? What kind of information can you get by passing the mouse arrow over a hypertext link?

2. Beginning at your home website, follow a path of hypertext links that interest you. How far away from your home site did you venture?

3. Refer to the URLs given for the popular search engines given in this chapter. Enter a very general keyword in a search engine of your choice. Using the strategies described in this

chapter, along with any noted in the search engine's help section, continue to narrow your search. How many modifications to your search string did it take until you were satisfied with your search results?

4. Choose one keyword string that interests you and enter it into at least three different search engines. How do the search results compare? What types of information would you have missed by using only one engine? What opinions are you forming about the features that define a good engine?

5. Add a bookmark for each site you find that interests you during your searches. For the browser you are using, determine the method for saving bookmarks, and save your bookmarks to a file. Import this file into the browser on another computer to use for future searching.

6. Find out what Telnet and FTP applications your school's system uses, and learn how to operate them.

7. Search for a remote computer location that has software for free download. Follow the directions on the site to download a program to your computer.

8. After exploring the World Wide Web for a period of several weeks, check to see if any "cookies" have been left on your hard drive by any of the websites you have visited. Set the **Preferences** on your browser to notify you if any site wishes to place a cookie on your system, and keep track of how often you are alerted. Try visiting a site without giving it permission to place a cookie and then go back again after accepting the cookie. Do you notice any differences in the information you see there?

9. Draft an acceptable use policy that schools could adopt to protect students during their Internet exploration. Search for online information on how other schools are handling acceptable use issues.

10. Review an Internet filtering application. Test it thoroughly to see what types of objectionable material it intercepts and what is allowed to pass through its screens. Does the software live up to its claims of safety?

BIBLIOGRAPHY

Anderson, B. (1996). The Internet: Trends and directions. *Behavioral and Social Sciences Librarian, 15*, 59–64.
Bjorner, S. (1997). Day tripping to Internet world. *Searcher, 5*(2), 50–61.
Bogyo, J. (1997). So you want to use the Internet in the elementary school. *Technology Connection, 4*(2), 10–12.
Brandt, D. S. (1997). What flavor is your Internet search engine? *Computers in Libraries, 17*(1), 47–50.
Carroll, R. (1997). Documentation of electronic sources. *Business Education Forum, 5*(4), 7–10.
Classroom Connect and TRUSTe (2000). *Parents' and teachers' guide to online privacy.* San Jose, CA: Author
Collis, B. (1996). The Internet as an educational innovation: Lessons from experience with computer implementation. *Educational Technology, 36*(6), 21–30.
Cowan, G. (1996). How the web works. *Social Education, 60,* 113.
DeZelar-Tiedman, C. (1997). Known-item searching on the World Wide Web. *Internet Reference Services Quarterly, 2,* 5–14.
Falk, H. (1997). World Wide Web search and retrieval. *Electronic Library, 15*(1), 49–55.
Federal Trade Commission. (1998, June). *Privacy online: A report to Congress* [Online]. Available: <http://www.ftc.gov/reports/privacy3/toc.htm>.

Hill, J. A., & Misic, M. M. (1996). Why you should establish a connection to the Internet. *TechTrends, 41*(2), 10–16.

Kafai, Y., & Bates, M. J. (1997). Internet web-searching instruction in the elementary classroom: Building a foundation for information literacy. *School Library Media Quarterly, 25,* 103–111.

Laverty, C. Y. C. (1996). Internet primer: Workshop design and objectives. *Internet Reference Services Quarterly, 1*(3), 35–53.

Lawrence, S., & Giles, C. E. (1999). Accessibility of information on the web. *Nature, 400,* 107–109.

Lindroth, L. (1997). Internet connections. *Teaching PreK–8, 27*(5), 68–69.

Mann, B. (1997, April). Stopping you watching me. *Internet World, 6,* 42–44.

Mondowney, J. G. (1996). Licensed to learn: Drivers' training for the Internet. *School Library Journal, 42,* 32–34.

Pierson, M. E. (1997). The honeymoon is over: Leading the way to lasting search habits. *Technology Connection, 4*(4), 10–12, 25.

Reed, J. (1995). Learning and the Internet: A gentle introduction for K–12 educators. *Distance Educator, 1,* 2, 8–11.

Sanchez, R. (1996). Students on the Internet: Can you ensure appropriate access? *School Administrator, 53*(4), 18–22.

Simpson, C. (1996). Full speed ahead on the Internet. *Book Report, 15*(2), 3, 5–7, 9–11, 13–14.

The Software and Information Industry Association (SIIA). (2000, August 3). Building the Net: Trends Report 2000. Washington, DC: Author. Retrieved September 29, 2000, from the World Wide Web: <http://www.trendsreport.net/>.

Tobiason, K. (1997). Tailoring the Internet to primary classrooms. *Technology Connection, 4*(2), 8–9.

Truett, C., Allan, S., Tashner, J., & Lowe, K. (1997). Responsible Internet use. *Learning and Leading with Technology, 24*(6), 52–55.

Vaughan-Nichols, S. J. (1997, June). Find it faster. *Internet World, 8,* 64–66.

Williams, C. (2000). *Internet access in public schools: 1994–1999* (NCES 2000-086). U.S. Department of Education. Washington, DC: National Center for Education Statistics.

CHAPTER 5

EMERGING TECHNOLOGIES

FOCUS QUESTIONS

1. In what ways are emerging technologies helping computers to mimic human capabilities?
2. How might computer innovations impact classrooms of the future?
3. What effects will the increased storage capacities of computers have on the transmission of information in various media?

Technological advancement is constantly offering many challenges to teaching and learning. With the advent of computers in science and industry, technological developments occur almost daily. The present and future are sometimes hard to distinguish: What was science fiction 10 years ago is reality today and will be obsolete in ten years. Engineering and computer science students are often told that their educations will be outdated by the time they graduate and enter their professional fields. The lightning speed of technological advancements in our age makes predictions of the future tentative and difficult. However, some technological trends have emerged over the past several years that permit us to speculate about how technology will revolutionize our society and our daily lives in the future.

One fact is certain: Computers are here to stay! The work of our complex society could not be accomplished without the speed and accuracy that computers allow. Also, the multifaceted work of computers in research and development, coupled with the research of scientists and engineers, will produce the next generation of computers, more capable than those in use today. Their work is oriented toward several areas: continued miniaturization, greater memory capacity, speech recognition and synthesis, enhanced graphics displays, as well as many emerging technologies.

One of the most noticeable characteristics of computers during the past twenty years has been their decreasing physical size. Many of the powerful computers of the 1960s were room-sized; in the 1980s, a home computer owner could own and operate an equally powerful personal computer that could be set up in the corner of a study or family room! The 1990s saw the introduction of portable computers and notebook-sized computers that fit into a briefcase or backpack. Currently, we are seeing the advancement of ubiquitous computing with palm-sized computers. What has accounted for this decrease in size of computer hardware?

INTEGRATED CIRCUITRY

The first generation of computers (1944–1958) relied on vacuum-tube technology, which was cumbersome and required huge amounts of energy. The second generation of computers (1959–1964) introduced transistor technology, an improvement over vacuum tubes. Still the distance between transistors kept computers relatively large and, more importantly, relatively slow. Consequently, the third generation of computers introduced the integrated circuit, a wafer of silicon on which thousands of transistors have been connected with tiny wires.

Integrated-circuitry technology improved so much that even more transistors could be integrated on a chip through the process of large-scale integration. As this occurred, computers became physically smaller, but retained their power, becoming even faster data processors. This trend continues with very large-scale integration. As integrated circuitry becomes more sophisticated, computer power can be housed in smaller and smaller pieces of equipment. And as the size of computer hardware decreases, so does the purchase price of such equipment. That means that a greater number of people than ever before can afford to have computer power at their fingertips.

An important result of integrated-circuit technology has been a wide range of micro-processors that perform many types of functions. A microprocessor is a small computer that has been programmed to carry out a set of specific tasks. For example, microprocessors now control fuel intake of automobiles, monitor cooking in microwave ovens, and perform calculations for owners of pocket calculators or personal data assistants. Many traditional household appliances will depend on computer power in the homes of tomorrow, as we shall explore later.

The amount of power that a computer has is directly related to the amount of data and instructions that can be stored in its memory. The greater a computer's memory, the more powerful the computer. Computer scientists are continually in the process of researching alternate memory systems to store a maximal amount of information in a minimum of space.

SPEECH RECOGNITION AND SYNTHESIS

Speech recognition refers to the computer's ability to recognize and interpret human speech (see Figures 5.1 and 5.2). Computers that recognize speech circumvent the need for a keyboard. A computer that recognizes speech and doesn't have a monitor uses the concept of a hologram to project text into space. This has a number of advantages.

For example, speech recognition just may make house keys obsolete and, at the same time, cut down on home burglaries. Imagine a computerized "lock" that opens doors only to those people whose voices it recognizes as members or guests of a household. Speech synthesis, on the other hand, refers to the computer's ability to duplicate sounds similar to the human voice. The speech synthesizers of today are rudimentary and often difficult to understand, but researchers are constantly improving their quality. Computer speech has the potential for great impact on the lives of people who are voice-impaired, and experiments are now being conducted with computers that speak for those who have no voice. Speech recognition capabilities continue to improve. Early speech recognition worked by the method of discrete speech. The user had to pause between words. Phone companies utilize this approach. Continuous speech recognition is more sophisticated. A user can speak

FIGURE 5.1   SpeechMagic—Phillips speech recognition engine.

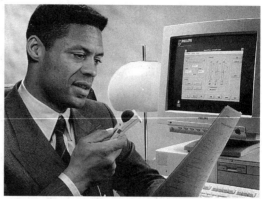

FIGURE 5.2   SpeechFlow—the PC-LAN–based digital dictation system.

in a natural rhythm with close to normal speaking pace. Speech and voice recognition software usually allows the computer to be "trained" to recognize your individual voice patterns, rhythm, syntax, and vocabularies. The legal and medical professions actively utilize this software. Legal briefs, letters, patient charts, and data collection are applications in practice. In education, Kurzweil and Microsoft have developed voice recognition products (see the websites listed after the bibliography at the end of the chapter). The future of this emerging technology is unlimited. We will see this technology applied to cars, appliances, and software; it will especially have an impact on educational software. This software will engage the learner in conversations that provide unlimited educational potential. A newer technology, "digitized" speech, has an improved, humanlike quality.

GRAPHICS

Yet another area of technological advancement is graphics. With the phenomenal popularity of video games, both at home and in game arcades, computer graphics is becoming a popular art form. Researchers are working to make computer graphics more sophisticated (see Figure 5.3). Graphics will display a wider range of colors and more realistic effects. This will also have a great impact on classroom computers; spectacular graphics displays attract children to the computer and hold their attention.

The personal computing era is giving way to the ubiquitous computing era, which is the availability of data and information generating, storing, transmitting, or processing information anywhere, anytime. In the future, more people will be using a variety of "information appliances," such as automobile navigational systems, personal digital assistants (PDAs), digital cameras, and mobile phones. Computers will be physically smaller and less expensive, have greater memory capacity, be able to recognize and produce speech, generate more sophisticated graphics displays as well as take advantage of other emerging technologies. As the price of computers declines, more and more people will take advantage of the seemingly infinite benefits of computer technology.

(a)   (b)

FIGURE 5.3   **(a) Image processing steps of human-interface system. (b) Human-interface system.**

OTHER EMERGING TECHNOLOGIES

The network computer, hand-held devices such as personal digital assistants and palm-sized PCs, flash memory cards, DVD, digital video, Internet 2, and wireless technologies are a few of the emerging technologies that will have an impact on education. The *network computer (NC)* is a fully functional, low-priced multimedia computer that accesses and uses internal and external networks. It works similarly to a television or telephone. Individual students would have their own NCs. Each NC is an intelligent system connected to networks and it gains all its power from the network. The unit cost is minimal and provides a means for web browsing, electronic mail, applications software, and educational software that is on the network. Students could do their assignments offline and download to the school network for teacher or peer review. The NC can potentially have a major impact on education.

Personal digital assistants (PDAs), or knowledge navigators, will become available to everyone. These represent smaller, more compact computers that function as message centers, personal secretaries, and passports to electronic networks to access and share information (see Figures 5.4, 5.5, 5.6, 5.7, 5.8, 5.9, and 5.10). *Palm-sized PCs* equipped with sensing probes will help students gather field data such as water or soil temperature. *Flash memory cards* are high-capacity diskettes with the ability to transfer data between information appliances as well as PCs. Flash memory devices such as Sony's Memory Stick will enable students to share digital pictures instantly and easily and SmartMedia cards to share CD-quality music. Flash memory devices will help students create and share electronic portfolios and multimedia presentations.

Digital Versatile Disc (DVD) is the next generation of optical media. Its impact is on multimedia, video games, music, consumer electronics, and entertainment. DVD is slowly expected to replace videotape because of its excellent video quality and its interactive potential. In essence, DVD technology's large data storage capacity provides for high-quality playback of video, audio, images, and text (see Figure 5.11). For PCs, DVD allows for

FIGURE 5.4   Sharp Personal Information
Organizer.

FIGURE 5.5   Personal Information Management
Organizer.

FIGURE 5.6   Email and Internet-ready hand-held
computer.

FIGURE 5.7   Cassiopeia—hand-held
computer.

FIGURE 5.8   Color personal digital
assistant (PDA).

FIGURE 5.9   Pen-based computing.

FIGURE 5.10   Wireless personal digital assistant (PDA).

FIGURE 5.11   Digital Versatile Disc (DVD) player.

high rates of data transfer, paving the way for the convergence of TV and the computer. Education will be able to combine the interactivity with high-quality video and sound into sophisticated interactive learning programs. Digital video has the capability to provide full motion, full screen, and full color for desktop computers. Quick Time is a common video file format for computers. The emergence of digital video will play an important role in the

FIGURE 5.12   Virtual reality for the Internet.

delivery of video on the Internet. In education, learning technologies and the World Wide Web (WWW) enable the integration, manipulation, and delivery of various media.

Internet 2 is a collaborative effort of the nation's leading universities, the private sector, and the federal government to develop the next generation of Internet technology and applications. This development will enable schools to send and receive high-quality programs that are now limited due to transmission and delivery capabilities. For example, video will be delivered full screen in real time (see Figure 5.12). Advancements in wireless technologies will impact classroom connectivity. With increasing frequency and ease, classrooms will be connected to a local-area network (LAN) and a wide area network (WAN) like the WWW. Placing network resources in the classroom will significantly impact students' access to real-time data exchanges. Wireless technologies combined with affordable hand-held and NC computers will make equipping every student with computing power a reality. Of course, these are only a few of the emerging technologies that will impact education.

APPLICATIONS OF TOMORROW'S TECHNOLOGY

We can see the roots of tomorrow's technology in the computers we use today (see Figure 5.13). For example, cities now use computers to monitor and control the flow of rush-hour traffic. This system cuts down on accidents and helps alleviate the frustration of bumper-to-bumper traffic in congested areas. Such systems are likely to be more widespread in the future. Many experts predict the use of autopilots in automobiles will soon be commonplace. Drivers will program their automobiles to deliver them safely to predetermined destinations. This will certainly decrease the number of deaths and injuries caused by traffic accidents in which human error is the culprit. Presently, computerized highway, road, and street maps are available for automobile dashboards.

Similarly, airplane pilots will be assisted by computer-controlled devices that regulate takeoffs and landings. Because most serious airplane accidents occur during either takeoff or landing, we can expect that these computer-controlled devices will save a substantial number of lives.

(a)   **(b)**

FIGURE 5.13   (a) Virtual reality headset. (b) Virtual reality is often a pleasant distraction from reality itself.

Health care is another area that will be greatly aided by computer power. Already hospitals use sophisticated computerized devices to monitor patients' vital signs. This allows health care professionals to be aware of unusual conditions that jeopardize human lives and to circumvent the devastating effects of such conditions. Research in this area will result in increasingly precise monitoring devices. Along with this, computers are being used to assist doctors in diagnosing illness. Given a set of symptoms and conditions, the computer draws from its memory of diseases an accurate diagnosis, prognosis, and treatment. Using state-of-the-art technology and telecommunications, doctors and surgeons are able to instruct, supervise, and direct sophisticated surgical procedures and diagnostic consultations from medical facilities thousands of miles away.

Law enforcement agencies will find it easier to locate and keep track of offenders. Complex monitoring devices will help police officers to detect violations of motor vehicle laws. Monitoring devices note speed limit violations, for example. In addition, centralized computers will keep track of records of law violations, and this will help law enforcement agencies to coordinate efforts in apprehending offenders who move from state to state to avoid prosecution.

Other government agencies will also rely on new and better computers. Employers will use computer terminals to record the earnings of their employees, and this information will be reported automatically to various tax authorities. This system will make tax evasion more difficult and tax reporting much easier.

DATABASES IN THE FUTURE

A natural consequence of the trend toward buying and using personal computers will make databases increasingly important in the future. Many databases exist today, serving the medical profession, the legal profession, and many other groups. These databases provide access through a computer terminal to vast amounts of information that would be too expensive and too bulky for most people to purchase and store. Databases have the additional benefit of being updated constantly so that the information they contain is the latest and best available. Consider, for example, how vital this is to a doctor who must treat an illness that is obscure or that is currently being researched. The doctor can access up-to-the-minute information about such an illness, and this information may mean the difference between life and death.

A number of general databases are in existence today. For example, many commercial vendors offer subscribers access to information on a wide range of subjects. For a monthly fee, subscribers can tap into the latest information on hobbies, health concerns, financial information, and an impressive number of other topics. All that the subscriber needs is a computer through which to receive this information.

As we have already mentioned, it is likely that libraries as we know them today will someday be obsolete. Rather than having to drive to a library, search through the stacks for the volumes we want, and then find that we may have to wait until those volumes are returned by another borrower, we will simply sit down at our home computer, type in a particular code, and then request the text we want to read. Should we desire to purchase a copy of that text for our home library, we will use a special printer to print a copy quickly.

Databases for special interests will develop rapidly in the future. Information of all kinds will be available at the touch of a finger. As society becomes more complex and more facets of our life are affected by technology, it will become essential that we have immediate access to accurate and constantly updated information. Databases will help us to stay fine-tuned to the world around us.

The emergence of a public networking system, the National Public Telecomputing Network, similar to the Public Broadcasting System, offers a broad range of information services and databases to schools, communities, and home microcomputer users. The Internet is an electronic superhighway allowing users access to universities and other large resource-sharing entities across the United States.

DATA COMMUNICATIONS

Another area destined for rapid and significant development in the future is *data communications,* or the transfer and reception of data by electronic means. Many computer users rely on data communications via network systems. This allows large corporate offices to keep in constant communication with branch offices. It allows for centralized record keep-

FIGURE 5.14   PCtel modem.

ing and enables a corporation to coordinate the efforts of all its branches to best meet the needs of its customers. It is an effective means of keeping business healthy. This trend toward communicating over data networks will continue to grow, becoming faster and more reliable than it is today (see Figure 5.14).

Government will certainly work toward developing more effective means of data communication. It is important for governmental agencies to keep in contact with each other, for remote military bases to maintain communication, and even for nations to monitor each other's activities. More sophisticated means of data communications, such as fiber optics and microwave, will make communication faster and more effective in the future.

ARTIFICIAL INTELLIGENCE

Along with databases and data communications, the field of *artificial intelligence (AI)* will undergo rapid changes and development. Artificial intelligence refers to devices capable of imitating human cognitive processes: thinking, remembering, learning, inferring, and so forth. For the past twenty-five years, researchers have been working to develop a "teachable" computer. Although today's computers process numerical data, the AI computers of the future are expected to process nonnumerical data with technology that is being developed all over the world.

In addition, future generations of computers with artificial intelligence are expected to be able to decode instructions given them in ordinary human language. They may be able to compile their own instructions to perform virtually any task they are asked (literally!) to perform. Researchers say that these computers will be available in the near future.

Much work that has been done by humans is now being performed by robots, and this is expected to increase in the future. The term *robot* calls to most minds an image of a metal humanoid similar to the tin man in *The Wizard of Oz* or the two characters in the *Star Wars* series, R2D2 and C3PO. Yet robots are highly sophisticated machines capable of performing many tasks. They are particularly well suited to jobs that are repetitive, dangerous, or difficult for humans to perform. Robots can be exposed to situations that might injure the health of human workers. In addition, they are capable of working 24 hours a day, 7 days a week, with little need for work stoppage. Although the initial purchase price of robots is high, robots are extremely cost-effective workers.

The advent of computerized robots in manufacturing raises an important issue. Many people fear computers because they believe that these technological wonders will make human workers obsolete. What will happen to the large percent of the labor force whose jobs are eventually automated? Actually, there will be plenty of employment opportunities available in the future, but the nature of those jobs will be different than the jobs today. This is why the retooling and retraining going on in business and industry are such enormous tasks.

According to the U.S. Bureau of Labor Statistics, the need for qualified people to work in computer-related careers will double in the next decade. Many experts say that that estimate is too moderate and predict that the demand for such workers will easily triple during the next three years. It is logical to assume, then, that those workers who find themselves displaced by automation on the job will be retrained to assume computer-related positions. The robots cannot exist, after all, without human workers to design, manufacture, operate, and maintain them.

But robots in industry are merely one facet of the fascinating field of artificial intelligence. The impact of AI on computers in the schools will be momentous. Very young children will be able to operate computers without the need for typing skills or knowledge of programming languages. They will be able to "teach" the computer to carry out the activities they want done. Because AI computers function as intelligent aids to their users rather than as merely programmable machines, computers will become more effective teachers, listening to the students, responding according to information stored in memory, and then storing information away for later use. They will no longer rely on rigidly defined software.

COMPUTERS IN THE HOMES OF TOMORROW

Some of the most significant changes that we will witness will take place in our own homes. During the past several years, there has been a significant increase in the number of microcomputers being purchased for home use. No longer is computer power an advantage enjoyed only by a few very large corporations. Indeed, the decreasing size and price of powerful microcomputers will result in microcomputers becoming standard household appliances (see Figures 5.15, 5.16, and 5.17). How will this affect our daily lives?

Microcomputers are capable of performing any number of routine tasks now done by humans. Many microcomputer users now monitor budgets and bank accounts with their computer systems. Their computers are faster and more accurate than the users are. Tomorrow's homeowner will not need to keep account books, budgets, and voluminous files of papers to maintain a close watch on household matters; the microcomputer will assume these tasks.

When it is not busy balancing the checkbook, the home computer will keep an electronic "eye" on other household appliances. It will regulate the climatic conditions inside and outside the house in order to maintain a comfortable environment with the least amount of fuel. It may be used as a recipe file to store family favorites. The microcomputer may serve to turn on lights, turn off the microwave oven when dinner is fully cooked, and keep an inventory of food items on the cupboard shelves, adding items to a grocery list as they are used.

FIGURE 5.15   **Philips Magnavox Internet TV terminal.**

FIGURE 5.17   **Forty-six-inch plasma wall hanging display for high-definition television (HDTV).**

FIGURE 5.16   **Plug-n-play Internet video camera.**

Because much of our shopping will be done via computer, the microcomputer will report its grocery list to a computer at the grocery store. The necessary items will be ordered automatically. Microcomputers may even perform comparative shopping for users, compiling lists of prices from various stores and determining which store is most economical for the items needed.

After dinner is finished, children will use the microcomputer to do their homework. They will be able to use learning technologies at home as well as in their classrooms. They can learn from mathematics simulations, microworlds, and knowledge networks on their home computers. Schools and parents will communicate with each other via the Internet to a greater extent. Teachers will recommend software to be purchased, borrowed, downloaded, or rented that meets the individual needs of children and substitutes for some of the more traditional kinds of homework assignments. Family members may access the local public library via computer and the Internet/WWW, search through the collection for a specific book or a favorite author, reserve the materials, or access an article electronically via the World Wide Web. Because the computer will be part of your television set or home entertainment unit, most, if not all, children will have home access to computers and the WWW. Parents and older sisters and brothers can take college courses via distance education. Even graduate and postgraduate courses will be available to microcomputer users. Best of all, students of any age can set their own pace for learning. The computer is both patient and challenging.

Because the computer will save its users many hours spent in dull household chores, personal computer owners will have more leisure time. Some of this time they may choose to spend enjoying the many fascinating and challenging activities available via the web.

There will be many sorts of activities to enjoy. Again, the computer can challenge all ages and levels of ability. It can play Go Fish with a very small child and chess with an adult.

If the user is not in the mood for games, then he or she may use the microcomputer to create art of many types. For example, a visual artist can use the graphics capability to create stunning displays. A writer can use the word processing capability to compose the Great American Novel or to write a sonnet. Musicians can compose complex pieces of music and then hear their compositions performed immediately by computerized music synthesizers.

As more and more people purchase home computers and experiment with their capabilities, more applications of computers in the home will become apparent. Home life as we know it is destined to change in the future as computers relieve us from routine, often boring chores that we now perform. More than likely, we will find the microcomputer no more intimidating than an oven or a refrigerator.

COMPUTERS FOR PEOPLE WITH DISABILITIES

One of the most promising areas of technological advancement to watch in the future is the research and development of devices to aid the population with disabilities (see Figure 5.18). Many such devices are under study today and will become more accessible as computer technology develops smaller and less expensive computers. Speech recognition is one of many future technological developments that will have a major impact on aiding the population with disabilities.

Learning technologies have proven extremely effective in special education environments. Slow learners are comfortable using computers to master academic subjects that have proven difficult for them in the past. Also, students who are paralyzed or suffer muscle impairment that prevents them from holding a pen are capable of writing essays and solving mathematical problems with a computer. Severely handicapped or special needs students can use computers to learn in their homes if they are unable to attend classes (see Figure 5.19).

Computers also help people with disabilities in other ways. Voice synthesizers allow the speech-impaired to communicate their thoughts, perhaps for the first time. Still other

FIGURE 5.18   Bausch and Lomb PC Magni-Viewer magnifies on-screen information 175 percent.

FIGURE 5.19 Voice mail with voice recognition to email software.

devices help the vision-impaired to read and generate written texts. Because artificial-intelligence research promises to make computers more capable of imitating human activities, more computer aids for those with disabilities are sure to be developed in the future (see Figure 5.20). This gives hope to many today.

COMPUTERS IN THE SCHOOLS

One of the most exciting and promising areas of technological advancements will be in our schools. As costs of information technologies (i.e., computers and web servers) decrease and the economic demand for computer-literate adults increases, school systems will build information infrastructures at the classroom level. Very young children will learn to use

FIGURE 5.20 Foot-controlled mouse.

computers not only for the purpose of becoming computer literate but also to study conventional academic areas such as mathematics, history, composition, science, and international languages (see Figure 5.21). Curriculum can be centered on "authentic" problems in real-world settings (Cognition and Technology Group at Vanderbilt, 1997). Indeed, every subject that is taught in schools today can be adapted to digital learning. The CEO Forum on Education and Technology (2000) defines digital learning as "the educational approach that integrates technology, connectivity, content and human resources." Programs such as math•ed•ology (see <http://www.thejournal.com>) by Technology Based Learning and Research were designed to provide teachers with anytime, anywhere professional development. Simulations will be designed to give teachers and students opportunities to problem solve and interact with other professionals outside of the school setting. Project-based inquiry, virtual communities-of-practice (Linn, 1997), and other forms of sophisticated pedagogies will support students' development of higher-order cognitive, affective, and social skills necessary for success in a knowledge-based economy.

Widespread use of learning technologies will have a radical effect on education. Historically, learning technologies have been associated with computer-assisted instruction (CAI), which has been primarily drill-and-practice software programs. Learning technologies have progressed from educational television to CAI to Intelligent CAI (ICAI) to videodisk to hypermedia to hand-held computer access (Duchastel, 1996). The next cycle will evolve hand-held computer access to ubiquitous computing and databases to distributed (networked) learning environments including media retrieval systems and web-based media management systems.

Perhaps most importantly, learning technologies will make education available to virtually everyone. Special needs students who cannot attend regular classes, for example, will be able to "attend" class via the microcomputer. Students will be able to take courses offered at schools 5 miles or 5,000 miles from their homes without ever having to travel to the sites where these classes are taught. Imagine being able to study physics with a professor from the Massachusetts Institute of Technology and philosophy with a professor from the University of California at Berkeley in the same semester. This will be commonplace in the near future.

(a)

(b)

FIGURE 5.21   **(a) Mathematica used to solve complex math problems. Here, as the string wrapped around the cubic is unwound, its end traces out an involute. (b) EasyCam videoconferencing kit.**

Learning technologies will allow for more individualized instruction. Instead of gearing most activities toward the average student, teachers can challenge gifted students and provide remediation for students who require it. The computer is a patient teacher that allows students to determine their own pace for learning, thus freeing the teacher to work with students on a one-to-one basis. The computer serves as a kind of instant learning center, suitable for a myriad of purposes. And, freed from the necessity of conducting routine drills and performing many management duties, the teacher has more time to be the vital human link between student and knowledge. The computer does not supplant teachers; it supports them.

With authoring programs, students are able to create and write their own information. The use of interactive media within the classroom will continue to expand, to further address multisensory learning channels, and to introduce the global range of perspectives brought to bear on an issue, problem, or concept. Online collaborative projects will develop teamwork skills. Most importantly, participating in these expanded learning communities and project-based learning activities might increase students' taking responsibility for their own learning. These skills will be consistent with the new workplace.

The current trend to merge the computer lab with the library or media center to create a digital media lab will continue. The media lab exists as both a physical space—a digital media lab—and a virtual space—a collection of web-based resources. The lab will provide access to existing resources and will support the creation of new customized media projects for the faculty, support personnel, and students as well as the community (see Figure 5.22). Tomorrow's media centers will include fewer shelves of books and periodicals and more digital storage and retrieval systems. The process of data storage and retrieval, or databases, will become vital links between information and the people who require that information.

FIGURE 5.22   Emerging technologies support the creation of new customized media projects.

THE FUTURE STUDENT COMPUTER

The future student computer will be a hand-held device or "palmtop" with Internet access, software programs, input devices, and many mathematical capabilities. The student palmtop will have a calculator, graphing capabilities, productivity tools for word processing and spreadsheets, geometry construction tools, simulations, algebra systems, and intelligent tutor capabilities. It also will be able to adapt to the user's interests and abilities and may even talk to you. This wireless device will have a touch screen option like a magic slate, allowing students to input or write without a keyboard. Battery life will be similar to pagers—lasting weeks. So merging the organizer, pager, TV, Internet, streaming video, voice recognition, and handwriting recognition will produce a very slim, lightweight student hand-held computer.

Many of the technologies listed previously will be available on the palmtop or be accessible via this computer and the Internet. Students will have access to resources or digital content required by the school for their academic success. Students will be able to access many of the historical archives as well as download required textbook materials as needed. No more big, heavy backpacks! Students' academic activities and assignments will always be with them and can be sent to the teacher and/or parent for evaluation. Special needs functionality will be an integral part of this hand-held computer as well. It is clear that future technologies will become more interactive, promoting exploration, problem solving, communication, and higher-order thinking. By 2005, every student will have his or her own hand-held computer. This will truly be anytime, anywhere learning.

Clearly, we are in the midst of a technological revolution. As we look around us daily, we often wonder whether we have accidentally stepped into a time machine that has carried us far into the future. The phenomenal advancements in technology that we have witnessed during the past 20 years are only the tip of the iceberg. What technological achievements lie in our future is anyone's guess! Because our technological society will have deep roots in math and science concepts, people of all ages will be expected to become both scientifically and technologically literate.

SUMMARY

In the future, we may expect to see rapid technological advancements in computers. Research and development is geared toward five areas in particular: continued miniaturization, greater memory capacity, speech synthesis and recognition, artificial intelligence, and enhanced graphics displays. Greater amounts of computer power will be built into physically smaller units that will be more affordable and, hence, more accessible to the average person. These smaller computers will be made more powerful by new systems of memory that allow for greater storage. Speech synthesis and recognition will make computers easier to use because they will be able to communicate directly with humans. Finally, improved graphics capabilities will make computers more attractive to those who wish to generate visual displays.

The computers of tomorrow will be used in a great number of applications, both social and personal. They help regulate traffic flow, control airplane landings and takeoffs, and monitor the vital signs of hospital patients. They serve to diagnose illnesses and prescribe treatment. In addition, they play a more important role in the educational system as a greater number of schools implement curricula that employ emerging information technologies.

We can also expect to see expanded use of databases by the general public. Databases give computer users access to up-to-the-minute information on a wide range of subjects. Not only are databases extremely useful to professionals such as doctors, lawyers, and law enforcement officers, but they also provide special-interest information on hobbies, first aid, and current events. Tomorrow's complex society will necessitate fast access to updated information.

Data communications, or the transfer and retrieval of data via electronic means, will develop to become an important way for large corporations to keep in constant contact with their branch offices. It will also be used more widely by government agencies and others who must maintain close contact with remote locations.

Yet another promising area of technological advancement is artificial intelligence. Future computers will be capable of imitating human cognitive activities such as thinking, remembering, and inferring. They will be able to compile their own instructions based on commands given them in ordinary human language, allowing more people to "program" computers without extensive knowledge of computer programming languages. Also, AI robots will continue to be used widely in industry, causing a significant shift of the labor force from industrial work to technically oriented jobs.

Home computers will expedite the work of homeowners by keeping records, maintaining budgets, and regulating household inventories. They will also serve as important learning tools either to supplement education received in traditional classrooms or to serve as a medium of taking classes via distance education. This access will be able to provide many forms of entertainment. More people will use their microcomputers to work at home without the need for traveling to a work site. DVD will combine the TV and PC into one home entertainment unit merging excellent video and sound capabilities with interactivity that will revolutionize home entertainment. Education will utilize this technological impact with parent, school, and home communication and interactivity. The classroom of tomorrow will bridge the current learning gap—the difference between available resources and classroom access.

People with disabilities will enjoy numerous new computerized devices that will improve the quality of their lives. Speech synthesizers, for example, will allow the speech-impaired to communicate orally.

The future holds great promise of technological advancements that will change our lives for the better.

LEARNER ACTIVITIES

1. Interview a computer scientist about the future of technology and write a summary of the discussion.

2. Write your own scenario of the technology-based classroom of the future.

3. Research predictions of future technology by several computer experts. Include any research findings on the success or lack of success of emerging technologies. Report on your findings.

4. Consider how the development of artificial intelligence will affect learning technologies.

5. Develop a unit of practice in which students explore the future of technology.

6. Write a report reviewing the literature on the role of learning technologies for special needs students.

7. Write a report on the potential impact of voice recognition on education.

8. Write a report on the impact that the Digital Versatile Disc (DVD) will have on the future of education.

9. Write a report on the implications of web-based instruction via the WWW on business, industry, and education.

10. Design a hand-held student computer. Include a drawing, size specifications, and capabilities and applications that this computer will possess.

BIBLIOGRAPHY

Artificial intelligence goes postal. (1997). *Science, 275,* 1073.

Austin, M. B. (1994). A comparison of three interactive media formats in an RTV/DVI computer-mediated lesson. *Computers and Education, 22,* 319–333.

Benedikt, M. (Ed.). (1991). *Cyberspace: First steps.* Cambridge, MA: The MIT Press.

Broadband Editor. (2000). Colorado State University expedites student research with library-wide wireless network. *T.H.E. Journal, 28*(2), 34–37.

CEO Forum on Education and Technology. (2000). *The power of learning: Integrating digital content.* Washington, DC: Author.

Cheng, D., & Yan, H. (1997). Recognition of broken and noisy handwritten characters using statistical methods based on a broken-character-mending algorithm. *Optical Engineering, 36,* 1465–1479.

Cognition and Technology Group at Vanderbilt. (1997). *The Jasper project: Lessons in curriculum, instruction, assessment, and professional development.* Mahwah, NJ: Lawrence Erlbaum.

Collins, H. M. (1990). *Artificial experts—Social knowledge and intelligent machines.* Cambridge, MA: The MIT Press.

Decker, R., & Hirschfield, S. (1992). *The analytical engine: An introduction to computer science using toolbook.* Belmont, CA: Wadsworth.

Dede, C. (2000). *Implications of emerging information technologies for states' education policies.* Commissioned paper for the Council of Chief State School Officers' Educational Technology Leadership Conference in January 2000. Available: <http://publications.ccsso.org/ccsso/publication_detail.cfm?PID=290>

D'Ignazio, F. (1990). Electronic highways and the classroom of the future. *The Computing Teacher, 17*(8), 2–24.

Duchastel, P. (1996). Learning interfaces. In T. Liao (Ed.), *Advanced educational technology: Research issues and future potential.* New York: Springer-Verlag.

East, P. (1990). On the basics of education in the 21st century. *The Computing Teacher, 17*(6), 6–7.

Finkel, L., Rawitsch, D., & Brady, H. (1990). Memories: A ten-year retrospective. *Classroom Computer Learning, 10*(8), 14–15, 18–31.

Gader, P. D., Keller, J. M., Krishnapuram, R., Chiang, J. -H., & Mohamed, J. A. (1997). Neural and fuzzy methods in handwriting recognition. *Computer, 30,* 79–86.

Girard, K., & Dillon, N. (1997). Market grows for voice applications. *Computerworld, 31*(32), 55–56.

Haugeland, J. (1986). *Artificial intelligence: The very idea.* Boston: The MIT Press.

Hofmeister, A. M. (1991). Expert systems and decision support in special education: Results and promise. *Educational Technology, 31*(10), 23–28.

Hughes, T. (1990). *American genius.* New York: Penguin.

Kim, G., & Govindaraju, V. (1997). A lexicon driven approach to handwritten work recognition for real-time applications. *IEEE Transactions on Pattern Analysis and Machine Intelligence, 19,* 366–379.

Kirkpatrick, S. N., & Biglan, B. (1990). AI in the elementary, middle, and secondary classroom. *The Computing Teacher, 17*(5), 14–19.

LaBarge, R. S. (1996). *DVD Today,* Vol. 1 [CD-ROM]. Crofton, MD: NB Digital Solutions.

Leedham, D. G., & Qiao, Y. (1992). High speed text input to computer using handwriting. *Instructional Science, 21,* 209–221.

Linn, M. C. (1997). Learning and instruction in science education: Taking advantage of technology. In D. Tobin and B. J. Fraser (Eds.), *International handbook of science education.* The Netherlands: Klewer.

Lundsten, A., & Doiel, R. (2000). Digital video and Internet2: Growing up together. *Syllabus, 14*(1), 12–16.

McCullough, M., Mitchell, W. J., & Purcell, R. (Eds.). (1990). *The electronic design studio: Architectural knowledge and media in the computer era.* Cambridge, MA: The MIT Press.

National Foundation for the Improvement of Education. (1991). *Images of potential.* Washington, DC: Author.

Patterson, J. C. (2000). How digital video is changing education. *Curriculum Administrator, 36*(6), 34–37.

Pearlman, R. (1989). Technology's role in restructuring schools. *Electronic Learning, 8*(8), 9, 12, 14–15, 56.

Roberts, G. I., & Samuels, M. T. (1993). Handwriting remediation: A comparison of computer-based and traditional approaches. *Journal of Educational Research, 87,* 118–125.

Schenkel, M. E. (1995). *Handwriting recognition using neural networks and hidden markov models.* Kontanz, Germany: Hartung-Gorre Verlag.

Sheingold, K. (1991). Restructuring for learning with technology: The potential for synergy. *Phi Delta Kappan, 73,* 17–27.

Sin, B.-K., & Kim, J. H. (1997). Ligature modeling for on-line cursive script recognition. *IEEE Transactions on Pattern Analysis and Machine Intelligence, 19,* 623–633.

Solomon, G. (1990). Learning to use the tools of the future. *Electronic Learning, 9*(5), 14–15.

Soloway, E., Grant, W., Tinker, R., Roschelle, J., Mills, M., Resnick, M., Berg, R., & Eisenberg, M. (1999). Science in the palm of their hands. *Communications of the ACM, 42*(8), 21–26.

Szuprowicz, B. O. (1995). *Multimedia networking.* New York: McGraw-Hill.

Tamashiro, R., & Bechtelheimer, L. (1991). Expert systems in the elementary grades: Developing thinking skills and independent learning. *The Computing Teacher, 18*(5), 21–26.

VRML industry microcosms in the making. (1998). *New Media, 8*(3), 21–24.

Wildstrom, S. H. (1997, September 22). PC, take a letter to Mr. Jones. *Business Week,* (3545), 18.

Williams, C. (2000). *Internet access in public schools: 1994–1999* (NCES 2000–086). U.S. Department of Education, Washington, DC: National Center for Education Statistics.

Willis, W. (1998). Speech recognition: Instead of typing and clicking, talk and command. *T.H.E. Journal, 25*(6), 18–22.

Ziegler, Bart. (1998, January 29). New generation of hand-held PCs inches closer to ideal. *Wall Street Journal,* p. B1.

WEBSITES

About Internet2 <http://www.internet2.edu/html/about.html>

Canon DV: DV Format <http://www.canondv.com/shared/dvinfo/dvinfo3.html>

Cappuccio, D. (1997). Network computers—Panacea and Pandora's box. Garter Research. Available: <http://gartner4.gartnerweb.com/public/static/consulting/tco/tv000032.html>

Communication Intelligence Corporation <http://www.cic.com>

Handwritten word recognition. Center of Excellence for Document Analysis and Recognition (CEDAR). Available: <http://www.cedar.buffalo.edu/Linguistics/hwwr.html>

Lexicus Handwriting Recognition Technologies <http://www.motorola.com/MIMS/lexicus/technologies/handwriting/>

Memory Stick Information <http://www.hightechproductions.com/memorystick.htm>

Panasonic DVD homepage <http://www.panasonic.com/PCEC/dvd/indexdvd.html>

Rawson, C. E. (1996, July 5). Breaking down the last document automation barriers! An overview of Natural Handwriting Recognition (NHR). Available: <http://www.infotivity.com/hwr.htm>

SmartMedia Technology Primer <http://www.pc-card.com/smartmedia.htm>

Sony DVD <http://www2.sony.com/SEL/consumer>

Srihari, S. N., & Kuebert, E. J. (1997, May 31). Integration of hand-written address interpretation technology into the United States Postal Service Remote Computer Reader System. Center of Excellence for Document Analysis and Recognition (CEDAR). Available: <http://www.cedar.buffalo.edu/Publications/TechReps/HWAIPaper/integration_of_hwai-2.html>

Ubiquitous Computing <http://www.ubiq.com/hypertext/weiser/UbiHome.html>

Zakon, R. H. (2000, July). Hobbes' Internet time line. Available: <http://info.isoc.org/guest/zakon/Internet/History/HIT.html>

Speech Recognition Sites

<http://www.hitl.washington.edu/publications/dissertations/Savage/home.html>

<http://www.kurzweil.com/pcapps/vppro/>

IBM Voice Systems <http://www-4.ibm.com/software/speech/>

Microsoft Speech Technology <http://www.research.microsoft.com/research/srg/>

Personal Communication Attendant <http://www.pcahome.com>

Speech Commander <http://www.voicecommander.com/index_main.html>

CHAPTER 6

RESEARCH ON TECHNOLOGY IN TEACHING AND LEARNING

FOCUS QUESTIONS

1. How do classroom teaching and learning behaviors alter as a result of introducing computers to the curriculum?
2. Does computer use lead to academic gains in all subject areas?
3. What are reasonable effects to expect from integrating technology in typical classrooms?

During his first week in office, President George W. Bush (2001) issued his education plan, *No Child Left Behind.* Addressing technology specifically in the section "Enhancing Education Through Technology," the President stated, "The Administration believes schools should use technology as a tool to improve academic achievement, and that using the latest technology in the classroom should not be an end unto itself." His plan calls for a streamlined performance-based technology grant program that sends more money to schools. It is anticipated that this action will strengthen previous efforts launched by the U.S. Department of Education's report, *Getting America's Students Ready for the Twenty-First Century,* which urged the nation's educational leaders to initiate changes to prepare our younger generations for success in the twenty-first century. This report supported the four "pillars" of technology:

1. All teachers in the nation will have the training and support necessary to help students learn to use computers and the information superhighway.
2. All teachers and students will have access to modern multimedia computers.
3. Every classroom will be connected to the information superhighway.
4. Effective software and online learning resources will be an integral part of every school's curriculum (U.S. Department of Education, 1996).

In support of this initiative, the Panel on Educational Technology (1997) published a series of strategic recommendations on the application of various technologies to K–12 education:

1. Focus on learning with technology as a tool, not about technology as a subject in and of itself.
2. Emphasize content and pedagogy rather than hardware use alone.
3. Give special attention to professional development for teachers on the effective use of technology.
4. Engage in realistic budgeting, so that computer technology is a part of ongoing operating budgets rather than a one-time expenditure.
5. Ensure equitable, universal technology access to all students, regardless of socioeconomic status, race, ethnicity, gender, or geographical factors.
6. Initiate a major program of experimental research to ensure both the efficacy and cost-effectiveness of technology use within our nation's schools.

Recent survey statistics reveal that these challenges have begun to be met. Ninety-seven percent of all teachers use computers at either home or school for professional responsibilities (Fatemi, 1999). Fifty-three percent of teachers say that they use educational software for instructional purposes, and 61 percent use the Internet for instruction. However, a key barrier to regular technology use appears to be access. Almost half of the teachers surveyed reported that there was software they would like to use but had no way of obtaining it through their districts, and an equal number found locating quality educational websites difficult and time-consuming. Somewhat surprising is the fact that newer teachers, those with less than five years' experience, are no more likely to use technology than are teachers who have been in the classroom over twenty years. This statistic hints at a more complex challenge than can be met by simply purchasing adequate hardware.

This chapter will first inform educators about characteristics unique to educational technology research so that results can be appropriately interpreted. It will then report an overview of recent findings on technology's effect on teaching and learning. Any expected change in classrooms as a result of technology hinges on teachers' perceptions and understandings of the potential benefits and barriers. Hence, an awareness of current research findings must be a part of the ongoing dialogue on the benefits of technology in the classroom.

INTERPRETING THE RESULTS OF RESEARCH ON TECHNOLOGY IN EDUCATION

Unfortunately, as the technology wave crashes into traditional educational practices, teachers are infrequently being made aware of the latest research findings. Dozens of articles are written every year on educational technology–related topics, and although the sheer amount of information can be staggering to new teachers, being aware of the mistakes and successes of others will help to establish sound practices. In order to integrate technology effectively into the lives of students, teachers need to be able to weigh the evidence. Do computers make students smarter? How do actual classroom teaching and learning behaviors alter as a result of introducing computers to the curriculum? Is this technological revolution really good for our children, or is this just education's attempt to stay up with the times? (See Figure 6.1.)

Changing Research Goals

As each new media type has become available to classrooms, educators, along with the general public, have been quick to jump on the bandwagon, hoping that real change in education may be possible this time. History shows, however, that many educational innovations have come and gone without satisfying the goals for improved student learning. Much of the past research on technology integration has focused on incorporating computers into traditional teaching methods (Berson, 1996) and allowing teachers to do what they normally do, but faster (O'Neil, 1995). Educators are discovering that it is no longer enough merely to place a computer in a classroom and say that students are "using" technology. It is the way computers are used rather than the actual machines themselves that contribute to learning (Proctor & Burnett, 1996; Roblyer, 1997). Researchers are beginning to look more at how technology might change basic teaching and learning processes to better address expectations for what students should learn, moving away from simply investigating whether students have higher test scores with computer-based instruction (Roblyer, 1996).

New Learning Theory and Practice

Any discussion of the inclusion of technology in classrooms should be informed by an understanding of current learning theories and practices that represent fundamental changes

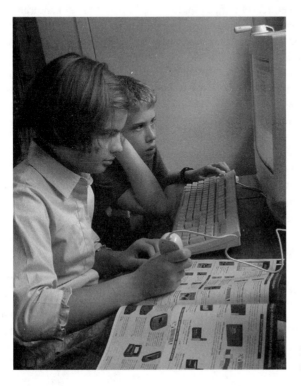

FIGURE 6.1   Do computers make students smarter?

in the ways teachers teach and learners learn. *Constructivism* is a learning theory premised on the understanding that people are participants in their own learning. There is no one true reality that must be imparted to learners, but rather individuals create their own knowledge based on how they relate new information to what they have previously experienced. *Social constructivism* additionally recognizes the value of social interactions in the learning process, meaning that people clarify personal conceptions as they interact with the understandings of others. *Engaged learning* is tied closely to constructivist underpinnings. Students learn best when they are active participants in the learning process, meaning that they make their own decisions, think critically about real learning problems and resources, and operate in contexts that are meaningful to them. Authentic, challenging, and multidisciplinary learning tasks allow students to grasp the subject matter better.

Teachers in constructivist and engaged learning classrooms must build rich learning environments filled with opportunities for authentic, project-based tasks as well as a variety of technology and nontechnology tools. They must then facilitate the management of a range of information by their students, rather than telling students what they need to know. Students need to have a say in what topics will be explored and ample interaction with peers, adults, experts, and others with whom they can test theories and confirm understanding. Students take ownership of their own learning, with teachers serving a supportive, rather than directive, role.

Clarifying the Research Variables

The changed goals for research on technology use, along with the increasing acceptance of constructivist and engaged learning principles, have implications for interpreting research results on the effectiveness of technology in education. Computers used in traditional classrooms, in which students are expected to converge upon predetermined correct answers, will have a different effect on student learning than computers used in classrooms in which students are expected to come to their own understandings of various concepts. Technology will be used for different purposes in each situation.

The following three factors must first be accepted to be able to interpret research on the effectiveness of technology in student learning (Honey, Culp, & Spielvogel, 1999):

1. *Technology* refers to more than computers, including a range of electronic methods and tools that can be used to support learning (see Figure 6.2).
2. The assessment of how technology impacts student achievement is a complex process that demands alternative methods to standardized assessments of isolated facts.
3. Classroom change correlates with other educational factors, such as teaching and learning roles.

Educators looking to the results of research for the answers about using technology for learning might start by isolating study variables through the following questions:

Who? Who are the leaders in student learning? Do students have ownership and direction in their own learning or are classroom activities primarily teacher-directed?

What? What technology is being used? Are students using productivity software, content-specific software, web-based tools, or scientific probeware?

**FIGURE 6.2   Technology refers to more than computers, including a range of
electronic methods and tools that can be used to support learning.**

Where? Where do students have access to technology? Regular, as-needed access to computers in the classroom will impact student learning differently than will limited, weekly visits to the computer lab.

Why? Why is technology being used? Is there a clear learning goal in mind, or is technology being used only for technology's sake?

How? How is technology used by students and teachers? Are electronic information sources used to supplement traditional instruction or as the basis for student-led, meaningful, inquiry-based learning?

Research reports do not always clearly specify the learning conditions in classrooms in which technology use is studied, so consumers of research must look carefully for clues. If none exist, the results should not be taken as a complete story but rather as one indication of technology effectiveness.

TEACHING WITH TECHNOLOGY

Teachers' actions largely influence their students' achievement. Therefore, an understanding of the academic effects of the use of technology for students should begin with an understanding of the impact of technology on the teaching profession. The types of teachers who use technology, how that technology use alters teaching practice, the effects on collegial relationships, and the stages of integration that teachers progress through when adopting technology as a part of their teaching are areas of recent investigation.

Technology-Using Teachers

Becker (1994) looked at how "exemplary computer-using teachers" differ from other teachers in the environment in which they teach, their personal computer experience, and their teaching habits. Using information from surveys of third- through twelfth-grade teachers, this study found four main requirements of a school environment that make it more conducive to exemplary computer users.

1. Teachers need to be surrounded by other teachers who use computers. Whether expert or novice users, teachers can benefit from the collegial sharing of ideas, resources, and teaching strategies with other computer-using teachers in their building.
2. Teachers benefit by working in a school in which computers are used for authentic, meaningful purposes, such as for writing for a real audience. Exemplary computer-using teachers are more likely to come from a setting like this than from one in which word processing is used only to accomplish predetermined skills or computers are used primarily for games.
3. Financial support for technology at both the school and district levels makes for more proficient computer users. Schools in which exemplary computer users were found frequently had a school or district computer coordinator who assisted teachers in getting started with technology integration. In addition, these teachers had available to them sufficient staff development opportunities, to instruct them in computer applications and integrate the computer into the content being taught.
4. A "resource-rich" environment supports expert computer users. Teachers often had smaller class sizes and fewer students per computer. It is unclear whether teachers were able to become exemplary computer users because they had smaller classes, or if they were given smaller classes because they were exemplary computer users.

When surveyed about their personal backgrounds, researchers found that these exemplary computer-using teachers, more than other teachers, spent a great deal of their personal time working on computers, staying after school, or bringing computers home. These teachers on the whole also had more training with using computers, higher levels of education, more experience teaching their current subject; and they tended to a large degree to be male. In practice, the teachers surveyed who fell into the category of exemplary computer users more often than others made conscious decisions to alter existing curriculum, eliminating less important topics to allow room for more computer-related endeavors. They allowed students some choice in their learning and encouraged teams of students to work together on computer assignments. Together, these data imply that both increased personal interest as well as greater amounts of experience, with computers and with general content knowledge, make for a teacher more apt to be successful in computer integration in the classroom. This is found in other studies that show that the amount of technology used by the teacher positively impacts student achievement in areas such as reading and math (e.g., Middleton & Murray, 1999). There is a strong need for training to maintain teachers' knowledge of new technology and its use in education, not limited to specially designated computer teachers, but extended to all teachers involved (Yaghi, 1996).

Changes in Teaching Practice

The Apple Classrooms of Tomorrow (ACOT) project involved giving every teacher and every student from test classrooms across the country two computers each, one to use at school and one to bring home (David, 1995). The intent was to create model, technology-rich learning environments in which teachers and students could use computers on a routine, authentic basis. Changes in teaching practices do not take place instantaneously (Ringstaff, Sandholtz, & Dwyer, 1995). ACOT researchers found that new technology is typically slotted into a place determined by old teaching habits. Teachers and students initially followed the traditional classroom patterns with which they were familiar (O'Neil, 1995). Gradually, over years of participating in the study, teachers began making noticeable alterations in the dynamics of the learning environments, based on the new thinking the technology sparked. Teachers were finding out that one person, whether it is himself or herself or a student, could not always be the expert on every facet of a new technology medium. Recognizing the potential for student involvement in the teaching of peers was a difficult shift for many teachers who had grown accustomed to the traditional teacher–student relationship structure. When teachers were able to move past that pervasive teacher-centered view of education, students and teachers, as communities of learners, were able to benefit from the range of individual areas of expertise represented by the entire group (see Figure 6.3).

Collegial Relationships

As teachers ventured through this learning process, they discovered new facets of relationships they shared with each other (Ringstaff et al., 1995). In a traditional school, teachers are fairly autonomous; once the classroom doors close, the majority of their time is spent with students. Teachers in the ACOT schools at first communicated primarily to commiserate about their unfamiliar experiences and to support each other. As they grew accustomed to having and using the technology, they supported each other using the hardware

FIGURE 6.3   Students and teachers benefit from the range of individual areas of expertise represented by the entire group.

and software, passed along instructional ideas and strategies, and ultimately collaborated with team members to develop innovative teaching methods and curricula. Technology was the topic of conversation and also the medium through which much of the communication was made possible.

Stages of Integration

Researchers were able to identify five distinct stages through which teachers new to technology developmentally progressed in their pursuit of technology integration (Sandholtz, Ringstaff, & Dwyer, 1997). The *Entry* stage was one of frequently painful growth as experienced teachers ran headlong into the very basic challenges that generally plague rookie teachers. Everyone involved was required to learn to live with very different classrooms than those in which they were used to teaching and learning. Teachers had to contend with students experimenting with new cheating techniques, technical problems, and the annoyances of classroom facilities not built for computers. At this initial stage, teachers found themselves reacting to the small issues and overlooking the larger issues involved with integrating the computers into effective instructional agendas. Teachers transitioned into the *Adoption* stage as they began to take more of a proactive stance toward meeting the challenges presented by the computers. They worked with students to learn to use the hardware and software and began learning from their mistakes to settle into tolerable patterns of classroom life, often accepting a level of movement and activity in the classroom that they might not have found acceptable earlier. Learning to use the technology tends to take precedence over the integration of content, with initial technology projects done with excitement and flash, but meaningful content integration taking perhaps years (Goldman, Cole, & Syer, 1999). In the *Adaptation* stage, teachers finally began making the technology work for them, instructionally and for administrative duties. The traditional lecture format perpetuated in classes throughout the study, but teachers were able to get past issues of teaching the technology and get back to teaching content. During the *Appropriation* stage, they were able to move beyond simply accommodating computers and squeezing them into the traditional daily routine and began to personally accept the new teaching possibilities technology offers. Ultimately, the teachers arrived at the *Invention* stage, at which they were not only ready but also eager to break out of typical, teacher-controlled classroom routines. At this stage, teachers communicated with each other a great deal, sharing ideas and innovations, and even bringing together groups of students for authentic project-based activities. Working with and learning from other teachers and students characterized this changed philosophy of education whereby technology became the medium for inquiry, collaboration, and constant reflection on what was being accomplished and what was yet attainable. At this final stage, teachers take advantage of new communication capabilities to play the roles of information consultants, team collaborators, facilitators, course developers, and academic advisers (Kook, 1997).

LEARNING WITH TECHNOLOGY

Those involved with educational policy decisions regarding technology issues are frequently concerned with one issue: Do the academic gains brought by the addition of computers into classrooms outweigh the financial expenditures necessary to equip classrooms? Unfortunately, those looking for quick answers will find none. The results from research into the effects of technology on learning are mixed. Whereas a large proportion of researchers are able to demonstrate positive academic results, others have shown no effects or even slightly negative impacts on achievement.

Overall Academic Effects

Similar to the ACOT study, a study of concentrated computer use took place in Union City, New Jersey, a largely ethnic and impoverished community in the most densely populated city in the United States (Honey, Culp, & Carrigg, 1999). The city embarked on substantive changes in class block length, increased in-service training for teachers, buildings renovation, and improved class libraries. Union City also began investing in technology resources so that it is now one of the most wired urban school districts in the country. Researchers found that these reforms impacted standardized-test performance, especially for those students with home and school access to technology. Writing was the area in which middle-grade students showed the greatest gains. Increased expectations and teacher preparation combined with other reforms to achieve such improvements. The researchers recommend that technology will have the greatest impact when other reforms happen in concert. Professional development in teaching approaches, not only for technology skills, must be offered to teachers. Students should be assisted in developing learning skills such as creativity through individualized tasks for all ability levels. Information-rich environments including technology and nontechnology tools should be available.

When compared with students in traditional classrooms, students in technology-rich ACOT classrooms were more apt to work together, which made school more interesting and, consequently, improved students' attitudes about themselves and their learning (Sandholtz, Ringstaff, & Dwyer, 1995b). Rather than merely fulfilling what was asked of them in assignments, these students surpassed original goals, challenging themselves to explore new and creative projects and often choosing to work during their free time. Teachers, in fact, had trouble at times getting students to move on to other projects. Students did not, as was feared at the outset, become solo workers in front of their personal computer screens. Instead, they developed and demonstrated the ability to use social interaction to enhance their learning by sharing knowledge and explaining processes as they were undertaken (see Figure 6.4).

Along with those for whom computers facilitated a richer learning experience, some students became just as bored with technology as they did with traditional teaching. This was the case when the technology was not used as just one of a selection of classroom tools but was focused on in an artificial manner. Students worked best when technology was not the topic itself but was integrated into the entire curriculum.

High school students who had unlimited access to technology during their entire high school careers matured into self-starting problem solvers and self-assured collaborators (Tierney et al., 1995). They were able to verbalize the role computers played in their growth as students, and they saw how the unique abilities they had gained during those four years had empowered them to future success.

A staggering number of studies on educational technology have examined the effects of a whole range of factors on success with technology, from student variables, such as gender and socioeconomic levels, to environmental variables, such as the type of technology

FIGURE 6.4   **Students do not become solo workers in front of their computers, but use social interaction to enhance their learning.**

being used. Academic and other gains made by various segments of students often appear to contradict each other; so, again, the reader is cautioned to interpret such findings as partial indication of effectiveness rather than as absolute truth.

Boys are more likely than girls to see themselves as computer users and to see the world of computer use as male-dominated, although behaviors related to computers do not generally vary according to gender (Whitley, 1997). Boys are more concerned with mastery of computer work and feel more relaxed while working with computers, possibly leading them to feel better about their performance of work on the computer. It is believed that differences in how boys and girls perceive their computer competence stem from boys having more opportunities, at home and at school, to use computers (Nelson & Cooper, 1997).

Having a home computer is associated with higher mathematics and reading scores, and in general, children from high- rather than low-socioeconomic-status homes, boys more than girls, and white students more than ethnic minorities, achieve the largest educational gains from home computers (Attewell & Battle, 1999). Other findings indicate that high school students' skill and experience with computers, parental education, access to computers, and even academic self-concept are all reliable predictors of student use of electronic communication tools (Fishman, 1999). Fifth-graders using an integrated learning system improved test scores, although in this case, lower-achieving students made the greatest gains, and boys and girls achieved equally (Mann, Shakeshaft, Becker, & Kottkamp, 1999).

Both regular and special needs students in technology-rich environments showed positive achievement in all subject areas in preschool through higher education, as well as improved attitudes toward learning and self-concept (Sivin-Kachala, 1998). Students who used educational computer games had more developed comprehension skills and outscored nongame-playing peers in both reading and math, possibly a result of experience with comprehending game instructions and performing game-related tasks (Mayer, Schustack, & Blanton, 1999). Technology has been shown to allow learner control, increase motivation, provide connections to the real world, and lead to increased achievement when tied to content standards and the needs of the learners (Valdez et al., 1999).

The Effect of Technology
on Language Achievement

Research into the effects of technology on student achievement in language arts has resulted in widely disparate findings. The quality of writing produced by second-graders on word processors improved over writing they produced using paper and pencil. In addition, their stories were longer than those that they wrote by hand (Jones, 1994). Students who first had experiences writing with the help of word processors showed signs that they maintained a higher level of writing even when they later wrote with paper and pencil. Sixth-grade students who wrote compositions on word processors showed few differences in quality and complexity of compositions, as well as the accuracy of grammar, from students who wrote compositions by hand (Nichols, 1996). Those students using word processors, provided they had ample keyboarding experience, wrote significantly longer compositions that those writing with paper and pencil. Using computers has no conclusive effects on either the quantity or quality of the writing of fifth-graders. This suggests that the difference in students' writing abilities will stem from their teachers' beliefs and dedication toward teaching writing rather than from the decision of whether to use computers (Dybdahl, Shaw, & Blahous, 1997).

A review of research on the effects of word processing programs on students' writing abilities shows that in general, writing using word processing programs improves students' attitudes toward writing, produces longer and more fluent written products, and allows students to revise their writing more easily and quickly than with paper and pencil (Reed, 1996). Despite this success, the potential problem with word processing programs is that they are not completely aligned to writing process theory. The programs offer an open area for drafting compositions, but do not prompt student writers to consider prewriting thoughts or specific revision activities. Teachers should understand the role of this software as a tool in the writing process, not a substitute for the process itself.

Technology allows students to enhance written words using multiple modalities through which to communicate, such as through video, animation, and sound effects (Baker & Kinzer, 1998). Word processing allows teachers to reevaluate composition methods by viewing the writing process as dynamic and recursive, rather than linear, as it frequently is when students use pencil and paper. Students who word processed rarely considered writing pieces finished, regularly returning to saved files to rework compositions. Peers collaborated more openly, offering feedback to writers as they passed by the computer monitors. These practices signal potentially dramatic changes in assessment, as traditional practices such as grading final papers might not measure student learning sufficiently. A caveat emerging is the tendency for students to put more focus on creating electronic presentations than on attending to the content of the paper.

Researchers have also investigated the effects of technology on reading comprehension. Students had higher comprehension scores after reading the electronic stories versus reading printed texts (Greenlee-Moore & Smith, 1996; Matthew, 1997). The interactive effects of the sound, animation, narration, and additional definitions that make up the electronic texts motivate students to want to read the stories again and again, something researchers found to occur less often with printed books. The educational potential of these stories is jeopardized when insufficient teacher guidance leads to the software being used solely for entertainment.

Ninety percent of kindergarteners using a computer-based reading readiness program achieved grade-level reading ability by first grade (Alfaro, 1999). Third- through sixth-grade students in a low socioeconomic community scored the same reading scores with traditional basal reading preparation and computer-assisted instruction (Hamilton, 1995). Students using computers in a collaborative context demonstrated superior depth of understanding and reflection, as well as improved reading and language scores (Scardamalia & Bereiter, 1996).

The Effect of Technology on Mathematics Achievement

Research into how computers have affected mathematics learning and teaching examines effects of programming, computer-assisted instruction, and tool software (McCoy, 1996). Students from primary to secondary grades who have programming experience score higher on measures of geometry knowledge and problem solving. A review of research found that experimental groups of students from third grade to high school, using fraction software, problem-solving software, and estimation software, scored significantly higher than did control groups (McCoy, 1996). Simulation programs that allowed students to explore mathematical environments actively were shown to be effective in helping students understand geometric notions and develop intuitive understandings of graphing. Students using mathematical software for algebra, geometry, and calculus were shown to have gained a better understanding of the topic (McCoy, 1996). The tools allowed students to actively participate in mathematical topics that otherwise might be considered stagnant or outdated (Blubaugh, 1995).

Students were more motivated and self-confident about subjects such as calculus, finding them to be more meaningful than they had previously thought (Rochowicz, 1996). Students in math courses in which computers were used were able to tackle more complex problems without spending time on routine exercises. High school geometry students using problem-solving software as part of their mathematics program scored significantly higher in both problem-solving and general performance areas than did students not using the software (Funkhouser, 1993). In addition, students found enjoyment in what they were learning, which motivated them to put more effort into their work. Other studies, however, found no difference between the achievement levels of students using computers in mathematics and those who were not, yet noted improved motivation and participation of the computer users (McCoy, 1996).

The professional development of the teacher and the frequency of home computer use were positively related to academic achievement in mathematics (Education Testing Service, 1998). Fourth-graders achieved better in mathematics when they had experience using math computer games, whereas eighth-graders did better when higher-order thinking skills were stressed. The positive aspects of technology use were more prominent for older students, equivalent to up to 15 weeks above grade level, than younger students.

The Effect of Technology on Science Achievement

Computers have been used in science classrooms in a variety of ways aimed both at helping students learn scientific facts and at giving them experience with the scientific process. As with other studies of academic achievement, results in the area of science are mixed. In one review of current literature on the topic (Weller, 1996), results span the range: Research shows that work with computer-assisted instruction packages allowed students to learn more than they would working in only a traditional lab setting, to computer instruction acting as a supplement to traditional instruction, to, finally, computer programs being not more effective than some styles of instruction, such as self-paced. Simulation software, and the more complex science "microworld" simulations, offers students opportunities to change understanding at the conceptual levels. Students in middle grades using simulations exhibited growth in conceptual understanding. Students were often able to transfer their understanding to written tests, on occasion outperforming students at much higher levels who had not had the benefit of learning with technology. Secondary students learning from simulations were shown to score higher on standardized science tests and to be capable of sharing rich scientific dialogue about the topic of a simulation. Studies on the effects of other technologies, such as interactive video and microcomputer-based laboratories, whereby actual data are measured and converted into digital information, and a number of others show similarly variable results (Weller, 1996). On the average, students receiving traditional instruction supplemented with computer-assisted instruction attained higher science achievement than did those receiving only traditional instruction (Christmann & Badgett, 1999).

The Effect of Technology on Social Studies Achievement

In a review of recent research involving the effectiveness of computers in social studies (Berson, 1996), drill-and-practice programs were found to be the most prevalent of applications used in social studies education. Use of this type of software was studied largely with secondary students, and results showed modest gains in recall-type skills and motivation. Simulation programs allowed students to go beyond the basic knowledge level to explore environments to which they might not normally be able to go. Although working with these programs also appeared to increase a student's ability to recall facts, students additionally showed improvement in problem solving, curiosity, and personal initiative and control. Computerized simulations resulted in students who could communicate better and at higher levels than those who did not use simulations in social studies (Willis, 1996). Databases were encouraging to the development of students' abilities to search for and analyze the extensive collections of current and historical data (Berson, 1996). Overall, computers allowed students access to information and motivated them to inquire and to learn.

The Effect of Technology for Students with Special Needs

In the areas of composition and reading, the literature has shown positive effects from using technology with students with mild and moderate disabilities (Fitzgerald & Koury, 1996). Improved comprehension, spelling, and collaborative practices were found, along with positive attitudes in students who used multimedia tools to compose. Current advancements in voice transcription technology do not allow students to compose a piece of writing completely via dictation, but other gains show promise.

Motivation, self-confidence, learning attitudes, and achievement of at-risk students were improved with cooperative-learning computer-search activities (Gan, 1999). Traditionally, schools have had lower expectations for at-risk students and have emphasized the acquisition of basic skills, often in special pullout programs or in lower-level tracks (Means, 1997). Students with special needs may require more coaching in computer-based activities, but they will benefit from the experience of learning with and from other students.

CHANGING CLASSROOM ENVIRONMENTS

The teachers in the ACOT study initially retained conventional ideas about how to physically arrange the classroom (Stuebing, Celsi, & Cousineau, 1995). Teachers began the study with certain convictions that students needed their own desks and teachers needed to see, at a glance, each of the computer screens in the class. As teachers allowed themselves to change with the potential technology presented, classrooms gradually shifted to allow space for presentations and work of variably sized groups, for increased communication, even around the somewhat cumbersome computer screens, and for flexibility in using the technology for multiple activities. These changes were brought about because of the addition of technology into the physical space of the classrooms, but the changes reflect a much larger transformation in the concepts of teaching and learning.

Laptop Computers

There is a growing movement to consider the use of laptop computers in educational settings, citing the appeal of the flexibility and individual access to technology that portable computers provide. Access to laptops has been shown to enhance academic gains among sixth-grade students who traditionally have not succeeded in school, with laptop users consistently outperforming nonusers (Stevenson, 1999). Students were found to perform better than nonlaptop-using peers in writing, reporting that computers allowed them to write better and longer (Rockman et al., no date). Laptops encouraged collaboration among students, working more often in groups and assuming a greater variety of roles teaching their peers and their teachers. Finally, these students were more confident, organized, and motivated. Laptop-using students were more likely to agree with the statement "Computers help me improve the quality of my schoolwork," whereas nonlaptop-using students agreed with the statement "I enjoy playing games on computers" (see Figure 6.5). Teachers who used laptop computers showed significant changes toward constructivist teaching practices, using discussion rather than lecture, encouraging student-led inquiry, and emphasizing thinking skills. They felt they had a greater sense of control over their classroom instruction and management of student learning and used computers more often with greater confidence.

CAVEATS

A growing concern among critics of technology use in education is that the charm of technology might not be so magical after all. Some argue that students become so focused on learning the tricks of a particular software that they are prevented from learning what the software is designed to teach (Oppenheimer, 1997). Another challenge is group computer work, which in reality involves one student centered in front of the computer screen with control of the

FIGURE 6.5   Laptop-using students are more likely to think that computers improve the quality of their work.

mouse at any one time. Other students may or may not be attending and participating in the decision-making process and, depending on the management of the computers in a classroom, may not get a turn in the "driver's seat" with any regularity. Students may have difficulty paying attention in a classroom filled with the variety of noises, activity, and distractions common to technology-enhanced rooms (Sandholtz, Ringstaff, & Dwyer, 1995b). Academic gains that appear to be an effect of technology may simply be a result of more time and effort devoted to students because of the newness of the medium (Weller, 1996).

The rate of technological advancement is staggering, and in order to provide the best education possible to students, hardware must be maintained, software must be upgraded, and staff must be kept trained in the most current practices. These issues might prove to be too great of a financial burden for the schools and districts to face regularly. There are clearly no easy answers for schools, so it follows that the best advice would be to consider these potential drawbacks as part of a complete and ongoing decision-making process regarding technology integration.

Observations from the ACOT study summarize well the need for caution as we form expectations about computers in the classroom (Sandholtz, Ringstaff, & Dwyer, 1997):

1. Teachers must be ready to make some changes in their teaching beliefs and methodologies in order to give innovations a chance.

2. Technology by itself cannot be expected to revolutionize education, but rather should be seen as one of a collection of tools that might spark and facilitate innovative thinking.

3. An environment of support and sharing will encourage teachers to take risks.

4. Any changes initiated by the introduction of technology to classrooms must be expected to occur over time and with a great deal of dedication and effort.

TEACHER AS RESEARCHER

The characteristics and trends in educational technology research should certainly be understood by classroom teachers, but more importantly, the growing body of research should signal a call for action. The interaction between the technology and the users is beginning to be seen as a conversation that is different with every user in every situation (Kozma, 1994), which presents difficulties for neat, convenient research. More qualitative, ethnographic-type studies are called for, but the dilemma is encountered that no easy, all-encompassing answer is available to apply to every situation (Roblyer, 1996).

Traditional educational research cannot keep pace with hardware and software development, yet teachers, who generally are on the forefront of innovative methods, often do not write their findings so that others can learn from their insight (Valdez et al., 1999; Willis, 1996). If classroom teachers participate in educational research, that research will be stronger as it reflects their daily lived experiences. Despite the requirements of normal duties, teachers' substantial participation in research is the only way to ensure meaningful and practical research results.

Even more important than enriching the literature base, the process of classroom research serves the vital function of helping teachers learn more about their own teaching by carefully observing their students (Painter, 2000). Teachers who research with colleagues, and even students, can further inform their own understanding, satisfy personal learning goals, and accomplish writing through collaboration.

SUMMARY

This chapter begins with a discussion of characteristics unique to educational technology research so that teachers will be able to interpret the findings. Researchers are beginning to pay closer attention to how technology can change teaching and learning processes to better address expectations for what students should learn, rather than simply investigating whether students have higher test scores with computer-based instruction. Current learning theories and practices, such as *constructivism* and *engaged learning,* represent fundamental changes in the ways we understand teaching and learning. Therefore, research findings should be read with an understanding of these new ideas. Educators looking to research findings for guidance about using technology for learning should first consider the variables in studies they read about.

Exemplary computer-using teachers have been shown to teach in different environments from other teachers and have greater personal computer experience, greater amounts of personal time working on computers, and unique teaching habits. Teachers in technology-rich classrooms followed the traditional classroom patterns initially, and then gradually began altering classroom practices and forming new collegial relationships. Researchers have identified distinct stages through which teachers new to technology progress in their pursuit of technology integration.

The results from research into the effects of technology on learning are mixed. Whereas a large proportion of researchers are able to demonstrate positive academic results, others have shown no effects or even slightly negative impacts on achievement. The effects of technology use on language, math, science, and social studies achievement, as well as effects for special needs students, have been recent areas of research.

As teachers learn about the potential of technology, they restructure their physical classroom environments to allow presentation space, group work space, and flexible space for multiple activities. There is also a growing movement to consider the use of laptop computers in educational settings, due to the appeal of their flexibility and individual technology access.

A growing concern among critics of technology use in education is that the charm of technology might not be so magical after all. Some argue that students focus on the software rather than the content and that students working in groups have unequal access.

Traditional educational research cannot keep pace with hardware and software development. Teachers, who are at the forefront of innovative methods, are urged to write about their experiences so that others can learn from their insights.

LEARNER ACTIVITIES

1. Watch both the local and national newspapers and popular news magazines over a month's time for news on educational technology. What are the current issues? How is research on technology's effectiveness being portrayed to the public?

2. Visit a local school and observe the level and amount of technology available. What is the school or district plan for integration? What evidence do you see of its progress?

3. Interview a teacher who has incorporated technology to some extent into his or her teaching. According to the teacher, what challenges have been faced?

4. Research technology's effectiveness in your intended area of specialty.

5. Make a list of how teaching in a high-technology classroom will be different than or similar to the education you had growing up. How will it change daily classroom activities?

6. How might universities and other teacher preparation programs better ready future teachers to take advantage of the technology they will surely have in their classrooms? How are strategies that will be used to introduce technology to students similar to those that can be used to familiarize teachers with it?

7. Write a note to the parents of your future students explaining your philosophy of technology integration.

8. How would you convince a colleague to utilize computer technology in his or her teaching repertoire?

9. What are your predictions for the future of technology use in education? Will schools always attempt to emulate the degree of technology integration that society achieves?

10. Play the devil's advocate role. Compose a brief argument against the purchase and use of computers in schools.

BIBLIOGRAPHY

Alfaro, R. (1999). The technology-reading connection. *Educational Leadership, 56*(6), 48–50.

Attewell, P., & Battle, J. (1999). Home computers and school performance. *Information Society, 15*(1), 1–10.

Baker, E., & Kinzer, C. K. (1998). Effects of technology on process writing: Are they all good? *National Reading Conference Yearbook, 47,* 428–440.

Becker, H. J. (1994). How exemplary computer-using teachers differ from other teachers: Implications for realizing the potential of computers in schools. *Journal of Research on Computing in Education, 26*(3), 291–321.

Berson, M. J. (1996). Effectiveness of computer technology in the social studies: A review of the literature. *Journal of Research on Computing in Education, 28*(4), 486–501.

Blubaugh, W. L. (1995). Use of software to improve the teaching of geometry. *Mathematics and Computer Education, 29*(3), 288–293.

Bush, G. W. (2001). Enhancing Education through Technology. *No Child Left Behind.* Retrieved March 14, 2001, from the World Wide Web: <http://www.ed.gov/inits/nclb/partx.html>

Christmann, E., & Badgett, J. (1999). A comparative analysis of the effects of computer-assisted instruction on student achievement in differing science and demographical areas. *Journal of Computers in Mathematics and Science Teaching, 18*(2), 135–143.

David, J. L. (1995). Partnerships for change. In *Apple education research reports* (pp. 45–46). Eugene, OR: International Society for Technology in Education.

Dybdahl, C. S., Shaw, D. G., & Blahous, E. (1997). The impact of the computer on writing: No simple answers. *Computers in the Schools, 13*(3/4), 41–53.

Education Testing Service. (1998). *Does it compute? The relationship between educational technology and student achievement in mathematics.* Wenglinsky, H. (Ed.), Policy Information Center. Princeton, NJ: Author.

Fatemi, E. (1999). Building the digital curriculum. *Technology Counts '99: Building the Digital Curriculum, Education Week, 19*(4), 5–8.

Fishman, B. J. (1999). Characteristics of students related to computer-mediated communications activity. *Journal of Research on Computing in Education, 32*(1), 73–97.

Fitzgerald, G. E., & Koury, K. A. (1996). Empirical advances in technology: Assisted instruction for students with mild and moderate disabilities. *Journal of Research on Computing in Education, 28*(4), 526–551.

Funkhouser, C. (1993). The influence of problem-solving software on student attitudes about mathematics. *Journal of Research on Computing in Education, 25*(3), 339–346.

Gan, S. (1999). Motivating at-risk students through computer-based cooperative learning activities. *Educational Horizons, 77*(3), 151–156.

Goldman, S., Cole, K., & Syer, C. (1999). *The technology/content dilemma* [Online]. Available: <http://www.ed.gov/Technology/TechConf/1999/whitepapers/paper4.html>.

Greenlee-Moore, M. E., & Smith, L. L. (1996). Interactive computer software: The effects on young children's reading achievement. *Reading Psychology, 17*(1), 43–64.

Hamilton, V. (1995). Computers and reading achievement (ERIC Document Reproduction Service No. ED 382 923).

Honey, M., Culp, K. M., & Carrigg, F. (1999). *Perspectives on technology and education research: Lessons from the past and present* [Online]. Available: <http://www.ed.gov/Technology/TechConf/1999/whitepapers/paper.html>.

Honey, M., Culp, K. M., & Spielvogel, R. (1999). Using technology to improve student achievement. *Pathways to School Improvement* [Online]. Available: <http://www.ncrel.org/sdrs/areas/issues/methods/technology/te800.htm>.

Jones, I. (1994). The effect of a word processor on the written composition of second-grade pupils. *Computers in the Schools, 11*(2), 43–54.

Kook, J. (1997). Computers and communication networks in educational settings in the twenty-first century: Preparation for educators' new roles. *Educational Technology, 37*(2), 56–60.

Kozma, R. B. (1994). Will media influence learning? Reframing the debate? *Educational Technology Research and Development, 42*(2), 7–19.

Mann, D., Shakeshaft, C., Becker, J., & Kottkamp, R. (1999). *West Virginia's Basic Skills/Computer Education Program: An analysis of student achievement.* Santa Monica, CA: Milken Family Foundation.

Matthew, K. (1997). A comparison of the influence of interactive CD-ROM storybooks and traditional print storybooks on reading comprehension. *Journal of Research on Computing in Education, 29*(3), 263–275.

Mayer, R. E., Schustack, M. W., Blanton, W. E. (1999). What do children learn from using computers in an informal, collaborative setting? *Educational Technology, 39*(2), 27–31.

McCoy, L. P. (1996). Computer-based mathematics learning. *Journal of Research on Computing in Education, 28*(4), 438–460.

Means, B. (1997). Critical issue: Using technology to enhance engaged learning for at-risk students. *Pathways to School Improvement* [Online]. Available: <http://www.ncrel.org/sdrs/areas/issues/students/atrisk/at400.htm>.

Middleton, B. M., & Murray, R. K. (1999). The impact of instructional technology on student academic achievement in reading and mathematics. *International Journal of Instructional Media, 26*(1), 109–115.

Nelson, L. J., & Cooper, J. (1997). Gender differences in children's reactions to success and failure with computers. *Computers in Human Behavior, 13*(2), 247–267.

Nichols, L. M. (1996). Pencil and paper versus word processing: A comparative study of creative writing in the elementary school. *Journal of Research on Computing in Education, 29*(2), 159–166.

O'Neil, J. (1995, October). On technology and schools: A conversation with Chris Dede. *Educational Leadership, 53*(2), 6–12.

Oppenheimer, T. (1997, July). The computer delusion. *The Atlantic Monthly, 280,* 45–62.

Painter, D. D. (2000). Teacher as researcher. *Learning and Leading with Technology, 27*(7), 10–13, 27.

Panel on Educational Technology, President's Committee of Advisors on Science and Technology. (1997, March). *Report to the President on the use of technology to strengthen K–12 education in the United States* [Online]. Available: <http://www.whitehouse.gov/WH/EOP/OSTP/NSTC/PCAST/k-12ed.html>.

Proctor, R. M., & Burnett, R. C. (1996). Computer attitude and classroom computers. *Computers in the Schools, 12*(3), 33–41.

Reed, W. M. (1996). Assessing the impact of computer-based writing instruction. *Journal of Research on Computing in Education, 28*(4), 418–437.

Ringstaff, C., Sandholtz, J. H., & Dwyer, D. C. (1995). Trading places: When teachers utilize student expertise in technology-intensive classrooms. In *Apple education research reports* (pp. 35–37). Eugene, OR: International Society for Technology in Education.

Roblyer, M. D. (1996). The constructivist/objectivist debate: Implications for instructional technology research. *Learning and Leading with Technology, 24*(2), 12–16.

Roblyer, M. D. (1997). Predictions and realities: The impact of the Internet on K–12 education. *Learning and Leading with Technology, 25*(1), 54–56.

Rochowicz, J. A., Jr. (1996). The impact of using computers and calculators on calculus instruction: Various perceptions. *Journal of Computers in Mathematics and Science Teaching, 15*(4), 423–435.

Rockman et al. (no date). *A more complex picture: Laptop use and impact in the context of changing home and school access* [Online]. Available: <http://www.microsoft.com/education/aal/research3.asp>.

Sandholtz, J. H., Ringstaff, C., & Dwyer, D. C. (1995a). The relationship between technological innovation and collegial interaction. In *Apple education research reports* (pp. 37–38). Eugene, OR: International Society for Technology in Education.

Sandholtz, J. H., Ringstaff, C., & Dwyer, D. C. (1995b). Student engagement revisited: Views from technology-rich classrooms. In *Apple education research reports* (pp. 29–30). Eugene, OR: International Society for Technology in Education.

Sandholtz, J. H., Ringstaff, C., & Dwyer, D. C. (1997). *Teaching with technology: Creating student-centered classrooms.* New York: Teachers College Press.

Scardamalia, M., & Bereiter, C. (1996). Computer support for knowledge-building communities. In T. Koschmann (Ed.), *CSCL: Theory and practice of an emerging paradigm.* Mahwah, NJ: Lawrence Erlbaum.

Sivin-Kachala, J. (1998). *Report on the effectiveness of technology in schools, 1990–1997.* Software Publisher's Association.

Stevenson, K. (1999). Learning by laptop. *School-Administrator, 56*(4), 18–21.

Stuebing, S., Celsi, J. G., & Cousineau, L. K. (1995). Environments that support new modes of learning. In *Apple education research reports* (pp. 27–28). Eugene, OR: International Society for Technology in Education.

Tierney, R. J., Kieffer, R., Stowell, L., Desai, L. E., Whalin, K., & Moss, A. G. (1995). Computer acquisition: A longitudinal study of the influence of high computer access on students' thinking, learning, and interactions. In *Apple education research reports* (pp. 31–32). Eugene, OR: International Society for Technology in Education.

U.S. Department of Education. (1996). *Getting America's students ready for the twenty-first century: Meeting the technology literacy challenge* [Online]. Available: <http://www.ed.gov/TechnologyPlan/NatTechPlan/title.html>.

Valdez, G., McNabb, M., Foertsch, M., Anderson, M., Hawkes, M., & Raack, L. (1999). *Computer-based technology and learning: Evolving uses and expectations.* Oak Brook, IL: North Central Regional Educational Laboratory.

Weller, H. G. (1996). Assessing the impact of computer-based learning in science. *Journal of Research on Computing in Education, 28*(4), 461–485.

Whitley, B. E., Jr. (1997). Gender differences in computer-related attitudes and behavior: A meta-analysis. *Computers in Human Behavior, 13,* 1–22.

Willis, E. M. (1996). Where in the world? Technology in social studies learning. *Learning and Leading with Technology, 23*(5), 7–9.

Yaghi, H. (1996). The role of the computer in the school as perceived by computer using teachers and school administrators. *Journal of Educational Computing Research, 15*(2), 137–155.

CHAPTER 7

SELECTING EDUCATIONAL RESOURCES

FOCUS QUESTIONS

1. What are the differences among software selection, review, and evaluation?
2. What considerations must a district make when forming a plan for software or educational website review?
3. What are the benefits and drawbacks to using a checklist-type form to review software?

The number of educational software titles is topping 17,000 (ISTE, 2000), and the number of new websites is increasing daily. Therefore, educators must have in place effective, planned processes for the critical investigation and acceptance of software and recommendation of websites for use in their classrooms so as not to waste valuable teacher time and district money on advertising hype. Many times software publishers forsake strong instructional design for colorful graphics and packaging (Hoffman & Lyons, 1997), and web content and quality can vary as greatly as it is easy to upload a website. The lines between educational software and educational websites are blurring, as many new software titles include web interactivity and websites offer engaging student activities. This chapter presents strategies for making decisions about both types of resources, first highlighting considerations that must guide any resource choices, and then suggesting an assessment process that takes into account the intended uses. An example Software Review Form is offered, with extensive descriptions for use and adaptation, as is a guide for reviewing educational websites. Finally, alternate review approaches are proposed that may provide both more useful and accurate information about potential resource uses as well as better accommodations of new multimedia software.

LEARNING RESOURCE ASSESSMENT TERMINOLOGY

Distinctions must first be drawn among several similar and potentially confusing assessment terms. McDougall and Squires (1995a) note the frequently interchangeable uses of the terms *evaluation, review,* and *selection* in the literature on educational electronic resources, and have, for clarity's sake, provided working definitions that distinguish the three. *Evaluation* is a specific process that aids in the actual development of software, occurring either during or immediately following the software development. *Review* refers to the more formal assessment of the performance and characteristics of a piece of software, usually for the purpose of disseminating the results to an audience of fellow educators. Organizations that exist solely to provide reviews of electronic resources to teachers are discussed later in the chapter. Finally, *selection,* according to these authors, describes the informal decisions teachers make daily with regard to what learning materials they will use in their classrooms. Based on their own experience and teaching styles and on what they know about the abilities and needs of their students, but without actually performing any structured review, teachers select what they think will work best. Because the audience reading this book will be most interested in strategies they themselves can use to make informed decisions about what software will work best in their classrooms, this chapter will focus primarily on district review procedures and individual electronic resource selection.

GUIDING PRINCIPLES BEHIND DEVELOPING
A RESOURCE REVIEW AND SELECTION PLAN

Depending on the extent of its use in the classroom, electronic resources have the potential to make quite an impact on the delivery and even the interpretation of a school or district's curriculum. For this reason, districts must have a clear plan for reviewing and selecting educational resources for use with students. In creating that plan, some basic principles must be considered.

At the outset of the entire selection process for electronic resources, it must be understood that merely sitting a child in front of a computer with an educational software title plugged into it does not constitute a sound educational plan. Doing this would allow a software publisher's goals and intentions to override those of the district and the classroom teacher, thus taking thoughtful control out of the hands of those closest to students. Resource use first must be consistent with the goals and objectives of not only individual classrooms, but also those of the school, the district, and the state. In addition, national curriculum standards should be consulted in formulating a plan for software use. Not only should the content be compared to local scope and sequence guidelines, but also the instructional design and the way in which the material is presented should be considered. The learning theories that underpin the content of a resource should match what is accepted in current educational literature and should correspond to what is accepted in the local communities. If a district embraces a constructivist educational philosophy, for example, it should seek educational resources that allow students to come to their own understandings based on their experiences. Often, an implicit set of values are embedded into the structure and content of a piece of software or website, and these values must also be carefully examined to see if they fit with the intended learning environment. In essence, electronic resources, like any other learning tool or activity, must match the purpose for which they will be used and must represent the best way to accomplish those particular educational goals. (See Figure 7.1).

Some basic understanding of the idea of evaluation is also helpful from not only those involved with district review but also teachers who will be interpreting the reviews for classroom use. Evaluation is a highly subjective process, no matter how specific and

FIGURE 7.1   Merely sitting a child in front of a piece of software does not constitute a sound educational plan.

criteria-based it aims to be. We make evaluations every day, such as whether we enjoyed a new restaurant or how well a tie looks with a shirt. Whoever is evaluating a software package is viewing it through the filter of his or her own unique perspective. The person's background experience, educational philosophy, and even personal interests play a role in determining how he or she will rate the software. Because we are human, there is simply no way around this natural subjectivity. The important point to make is that anyone who reads a review of software, or hears of an opinion on anything for that matter, must always consider the source of the review and again filter it through his or her own perspective. Because one evaluator dislikes a program does not necessarily mean that it is completely unusable for all purposes. Take all reviews under consideration and proceed according to your individual beliefs.

A SOFTWARE REVIEW AND SELECTION PROCESS

With the regular influx of new software to educational markets, school districts must have an organized process for how new software will be assessed and how decisions regarding purchase and usage will be made. One of the first steps is to obtain software copies for review purposes. This can generally be done by contacting the software publishers directly (the appendix gives a list of publisher contacts). Many universities and state departments of education maintain review sites with software available for checkout.

The next part of the process that should be considered is who will actually have the first look at a new piece of software. Will curriculum policy administrators review software for the entire district? Will a committee of teachers representing their curricular areas or grade levels serve as reviewers? What role might parents or community members play in the process? Will students be observed using programs or will their opinions or comments be elicited? Although involving students in reviewing will add an extra step to the process, it promises the benefit of a very different rating than those that teachers or parents will provide (Reiser & Kegelmann, 1994). It is important for this flow of review information to be made clear to the teachers who will have the direct experience of planning for and using each piece of software. Every teacher should have a clear understanding of how diligently and by whom a new software package has been reviewed. If there are comments available from district reviewers, a plan should be in place for disseminating the review information to teachers. If little local review has been performed, teachers should likewise be made aware of how much of the burden of selection and review falls to them.

Reviewers need some kind of a standard form on which review comments can be recorded and compared to comments about other programs. The easiest and most common method of assessing software is to use a checklist. The checklist form might contain any number of criteria to be examined and rated, sometimes with a simple yes or no and sometimes by choosing from a range of scores for each area. Forms can provide space to encourage longer answers regarding specific problem areas or ideas for integration of the program into curriculum. Later in this chapter, some objections to the checklist method of reviewing software will be raised, but it still remains the most straightforward way to compare results from several evaluators on several software titles.

Finally, a district software review plan needs to include some way of getting the review information for accepted packages into the hands of the teachers who will be using the software to teach. Knowing that the package was accepted is not enough. Teachers have a right to all information known about a program so they can make informed decisions about how to best use the program to facilitate student learning.

A good general review sequence like the one shown in Table 7.1 will ensure the best use of evaluator time and at the same time will result in the most consistent and reliable results.

SOFTWARE REVIEW ORGANIZATIONS AND OTHER REVIEW INFORMATION

To assist educators in making software selection decisions, a number of organizations exist solely to review and share information about new software packages. The *Educational Software Preview Guide* (Educational Software Preview Guide Consortium) is distributed annually by the International Society for Technology in Education (ISTE). The Consortium members meet annually to compile reviews and to make specific recommendations that guide educators in purchasing and using software packages. Although the *Guide* is not meant to be a guarantee for educators to purchase the recommended software without first reviewing it themselves, it does provide a comprehensive and accurate starting point, based on established subjects, modes, and a rating system.

Table 7.2 gives purchase contacts for this guide, along with the Internet addresses for a number of additional review sites available on the World Wide Web. (See Figure 7.2.)

TABLE 7.1   Sequence of Software Review

1. As a software package is received, first check it briefly to determine that there are no major technical flaws and that it includes complete documentation. If there are such technical problems, send the program back to the vendor with specific information describing the encountered problems.

2. If no problems are discovered, proceed by reading the program documentation thoroughly. To completely test the program's capabilities, run it three additional times: once to determine the program flow; next making as many mistakes as possible; and finally responding exactly as instructions indicate, making as many correct responses as possible. Test all program options, such as printing or playing video segments, and try every navigable path.

3. Try software with an appropriate student audience, if desired. As the students participate in the evaluation process, note both their actions and their comments.

4. Record the evaluation on a standard review form, such as the one presented later in this chapter, to encourage comparable results.

5. Make evaluation information available to teachers. One efficient way to organize these reviews is to compile evaluations into one cohesive database of titles. Distribute the database to teachers in either print or electronic form.

TABLE 7.2   Educational Software Reviews

ISTE	WORLD WIDE WEB
Educational Software Preview Guide Customer Service Office 480 Charnelton Street Eugene, OR 97401-2626 Order Desk: 800-336-5191 Order Fax: 541-302-3778 www.iste.org	**The School House Review** <www.worldvillage.com/wv/school/html/scholrev.htm> **SuperKids Educational Software Review** <www.superkids.com/aweb/pages/reviews/reviews.html> **Way Cool Software Reviews** <www.ucc.uconn.edu/~wwwpcse/wcool.html>

FIGURE 7.2
SuperKids Educational
Software Review
<www.superkids.com>.

AN EXAMPLE EDUCATIONAL SOFTWARE REVIEW FORM

This form is appropriate for district review purposes and allows software reviewers to assess the complete software package, including both content and technical considerations. It is easily modifiable so that districts can match it to their existing district goals and curriculum objectives. For the more informal software selection that classroom teachers perform, a form as detailed as this would most likely not be time-efficient. Teachers, however, should be familiar with the review categories and types of items that are considered here as they make those important decisions in selecting software.

This form was designed to be easy to use, yet descriptive enough to provide true indications of quality software. It first solicits basic identifying information that should be readily apparent from the program packaging and accompanying documentation. The form then asks the evaluator to rate how well the package satisfies a series of criteria statements grouped by category. These category groupings do not imply that these often interrelated areas are independent of each other, but rather they are intended to aid the evaluator in understanding the structure of the evaluation process. The final section of the form provides for a graphical summary of all the section evaluations. It allows the evaluator not only to see in an instant the overall rating for the program but also to compare two programs with just a glance.

Identifying Information

The first few items you will need are the obviously necessary title, publisher, and price of the software, without which the evaluation process would become an unlabeled mess. Giving the date the package was reviewed helps to ensure that the most recent versions of software are being considered, and providing the reviewer's name becomes important when a number of different people are participating in the review process.

System Requirements.   The list of system requirements is usually listed on the software box or in the installation directions. Be specific when listing this technical information so that if there are problems with the operation, you will have a handy reference describing the system with which you are working. Most districts have computers with a range of capabilities, so evaluators may want to try each software on a number of different machines to get a complete performance picture.

Grade Levels.   The grade level that is posted on the package documentation should be used only as a general guide for use. Often, what your students are able to accomplish may fall above or below the listed grade levels. Reviewers, therefore, should always consider how each package might be used with students outside the stated grade-level range. Sometimes students might not benefit from the intended task at their level, but may be able to use the program to accomplish some other goals. For instance, a reading program might be below the reading levels of some fourth-graders, but the program might be creatively used with the students to explore writing in a particular genre.

Subjects.   The subject section is extensive and is based on the subjects considered in reviews for the *Educational Software Preview Guide* (ISTE, 2000). Providing the evaluator with an entire list of subjects, as opposed to just a blank line on which to fill in the subjects, prompts the full consideration of the range of possible subject areas. Because many software packages cross curricular lines, check all the subject areas that apply. Other subjects that apply to a particular district or purpose can also be added to customize this list.

Modes.   The purpose for which the software was designed is described by the modes (ISTE, 2000). One piece of software can be classified under several modes because most software can be used in several different ways.

Program Description.   Describe briefly the content that is covered by the program. This description is generic, omitting any evaluative opinions, and is similar to the description that might be found on the back of the software package. This type of description might be helpful if compiling a database of all of the software reviewed to give teachers some idea of what this program is about.

Content and Technical Information

This section consists of a series of criteria that describes what might be expected in a quality software program. Read each statement carefully, and circle the number that best describes your rating of this program for each indicator. Scores represent a range from zero meaning Poor to a score of five meaning Excellent. Circle *N/A* if the indicator is not applicable to this program for any reason. For each section, then circle the score that best summarizes the program's performance on all of the indicators. This gives the evaluator a quick summation of a program's performance in each area.

Documentation and Supplementary Materials.   Software is generally sold with some accompanying materials, including installation procedures, teacher's guides, student workbooks, and even the box itself. These items should make the use of the program easier and more effective. Were you able to install and operate the program successfully according to the supplied directions? In order for the program to be effective, it should have some stated educational objectives. Even if teachers can think of alternate instructional purposes for the program, objectives that are clearly stated give the program credibility and give teachers a starting point.

Program Content.   The content is the heart of the program and determines in many ways just how useful the program will be. Indicators here ask you to consider how well the program authors have matched the content to the stated objectives. Does the way in which the instruction is presented reflect current research, and does it allow for a variety of learners? You must also decide if the content appears up-to-date and is free from errors and unwanted stereotypes.

Presentation.   The way in which the instruction is presented can make or break a program. If the content is developed logically, with relevant examples and illustrations, students have a better chance of making meaningful connections. It is a given that spelling, punctuation, and grammar be correct, but what a student sees on the screen must also be clear and shown with enough variety to keep the interest of the intended audience.

Effectiveness.   What ultimately matters with any instructional tool or strategy is whether it leads to student learning. This category is best judged by incorporating student participation into the review process. Do students appear to have a grasp on the concepts covered in the program following its use? Are they able to apply what they have learned, and does it seem that they are now interested in the topic? A very important indicator in this section asks you to decide whether the instructional software medium is appropriate in teaching this particular content. Some nontechnical solutions do a better job of encouraging the learning process than do many software programs.

Audience Appeal and Suitability.   For this section, you will want to consider how closely what the program offers fits the needs of the intended audience. Rate whether the way the content is organized and presented will hold the interest of these students, and if once their interest is piqued, they will be able to read and respond as needed. Decide if the visual aids are appropriate for this audience, and if the time spent on content instruction fits with what you know about the attention span of your student group.

Practice/Assessment/Feedback.   How does this program account for the learning it promotes? Good instructional design demands that the practice and the assessment be aligned with both the stated objectives and with the instruction. Feedback should be related to student responses and should occur immediately after a response in order to reinforce or remediate as needed. Depending on your personal or district philosophy of education, you may want to note the inclusion of alternative practice and assessment methods, such as portfolio compilation or collaborative learning.

Ease of Use.   The most well-designed instruction is rendered meaningless if a student cannot access it easily. For this section of the evaluation, reflect on how easy it is to work through the program. Are there directions and a **Help** screen available from every screen? Are these items thorough and easy to understand? Consider, also, how much control the user has to navigate at his own speed and to go wherever he wants to go.

User Interface and Media Quality.   Ideally, all of the media elements, such as graphics, audio, video, and animations, combine to create a virtual learning environment. Rate whether the environment created is appropriate for the intended learning audience. Are these media elements used to heighten student interest and promote instruction, or are they merely decorative? Additionally, evaluate the quality of those media elements. Do they appear to utilize the latest technical capabilities? Do the media elements function without technical problems?

Evaluation Summary

The last two sections of this evaluation form ask you to summarize the ratings you have made so far. Frequently, the only part of an evaluation that an end user sees is the final rating, so it is helpful to boil down the information to a more concise format. This review instrument offers both a graphical and verbal summary. At the end of each section, you circled a summary score that best illustrated how the program performed on those particular indicators. Now, simply transfer those scores to the Section Summary Graph by shading in the score for each section. This creates a visual representation of the overall program rating, making it easy to see at a glance how the program rates and allowing for easy comparison of multiple programs. A district may want to set a rating minimum for acceptance of a package.

The other evaluation summary is an open area for you to record your Overall Evaluative Comments. This gives you the chance to explain the strengths and weaknesses of the program, including any areas that might not have been represented by the indicators on the evaluation form. These comments might be the deciding factors between two programs with very similar numerical ratings, so be persuasive and complete.

The form in Figure 7.3 can be duplicated and modified for educational software review purposes.

FIGURE 7.3   Educational Software Review Form.

Software Title:	
Publisher:	Price:
Reviewer:	Review Date:

SYSTEM REQUIREMENTS:	GRADE LEVELS:
Platform:	PreKindergarten
Processor:	K–2
RAM:	3–5
Hard Drive:	6–8
CD:	9–12
Other:	Adult
	Teacher Tool

SUBJECTS:

Art:	Keyboarding	Science:
☐ Music	☐ Language Arts	☐ Biology
☐ Performing Arts	Math:	☐ Chemistry
☐ Visual Arts	☐ Advanced	☐ Earth Science
☐ Computer Science	☐ Algebra	☐ Environmental Ed./Ecology
☐ Cross Curricular	☐ Geometry/Measurement	☐ General Science
☐ Early Childhood/Preschool	☐ Number	☐ Physics
☐ Health/Phys. Ed./Recreation	☐ Probability/Statistics	☐ Scientific Method/Lab Equip.
☐ Internet/WWW	☐ Multimedia Production	☐ Space Science
Instructional Tools:	☐ Problem Solving/Logic	☐ Social Studies
☐ Authoring Systems	☐ Reference Library	☐ Test & Testing
☐ Class Management	☐ School to Work	☐ World Languages (non-Eng.)
☐ Comp. Assisted Drafting		
☐ Computer Utilities		
☐ Desktop Publishing		
☐ Image Generator		
☐ Personal Productivity		

MODES:

☐ Authoring System	☐ Education Game	☐ Problem Solving
☐ Bilingual	☐ Exploration	☐ Reference
☐ Computer Programming	☐ Guided Practice	☐ Simulation
☐ Creative Activity	☐ Internet	☐ Tool
☐ Demonstration/Presentation	☐ Limited English Proficient	☐ Tutorial
☐ Drill & Practice	☐ Multimedia	

(continued)

FIGURE 7.3 CONTINUED

PROGRAM DESCRIPTION: (Briefly describe the content of the program.)							

DOCUMENTATION & SUPPLEMENTARY MATERIALS:							
Necessary technical documentation is included.	N/A	0	1	2	3	4	5
Objectives are clearly stated.	N/A	0	1	2	3	4	5
Learning activities that facilitate integration into curriculum are suggested.	N/A	0	1	2	3	4	5
Materials for enrichment and remedial activities are provided.	N/A	0	1	2	3	4	5
Section Summary:	**N/A**	**0**	**1**	**2**	**3**	**4**	**5**

PROGRAM CONTENT:							
Instruction matches stated objectives.	N/A	0	1	2	3	4	5
Instructional strategies are based on current research.	N/A	0	1	2	3	4	5
Instruction addresses various learning styles and intelligences.	N/A	0	1	2	3	4	5
Information is current and accurate.	N/A	0	1	2	3	4	5
Program is free of stereotypes or bias.	N/A	0	1	2	3	4	5
Section Summary:	**N/A**	**0**	**1**	**2**	**3**	**4**	**5**

PRESENTATION:							
Information is presented in a developmentally appropriate and logical way.	N/A	0	1	2	3	4	5
Illustrations and examples are relevant.	N/A	0	1	2	3	4	5
There is appropriate variety in screen displays.	N/A	0	1	2	3	4	5
Text is clear and printed in type suitable for target audience.	N/A	0	1	2	3	4	5
Spelling, punctuation, and grammar are correct.	N/A	0	1	2	3	4	5
Section Summary:	**N/A**	**0**	**1**	**2**	**3**	**4**	**5**

EFFECTIVENESS:							
Students are able to recall/use information presented following program use.	N/A	0	1	2	3	4	5
Program prepares students for future real-world experiences.	N/A	0	1	2	3	4	5
Students develop further interest in topic from using program.	N/A	0	1	2	3	4	5
This is an appropriate use of instructional software.	N/A	0	1	2	3	4	5
Section Summary:	**N/A**	**0**	**1**	**2**	**3**	**4**	**5**

AUDIENCE APPEAL & SUITABILITY:							
Program matches interest level of indicated audience.	N/A	0	1	2	3	4	5
Reading level is appropriate for indicated audience.	N/A	0	1	2	3	4	5
Examples and illustrations are suitable for indicated audience.	N/A	0	1	2	3	4	5
Required input is appropriate for indicated audience.	N/A	0	1	2	3	4	5
Necessary completion time is compatible with student attention.	N/A	0	1	2	3	4	5
Program supplies remediation or enrichment when appropriate.	N/A	0	1	2	3	4	5
Section Summary:	**N/A**	**0**	**1**	**2**	**3**	**4**	**5**

FIGURE 7.3   CONTINUED

PRACTICE/ASSESSMENT/FEEDBACK:								
Practice is provided to accomplish objectives.	N/A	0	1	2	3	4	5
Practice is appropriate for topic and audience.	N/A	0	1	2	3	4	5
Feedback corresponds to student responses.	N/A	0	1	2	3	4	5
Feedback is immediate.	N/A	0	1	2	3	4	5
Feedback is varied.	N/A	0	1	2	3	4	5
Feedback gives remediation and reinforcement.	N/A	0	1	2	3	4	5
Remediation and reinforcement is positive and dignified.	N/A	0	1	2	3	4	5
Assessment is aligned with objectives.	N/A	0	1	2	3	4	5
Open-ended responses and/or portfolio opportunities are promoted.	N/A	0	1	2	3	4	5
Collaborative learning experiences are provided for.	N/A	0	1	2	3	4	5
Section Summary:	**N/A**	**0**	**1**	**2**	**3**	**4**	**5**

EASE OF USE:								
User can navigate through program without difficulty.	N/A	0	1	2	3	4	5
Screen directions are consistent and easy to follow.	N/A	0	1	2	3	4	5
Help options are comprehensive and readily available.	N/A	0	1	2	3	4	5
Program responds to input as indicated by directions.	N/A	0	1	2	3	4	5
Title sequence is brief and can be bypassed.	N/A	0	1	2	3	4	5
User can control pace and sequence.	N/A	0	1	2	3	4	5
User can exit from any screen.	N/A	0	1	2	3	4	5
Only one input is registered when key is held down.	N/A	0	1	2	3	4	5
Section Summary:	**N/A**	**0**	**1**	**2**	**3**	**4**	**5**

USER INTERFACE AND MEDIA QUALITY:								
Interface provides user with an appropriate environment.	N/A	0	1	2	3	4	5
Graphics, audio, video, and/or animations enhance instruction.	N/A	0	1	2	3	4	5
Graphics, audio, video, and/or animations stimulate student interest.	N/A	0	1	2	3	4	5
Graphics, audio, video, and/or animations are of high quality.	N/A	0	1	2	3	4	5
Section Summary:	**N/A**	**0**	**1**	**2**	**3**	**4**	**5**

SECTION SUMMARIES:

Documents	Content	Presentation	Effectiveness	Appeal/ Suitability	Practice/ Assessment	Ease of Use	Interface/ Quality
⑤	⑤	⑤	⑤	⑤	⑤	⑤	⑤
④	④	④	④	④	④	④	④
③	③	③	③	③	③	③	③
②	②	②	②	②	②	②	②
①	①	①	①	①	①	①	①
⓪	⓪	⓪	⓪	⓪	⓪	⓪	⓪

OVERALL EVALUATIVE COMMENTS

EDUCATIONAL WEBSITE REVIEW GUIDELINES

This guide was designed with parallel categories to the Software Review Form to demonstrate the similarity of reviewing any educational resources. Ratings can be scored and tallied as with the Software Review Form, although because websites are more often reviewed by teachers, rather than at the district level, these items may be best used simply as a general guide. As with the Software Review Form, please feel free to modify it to meet your specific needs (see Table 7.3).

OBJECTIONS TO CURRENT REVIEW PRACTICES
AND FUTURE TRENDS

Checklist review forms, such as the ones presented in this chapter, have historically been the most common way of recording software evaluations performed by multiple reviewers. In recent years, however, voices in the research field have raised concerns over the validity of relying solely on these checklist evaluations in light of modern educational philosophy and with regard to new multimedia technology.

McDougall and Squires (1995a) suggest that checklists are truly useful only in the *evaluation* of software, which has previously been defined as the specific process that aids in the development of software and occurs either during or immediately after the software development. Generic checklists, they contend, are not helpful in the review or selection of software because checklists are incapable of describing the context and surrounding activities to which software might contribute. In their critique of software, the researchers summarized other problems found in research on checklist use to include the focus on technical issues rather than educational issues, the difficulty in assigning importance to certain items over others, the obstacles in recognizing a variety of teaching strategies, and the inability of one set of criteria to effectively define a number of different content areas.

A review plan they propose instead of the checklist method stresses the consideration of classroom activities, teaching and learning roles, and curriculum issues over the attributes of software packages (Squires & McDougall, 1996). By examining the interaction of the perspectives of the student, the teacher, and the software designer, this new paradigm allows for a comprehensive view of learning, curriculum, and pedagogical issues, promoting new ideas, rather than mere descriptions (McDougall & Squires, 1995b).

Squires and Preece (1996) propose that when checklists separate evaluative categories, it implies that issues of program usability and learning are separated. The authors propose a "Jigsaw" model that provides for software to be evaluated with the ideas of learning interrelated with how a program is actually used.

Nicholls and Ridley (1997) posit that the new interactive multimedia programs that are becoming the norm in the software industry are so different from text-based learning materials that accordingly they need different methods of review. They contend that these types of programs allow such a range of navigational freedom throughout a variety of media and information that the software creators cannot actually predict just what type of learning experiences are possible. Students will actually be constructing the learning experience as they go. Multimedia software must be looked at like a work of art in the way that

TABLE 7.3   Educational Website Review Guidelines

DOCUMENTATION AND CREDIBILITY

Site author information is clearly stated, including name and contact information.
Site author has provided credentials, if necessary.
Information sources are indicated, as necessary.
Date of latest site revision is provided.
New information is highlighted.
Fees or names are not requested to use site.

CONTENT

Site title represents content.
Purpose or goals of site are clearly stated.
Content can be used for various learning styles and intelligences.
Site has links to other relevant sites.
Information is current and accurate.
Content is free of stereotypes or bias.

AUDIENCE APPEAL AND SUITABILITY

General appearance of site is appealing to target audience.
Language is developmentally appropriate for target audience.
Text and graphics are appropriate for target audience.
Content of linked sites is appropriate for target audience.

EASE OF USE, NAVIGATION, AND ACCESSIBILITY

Users can navigate through site without difficulty.
Help features and site map are available and easy to access.
Information is well organized.
Links back to homepage are included on each succeeding page.
Links to other sites are relevant.
All links work.
Few large graphics increase download speed.
Directions given for downloading any needed plugins.
Site functions in variety of browsers.
Site is accessible to individuals with disabilities.

USER INTERFACE AND DESIGN

Navigation options are clearly marked and self-explanatory.
Spelling, punctuation, and grammar are correct.
Text is clear and in a font suitable for intended audience.
Media elements (e.g., graphics, audio, video, animation, databases, JavaScript) are used to
   enhance content, as appropriate.
Media elements (e.g., graphics, audio, video, animation, databases, JavaScript) are of high quality.
Design creates stimulating environment.
Design elements are consistent on all pages.
Advertising is either nonexistent or does not interfere with content.

CLASSROOM VIGNETTE

Mary Farnelli is one of three teachers at her high school who serve on the District Technology Review Committee. Her experience as a journalism and creative writing teacher allows her to select software that effectively handles the instruction of composition and other related topics, a combination she finds too infrequently in the software that has been coming in for review over the two years she has served on the committee.

The committee meets once a month and brings together teachers from around the K–12 district. Every third Tuesday, the teachers meet to see what new software review copies have been received by the district technology coordinator that month. The coordinator, Amy Ramirez, introduces each program by reading what is listed on the package box and documentation, and from these descriptions, teachers volunteer to take the titles with them to review. Sometimes the teachers who take a program have students in the stated grade-level range, and other times teachers are enticed by the flashy packaging or program features.

Software that has been reviewed during the last month is also brought back for discussion. At this time, the reviewing teacher offers a few brief comments and then suggests which other teachers might want to review it. Sometimes the reviewer does not like the software package and wants a second opinion. Other times, the original reviewer may feel that the program might apply to grade levels or subject areas other than those listed on the package. According to the official district review process, a piece of software must receive at least three "Excellent" reviews to be accepted, so a minimum of three different teachers must find value in a program in order for it to be proposed to the school board for purchase.

This week, a fourth-grade teacher has a multimedia production program that he highly recommends. He wants a middle or high school teacher to consider it, also, because he has thought of some other uses for it, such as scriptwriting and dramatization. Mary volunteers to take it with her to look at, remembering that the program sounded interesting when it was introduced at the last meeting. As she walks out of the meeting, she is already planning for how she can perform a thorough review by having students assist her in looking at this software.

there is the potential for interpretation of a higher level of intellectual meaning. The authors are exploring ways in which the potential for these unpredictable individual learning experiences might be assessed.

The lesson educators should take from this shift in evaluation thought is that existing checklists might need to be modified to include more consideration of the learning contexts and the specific types of media being evaluated. Educators need to remember that they are the consumers. If software publishers want to continue to sell new products, they will have to fit the curriculum demands of the end users.

SUMMARY

To ensure the purchase and effective use of quality educational resources, districts and schools need to formulate an established plan. Whether it is a committee reviewing the software at the district level or a teacher selecting the best website to fit with a particular lesson, it is imperative to consider the way the resource addresses the goals of classrooms, schools, districts, and states.

Many outside organizations publish reviews of software, both in print and on the Internet, but educators will want to examine all electronic curricular material closely to see if it fits their needs. Everyone involved in the process of evaluating resources for educational purposes must understand that all evaluation rests to a large degree on subjective methods. Having a set process and a standard review form of which all participants are informed will help to make the results of reviews somewhat comparable across reviewers.

Checklists are the most common method for recording observations on software and website strengths and weaknesses. Generally, checklists require reviewers to respond to a range of questions from discrete yes-or-no items to longer narrative descriptions. Checklist review forms should be modified to fit the specific needs of the evaluation purpose.

Some experts say that using checklists to evaluate software focuses the reviewer unnecessarily on technical issues rather than educational concerns. Proposed alternative review methods involve the consideration of instructional context and potential for individual construction of knowledge.

LEARNER ACTIVITIES

1. Have at least three people in different positions in the educational system (such as a student, parent, administrator, or community member) review the same piece of software. How do their reviews compare and contrast?

2. What modifications would be needed to use the Software Review Form in this chapter with students as the reviewers? Choose a target student audience, and list changes you would make to allow students to use the form to review software independently.

3. Find an example of a poor educational website. What makes the resource of poor quality? Are there any redeeming qualities?

4. Go to the software review websites listed in this chapter. Bookmark them for easy return. How do these review sites compare with the information presented in this chapter?

5. Look up reviews of educational resources published in educational technology journals. What are the review procedures? Are the reviews comprehensive enough to convince you to purchase the recommended titles?

6. Write a complete review of a piece of educational software and submit it to the software editor of an educational technology journal.

7. Research a school or district electronic resource review process. What types of people are involved in the process? How is review information disseminated to teachers?

8. Use the Educational Website Review Guidelines to review a website listed in Chapter 9.

9. Host an email forum with several peers or colleagues on the overall quality of educational software being produced today. Have participants send their responses to all in the "conversation" to keep everyone involved. Direct the ongoing discussion by sending questions soliciting perceived strengths and weaknesses of software that people have seen or used.

10. Is it possible to review one electronic resource for all audiences and purposes? Compose a position paper on the topic, discussing the problems with generic software reviews.

BIBLIOGRAPHY

Association for School Curriculum and Development. (1998). *Only the best.* Alexandria, VA: Author.

Educational Software Preview Guide Consortium. (1998). *1998 educational software preview guide.* Eugene, OR: International Society for Technology in Education.

Graf, N. (1996). Making the CD-ROM choices. *Book Report, 15*(2), 13, 15, 23.

Hakkinen, P. (1996). Software designers and teachers as evaluators of computer-based learning environments. *Machine-Mediated Learning, 5*(2), 135–148.

Hoffman, J. L., & Lyons, D. J. (1997). Evaluating instructional software. *Learning and Leading with Technology, 25*(2), 52–56.

International Society for Technology in Education. (2000). [Description of the *Educational software preview guide*]. Available: <http://www.iste.org/Bookstore>.

McDougall, A., & Squires, D. (1995a). A critical examination of the checklist approach in software selection. *Journal of Educational Computing Research, 12,* 263–274.

McDougall, A., & Squires, D. (1995b). An empirical study of a new paradigm for choosing educational software. *Computers and Education, 25,* 93–103.

Nicholls, P., & Ridley, J. (1997). Evaluating multimedia library materials: Clues from hand-printed books and art history. *Computers in Libraries, 17*(4), 28–31.

Reiser, R. A., & Kegelmann, H. W. (1994). Evaluating instructional software: A review and critique of current methods. *Educational Technology Research and Development, 42,* 63–69.

Shade, D. D. (1996). Software evaluation. *Young Children, 51*(6), 17–21.

Squires, D., & McDougall, A. (1996). Software evaluation: A situated approach. *Journal of Computer Assisted Learning, 12,* 146–161.

Squires, D., & Preece, J. (1996). Usability and learning: Evaluating the potential of educational software. *Computers in Education, 27,* 15–22.

Sturm, J. M. (1997). How to select appropriate software for computer-assisted writing. *Intervention in School and Clinic, 32*(3), 148–161.

CHAPTER 8

EDUCATIONAL SOFTWARE TYPES

FOCUS QUESTIONS

1. What are the defining characteristics of each type of software?
2. Besides type, what other software characteristics do teachers need to consider?
3. How can educational software be effectively integrated into a standards-based curriculum?

When schools allocate funds to bring technology into classrooms, one of the next purchases that quickly follows the hardware buys is that of educational software. Each piece of software, in its own unique way, allows a computer to help students reach specific learning goals. Some software is designed to be used with large groups of students aided by much teacher involvement, and others are best used with small groups or individuals interacting directly with the computer. One of the most difficult challenges teachers face is meeting the individual needs of all students. With a varied assortment of educational software at hand, teachers are able to individualize instruction to enrich or remediate as is necessary for student success.

A standards-based curriculum ensures students' continued growth according to identified goals, objectives, and standards, along with those strategies that will enable attainment of those outcomes. Those strategies now include the use of educational software. Teachers who understand how software might best be integrated into a standards-based curriculum will need to be aware of the different types of software that are available. This chapter defines and illustrates some of the common categories. In order to be an effective facilitator of software use in the classroom, however, it is not necessary for teachers to discern exact differences among the categories. In fact, most of the descriptors of the categories overlap and most software titles can be easily classified in a number of different software categories. In an attempt to provide full-service educational solutions, newer software includes components of most of the different software types grouped together in one integrated learning environment. Distinctions can be further blurred by the various terms used in the software industry to describe similar categories. Use the alphabetical listing of software types in this chapter as a guide to understanding the terms that are used when discussing software, but do not misunderstand this to be a definitive list of all that is possible in software. Most of the software titles that are featured in Classroom Vignettes could also be classified in other categories, but they are used here to illustrate specific characteristics of each type. See the appendix for contact information on software companies.

DRILL-AND-PRACTICE/INSTRUCTIONAL
GAME SOFTWARE

Category Description

In general, drill-and-practice software allows learners to come in contact with facts, relationships, problems, and vocabulary that they have previously learned until the material is committed to memory or until a particular skill has been refined. The best drill-and-practice software possesses an interesting format that encourages repeated use by students, thus establishing the stimulus–response association required for memorization of certain facts. Sequential learning tasks and immediate feedback assist the student in the mastery of the skill.

Drill-and-practice programs are available in a range of sophistication. Simpler programs offer students the same type of practice they might receive using flashcards. Students receive a series of items, answer each one in order, and receive feedback based on how they responded. If students receive a mastery score on the selection, they move on to the next harder set of problems.

More advanced drill-and-practice programs attempt to serve each student with questions that are at the appropriate level of difficulty. A program might begin with some sort of a pretest in order to place a student at a proper beginning location. As the student answers questions correctly, the program automatically branches to more difficult subject matter, and students answering incorrectly are quickly brought to material at a lower level. This adaptive design allows students to work as closely to their own developmental level as possible so that they are constantly challenged to perform tasks that are not too frustratingly simple or complex.

Quality drill-and-practice programs utilize brief, effective feedback for both correct and incorrect responses, either giving students another chance for incorrect answers or giving positive, motivating reinforcement for correct responses. Students should be able to control the rate of the program, taking as long as they need to answer a question. They should also have the ability to quit the program at any time and resume at the place they left off when they return.

Instructional games can be very similar to drill and practice, but have added increased motivation by having game rules, an entertaining environment, and competition to be the winner. Students may be more willing to work at practicing skills if they know they can do so by playing a game. Depending on the particular game, students can compete against the computer or against other students. Some instructional games take on the form of many traditional games, such as board games, logic games, adventure games, or word games, whereas others are originally created as software.

Practical Integration

Critics of classroom computer use often aim the brunt of their skeptical comments toward drill-and-practice software. Many of the early drill-and-practice programs were known as "drill and kill" because they presented the same isolated skills in the same way to every user, creating boring, impersonal learning environments. Because drill and practice was the first type of educational software brought into regular use by teachers, it was often used as a learning device rather than as a practice device by teachers unfamiliar with the potential of the media. As educational philosophy steers away from behaviorist principles toward more constructivist views of students constructing their own meaning, the practical use of all educational software must follow suit. Drill-and-practice software can be an effective tool if used as one of many educational tools, as appropriate, to meet specific educational goals.

Drill-and-practice software is ideal when students need to practice discrete skills. The electronic mode can be more motivating than a paper-and-pencil counterpart, and the feedback to student responses is immediate. It can be used repeatedly without the need for teachers to grade papers or keep direct track of progress.

Drill and practice is usually thought of for aiding math skills because the largely unambiguous nature of basic math facts lends itself to the right or wrong format. It can also be effective in areas that take advantage of gamelike formats, contextual clues, rhymes, and riddles, such as vocabulary, historical dates, and scientific definitions.

Educational games can be used just as drill-and-practice software might be. Skills that have already been introduced can be practiced and strengthened. Although it is true that students may be more motivated to use instructional games, you must constantly evaluate whether the learning experience is purposeful. Students may have mastered the instructional objectives of a game long ago, but may still enjoy playing. Too much playing might lead to an abuse of the game format. Take time to make sure that the use of gamelike software is balanced with other relevant learning opportunities. Because many games may be violent or may tend to encourage aggressive playing behavior in the classroom, preview all content and monitor program use to see that it is serving a meaningful place in the instructional sequence of your classroom.

■ ■ ■ ■ ■ ▨▨▨▨▨▨▨▨▨▨▨▨▨▨▨▨▨▨▨▨▨▨▨▨▨▨▨▨▨▨▨▨▨▨▨▨

CLASSROOM VIGNETTE

Carlos, Whitney, Tiffany, and Cari, kindergartners in Mrs. Hassam's class, began the year well above other students in their mathematical abilities. By midyear, they could count by 1s, 2s, 5s, and 10s with fluency and could write numbers past 100.

To encourage their continued progress, Mrs. Hassam began introducing them to some basic place value concepts. She used base-10 blocks to illustrate the relationship between 1s, 10s, and 100s, and within a short amount of time the four were trading place value digits with confidence. Following the work with the concrete manipulatives, Mrs. Hassam connected what they were capable of with the blocks to numerical writing.

When the four students reached an independent level of familiarity with place value concepts, they began working with Mighty Math Carnival Countdown (Edmark). With the Bubble Band, they could trade 10 bubbles for one big tens bubble or trade 10 tens bubbles for a hundreds bubble. The students were able to practice place values at their own pace, allowing Mrs. Hassam to work with other students on other math instruction.

INTEGRATED LEARNING SYSTEMS

Category Description

Integrated Learning Systems (ILSs) have offered schools comprehensive instructional and management features for decades. Largely traditional in methodology, the expensive ILSs are networked software compilations that address objectives in the core curriculum areas. Pretests, instruction, practice, and posttests are designed to be aligned with national or district curriculum goals. Students typically work independently, and their progress is tracked and reported automatically. When they have mastered a particular set of objectives, they advance to the next section. Teachers can monitor students' performance by examining reports printed out by the system and can choose to supplement the electronic instruction as necessary.

Practical Integration

The adoption of ILSs often makes the transition to using technology easier for schools because the curriculum is completely prepared. This packaged approach, however, may not always allow for easy integration into other outside curriculum. The software systems are generally intended to stand alone as the sole source of instruction. The systems follow a typically behaviorist approach to learning, funneling all students through a linear presentation of the curriculum. Some newer ILSs include real-world scenarios and projects to present skills in context (e.g., Wasatch Interactive Learning at <http://www.wasatchnet.com/welcome.html>). The easy mistake many schools make is assuming that when technology is brought into their classrooms, these curriculum delivery systems will adequately replace their teachers. Another misconception is that the introduction of ILSs satisfactorily prepares students with technology skills. Just because students access lessons or assessments using the computer does not mean they are gaining important communication, information management, and problem-solving skills that broader technology use can help to develop.

Care must be taken to ensure that the instructional format and content provide the best learning opportunity for each student. Current beliefs about the variety of learning styles found in any group of students lead to the understanding that any one method will likely not be sufficiently individualized to be successful. The human teacher is needed to orchestrate ILS use so that the most instructional benefit can be derived by each student.

If your school has adopted an ILS, be prepared to assume the role of an instructional facilitator. Be aware of the content and format of the software so as to anticipate student needs and questions. Rather than relying solely on the automatic records of each student's progress, investigate further to be sure that students are getting the instruction they need.

PROBLEM-SOLVING SOFTWARE

Category Description

Problem-solving software requires students to apply higher-order strategies and synthesize knowledge from multiple curricular areas in order to solve problems. Students can test hypotheses, learn from mistakes, and refine skills as they gain mastery of problem-solving

CLASSROOM VIGNETTE

Mr. Medina's third- and fourth-grade multiage class has been working hard over the last several weeks to learn basic multiplication facts. They have looked for equal groups of items in their everyday world, compared the patterns they found to fact patterns on a times table, and practiced with flash cards. Students have gained varying amounts of fluency with the facts and will continue to do so over the course of the rest of the year.

Today, Mr. Medina has set up several stations through which students will spend the morning rotating in order to gain even more experience and confidence with the facts. One of the stations is located at the two classroom computers, on which he has loaded Mega Math Blaster. This program allows students to practice, among other topics, multiplication facts in an arcade game format. Students compete in an outer space environment to solve problems at one of six difficulty levels (see Figure 8.1).

Because this is new software for students, Mr. Medina explains it briefly to the whole class. He sets up the context of the program by explaining the need to rescue the main character from Gelator, the Brain Drainer. He then goes over to show the first group at the station some of the basic operations, such as how to log-in, what levels might be most appropriate, the training on the game rules, and how to view the high scores. He has looked at the program himself a couple of times and so knows the general layout enough to get the students started. This group's job will then be to train the group that follows them how to operate the software, a peer-teaching strategy Mr. Medina frequently uses when introducing new software.

Matthew, Sara, Nicole, and Juan play at the game for the half hour they are at that station. They're animatedly involved, building strategies as they go. Sometimes they are so excited with winning that they yell out loud, and then quickly shush each other, giggling as they look around to find Mr. Medina. When their time is up, they reluctantly give up their seats at the computer and show the next group how to play.

FIGURE 8.1   Mega Math Blaster.

techniques. Software of this type can provide practice in solving problems by modeling general critical thinking steps, by focusing on specific subject-area issues, or by creating an open environment in which students can discover their own strategies. Whatever the method, problem-solving software affords the user more freedom than does drill-and-practice or

■ ■ ■ ■ ■ ■

CLASSROOM VIGNETTE

Ms. Brown always stresses problem-solving strategies to her upper elementary students and makes an effort to use word problems to illustrate real problem situations. Midway through the fall semester, she notices that although her students are largely successful with solving math problems on paper, they are not always able to describe in words how they solve the problems beyond pointing to the problems and saying the numbers. She decides to try some problem-solving software called Fizz & Martina's Math Adventures (Tom Snyder Productions) as another tool to provide a useful context for their learning (see Figure 8.2).

Over the course of two weeks, she introduces her class to Fizz and Martina and the other characters in Mr. Barney's math class. Mr. Barney loves to tell stories, which always involve some type of math problem. On the videos included in the program, Mr. Barney encourages students to take notes of any numbers they encounter during the stories. What intrigues Ms. Brown the most about the program is that not only does it help students to gain practice in team problem-solving skills but it also requires effective discussion techniques. Students have to be able to describe their problem-solving strategies without looking at their notes, so they learn to assist team members to verbalize their teams' thinking.

Ms. Brown soon sees students excited about the program and hears them talking about the Blue Falls Elementary characters well after they finish using the computer. Speaking with students individually over the next several weeks proves two things to Ms. Brown: Not only are the students demonstrating proficiency with problem-solving strategies, but also they are feeling confident about what they know. One student even offers to show students in another class how to use the software.

FIGURE 8.2   Fizz & Martina's Math Adventures.

tutorial software, but may or may not present the real-world context that characterizes simulation software.

A useful framework for understanding the definition of problem-solving software classifies programs in terms of *learner control.* Some programs give little control to the user beyond the ability to make logical guesses, one at a time. Other programs provide for full learner control, with the user deciding exactly what he or she will do next and moving freely from one activity to another. Good problem-solving programs promote the development of logical systematic thinking patterns and transcend the boundaries of simple tutorial or drill-and-practice software.

Practical Integration

Effective problem solving is built by continuous practice and experience in a variety of meaningful situations. This understanding must be clear in teachers' minds as they plan a place for problem-solving software in the daily workings of a classroom. No software can be used as the sole tool for developing students' critical thinking abilities. Instead, software should be seen as one effective component in a repertoire of activities that promote the acquisition of higher-order thinking skills. Whether a piece of software is used to appropriately extend a lesson or a particularly strong program inspires continued class work away from the computer, teachers must plan for extensive electronic and nonelectronic chances for students to think critically.

REFERENCE SOFTWARE

Category Description

In years past, when students needed to conduct research, they were required to go down to the library to peruse heavy encyclopedic tomes. Technology has brought both the storage capabilities to gather volumes of facts onto one small CD-ROM and the media variety with which to effectively bring life to static reference material. Reference software can take the form of any traditional reference works, such as dictionaries, encyclopedias, and thesauri. Other reference software presents extensive collections of information on a focused topic.

Practical Integration

Electronic reference works can be utilized just as traditional reference material would be. Depending on the particular learning activity, students might refer to software as needed to answer specific questions. They also might openly explore a multimedia reference without specific goals to guide their learning. The multimedia components of reference software present information in graphic, audio, video, or other alternate formats that allow uniquely unlimited access to students who might not be developmentally able to contend with the text version of the information.

SIMULATION SOFTWARE

Category Description

Educational simulations allow students to experience events or phenomena that they are not able to witness personally and that would be too difficult or too dangerous to duplicate in a classroom setting. Software can simulate manipulating objects, performing a set of

CLASSROOM VIGNETTE

Max had chosen to study dinosaurs for his independent project. He remembered learning about them when he was in kindergarten, but he just saw a movie about them, and now he really wanted to become an expert. He already knew a lot of dinosaur names, and he wanted to learn more about how each type of dinosaur lived.

He is sitting in front of Eyewitness Virtual Reality: Dinosaur Hunter, the new software his teacher sent him to the library media center to use (see Figure 8.3). An older student just showed him how to move around in the program, and now he is exploring on his own. He hungrily studies the bright pictures and watches the videos and animations. He sees how paleontologists dig for and piece together fossilized bones, and he feels like he is actually participating in the field project. He remembers a few times to write down some notes, but he mostly only takes in the wonder of the multimedia-designed research environment.

The next day and the day after that, Max heads down to the media center to research dinosaurs. After just a couple of days, he knows his way around the "dinosaur museum" and can name a great number of dinosaur facts. He is even starting to think of ideas for how he might show his class what he has learned in his research.

FIGURE 8.3   Eyewitness Virtual Reality: Dinosaur Hunter.

procedures, or acting in a given situation. Real processes can be slowed down or speeded up to study the effects of artificially tinkering with the variables.

Simulations provide contexts rich for meaningful individual learning construction. Like life experiences, simulations require the synthesis of many skills and understandings, making for true cross-curricular learning. Students must use what they know in ways that force them to confirm and expand their understanding. Simulations allow students to make and be affected by their own decisions. Guided by data provided by the software, the stu-

CLASSROOM VIGNETTE

When he saw Decisions, Decisions: The Environment (Tom Snyder Productions) on the list of software the district had recently purchased, Omar Mahesh knew it was ideal for his seventh-grade government class. The software is a role-playing simulation of a small-town pollution crisis during a political campaign. Students use the briefing books provided with the software to represent four different expert viewpoints—including an environmentalist, an economist, a scientist, and a campaign manager—to advise the fictional candidate on environmental issues.

Mr. Mahesh divides students into groups of four so that the random number generator can control turn taking. With his students armed with their briefing books and gathered in teams around the television monitor at the front of the room, Mr. Mahesh begins the simulation introduction.

As students learn about the pond being polluted, the software prompts student groups, acting as the mayor of the town, to set goals in priority and then, acting as the advisers, to look up information in the briefing books. Based on this advice, groups decide how to act and evaluate consequences of those actions. Just as in real life, single decisions lead to new problems, and students continue with the simulation over several class periods. On an especially contested decision in the classroom, several students suggest further time to think and do some outside research. At students' suggestions, Mr. Mahesh broadens the activity to include parent interviews and Internet research before resuming the simulation. With amazing timing, a pollution issue appears in their own town newspaper just a couple of weeks after their study. Mr. Mahesh is pleasantly pleased when students demonstrate some of the same careful problem-solving habits developed during the simulation to debate the real environmental situation (see Figure 8.4).

FIGURE 8.4 Decisions, Decisions: The Environment.

dent becomes an active player in the scenario, selecting certain options or taking risks, and then witnessing the results of his or her decisions. Their involvement in a simulated situation lets students experience some of the feelings and problems associated with participating in the actual situation. They see the reasons for developing good strategies and therefore begin to think in a more organized fashion.

Good simulations build realistic, yet appropriately unpredictable environments. They combine text with a selection of media elements that create engaging, content-rich situations.

Practical Integration

Simulation software prompts active discussion and encourages cooperation toward common goals. Depending on the situation being simulated, the software can be effective with a variety of student groupings. Entire classes can work together, collaboratively making key decisions. Small groups of students can explore situations separately and then later compare notes to see how others performed under the same circumstances.

In science labs, student can pour and mix dangerous chemicals via simulation, so mistakes do not blow up the classroom. Through the simulation, students can begin to make the fine discriminations needed for proper handling of chemicals. It is also possible to simulate experiments that are too expensive, complicated, or time-consuming to replicate in school laboratories, such as building models of the systems in the human body (Coleman, 1997). Simulations provide for more student involvement than is possible through a reading assignment or lecture.

Social studies simulations can help students reenact historical events, learn about other societies, or experience governmental procedures, such as elections and lawmaking. When running simulation software, students must first understand certain information and concepts so that they can then analyze situations and make wise decisions; therefore, learning becomes more relevant and useful to them.

Simulations can also be used to train students in the operation of tools and different types of equipment. Such training allows students to practice skills and procedures needed to operate the equipment safely and accurately—without danger to themselves or to the equipment.

Social studies, science, business, and vocational simulations can be valuable learning devices if their use is wisely integrated into the curriculum at appropriate times. Simulations do not serve as stand-alone units, but are most effective when used to illustrate and use skills, ideas, and experiences that have first been explored by other means. Students must be prepared with both knowledge of the content and an understanding of how to operate the simulation itself, preparation they would undoubtedly receive in advance of the corresponding real-life situation.

When having students work in a simulated environment, you must ensure that they understand the shortcomings of the software. No matter how realistic the representation of the life situation it remains merely a simulation and is thus not entirely accurate or sufficiently complex. Discussing decisions and consequences with others who have used the program can help students to connect the simulation with reality.

TOOL SOFTWARE

Category Description

Software tools help teachers and students become efficient and productive managers of textual, numerical, and graphical information. Because tools are not as content-specific as other software types, they can extend what humans are able to do in virtually any curricular or management area. Just as teachers and students use pencils, for example, as tools in innumerable daily activities, so, too, can the word processors, spreadsheets, databases, graphics, and authoring programs be used. Other tools lend themselves to a particular content area, but allow users of many different ages to create or do something unique. Tools such as these will be used by students all their lives in most professions. The general skills and habits they learn by using software for various learning tasks will be transferable to other software they will be required to use in their future.

Practical Integration

Software tools afford quite a bit of freedom to teachers in how technology can be integrated into various learning tasks. Whereas other content-specific software, such as drill and practice or tutorials, is appropriate only for a particular subject area or developmental level, productivity tools can be used across grade levels and across subjects. Children using this type of software are more in control of the operation of the program than they might be with other types of software. The processes and products can be more customized.

Your students might use word processors to record information they have researched or to write creatively. They may compose letters directly on the word processor or may type in field notes after having scribbled them down on paper. With spreadsheet programs, students can study the relationships between amounts of money or can learn to schedule time. Students might organize research content using a database program. With graphics software, students can explore geometric relationships, geographic features, and artistic representations.

Internet tools, such as HTML editors, are making up an increasing share of the tool software. The creative production versatility of authoring software is developed to a great extent in Chapter 16.

Teachers should also be using productivity tools to support their efforts as teachers and managers of student information. Specific tips for using software as an aid to classroom administration can be found in Chapter 15.

TUTORIAL SOFTWARE

Category Description

Tutorial software utilizes written explanations, descriptions, questions, problems, and graphic illustrations for concept development. Concepts are intended to be learned without any other instruction efforts, thus existing as a stand-alone form of instruction. This presentation of instruction differs from drill-and-practice software, which provides only practice and assessment. Students are given opportunities in tutorials to gain experience with new concepts much like they would when learning with a living and breathing teacher. Often computerized or traditional written pretests are included with tutorial software to determine the most appropriate level of lessons for a particular student. After the tutorial portion of a lesson has been presented, drill-and-practice exercises are offered. In some cases, the student has total control of the number of exercises. Finally, a posttest for each objective or

CLASSROOM VIGNETTE

The new concept for the ninth grade at Inez Guerrera's high school involves team planning for interdisciplinary curriculum. Teachers now partner, with history and language, and math and science, working together, and students attend two-hour block sessions for more focused and intensive study. Inez has taught ninth-grade language for the last seven years and has developed a friendship with Beverly Middleton, a ninth-grade history teacher. The partnership is welcomed on both ends.

In planning for joint projects during the summer, the two teachers decide on using selected literature pieces to exemplify historical periods. Inez reads of the History through Literature series (Clearvue) and in particular the Civilization and Writing episode (see Figure 8.5). Inez and Beverly see a useful connection between history and language development as they preview the software. They then decide that it will best be used once the reading has begun as an enrichment to the context. During the first month of school, ninth-graders start reading Homer's *The Iliad.* As they learn about the characters Achilles and Hector, they simultaneously learn about the historical setting of the novel.

Students can use the software to read historical summaries and listen to narration, accompanied by relevant video and photos. Keywords are highlighted and linked to glossaries, and students can take quizzes of any length and any time limit, as determined by the teacher. The presentations include quotes from notable literature selections, such as *The Iliad.* Over the next several weeks, students work individually or in pairs to view the software chapters and reflect on the relations to their readings. Not only do students learn about literature and history, but they also experience the two in tandem and with the logical relations in context.

FIGURE 8.5   History through Literature.

group of objectives determines mastery. Student scores may be displayed as the lesson ends, as well as suggestions for further study and practice.

Very basic tutorial programs present information and practice in a strictly linear fashion, similar to ways students would learn by themselves using a book. *Linear tutorials* present a series of screen displays to all users, regardless of individual differences among the students. There are very few reasons for these "page-turner" programs to be in electronic form because they utilize little of the technical capacity of computers. *Branching tutorials,* on the other hand, do not require all users to follow the same path, but direct students to certain lessons or parts of a lesson according to results of computerized pretests and posttests, or to student response to embedded questions within the program.

Tutorial programs that are designed to take full advantage of the medium should allow for students to interact with the programs continually as they practice new information. Good tutorials also allow individual students to work at their own pace, reviewing material as needed and moving ahead quickly when they fully understand a new concept. It does the learner no instructional good when a program advances to the next screen if the learner is not ready to go on. Adequate practice must be given following instruction, but prior to assessment. The author of the tutorial must try to predict all possible correct responses and allow for insignificant misspelling and capitalization errors. The program must respond intelligently to incorrect answers, predict the most common incorrect answers, and offer specially tailored explanations and learning experiences according to which incorrect answers were chosen by the student. In addition, computerized tests must be as valid and reliable as their written counterparts. This is so that students are not subjected to material they have already learned and so that learning can be evaluated fairly and accurately. A management feature allows teachers to track student progress and step in if human instruction or redirection is warranted. In short, tutorial software requires the thorough instructional design that would be required of any good lesson a teacher would present in a traditional manner.

Practical Integration

In a busy classroom with dozens of different learning levels and styles, teachers can use tutorials to supplement their instructional efforts. Tutorial programs can teach students who require additional instruction on a topic or can allow more time to work through concepts at a slower pace. Instruction can be planned in a presentation style that complements what is available in a tutorial, so that students for which one style is not effective will have an alternative method to learn. Tutorials can open up learning opportunities to students in smaller or rural schools. If there are no teachers trained to provide instruction in higher-level math or science courses or certain languages, students can use tutorial software to learn what they would otherwise miss.

WEB-BASED SOFTWARE

An increasingly viable resource for teachers is web-based software, made possible through the latest web technologies that provide the sophistication found on most CD-ROM–based software. The programs, available largely for free on an endless variety of content websites, are designed to be used entirely online. Web-based software generally requires the downloading of Internet plug-ins; however, the user typically is led to the download site automatically. Teachers are cautioned that this software is not necessarily designed for educational purposes. However, these *edutainment* games, part education and part entertainment, can be used effectively for specific purposes with clear planning. Depending on the purpose and provider of the software, teachers will find varying levels of supportive recommendations for classroom use.

The following is a selection of the most exciting web-based software currently available. The listed selection may change by press time, so teachers are encouraged to search for the latest resources.

AMAZING-SPACE <http://amazing-space.stsci.edu/>
The Space Telescope Science Institute, operator of the Hubble Space Telescope, employs science teachers, scientists, and engineers to develop interactive web-based lessons based on a variety of space-related concepts.

CLICKING ANASTASIA <http://www.lostsecrets.com/>
Students follow the story of Nicholas Romanov, former Tsar of the Russian Empire, his wife Alexandra, and their five children, killed by communist revolutionaries. The mystery that remains is the location of the Tsar's lost millions of diamonds and gems. Students can participate in interactive problem solving, receiving clues via email.

FUNSCHOOL <http://www.funschool.com/>
Provides over 500 free online games based on educational concepts in a safe, interactive, and entertaining environment.

KIDSPSYCH <http://www.kidspsych.org/>
This site was actually designed for parents to help children develop cognitive thinking skills and deductive reasoning, but it has great potential for the development of the same skills in the classroom.

SECRETS AT SEA <http://www.secretsatsea.org/>
Fourth- through seventh-grade students can participate in an online ocean adventure examining unusual behaviors by killer whales.

SPYWATCH <http://www.bbc.co.uk/education/lookandread/>
Spywatch is based on the popular BBC television series, set in a country village in World War II. Students develop phonics, spelling, and story-writing skills as they follow the adventures of a group of evacuees and investigate a range of spy suspects.

SUMMARY

Educational software allows teachers to use computers as versatile instructional aids to meet the individual needs of their students. Teachers can get a better understanding of how to incorporate software into a standards-based curriculum by considering the types of software that are available: drill and practice/instructional game, Integrated Learning Systems, problem solving, reference, simulation, tool, and tutorial. Although knowledge of the software types is helpful for planning, teachers should know that the categories tend to overlap and many software pieces can be easily described by the descriptors of several of the categories. Drill-and-practice software allows students to work with information they have previously learned, getting immediate feedback to assist in skill mastery. Instructional games provide practice similar to that found in drill-and-practice software, but structure it in a game format, with rules and a competitive environment. Integrated Learning Systems offer complete, networked instructional, assessment, and management packages. Problem-solving software requires logical thinking on the part of students and assumes that some previous concept development has taken place. The continuing development of logical thinking is an important goal for problem-solving software. Reference software brings together great amounts of facts and illustrates them with a variety of media elements, such as graphics, animations, video, and audio.

Computer simulations allow students to experience real-life events in the safety of the classroom. Decisions must be made to affect the outcome of the simulation, so the student tends to become an involved and interested learner. Software tools are not as content-specific as other types of software, meaning students and teachers can use them across the curriculum to manage all types of information. Tutorials attempt to aid concept development by carefully presenting instruction and feedback. Students can utilize tutorials for remediation or enrichment, and they are especially useful when teachers for a specialized topic are not available.

LEARNER ACTIVITIES

1. Look at some newspaper ads and make a list of the features that appear most desirable in the educational software that is advertised. Do these features appear educationally sound or does flashiness seem to be selling more software?

2. Identify all of the software currently available on the market that could be used for your intended teaching area or grade level. Comment on the selection available to learners in your area.

3. Choose one specific piece of software and write a lesson plan for how you would integrate it into a complete instructional sequence. Be sure to include the instruction or other preparation that would precede the software use and how your students would follow up their experiences with the software.

4. Summarize the advantages and disadvantages of teaching a particular concept with and without educational software.

5. Describe the different strategies that would be needed to facilitate effective use of educational software by different-sized groupings of students.

6. Observe a traditional lesson taught to students of the level you plan to teach. What type of software would be appropriate to assist students with practicing or extending this topic? How might you convince the teacher to include educational software in his or her instructional repertoire?

7. Discuss how educational software changes the roles of teachers and students.

8. List five software companies and describe the apparent educational philosophy of each based on an examination of a selection of their current software.

9. Review the literature on the effectiveness of educational software since 1990 and summarize the research results.

10. List all the sources you can identify that teachers and students can use to find out information on how to use specific software.

BIBLIOGRAPHY

Adams, P. E. (1996). Hypermedia in the classroom using Earth and space science CD-ROMs. *Journal of Computers in Mathematics and Science Teaching, 15*(1–2), 19–34.

Allen, D. (1996). Teaching with technology: Problem-solving strategies. *Teaching PreK–8, 27*(3), 14–16.

Coleman, F. M. (1997). Software simulation enhances science experiments. *T.H.E. Journal, 25*(2), 56–58.

Frye, B., & Frager, A. M. (1996). Civilization, Colonization, SimCity: Simulations for the social studies classroom. *Learning and Leading with Technology, 24*(2), 21–23, 32.

Ivers, K. S. (1996–1997). Desktop adventures: Building problem-solving and computer skills. *Learning and Leading with Technology, 24*(4), 6–11.

Jenkins, D. (1996). Have more fun teaching physics: Simulating, stimulating software. *MultiMedia Schools, 3*(5), 42–47.

Johnson, J. M. (1996–1997). Software for an evaluation workshop. *Learning and Leading with Technology, 24*, 48–50.

Mobley, E. D. (1996). Interactive multimedia in the music classroom. *Music Educators Journal, 82*(4), 22–24, 54.

Schatz, S. (1996). Show/Do/Cue: A model for training use of software tools. *T.H.E. Journal, 24*(2), 86–89.

White, C. S. (1996). Multimedia products for U.S. history. *Social Education, 60,* 379–383.

CHAPTER 9

INTEGRATING WORLD WIDE WEB RESOURCES

FOCUS QUESTIONS

1. What considerations must be made to successfully integrate an online resource into a comprehensive lesson sequence?

2. How can understanding a framework of information make it easier to categorize and use Internet resources?

3. How can specific content resources be integrated?

As schools around the world establish connections to the Internet, and teachers and students gain proficiency with navigating through the vast quantities of readily available information, the true educational potential of the World Wide Web can finally begin to be understood. The web can be a dynamic tool capable of assisting educators in propelling learning to exciting and compelling levels and of bringing education to any students, anywhere, at any time (Ellsworth, 1997). Students can learn from experiences and communication that would never be possible within the scope of an isolated classroom. But instructional resources on the web should never be mistaken as substitutes for the skill and intuition of human teachers, or even thought of as replacements for traditional methods of instruction. Instead, these resources, when used appropriately, should be considered as rich enhancements of a complete educational plan.

CONSIDERING THE INSTRUCTIONAL USE OF ONLINE RESOURCES

The key to the effectiveness of any instructional tool lies partly in the tool's unique attributes, but to a larger degree in how the tool is actually utilized. This is very much the case with educational Internet resources. No matter how flashy or cute or seemingly educationally relevant a website or other resource is, if time is not taken to carefully plan for its use as part of an entire instructional sequence, the potential benefits to learners may be squandered. The first step in planning learning experiences that involve online resources is to consider the goals not only for one specific activity but also for the class and even the school as a whole. Ross (1995) offers the questions in Table 9.1 as starting points to the planning.

Understanding the place of an Internet-based activity within the larger scope of an entire curriculum will help teachers plan meaningful and effective learning experiences. Projects should be organized and well defined, just as a traditional lesson taught without technology would be (Barron, 1996). The structure of the lesson should fit with an individual teacher's teaching style and philosophy. If child-centered work is common in a particular classroom, for instance, then child-centered work should be considered for an Internet-based lesson. Of course, this should not discourage teachers from exploring new methods and letting the technology facilitate change in their teaching. It simply must be understood that any change that occurs is not the sole result of the use of any technologies. The Internet can supply the resources to motivate teachers and open their minds to the world around them available online, but this will happen only with the conscious desire of teachers to change their teaching.

PLANNING A LEARNING EXPERIENCE

The planning sequence that is necessary to make the most out of an Internet-based lesson is virtually the same as the thoughtful planning that goes into any other quality lesson (Tomei, 1996).

First, define the goals of the lesson. Understanding exactly where a lesson fits into a curricular sequence, taking into account what experiences students have had prior to this lesson and what expectations are held for them following the lesson, will make more efficient use of your time spent searching for Internet resources.

After lesson goals are solidified, locate the online information that will be necessary for the lesson. The time and effort involved at this stage can be extensive, depending on a teacher's familiarity with locating web resources, the amount and quality of information

TABLE 9.1   Questions to Consider When Planning for the Use of Internet Resources

1. What is the educational goal I want my students to achieve?
2. Is this a worthwhile educational goal, whether it be accomplished using electronic or traditional means?
3. Am I trying to make my educational goals conform to the available technology, or am I using these tools to more effectively meet my instructional goals?
4. When compared to other available tools, does this electronic tool effectively assist in obtaining this goal?
5. Can this goal be reached just as effectively using more traditional methods?
6. Is this electronic medium an effective way to teach an educational goal, or is this activity just a skill-building exercise in the use of the tool?

available on the topic, and the ways and extent to which resources will be used in the instruction. Sometimes the time required to locate quality resources discourages teachers from using the web to teach. The best advice is to start with sites that have been recommended or with larger "jumping off" sites (discussed later in this chapter). The next steps can involve conducting a web search for information relating to your topic (see Chapter 4 for searching strategies). Because the quality and age appropriateness of websites vary, you will want to explore the entire site thoroughly prior to ever having students use all or parts of it.

Refer to the online resource evaluation information in Chapter 7. Select several sites, including teacher background information, lesson plans, and student activities. At this point, you will also want to consider nonelectronic information sources to complement the online information.

Next, plan the lesson, beginning with specific learning objectives, content, procedures, and assignments. The form of the lesson plan can vary, from something extremely structured to something with flexible parameters, again according to your teaching philosophy. Consider whether teacher resources will be used as a demonstration with the whole class, with a small group, with partners, or even with students working individually. These decisions will depend on the concepts you are teaching and the strategy that will be the most effective with your students.

A FRAMEWORK OF EDUCATIONAL RESOURCES

The task of sifting through online resources can be a daunting one for teachers with often overwhelming professional responsibilities. Finding useful online information and understanding where it might be integrated into an established curriculum can best be accomplished by examining the sites according to a categorical framework. Berenfeld (1996) proposes comparing the scope of the information environment of the Internet to that of the natural environment of living things, commonly referred to as the "biosphere." Because the information environment grows and changes and is based on interdependence of its components, just as is the biosphere, he has coined the term *infosphere*. Based on this systemic view of the information environment, as well as on the proposed organizational models of both Berenfeld and Ellsworth (1997), this chapter presents examples of World Wide Web resources organized into a framework of infosphere processes: planting information, harvesting information, and cultivating information. The ideas for use suggested here should not be taken as comprehensive, but are meant only to spur thinking about integration.

PLANTING THE INFORMATION

That which will eventually be harvested can be so only because it was once planted. The environment of the Internet was built on the idea of free contribution of ideas, and even students can help in this regenerative process by planting their own seeds of information that will propagate the online resource supply.

Students crave authentic audiences for their work. When they have learned something, it only makes them understand it better to show someone else. With the World Wide Web, students are no longer limited to writing for classmates or family members to read.

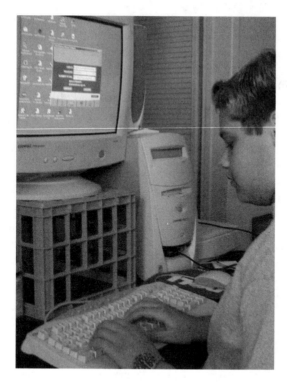

FIGURE 9.1   Websites dedicated to publishing the writing of students are easy ways to let students see their work published.

They can easily publish their work for the world audience. Reports, stories, poems, and school periodicals can be published easily on a server at the school or district (see Chapter 10 for information on creating educational websites).

There also exist websites dedicated to publishing the writing of students (see Figure 9.1). Because such sites are already created and require only following directions to submit a piece of writing, they are easy ways to let students see their work published.

HARVESTING THE INFORMATION

Life is made possible in our biosphere because of the ability of each living thing to gather, or harvest, what is needed for survival. Educators using the Internet for educational purposes have at the click of a button the ability to harvest general educational information, content information, insights into what others have experienced, and research on an unlimited number of topics. Although examples are given to illustrate each category, most web resources could in actuality be classified in a number of categories.

Jumping Off Sites

The vastness of the World Wide Web can be intimidating. Many times, teachers simply need a safe, informative place to get started. These "jumping off" sites provide links to a great variety of educational resources, from very general to topic-specific. Someone at each sponsoring organization has done the searching "footwork," meaning that you can benefit from a convenient organized collection.

EDUCATION WORLD <http://www.education-world.com/>
Education World boasts a searchable database of over 50,000 educational resource sites (see Figure 9.2). In addition, the site maintains current features on monthly lesson plans, timely education-related news items, administrator articles, curriculum ideas, educational books, and reviews of online educational resources.

EDWEB <http://edweb.gsn.org/>
EdWeb provides links to resources on educational reform and information technology. Success stories about real teachers using computers in classrooms are available, and a discussion area allows for the sharing of topical information among educators.

KATHY SCHROCK'S GUIDE FOR EDUCATORS <http://school.discovery.com/schrockguide>
Known by teachers since the World Wide Web was introduced, Kathy Schrock's Guide for Educators is for teachers, students, and parents. Its vast array of web resources are logically categorized and well-described.

LIGHTSPAN.COM <http://ightspan.com>
Lightspan.com is organized to provide extensive Internet resources, including teacher activities, software guides, examples of exemplary school computer uses, and classroom Internet projects. The site is searchable and is well-maintained to provide current links to a large variety of educational resources.

MARCOPOLO <http://www.wcom.com/marcopolo/>
The MarcoPolo program is a partnership between The WorldCom Foundation and national content organizations to produce content-specific educational websites. The sites present lessons, activities, and reviewed web resources for the K–12 classroom that have been developed by leading content experts. A selection of the partner websites is described here under the appropriate content.

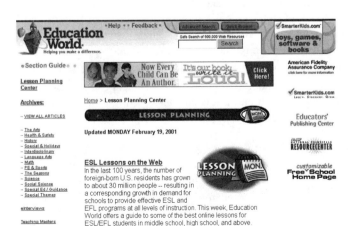

FIGURE 9.2   Education World.

U.S. DEPARTMENT OF EDUCATION <http://www.ed.gov/>
The homepage of the U.S. Department of Education provides timely news regarding the state of education in our country, answers to frequently asked questions, links to related governmental officials, updates on legislation, application information for federal grants, and links to federally funded publications. There are hints for teachers and researchers who use the site, and a search feature allows you to search the expansive site for specific information.

Content Resources

The largest category of educational resources on the World Wide Web, and those that are most easily incorporated into instructional plans, are those sites providing some type of content information. National organizations, research institutions, or even individual Internet users with a great interest in a particular topic might maintain these sites. The quality and extent of information will vary greatly between sites, necessitating thorough preview by teachers before students are asked to use them. These types of content sites can be used as minimally as a supplemental or enrichment resource or can supply the backbone of a series of lessons.

Language Arts

CHILDREN'S LITERATURE WEB GUIDE <http://www.acs.ucalgary.ca/~dkbrown/index.html>
This is a complete resource locator for those who teach literature to children. The site compiles an annual guide to newly published literature and points the user to annual award lists, such as Newbery and Caldecott. There are discussion areas, links to other children's literature online resources, a multitude of teaching ideas, and lists of current children's best-sellers. Still more links guide users to information on recommended books, authors, and movies based on books, as well as further resources for teachers, parents, and students.

Teaching Tip: Have book clubs in your class select their readings from a list you approve and join a discussion list about the author.

EDSITEMENT <http://edsitement.neh.gov/>
This partnership of the National Endowment for the Humanities and MarcoPolo is the center for humanities resources, lesson plans, and activities on the web. Separate sections on literature, foreign language, arts, and history create a complete selection of information organized by grade level.

Teaching Tip: High school foreign-language teachers can begin with the provided resources and then branch out to related sites to bring to life the unique cultures students are learning about.

SHAKESPEARE WEB <http://www.shakespeare.com/>
Whether used to enrich an established curriculum or to spur an individual interest, many gems of information can be found on Shakespeare Web. Itineraries on a traveling Shakespearean theater company and tidbits on Shakespeare history are highlights.

Teaching Tip: Use this site at the beginning of a middle school Shakespeare unit to research background history.

Mathematics

THE GEOMETRY CENTER <http://www.geom.umn.edu/>
Funded by the National Science Foundation, the Geometry Center develops methods in which technology can be used to visualize and communicate mathematics and related sciences. Serving both academic and industrial fields, this site provides links to geometry references, software, course materials, and distance learning resources. Current projects include such areas as spacecraft design, solar system visualization, and satellite constellation visualization.

Teaching Tip: Have intermediate math students work together to design a space station using geometrical principles. Encourage them to check back with this site frequently to verify calculations and confirm hunches.

ILLUMINATIONS <http://illuminations.nctm.org>
Presented by the National Council of Teachers of Mathematics (NCTM) in partnership with MarcoPolo, Illuminations is a wealth of interactive multimedia lessons, video teaching vignettes, and innovative lesson plans centered on the NCTM standards.

Teaching Tip: Use the imath interactive figure for investigating triangles with the whole primary class. Then have students find triangles in your school.

MEGA-MATHEMATICS <http://www.c3.lanl.gov/mega-math/>
Mega-Mathematics, a product of Los Alamos National Laboratory, brings very complex mathematical concepts to students in understandable, original ways. Lessons on such topics as colors, graphs, infinity, and algorithms are outlined completely so that teachers are prepared to facilitate the lessons. Lesson components include activities, vocabulary, background information, key concepts, evaluation ideas, relation to NCTM standards, preparation and materials, and indications for further study.

Teaching Tip: Have small groups of students work independently through the "A Usual Day at Unusual School" play. Encourage each group to record their thinking processes on paper. Have groups prepare charts to share their strategies with the rest of the class at the end of the activity. How do the strategies compare?

Science

THE FRANKLIN INSTITUTE ONLINE <http://sln.fi.edu/tfi/welcome.html>
The Franklin Science Museum's online presence is a must-see resource that not only allows a glimpse into the real museum but also gives teachers and students rich learning activities. Content units, problem-solving opportunities, resource "hot lists," and multimedia enhancement are among the many learning resources (see Figure 9.3).

Teaching Tip: Use "The Heart: An Online Exploration," in the Learning Resources section, with younger students studying basic circulatory properties or with older students studying advanced human anatomy and physiolology. Students can read the

FIGURE 9.3   **The Franklin Institute Online.**

text of the units independently or with a partner. Consider projecting the photo slide shows in front of the whole class as discussion prompts.

OLOGY <http://ology.amnh.org/>

The American Museum of Natural History presents Ology to demonstrate its belief that "everybody wants to know something." The Ology website tells children that if they are curious about something, they are "ologists." The highly interactive and informative resource links students with expert scientists in engaging content-based investigations.

Teaching Tip: Have students collect, sort, and compare "ology cards" to explore more about the specific content, such as the dinosaur varieties in the Paleontology exhibit.

SEAWORLD/BUSCH GARDENS ANIMAL INFORMATION DATABASE
<http://www.seaworld.org/>

Sea World and Busch Gardens maintain this vast website in order to provide an enthusiastic, imaginative, and intellectually stimulating atmosphere for students. Within the site, learners will encounter a list of animal information that spans animal rescue to zoological park careers, hitting sea turtles, penguins, and even Clydesdales along the way. Teachers can depend on numerous lesson resources and activities designed by the Sea World Education Department. Current animal-related news and "Ask Shamu," a frequently asked questions area on animals, round out the resource.

Teaching Tip: Have PreK students choose an animal and work with older "buddy" classes to research their animals. Prereaders can illustrate using photos from the website as guides. Older students can synthesize factual information into a format their younger buddies can understand.

VOLCANOWORLD <http://volcano.und.nodak.edu/>

Learn about volcanoes from the experts! This NASA-supported site is loaded with everything you ever wanted to know about volcanoes (see Figure 9.4). You can find the latest information on currently erupting volcanoes, observatories, and monuments, and research on the topic. Learners can access pictures, videos, stories, games, and activities, and they can even send a message to a real volcanologist. Teachers have available extensive lesson plans, and anyone can arrange to be alerted through email of any new eruptions.

Teaching Tip: Use the email alert system to have your students embark on a yearlong project to track volcano eruptions. Locate eruptions on a map, use the web to research the countries in which the eruptions happen, and use details to construct detailed scenarios predicting how the eruptions will impact the affected communities.

Social Studies

THE AMERICAN CIVIL WAR HOME PAGE <http://sunsite.utk.edu/civil-war/warweb.html>

The American Civil War Home Page gathers together in one place hypertext links to the most useful electronic files about the American Civil War. The lengthy list of links points to resources on time lines, photographs, specific battles, original documents such as letters and diaries, information on state participation, reenactment groups, and other Civil War organizations.

Teaching Tip: Students can use the vast resources available from this site to plan the sequence of a Civil War unit. After a couple of hours exploring the information available, have students develop concept maps about what they know about the Civil War. Then encourage them to plan how best to "fill in" the gaps in their understanding.

CONGRESS.ORG <http://congress.org>

This federal site links learners with information on activity in the legislative branch of the government. There is a directory of members, a calendar of events, and a list of legislative committees (see Figure 9.5).

Teaching Tip: Secondary government students can compare information on this site with online news sources and state government sources to interpret different versions of the same events.

FIGURE 9.4   Volcano World.

FIGURE 9.5   Congress.org.

ECONEDLINK <http://www.econedlink.org/>

EconEdLink produced by the National Council on Economics Education highlights the economics standards through real-world scenarios. The site provides lessons on authentic, up-to-date economics topics, real financial data, and economics-related news. This is a MarcoPolo partner site.

Teaching Tip: Use the lessons in EconomicsMinute to enrich weekly current events studies by encouraging students to think beyond the news to consider the economic implications of events.

NATIONAL GEOGRAPHIC XPEDITIONS <http://www.nationalgeographic.com/xpeditions/main.html>

Xpeditions brings the National Geography Standards to life in innovative ways that make the most of emerging web technologies. Students can use the atlas to search for global locations and print detailed maps of any location in the world. They also can locate relevant websites to be used to meet the geography standards and explore at home with their families through readings, games, and virtual field trips. By visiting the stunning virtual world of the Expedition Hall, the geography standards come to life in compelling and intriguing ways. Xpeditions is a MarcoPolo partner site (see Figure 9.6).

Teaching Tip: As part of a unit on international relations, use the Culture Goggles feature with the whole class. Have students make predictions about how each of the cultures will respond.

Arts

ARTSEDGE: THE NATIONAL ARTS AND EDUCATION INFORMATION NETWORK <http://artsedge.kennedy-center.org/artsedge.html>

Operating under an agreement between the Kennedy Center for the Performing Arts and the National Endowment for the Arts, and supported by the U.S. Department of

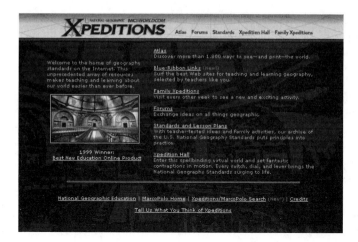

FIGURE 9.6
Xpeditions.

Education and MarcoPolo, this massive site is designed to help artists, teachers, and students communicate to support the arts in the K–12 curriculum. The listed projects, performances, and study guides are given to further the stated mission: to connect people to people, to connect people to information and resources, and to build a new base of knowledge in arts and education (see Figure 9.7).

Teaching Tip: Rather than having art students create projects and simply hang them up in the hallway, have students communicate with other classes around the country who are working on similar projects. Comparisons among techniques of artists at different locations can be valuable in the development of artistic skills.

METROPOLITAN MUSEUM OF ART <http://www.metmuseum.org>
The Metropolitan Museum of Art, one of the largest and best-known art museums in the world, presents on this website collections of several hundred thousand exhibits at any given time. Exhibits cover world culture from prehistory to the present. The site features a calendar that details special exhibits, concerts, lectures, films, and other museum activities.

FIGURE 9.7   ArtsEdge: The National Arts and Education Information Network.

Teaching Tip: This is an excellent resource to study the art of presenting an exhibition. Students could be asked to look beyond the breathtaking museum content to focus on the professional presentation style, organization, resources, and other strategies in order to plan for their own school exhibits.

PLAY MUSIC <http://www.playmusic.org/>
PlayMusic.org is produced by the American Symphony Orchestra League. The site allows students to learn about each family of instruments in an orchestra, with specifics about each instrument. Students can meet composers and musicians and listen to classical selections from well-known composers. They also can meet individual mentors according to instrument.

Teaching Tip: Partner with music teachers to have students do research on specific instruments.

Experience Simulations

In these days of budget cutbacks, "frivolities" such as field trips are usually some of the first luxuries to go. Students, therefore, are not able to experience firsthand much of what their own community has to offer, let alone the richness and diversity that the world can show them. Through online communication, students can experience vicariously what they cannot see in person. Pictures and stories bring remote events and foreign parts of the world to vivid life through the computer screen.

ADVENTURE ONLINE <http://www.adventureonline.com/>
From this site, students can follow modern-day explorers as they conquer the world's challenges. Current expeditions include a family retracing Magellan's original travel routes, the first attempt to circumnavigate the world's largest island by dogsled and kayak, and the first ever descent on kayaks down the Nile River. Students live the adventures through the explorers' journals, facts, and email.

GLOBAL ONLINE ADVENTURE LEARNING SITE (GOALS) <http://www.goals.com/>
Through virtual field trips, GOALS lets students experience travel, adventure, science, technology, and nature (see Figure 9.8). Students can ride along with the first woman from the United States to sail around the world and the first transoceanic rowing expedition, among other adventures. Students can learn through reports, pictures, audio clips, and activities based on the actual exhibitions.

Research Tools

ASKERIC <http://ericir.syr.edu/>
The Educational Resources Information Center (ERIC) is a federally funded national information system that provides a variety of services and products on a broad range of education-related issues. The AskERIC website gives access to education information to teachers, librarians, counselors, administrators, parents, and others (see Figure 9.9). Abstracts of professional journal articles and other educational documents can be searched in order to conduct research on hundreds of search terms.

FIGURE 9.8   Global Online Adventure Learning Site (GOALS).

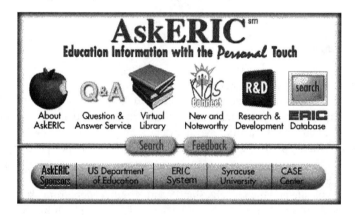

FIGURE 9.9   AskERIC homepage.

LIBRARY OF CONGRESS <http://www.loc.gov/>
The heart of America's library is its collection of documents, photographs, movies, and audio selections that tell the story of our country. There are also links from this site to legislative information, special national exhibits, and tips and tools for librarians and researchers (see Figure 9.10).

CULTIVATING THE INFORMATION

The planting and harvesting that keep the natural life cycle going are not always composed of separate one-sided efforts. The most exciting aspect of the Internet is the potential for collaborative work among learners. Students in different geographic locations can combine thoughts and talents to learn and discover together. Email is one way this collaboration might occur. (See Chapter 3 for more information on the educational applications of email.) A growing number of websites now offer the chance for classes to participate in organized online projects.

FIGURE 9.10   Library of Congress.

I*EARN <http://www.jearn.org/index.html>
I*EARN (International Education and Resource Network) is a resource of project-based learning involving students and teachers in ninety countries in multiple languages. Students and teachers have the opportunity to discuss issues, conduct research, and share opinions with people from diverse cultural perspectives.

KIDPROJ <http://www.kidlink.org/KIDPROJ/>
KIDPROJ is a site at which teachers and youth group leaders from around the world can plan activities and projects for students (see Figure 9.11). It has been set up for the exchange of curriculum-based activities and other projects among a community of kids and a world of ideas.

SUMMARY

The World Wide Web can be a source of unlimited resources that can bring exciting learning opportunities to students anywhere at anytime. In order to effectively and meaningfully

FIGURE 9.11
KIDPROJ on the
Kidlink Network.

■ ■ ■ ■ ■ ▬▬▬▬▬▬▬▬▬▬▬▬▬▬▬▬▬▬▬▬▬▬▬▬▬▬▬▬▬▬▬▬▬▬▬▬▬▬

CLASSROOM VIGNETTE

"How many of you have ever been to the ocean?" Mr. Pace asked his third-graders that morning. Five or six sure hands went up, along with a few other tentative ones, and the teacher proceeded to elicit stories from the experiences of these students. Other children said they had seen the ocean on TV and still others had read about it and seen pictures in books.

"Well, I have a way to take you to the beach, without even leaving our classroom." And as sounds of disbelief filled the classroom, Mr. Pace proceeded to explain their new project.

He told them about the teacher from California he met at the conference he attended last month. She also teaches third-graders, and her school just happens to be very near the beach. The two teachers agreed to try a collaborative project to have their students teach each other about their respective climates—Mr. Pace's class about the mountain region in which its community was nestled and Ms. Garcia's class about its beach. He explained how each class would research the other environment, using information from the World Wide Web, as well as more traditional media such as books and videos, and report on what they think it is like to live there. Then the classes would read each other's work and use their own personal experiences to help them edit for correctness.

Mr. Pace's class began that day with brainstorming a list of everything they knew about the beach and the ocean. They offered ideas on what they thought kids did for fun and even what kinds of clothes they probably wear. Based on these ideas, the teacher later spent the afternoon searching the Internet for beach-related informational sites and bookmarking those sites that were appropriate for his students' reading and understanding levels. Combined with the books he had already gathered from the library, and two videos that he reserved from the district media center, he was ready to begin facilitating his students' exploration into life on the beach.

Over the next several weeks, students worked in pairs to investigate what the selected web pages had to offer. They took notes, and they discussed and argued over what the most important information was. Eventually, students wrote, individually and as a whole class, what their impression of living near the beach must be like. When their thoughts were complete, Mr. Pace posted their drafted text onto their class website.

While Mr. Pace's class had been researching life on the beach, Ms. Garcia's class had been doing the same regarding life in the mountains. Now, each class had an initial report posted on the web, and their jobs switched from researchers to editors. Students in both classes spent time reviewing the other class's site in detail, writing up a list of comments and suggestions to send to their partner class. Each class also gathered pictures showing themselves in their surroundings to be scanned in and sent to the other class for its final website. The comments were emailed with the image files as attachments.

Mr. Pace's class eagerly listened as he read Ms. Garcia's class's comments about their research. They found that they were accurate about most of the facts, but needed to add some details regarding the specifics about the particular beach Ms. Garcia's class was most familiar with. They were surprised at how many things were similar even though they lived in such different places. Within several days, the class had amended its website and had developed a fairly complete vision about what it was like to live on the beach.

integrate an online resource, teachers must first thoroughly plan a place for it in the comprehensive curricular sequence. Similar to preparing to teach a traditional lesson, it makes sense first to consider the goals of the lesson. Once appropriate websites are found that will help meet those goals, they can be included in the lesson plan. Thought should also be given to ways in which technology will affect the facilitation of the lesson and can assist the assessment of learning.

Categorizing available web resources according to a framework makes planning for their use a more realistic task. The Internet can be thought of as an information environment, similar in process to the biological world in which we live. Learners can participate in processes of planting, harvesting, and cultivating information on various websites with potential educational application. Considerable time and effort are required to find appropriate websites to include in the lesson plan.

LEARNER ACTIVITIES

1. Using the questions given in Table 9.1 of this chapter, list a lesson that could be taught effectively using Internet resources and one that could just as effectively be taught through more traditional means. What lesson characteristics might indicate an easy, successful use of Internet resources?

2. Write a lesson plan that integrates information from at least two web resource sites.

3. Visit the content sites listed in this chapter. How are these sites set up? What level of involvement should a teacher have for your intended level of students to use each site successfully?

4. Do a web search for resources that would give contact information. How applicable are these types of sites to your area of teaching interest?

5. Look in the popular educational technology journals. What type of guidance do the articles supply for teachers? Are there complete lessons that you could use unaltered? How much customization will other ideas take to put them into practice?

6. Find an online interactive project for students at your level. How much participation does this project involve? How many suggestions are there for outside activities?

7. How can content resources from two different areas be integrated?

8. Should you start with planning a content lesson and add in World Wide Web resources, or start with the resource and plan the lesson around it? When would each strategy be appropriate?

9. What styles of teachers would not seem to lend themselves to easy integration of online resources? How might these teachers be convinced that such quality information is available on the web?

10. How can the infosphere metaphor be used to teach students about the Internet as a learning tool?

BIBLIOGRAPHY

Barron, A. E. (1996). *The Internet: Ideas, activities, and resources.* Tampa, FL: Florida Center for Instructional Technology.

Battle, R., & Hawkins, I. (1996). A study of emerging teacher practices in Internet-based lesson plan development. *Journal of Science Education and Technology, 5,* 321–342.

Berenfeld, B. (1996). Linking students to the infosphere. *T.H.E. Journal, 23*(9), 76–83.

Bogyo, J. (1997). So you want to use the Internet in the elementary school. *Technology Connection, 4*(2), 10–12.

Dickinson, K. (1997). Distance learning on the Internet: Testing students using Web forms and the Computer Gateway Interface. *TechTrends, 42*(2), 43–46.

Education World. <http://www.education-world.com>.

Ellsworth, J. B. (1997). Curricular integration of the World Wide Web. *TechTrends, 42*(2), 24–30.

Harrington-Lueker, D. (1997, September). *Web high.* Electronic School, A26-A29.

Kalmbacher, S. (1996). The Internet: Logon to lesson planning. *Schools in the Middle, 5*(3), 19–22.

Kimeldorf, M. (1995). Teaching online: Techniques and methods. *Learning and Leading with Technology, 23*(1), 26–31.

Milheim, W. D. (1997). Instructional utilization of the Internet in public school settings. *TechTrends, 42*(2), 19–23.

Nicholson, D. (1996). Class projects on the Internet. *Education in Science, 170,* 10–11.

Norman, K. (1996). Introducing students to the World Wide Web. *Teaching Music, 3*(5), 34–35.

Ross, P. (1995). Relevant telecomputing activities. *The Computing Teacher, 22*(5), 28–30.

Tobiason, K. (1997). Tailoring the Internet to primary classrooms. *Technology Connection, 4*(2), 8–9.

Tomei, L. A. (1996). Preparing an instructional lesson using resources off the Internet. *T.H.E. Journal, 24*(2), 93–95.

CHAPTER 10

DESIGNING
ONLINE INSTRUCTION

FOCUS QUESTIONS

1. What planning is necessary prior to establishing web-based instruction?
2. What are some strategies for keeping the documents of a website organized?
3. Why is regular maintenance vital to a quality website?

Teachers at all levels are discovering the possibilities for facilitating meaningful learning with World Wide Web resources. Students working at a distance or at a different pace than others, as well as those in a more traditional learning environment, are able to use the web as the actual method of instruction. The more time educators spend working with this instructional and informational mode, the clearer it becomes what types of interactive lessons and communication are conceivable using the web. Once teachers know what can be done, it is only a matter of time before they become comfortable enough to want to start planting their own seeds of information in the web environment. This chapter gives all the information needed to create well-planned, meaningful web-based instructional or informational sites.

TYPES OF ONLINE INSTRUCTION

Online instructional materials span the range from supplemental—whereby the online materials are used as resources for a traditional face-to-face course—to distance education—in which case students are separated from the instructor and from each other by a distance and the entire course is delivered online. Most uses for online learning materials fall somewhere between these two extremes. However, teachers must carefully consider their instructional goals and intentions prior to investing the time and money to create online learning materials.

Online Instruction as a Supplement

Chapter 9 introduced the integration of web-based educational materials into an established curriculum. Recent software advances make it easier than ever for classroom teachers to create their own online materials, anything from study guides for students to information sites for parents. The degree to which student learning is dependent on these online materials rests on the instructional goals. A teacher might use a history outline on his class website to teach a lesson in class, have partners use a scavenger hunt that he created on literature resources, or require students to log on from home for homework information. In all of these instances, students attend school daily and use the online instructional materials as a supplement to other instructional materials. Reliance on an online format should be based on a pedagogically sound reason; teachers are cautioned not to feel pressured to post duplicate materials online if another nontechnical strategy is more appropriate.

One recently accepted and systematized form of online instruction is the WebQuest. Dodge (1995) defines a WebQuest as "an inquiry-oriented activity in which some or all of the information that learners interact with comes from resources on the Internet...." Rather than allowing students to endlessly "surf" through websites, these online lessons instead encourage learners to seek specific information from the web. They then analyze it, synthesize it, and use it for some end project. Teachers design WebQuests with the following components:

1. Introduction
2. Task
3. Information sources
4. Process
5. Guidance
6. Conclusion

WebQuests can be designed as either short-term knowledge acquisition tools for one to three class periods or longer-term knowledge refinement activities that can take up to a month. Students can be asked to use web resources solely or can integrate electronic, paper-based, and human resources. For examples, rubrics, and further information on the WebQuest process, see The WebQuest Page at <http://edweb.sdsu.edu/webquest/webquest.html> and WebQuests and More at <http://www.ozline.com/learning/index.htm>, or conduct a web search for WebQuests.

Online District Information

Districts maintain informational websites to report everything from resources for new parents to updates on school board meetings to secure access to student grade reports. Such sites are a great convenience for parents with home computer access because parents can have their questions answered at any time from wherever they are. Mandatory web use is not yet typical of most school districts because home computer use cannot be guaranteed. Districts, then, offer such information as a supplement to more traditional parent resources.

DISTANCE EDUCATION

As the availability of Internet resources ushers in changes in traditional forms of education, it simultaneously offers a new dimension to some alternative forms of education already moving past the four walls of a classroom. Distance education is literally defined as "the delivery of the educational process to receivers who are not in proximity to the person or persons managing or conducting the process" (Lewis, Whitaker, & Julian, 1995, p. 14). It has existed in some form for years, often serving students in rural areas who were not able to reach a school or students who for some health or behavior reasons could not attend traditional school.

The correspondence model of distance education, which has served as the defining model of the field, was usually built around the teacher sending out course materials via regular mail. Upon receiving the materials, the student worked independently to complete the assignments and then mailed them back to the teacher for grading. The technology that most aided this educational exchange was the telephone, giving students and teachers a chance to discuss necessary topics of concern. Although this arrangement allowed some school participation for large groups of students who otherwise would not receive education at all, it amounted essentially to a strict delivery of education, with a minimum of guidance aimed at actually inciting learning (Berge & Collins, 1995).

With the advent of a global network of telecommunications, distance education has had new life and possibilities breathed into it. No longer is learning away from a traditional classroom the exception, but rather it is becoming a learner-centered standard many educational models strive to replicate. No longer are remote students left to struggle through learning on their own with only occasional phone contact with their teacher. Email and chat groups have provided a forum for relevant, content-rich, supportive online discussions between teachers and students as well as among students. Instead of sitting isolated at home working on assignments by himself, the distance learner can experience the feeling that he is part of a collaborative group of learners, a member of a class that is right there in the room with him. This feeling is called "social presence" (Mason, 1994). The rich assortment of resources that can be found on the World Wide Web augments static distance learning materials and creates an indefatigable research environment.

As students gain greater access to computer hardware and connections to the Internet, the chances for them to learn at a distance from one another increases. Students in small districts who would normally have a limited selection of courses available to them will soon be able to learn from content experts anywhere in the world. Adults who desire additional education will be able to fit the courses they need into a time schedule that fits with their work constraints. Parents who choose to teach their children at home will have available a world full of content and the chance for social contacts that will enrich their children's learning environment.

The near future holds promise for virtual schools, at the university, secondary, and even lower levels. Countless university courses are currently web-supported, offering some portion of their content online, and many are rapidly moving toward complete operation from a distance. A number of high schools are also now offering curricula online. Through a challenge grant funded by the U.S. Department of Education, the Virtual High School project is offering 30 online courses to 600 high school students in 13 states (Harrington-Lueker, 1997). By pooling resources and educator expertise, the range and number of courses that can be offered to students are greatly enhanced. What a student can learn is no longer limited by the knowledge of individuals who are employed at one particular school building. As people experiment with the types of learning that are possible through the Internet to students at a distance, and as it becomes easier for educators to use and contribute to the online world, the structure of learning undoubtedly will change. Where now many distance courses are designed to closely resemble instruction that occurs face to face, new learning theories will be depended upon to guide new forms of learning for the online world.

GETTING A MENTAL PLAN

Creating a website requires more than just the task of tagging it with the HTML code. The usefulness of countless websites accessible now in the online world is questionable. Some prove to be difficult to navigate through, others are visually confusing, and still others contain inaccurate or outdated information. Rushing out and posting just any old website for the sake of saying you or your school has one does not contribute to the cooperative information base of the web. Instead, it will ultimately serve as a waste of your valuable professional time. You will want to take care that the instructional site you are considering serves your intended purpose in a way that is appropriate for your anticipated audience.

Begin first by asking yourself some questions that will help to define your goals for this instructional site. Harris (1997) has suggested the following starting points:

1. Who will be interested in exploring the site?
2. What types of information should be available at the site to address the interests of different audiences?
3. How should this information be presented so that it is maximally helpful to identified project participants and/or to those just browsing through the site?

Audience

If you are designing a site that will provide content information for your students to use for instruction, it will be organized very differently than will a site meant to update parents or other outside community members on school announcements. If you are considering showcasing your students' writing, your site will have distinctive characteristics if the writing is done by kindergartners as compared to that done by sophomores. A website can serve many audiences by directing visitors to different sections. Think carefully about who will be accessing your site most often so that your planning can be efficient and audience-specific.

Types of Information

Primary to the planning of any website should be a consideration of the content the page is being designed to present. Without this forethought, the collection of pages you will be creating will resemble an art project more than the meaningful informative base it could be (Tennant, 1997). A classroom homepage will likely be viewed by parents or others interested in what students in the class are learning and doing. This type of page might include descriptions of projects, pictures of classroom events, or possible ways parents can extend the learning at home. A website meant to provide a thematic starting point for other classes would need to dedicate a certain amount of space to background information and facts pertaining to the project. If people find what they are looking for on your site, they will be more likely to come back to visit again. Inviting comments from visitors about the site and suggestions for what else they would like to see will help you to keep your site updated and relevant.

A word must be said here regarding the privacy of minor students. It is imperative that school districts adopt guidelines for posting student information online. Many districts deem it acceptable to include student first names but not last names on class websites. Photos showing students' faces might be allowed if parental permission has first been obtained. Other personal information about minor students is generally not acceptable except in special cases with parental permission or when the pages containing the personal information are password protected. Teachers are urged to become familiar with their districts' privacy policies prior to creating online classroom materials.

Presentation Strategies

There is an infinite number of ways to arrange the information on a website. Viewers may be required to scroll down the page through long chunks of text, or links can take viewers directly to other pages of information. Sometimes, your students might want to write the text of the page themselves. Other times, it might make more sense to provide a link to another established site that has already compiled an excellent treatment of the topic.

Based on your answers to these types of planning questions, you will begin to define the purpose of your proposed website. A website can take many forms in order for it to serve your identified purpose. One of the easier sites to begin with is a class homepage providing information to parents. Such a page might be organized, as would a newsletter that might be sent home, with such items as homework assignments and upcoming announcements.

In addition to these basic inclusions, website functions will also fall into the categories of web resources presented in Chapter 9. Written stories can be published for all to see and collaborative projects with other classes can be managed via your website. You might design an instructional site that provides content information your students need for class, or you might supply thematic information to keep parents apprised of what is happening in school. Field trips and other experiences can be documented through digital photographs and written reflections to share with other classes who may not have made the same trip or who may not be familiar with your area of the country. Unlimited amounts of online resources can be compiled by and for your students.

THE DESIGN PROCESS

With a good mental plan for what your site needs to include, your next move is to plan how you want the site to appear to others who will view it. It would be easy to skip this planning step in favor of getting right to the web design, but your valuable time could be wasted trying to visualize what you want the site to look like at the same time you are creating the site documents. A small amount of planning time up front not only will save time later but also will make for a more organized and easy-to-use website.

Study.   Begin by closely examining other websites you visit. Look at how the designer has laid out the text and graphics. Is it aesthetically pleasing or does it appear that page elements were just dropped in randomly? Are the graphics serving an obvious educational purpose or do they appear to be there for decoration only? Is the font size and style appropriate for the content? As you move around from page to page, is the navigation intuitive and well-organized. Once you get to another page, is it easy to get back to where you started?

Sketch.   When you have seen what is being shown on others' pages, sketch out what you envision for your page on a storyboard or a sequence of screen layouts. Your storyboard can be very rough or extremely detailed, as long as it gives you an idea of where text will be located, what size and other formatted text will be used, where graphics will be integrated, and how the navigational path is planned (see Figure 10.1). A simple, clean layout is the best place to start, as more complexity can be added later if desired.

Use specially formatted text, such as **boldface** or *italics,* judiciously. An overly formatted page is difficult to read, and your user might spend more time concentrating on the abundance of special text rather than on the content of the page. Images should also be chosen carefully. Large graphics take a long time for the browser to load, which slows down the use of your website. Make sure that every picture serves a purpose in your layout and overall goals, rather than just providing meaningless clutter. Your page will appear even more organized if you plan all the pages to have a consistent look and feel, such as by using the same background color or coordinating graphics throughout the entire site.

Plan Navigation.   List in your storyboard the URLs for any hypertext links you would like to create. Good web design calls for fitting the link seamlessly into the text, rather than telling the user to "Click Here." Include links that enrich the information on your site, but not so many that the user is constantly thrown offtrack. The linked resources should directly pertain to the goal of the lesson or informational piece.

Just as you create hyperlinks to other outside resources, you can also link your homepage to other pages in your own website. Connect pages within your storyboarded site with arrows showing the paths for how the user will be able to travel through the pages (see Figure 10.2). Plan a simple navigational path. You do not want people who visit your site to be lost wandering around between your pages. Make sure you include a link back to your homepage on every other page in your site. Add to your storyboard any custom colors

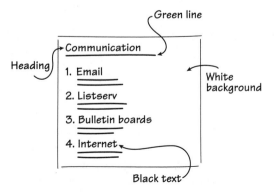

FIGURE 10.1   Sketching a storyboard for a web page.

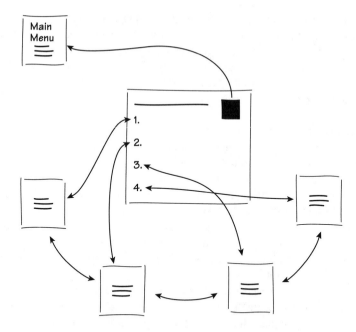

FIGURE 10.2   A storyboard showing the navigational path for a website.

you plan on using to help you get an idea of whether the color scheme is visually pleasing and appropriate for your intended audience. The background color or image should be in high contrast to the text, such as light text on a dark background or dark text on a light background. Your students will be less likely to succeed in their web learning experience if they must struggle to make out what the page says. Finally, plan to place your name or school name and the date in a prominent place on the page so that people accessing your page will know how current the information is and how to contact you should they have comments or questions.

Plan Organization.   To ensure an organized and easily modifiable website, it makes good sense to keep a record of the filenames of the HTML documents you create. Cafolla and Knee (1996–1997) recommend documenting the following information to create a complete record:

- Page titles
- Source of each link and the reasons it was selected
- Source of the graphics
- Size and type of graphics
- Width of horizontal lines

Even as you storyboard, jot down filenames you plan on giving to these pages. Keep to brief, logical filenames so you will remember what each page is by the name alone. Always use lowercase filenames to make it easier for your users to access your site with a browser. Web addresses are case-sensitive, so someone trying to find your site at "myhomepage.html" will not get there if it is actually named "MyHomepage.html." At this point in your planning, this record will serve as a checklist to guide your page creation. Later, when you are updating your site, it will streamline your job by reminding you of the filenames and the organization of the files.

INVOLVE STUDENTS IN WEB DESIGN

What better way to teach students about the Internet and instill some pride and confidence in their own work than to have them participate in the designing of a website. All of the aspects of website creation discussed in this chapter can be accomplished by students as well as by adults, and at times might even be handled better by students. The complete process can prove to be a valuable cross-curricular project. Depending on the abilities of the students, they can gain practice with written language and with measurement, such as with graphic sizes as they work with the page design and layout. They can do the background research, both on the content to be presented on the site and on websites to which links will be created. Participating in the process from the beginning through completion will teach students about follow-through and accomplishment. Some schools are even able to offer students their own individual homepages on which they can publish their writing for an authentic world audience.

THE DEVELOPMENT PROCESS

Now that you are armed with both a mental concept and a visual plan, you are ready to begin creating the actual documents that will make up your instructional site. Remember from Chapter 4 that a web page is a text document that uses HTML tags to tell the browser software how to display the page (see Figure 10.3).

Web documents can be saved either to a disk, the hard drive, or some other location, using the document names you previously planned on your storyboard. Files saved with the proper ".html" extension can be viewed in a web browser when saved to your local drive during development. However, they must be uploaded using file transfer software (see Chapter 4) to a web server to be available for others to view online.

In the not-so-distant past, the only way to create web-based documents was to manually code the text document with the correct HTML tags. Although this is not a difficult process, the work can be tedious and prohibitively time-consuming. Even most web development purists now take advantage of new software solutions for creating web documents. All of these tools allow you some range of capabilities to format documents, paragraphs, and characters, as well as to insert hypertext links, multimedia elements, and more advanced scripting.

Web editing tools are to web-page creation as calculators are to computation, or even as electric mixers are to baking. The results are quicker and easier with the tools of convenience, although there are those who might say that those basic skills you learn doing it the "old-fashioned" way lead to a better end product. When HTML editors first hit the market, they were able to format with only the basic tags, but could not be counted on to produce some of the more advanced formatting. As is always the case with innovation and progress, however, the more recent editors are able to handle the more complex HTML programming, making web-page creation accessible to even those with no HTML knowledge whatsoever.

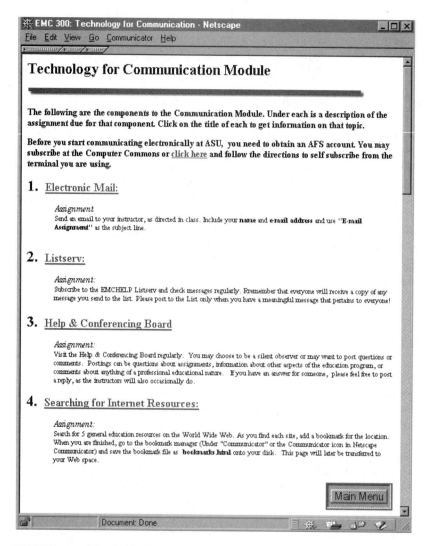

FIGURE 10.3   The finished web page.

This is good news for teachers who want to try their hand at designing web-based instruction, but fear their busy professional lives will prevent them from learning a complicated coding language.

HTML editors look and act very much like word processors. The ease of operation is based on a convention called WYSIWYG, the acronym for "What You See Is What You Get." Rather than seeing a mess of tags identifying various types of formatting, you see on the screen the actual formatted results. If you want a title to be centered, for example, the program shows it to you centered. Without you realizing it, the **<CENTER>, </CENTER>** tags are being added into the actual HTML document behind the scenes. Editors automatically insert the document formatting and allow you to choose any other of the paragraph and character formatting that is available by clicking on toolbar buttons for each of the procedures. Images can be easily inserted by clicking on the image button and identifying what image file you want. To create text that is hyperlinked, simply highlight the text, click on the link button, and type in the URL or other destination location. Whenever you want to view the actual HTML tags, you can usually click on a button to view the source of the document, and here you will notice all of the tags that have been inserted into the document (see Figure 10.4).

Web Editing Software.   Editing software is now available in a range of stand-alone pro-grams. The most basic offer a simple, intuitive tool that teachers and students can use with little training and a short learning curve (e.g., Page Composer, a free component of Netscape Communicator, at <http://www.netscape.com>, or Claris HomePage at <http://filemaker. com>). These programs allow for the construction of attractive and effective web pages com-plete with multimedia elements. More sophisticated software offers increased flexibility and a greater range of new web capabilities (e.g., Macromedia Dreamweaver, <http://www. macromedia.com>). Advanced features allow you to insert precoded objects such as frames, navigation bars, email links, and symbols. Some software uses layers so that objects and text can be moved freely in design, and many offer templates for preset coordinated color schemes. Site maps continue the good organization that was begun during the planning stage by automatically linking new files as the site is built. Other software focuses on site manage-ment, rather than individual page creation only (e.g., Microsoft FrontPage, <http://www. microsoft.com>). Sites are created and updated as a whole structure, making it easier for entire schools or districts to collaborate on consistent site creation (see Figures 10.5 and 10.6).

Productivity Software.   Most new productivity tools (e.g., Microsoft Office) give you the option to save documents as web pages. This means that teachers can do two jobs at once: generating materials on a word processor for classroom use, for example, and then saving another version of the same materials to be placed on the class website. One distinct advantage is that teachers reluctant to learn new software can contribute to online learning environments using the software with which they are already familiar.

Online Web Editors.   Some of the most exciting web advances for teachers are online web editors. These tools (e.g., Yahoo! GeoCities at <http://geocities.yahoo.com/home> and

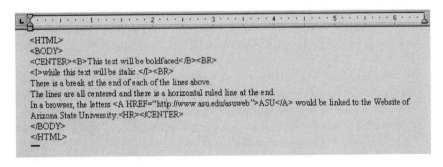

FIGURE 10.4   A sampler HTML document showing document, paragraph, character, and hypertext reference tags.

FIGURE 10.5   The sampler HTML document in Netscape Page Composer.

FIGURE 10.6   The way the tagged document would appear in a browser.

Quia at <http://www.quia.com>) are generally free if teachers and districts are willing to see some advertising on the pages. The tools provide wizards for step-by-step page creation in minutes, yet also allow quite a lot of customization with HTML tags. Some even let you drag and drop objects, similar to the more advanced stand-alone software, and give plenty of interactive tools such as guest books, page counters, feedback forms, and streaming media. Finally, teachers can add and update favorite links and upload photos with little effort.

Course Management Software.   The most sophisticated solution for creating online learning environments is course management software (e.g., WebCT at <http://www.webct. com/> and Blackboard at <http://www.blackboard.com>). These software systems are not typically an option for the classroom teacher independently, not only because the cost would be prohibitive but also because these tools are designed to function as a larger system-wide effort. Course management software can be used either to create professional-quality course supplements or to convert entire courses to online format to be offered at a distance. In-structors are not required to invest a lot of time, resources, or technical expertise with this software. They are provided with design templates to present students with a consistent interface; a comprehensive set of communication tools, such as email and discussion boards; and administrative tools, such as online assessments, to help manage student grading and reporting. Students can customize their own homepages to access appropriate communication tools, course information and assignments, educational resources, and personal and school calendars.

PRACTICAL CONCERNS

Server Storage

Local Server Space.   Your district or school likely already has a web presence and possibly even procedures for hosting individual classroom web materials. The procedure might entail your sending your files to a committee for review or to a server administrator to upload. Find out the policies prior to beginning your web design and development, because some districts have adopted web software and consistent procedures that may affect your capabilities.

Free Hosted Server Space.   An increasing number of public and educational websites offer free web pages (e.g., Yahoo! GeoCities at <http://geocities.yahoo.com/home> and Quia at <http://www.quia.com>). Once registered, the sites allow you to have ample space on their servers to host multiple web pages with some multimedia elements. You will have your own URL that students and parents can use, as well as some ability to upload new documents and updates via FTP, sometimes with the assistance of an easy-to-use wizard.

MAINTAINING A QUALITY WEBSITE

If you are taking the time to design and create a website, you will want to be sure that you are posting a quality product and that the pages stay in good condition as time goes by. Make the time to check your site when you think you are finished constructing it, and then set a regular schedule of making updates and improvements.

Check Your Site

Just as you might have someone proofread something you have written, have someone who has not seen your website previously and who is able to provide candid comments navigate completely through the site. Have that person first check for basic spelling and grammatical errors. Putting a page on the Internet with these types of errors is reprehensible and reflects poorly both on you as a web designer and on your school as a quality educational institution. Have your test user also check all of the navigational paths to make sure that every link goes where it says it does and that the routes are intuitive and allow for easy return to the homepage. You may have forgotten along the way to add a URL or check to see if resource sites were still operable. This way you will find it before your students or parents have the chance to become confused. It is important, also, to get an outside opinion on the page layout and color scheme. When you have worked with a page for quite a while, you may not even realize that the graphics make it hard to follow or that the font color is difficult to see on your chosen background.

Update Your Site

In the online world, information frequently changes, making it necessary for you to keep up or risk letting your site become antiquated. Skeletons of websites that are no longer functioning or current litter the Internet, slowing down search engines and proving endlessly frustrating to busy people looking for timely information (Tennant, 1997). Websites to which you have linked may be there one day and may vanish the next. If your links go nowhere, the learning goals you have for your students will not be achieved. Go through to check your links regularly, deleting or adding any as necessary. If your site contains content information, be on the lookout for any new developments in the field that should be included in your selection. New research or discoveries keep the site current and keep your audience motivated. As your class changes its thematic concentration, change your page to fit its studies. Any other timely data, such as announcements of upcoming events or homework calendars, must be kept up-to-date for the site to be fully functional.

Improve Your Site

As you browse through other websites, you may notice design features or instructional sequences that might add to your site's functionality or appearance. Do not be afraid to make changes, either subtle or drastic. Just because you liked that lime-green background when you originally designed the site does not mean it still serves your purposes today. Any good instruction must be flexible enough to accommodate new ideas. Changing the look and feel of your site will keep it fresh and keep regular visitors coming back.

SUMMARY

Once teachers are familiar with integrating online resources into traditional instructional modes, they are ready to try exploring how to design web-based instruction. Planning ahead of time will ensure a site that serves your intended purpose for your anticipated audience. Sketching out a storyboard will help to visualize what the website will look like and how it will be organized. To be helpful in the planning process, a storyboard should include text location, text attributes, graphics, and color. Arrows connecting the cells of the storyboard show the possible navigational paths.

Web documents are created using HTML code that gives directions to the web browser for how to display the page to the viewer. New software advances make it possible for users to create web pages without knowing HTML. Web editing software, productivity software, online Web editors, and course management tools provide a range of features to develop online materials.

HTML tags describe formatting for the entire document, a paragraph, or individual characters. Other tags instruct the browser to insert hyperlinks or images.

Completed websites must be maintained to ensure they remain quality learning and information tools. On a regular basis, inspect your site for accuracy and functionality. Replace outdated facts or linked sites and determine if improvements are needed.

CLASSROOM VIGNETTE

The fifth-graders from Mrs. Tabor's class are settling in on the floor next to their first-grade "buddies" in Miss Gomez's room. For five weeks, each of the classes has been studying "Habitats," both with age-appropriate assignments in their own rooms and integrated projects together. They are now preparing to go on their field trip to the museum next week. Mrs. Tabor and Miss Gomez have decided that a great way to share their trip experience with the other classes at school, as well as with the students' families, would be by putting up a website detailing what they have learned and what they see at the museum. They plan on taking the digital camera on the trip, so any pictures they take on the trip can be automatically inserted into the web page.

Prior to meeting together, each of the two classes separately has already brainstormed long lists of what they have learned so far in this habitat unit. Now, the two classes sit looking at both charts of data, ready to make some decisions on what they want to include in their website. The teachers lead the discussion, with students from both classes offering their ideas. Finally, through much discussion, a list of core learnings is decided upon.

Now comes the job of designing their site. Using a projection system with her classroom computer, Miss Gomez shows several different websites she has found that are useful in pointing out to students layout features and color combinations. The classes talk about what types of pictures they will be able to use and how to best showcase student writing. Working with their buddies, the students then sketch out on chart paper their ideas for how their website might be arranged. It is too large of a job to finish in one sitting, but over the next couple of days before the field trip, the classes compare all of the proposed page designs to decide on a final layout. It is also decided that each student will contribute some of his or her writing for the project, and several students have artwork on habitats that will be scanned in using the scanner down in the media center.

Back in their own classroom following the field trip, the fifth-graders learn how to use an HTML editing program. Together with Mrs. Tabor, they make a class practice website to get the feel for how to use the program. Over the next several weeks, the fifth-grade students bring their first-grade buddies in to work on converting their writing to HTML and laying out their individual pages. When the website is finished, the two classes have a dynamic record of their trip and all that they have learned that can be viewed and used by other classes and even parents at home.

LEARNER ACTIVITIES

1. Create a simple storyboard of a lesson that incorporates at least two thematic online resources.

2. What schools in your area offer courses through distance education? Are there single courses available, and can entire degrees be completed from a distance?

3. Set up an account on a website that offers online web editing tools and free web-page hosting, such as Yahoo! GeoCities at <http://geocities.yahoo.com/home> or Quia at <http://www.quia.com>.

4. Using an actual newsletter that a classroom teacher has sent home in printed form as a template, create an electronic newsletter website.

5. Find a classroom homepage on the World Wide Web. What types of items are included? How well is it organized? Is there quality instruction or mainly just informational items?

6. Find an educational website. Have two students from your level of interest go through the website following all of the instructions that are given. Record their progress and their comments. What improvements do you think would be warranted based on their results? What improvements do they suggest?

7. Survey a group of parents to see how many would make use of an informational class website if their children's classes had one available. Do this group's responses seem to fit with the impression the media give of parents' attitudes toward technology integration in the schools?

8. Familiarize yourself with your school or district's adopted web software and procedures for web-page hosting.

9. Find out the procedures at your school for saving web documents to a web server.

10. Research what the experts recommend when designing web-based instruction. What considerations make for good instruction across grade levels and topics? What specific attributes are relevant to your chosen level or area?

BIBLIOGRAPHY

Barkhouse, N. (1997). Grasping the thread: Web page development in the elementary classroom. *Emergency Librarian, 24*(3), 24–25.

Berge, A. Z., & Collins, M. P. (Eds.). (1995). *Computer mediated communication and the online classroom* (Vol. 3). Cresskill, NJ: Hampton Press.

Burgstahler, S. (1997). Teaching on the Net: What's the difference? *T.H.E. Journal, 24*(9), 61–64.

Cafolla, R., & Knee, R. (1996). Creating World Wide Web sites. *Learning and Leading with Technology, 24*(3), 6–9.

Cafolla, R., & Knee, R. (1996–1997). Creating World Wide Web sites. Part 2: Implementing your site. *Learning and Leading with Technology, 24*(4), 36–39.

Cafolla, R., & Knee, R. (1997). Creating educational Web sites. Part 3: Refining and maintaining the site. *Learning and Leading with Technology, 24*(5), 13–16.

Descy, D. E. (1997). Web page design. Part one. *TechTrends, 42*(1), 3–5.

Descy, D. E. (1997). Web page design. Part two. *TechTrends, 42*(2), 3–5.

Descy, D. E. (1997). Web page design. Part three. *TechTrends, 42*(3), 7–9.

Dodge, B. (1995). *Some thoughts about WebQuests.* [Online]. Available: <http://edweb.sdsu.edu/courses/edtec596/about_webquests.html>.

Harrington-Lueker, D. (1997, September). *Web high.* Electronic School, A26–A29.

Harris, J. (1997). Content and intent shape function: Designs for web-based educational telecomputing activities. *Learning and Leading with Technology, 24*(5), 17–20.

Hill, J. R., Tharp, D., Sindt, K., Jennings, M., & Tharp, M. (1997). Collaborative web site design from a distance: Challenges and rewards. *TechTrends, 42*(2), 31–37.

Lewis, J., Whitaker, J., & Julian, J. (1995). Distance education for the 21st century: The future of national and international telecomputing networks in distance education. In A. Z. Berge & M. P. Collins (Eds.), *Computer related communication and the online classroom* (Vol. 3, pp. 13-30). Cresskill, NJ: Hampton Press.

Mason, R. (1994). *Using communications media in open and flexible learning.* London: Korgan Page.

Monahan, B., & Tomko, S. (1996). How schools can create their own web pages. *Educational Leadership, 54*(3), 37–38.

Quinlan, L. A. (1997). Crafting a web-based lesson. Part two: Organizing the information and constructing the page. *TechTrends, 42*(1), 6–8.

Richardson, E. C. (1996). Site construction. *Internet World, 7*(4), 62–64, 66.

Scigliano, J. A., Levin, J., & Horne, G. (1996). Using HTML for organizing student projects through the Internet. *T.H.E. Journal, 24*(1), 51–56.

Tennant, R. (1997). Web sites by design: How to avoid a "pile of pages." *Syllabus, 11*(1), 49–50.

CHAPTER 11

TECHNOLOGY INTEGRATION IN THE CONTENT AREA

FOCUS QUESTIONS

1. How can teachers use technology in the content areas?
2. What factors must the teacher consider when planning to integrate technology?
3. What are the benefits to using technology for content areas?

Chapter 1 presented profiles of technology-literate teachers and students. Of course, it is ideal when students are introduced to computer literacy topics and learning technologies in their earliest school experiences. The knowledge they gain then serves as a foundation for continued technology-based learning through high school and even into adulthood.

Perhaps the most important concept for students to grasp is that the computer is a powerful tool for getting work done. When computers are used across the curriculum, students begin to appreciate the vast range of tasks that computer power can accomplish. The computer no longer appears to be a technological enigma that can be understood by only science and math wizards. Students come to view the computer as a manageable and multifaceted tool for writing essays and stories, performing sociological and scientific research, solving mathematical problems, and learning more about any subject they wish to study.

Teachers of all content areas can foster this attitude in their students by designing instruction that integrates technology as a tool for learning rather than relying on technology as a delivery mechanism. This presents quite a challenge to teachers who are themselves novice technology integrators or who specialize in subjects that are not traditionally associated with technology-based learning activities. Remember, the emphasis is not on learning a software application such as PowerPoint, but how to use the technology to solve problems. This chapter presents sample learning activities for five major content areas: mathematics, science, language arts, social studies, and special education. It is our hope that teachers will use these activities as a springboard for their own creativity.

FORMULATING LEARNING ACTIVITIES

Teachers will find that the process of designing learning activities that integrate technology is very similar to designing traditional lesson plans. Many of the same factors must be taken under consideration, whether students work with computers or with pencil and paper. In formulating learning activities, the teacher tries to answer a series of questions:

- For what ages or grade level is this activity appropriate?
- What is the purpose of the activity?
- What will students know or be able to do after completing the activity? What materials are required to perform this activity?
- What preparation is required on the teacher's part? On the students' part? What knowledge, skills, and concepts are necessary for students to complete the activity successfully?
- What tasks are most effective in teaching the topic?
- How will student learning be assessed and at what points during the activity?
- What extensions might be useful in reinforcing or expanding knowledge gained through the activity?
- What comments will contribute to greater success of the activity?

Most teachers are accustomed to considering these factors in creating learning activities. There are additional factors that can make or break the technology-based learning experience. Other questions a teacher might address follow.

- How will my classroom change or adapt when I integrate technology?
- Which technology is best suited for meeting the learning purpose?
- How can technology be used to optimize learning?
- What aspect of the computer's capabilities make it the best tool to use? To a large extent, activities must be tailored according to the hardware and software resources available in the individual teacher's classroom, school, or district.
- How can an activity meet both curriculum standards and the National Educational Technology Standards for students?
- What if there is limited access to the technology? Do students have access to computers in the classroom so that the only person controlling the amount of computer time is the classroom teacher?
- If so, how many computers are available?
- Can the entire class participate in the activity at the same time or will students need to work in shifts?
- Will students work individually, in pairs, or in larger groups?
- If computers are available in a central setting such as the media center, what constraints are placed on computer time for students?
- Will students work during normal class hours or will they schedule computer time outside of normal class hours?

These factors will determine how practical a given activity is for a particular class.

Most educational software is on CD-ROM. Usually, these programs are hybrid versions, meaning that the CD will run on a Macintosh or PC computer. Be sure to read machine requirements carefully before attempting to run the software on your computer. In addition, be sure to read the *read me file;* often, specific steps are required to have the software sound, video, and printing to work properly. One final note: Burning a backup copy of the CD is recommended as a safety precaution in case the original CD is lost or damaged.

The same precaution applies to software that requires students to store their work on disks. Have students save their work twice: first on their own disk and second to a shared network folder. Make it a habit to back up the shared network folder on a portable medium such as a zip disk or CD.

All the learning activities presented here have been designed for flexible use. That is, they can be tailored easily to meet the special needs of an individual teacher or class. Teachers can simplify a complex activity for younger or less experienced students by providing or even inputting data before the activity begins. On the other hand, a relatively simple activity becomes more challenging if students are required to research and key in data on their own. Teachers can also customize the activity by changing the topic. For example, the learning activity for researching scientists is also useful for researching writers, historical figures, athletes, and so forth.

Another feature of the learning activities in this chapter is that they are uniform in format following ISTE's *National Educational Technology Standards for Students: Connecting Curriculum and Technology* (2000). It is recommended that teachers decide on a standard format for designing learning activities. Doing so makes it easier to share learning activities with other teachers who want to integrate technology in their own classrooms.

The format of the learning activities incorporates the following subheads.

Activity Title. Title of the activity.

Grade-Level Range. This is an indicator of the age or grade level for which the activity is considered appropriate. It should be used as a guideline only, not as a hard and fast rule. The level of difficulty of the activities can be adjusted for different grade levels or even different ability levels within the same class. Gifted students and those with prior computer experience will probably be quite successful with activities aimed at higher grade levels.

Purpose. A simply stated goal or set of goals that the lesson should accomplish.

Description. A summary of what students will do. Of course, in a very real sense, all technology-based lessons share an important objective: to help students become comfortable and competent in using technology as a tool.

Activity Preparation. This section lists the preparation required before the activity is undertaken. The teacher needs to determine whether sufficient access to technology and learning resources exists to carry out the activity.

■ Do computers have enough memory to run the learning technology?
■ Is the software or digital media readily available or must they be ordered externally?
■ Does the activity require tools and resources such as textbooks, web pages, guest speakers, and so on? A critical consideration under this category is whether there is an available source of data that students will need to complete the activity.
■ Do students have network access to a database or will they be required to do library research before beginning computer work?

Activity Procedure. This section is a step-by-step description of the activity in which students will participate. Sometimes the activity does not require hands-on work on the computer but instead calls for collaboration, research, discussion, and other activities that are part of the learning experience.

Tools and Resources. Lists the identified software, hardware, websites, and other materials needed to support the learning activity.

Assessment. This section presents ideas for assessing student learning.

Comments. Provides additional information pertinent to the success of the activity or suggestions for varying the activity for use in another content area or with a different group or level of students. In addition, you may want to include special comments or notes that indicate potential problems and solutions.

Under each of the five content areas included—mathematics, science, language arts, social studies, and special education—two activities are given. The first is recommended for elementary classes, the second for secondary classes. Again, the teacher can adjust the level of difficulty of the activity to classroom needs. In some instances, commercial software has been identified, but alternatives have also been listed whenever possible.

LEARNING ACTIVITIES FOR MATHEMATICS

Because of its number-crunching ability, the computer is an excellent tool for use in teaching mathematics. Much of the educational software on the market today was written to teach mathematical principles. For that reason, the classroom teacher should have little difficulty in locating effective math packages. The activities in this section enable the teacher to use applications software—spreadsheet—to solve mathematical problems in much the same way a businessperson uses a spreadsheet to make predictions and plans.

Activity Title: **Avery's Skateboard**

Grade-Level Range: 3 to 6

Purpose.   In this activity students

- Explore a range of estimation strategies
- Problem solve with a spreadsheet application
- Create formulas to solve a linear equation
- Show different ways spreadsheets can be used
- Address the following National Educational Technology Standards (NETS) for Students Standards: 3—Technology productivity tools; 4—Technology communication tools; and 6—Technology problem-solving and decision-making tools

Description.   Students apply what they know about a spreadsheet application to solve a mathematical problem. Students use a spreadsheet to structure their problem–solution thinking. Students explore new uses for spreadsheets.

Activity Preparation

- Develop formulae for solving the problem.
- Create spreadsheet template.
- Gather examples of problem solving with spreadsheets.
- Prepare a handout with a clear statement of the problem.

- Invite a parent who is an accountant to talk to the class about his or her career and how he or she uses technology to solve problems.

Activity Procedure

1. As a class, review and discuss the spreadsheet concepts of row, column, and cell.
2. Have the invited speaker introduce the descriptive language appropriate to the problem and related to accounting: words and terms such as *cost, save, buy, spend, debit,* and *credit.* Speaker presents a sample problem from work and demonstrates how he or she thinks through a problem and the tools he or she uses.
3. Introduce the problem students will be working on:
   - Each week Avery receives an allowance of $5.
   - Avery wants to save part of her allowance to buy a skateboard, which will cost $60. She also wants to spend part of her allowance on candy and part on video games, which costs 25 cents a game.
   - If Avery plays six video games each week and spends $1 for candy, how many weeks will she have to save in order to buy her skateboard?
   - How many weeks if she stops buying candy and plays four video games each week?
4. As a class, discuss different computational tools (calculator, paper-and-pencil algorithm, or mental strategy) that could be used.
5. Working in groups of three or four, students estimate a solution set. Encourage them to explain their thinking frequently as they estimate.
6. Groups share with the whole class their computational estimation strategies.
7. Using a spreadsheet, small groups of students format the worksheet and input the problem data and formulae. Check their skills and understanding of how a spreadsheet works as they are doing the activity. Have your template ready for students who need assistance.
8. Groups share their spreadsheets with the whole class. Encourage them to explain their thinking as they present their findings and the formulae they used.
9. Compare and contrast their spreadsheet strategies as well as with their estimation strategies.
10. Ask each student to create a similar problem and spreadsheet solution.
11. Students email the problem to another student and arrange a chat time to discuss the solution.
12. As a class, discuss alternative uses for spreadsheets. Share an example you found on the Internet and the search strategy you used. Ask them to find examples by asking their families and searching the Internet.
13. Keep a visible record of students' spreadsheet examples.

Tools and Resources

SOFTWARE
- Spreadsheet, presentation

WEBSITES
- Spreadsheets in the Math Class <http://www.math.byu.edu/~lfrancis/readings302/Spreadsheets.html>
- Spreadsheets for images <http://graphics.stanford.edu/papers/spreadsheets/>

- Using Spreadsheets to Keep Track of Students' Grades <http://www.math.berkeley.edu/~zach/teaching/grades.html>

OTHER
- Presentation equipment to display students' spreadsheets to the whole class (large-screen monitor, LCD panel, or classroom television connected to a computer)

Assessment.   Observe students working in groups and individually. Keep anecdotal notes on students explaining their thinking. Evaluate students on their ability to use spreadsheets, determine and explain solutions, and discuss alternative estimation strategies.

Comments.   An interesting variation of this lesson is to divide the class into two groups. One group will use the spreadsheet to solve the problem while the other group uses pencil and paper. This helps students appreciate the tremendous speed at which computers can perform mathematical calculations.

Activity Title: Slippery Oil Prices

Grade-Level Range: 7 to 12

Purpose.   In this activity students

- Use a variety of resources to gather information
- Use spreadsheets to organize data
- Explore data for patterns
- Represent data using graphs
- Make predictions of a future trend based on oil price data
- Discuss and defend their predictions with other students
- Address the following National Educational Technology Standards (NETS) for Students Standards: 3—Technology productivity tools; 4—Technology communication tools; 5—Technology research tools; and 6—Technology problem-solving and decision-making tools

Description.   Students access current information on oil prices from a variety of print and media sources including the Internet. Students enter the data into a spreadsheet and use the chart tool to graph the data. They then examine the graphs for patterns in oil prices and extrapolate the data to make predictions. Student groups present their predictions to the class using multimedia authoring software.

Activity Preparation

- Students need to be familiar with basic operations of a spreadsheet package.
- Invite a guest speaker to explain how he or she uses spreadsheet as a prediction and decision-making tool in his or her career field.
- Create a website with a History of the Spreadsheet time line and links to spreadsheet and data analysis tutorials.
- Create an email list of experts willing to answer questions and discuss students' findings.
- Develop a data collection worksheet.

Activity Procedure

1. As a review, introduce the activity with an historical overview of the spreadsheet from its invention in the 1970s as an accounting tool to its continually expanding applications as a prediction instrument and decision-making tool.

2. As a class, discuss the wide range of current uses of the spreadsheet in business, government, and research. Make connections to other curriculum areas as well.

3. Have the invited speaker explain how he or she uses a spreadsheet in business, government, or research.

4. Introduce the task with a discussion about trends and graphs. Invite the speaker to participate in the discussion.

5. Working in groups of three or four, students collect data about oil prices from the media center (library) and online resources on the Internet.

6. Groups share with the whole class the data and sources they have found.

7. Discuss the pattern of oil prices for a six-month period.

8. Students record their data findings on a spreadsheet.

9. Students research the pattern of oil prices for a prescribed period of time (e.g., six months, one year, five years). Using the spreadsheet's chart tool, students represent data in a variety of graphs.

10. Students assess the trend in oil prices.

11. Working in groups of three or four, students share their graphs and discuss possible reasons for patterns they detect. Encourage students to explain their reasoning. Groups email a question or a brief presentation of their analysis with a graph to an expert for feedback.

12. Students use the spreadsheet to predict future oil prices for a prescribed period of time and speculate how this trend might affect gasoline prices. Using the results, students generate line graphs of the pricing trend and write a prediction rationale.

13. Working in groups of three or four, students share and discuss their predictions and graphs.

14. Groups synthesize their findings to create a group prediction, rationale, and graph. Groups create a multimedia presentation for the class using software such as Power-Point or HyperStudio, presenting their future trend and the rationale for their prediction.

15. As a class, discuss possible uses of the spreadsheet as a prediction and decision-making tool.

Tools and Resources

SOFTWARE

- Spreadsheet, graphics, presentation, or multimedia authoring (PowerPoint, HyperStudio)

WEBSITES

- Energy Information Administration: Energy Price Statistics <http://www.eia.doe.gov/analysis/price.htm>
- Verleger, P. K., Jr. (2000, April). Third oil shock: Real or imaginary? Consequences and policy alternatives. *International Economics Policy Briefs,* Number 00-4. Available: <http://www.iie.com/NEWSLETR/news00-4.htm>
- Industry Analysis—United States-Energy <http://www.corporateinformation.com/ussector/Energy.html>

- Statistics—The Facts and Figures of Oil and Gas <http://www.api.org/fas/>
- Collection of PowerPoint slides by Jamie MacKenzie that identifies the trends in future supplies and consumption patterns of crude oil <http://www.igc.org/wri/powerpoints/oil/index.htm>
- Crude Oil and Natural Gas Prices <http://www.oilprices.com/>
- Oil Price History and Analysis <http://www.wtrg.com/prices.htm>
- WTRG Economics <http://www.wtrg.com/index.html>

OTHER
- Presentation equipment to display students' presentations and graphics to the whole class (large-screen monitor, LCD panel, or classroom television connected to a computer)
- Printer for generating hard copies of student graphs and charts
- Data collection worksheet

Assessment.   Evaluate students on their ability to graph data, explain and defend their predictions, and work productively in a group. Develop a rubric with students for scoring the independent spreadsheets and predictions and the group presentations.

Comments.   A WWW search can provide students with more information regarding oil sources that can be built into a spreadsheet file. This lesson can be adapted for a class in geography, political science, or economics as part of a study of major oil-producing nations.

LEARNING ACTIVITIES FOR SCIENCE

There are many applications of technology in the science laboratory and classroom. In fact, some of our most innovative technological developments have come from computers that were designed for scientific applications. Therefore, it is appropriate that science teachers demonstrate to their students what a powerful tool the computer can be in furthering scientific investigation.

Activity Title: **The Weather Report**

Grade-Level Range: 2 to 5

Purpose.   In this activity students

- Plan and conduct a simple investigation
- Apply their understanding of data collection
- Generate bar graphs and pie charts
- Gather and analyze information
- Observe differences in weather conditions for different geographical locations
- Share their results with peers
- Address the following National Educational Technology Standards (NETS) for Students Standards: 3—Technology productivity tools and 5—Technology research tools

Description.   Students collect data on weather conditions. They observe, graph, and write about local weather for a month. Small groups synthesize their findings to demonstrate the relationship between weather and geographical location. Groups share their projects by creating a multimedia presentation.

Activity Preparation

- Students need to be familiar with the process of generating bar graphs or pie charts.
- Students understand the rudiments of systematic collection of data.
- Prepare a student worksheet listing the types of weather to be observed (sunshine, rain, clouds, snow, wind, and so on) and the days of the month during which weather will be observed.
- Gather resources (books, maps, CDs, weather videos, Internet sites).
- Invite a local climatologist to present and discuss weather concepts.
- Create a large outline of your state map. Create symbols for different types of weather (sunshine, rain, clouds, snow, wind, etc.) and different types of geographic features (mountains, lake, valley, river, grassland, plain, delta, desert, cape, rain forest, etc.).

Activity Procedure

1. Introduce the activity by placing a marker on a large state map indicating where the students live. Ask students to identify other cities or towns in the state. Hand out the weather worksheets and explain the project.
2. Begin each class by reminding students to observe the weather and record the data on their worksheets. Have a student select the appropriate weather symbol for the day and place it on the map.
3. Assign students to groups with three or four members, divided according to different state regions. On a weekly basis, have the groups locate weather sources to collect data on their assigned regions.
4. Encourage students to record weekend weather conditions at home and add these data to their worksheets as well.
5. Have students collect data for a prescribed period of time (e.g., one month).
6. After students complete data worksheets, assist them in entering the data into a graphing program as the basis for a pie chart or bar graph showing the number of sunny, rainy, cloudy, snowy, and windy days during the month.
7. Display students' graphs on a bulletin board for easy comparison.
8. Have each group complete its group worksheets and enter the data into a graphing program to create a pie chart or bar graph. Display group graphs.
9. As a class, discuss geographical differences of the state regions. Use Internet resources to locate landscape pictures. Have students place the appropriate geographic symbols on the state map.
10. Working in their region group, students discuss the differences between the region and local graphs and why they are different. Have each group reach a conclusion about the weather patterns for the month and prepare a short presentation for the class.
11. Following group presentations, discuss the conclusions and trends. Use weather sites on the Internet to show national and global weather patterns. Discuss how climatologists

use computers to gather, calculate, and display weather data. Ask students to write a general description about weather patterns they observed.

12. Invite a local climatologist to speak to the class and bring samples of computer-generated displays of weather data.

13. Encourage students to continue collecting data over a longer period of time so that their body of data is larger. Have them select a city in another country to observe its weather pattern. The Internet is an excellent source for up-to-date information for class projects and research.

Tools and Resources

SOFTWARE

- Graphics (or enter data into a spreadsheet and use the chart tool), presentation

WEBSITES

- National Climatic Data Center <http://www.ncdc.noaa.gov/>
- Climate Prediction Center <http://www.cpc.ncep.noaa.gov/>
- National Weather Service Homepage <http://www.nws.noaa.gov/>
- Weather Learning Resources <http://www.exploratorium.edu/ti/resources/weather.html>
- Weather Channel's website <http://www.weather.com/homepage.html>
- University of Michigan's Weather Cams <http://cirrus.sprl.umich.edu/wxnet/wxcam.html>
- Weather: What Forces Affect Our Weather? <http://www.learner.org/exhibits/weather/>
- 3D Atlas <http://www.3datlas.com/>

OTHER

- Presentation equipment to display students' graphics to the whole class (large-screen monitor, LCD panel, or classroom television connected to a computer)
- Printer for generating hard copies of student graphs and charts
- Data collection worksheet

Assessment.   Compare the students' graphs. Compare the group graphs. Are they similar? What accounts for differences between graphs? Use a rubric to score individual graphs, data collection worksheets, writing assignments, and group presentations and graphs.

Comments.   Older students may enjoy trying to predict the weather. Have students contact a website of your region of the National Weather Service for normal and record-setting weather conditions in your area within the past year. Students can use data to make weather predictions and then observe the actual weather to determine the reliability of their predictions. Check with your local television station for possible software. Using a weather radio and an LCD panel will allow students opportunities to be classroom meteorologists and give weather reports just like on television.

Activity Title: **Who's Who in Science**

Grade-Level Range: 6 to 12

Purpose.   In this activity students

- Explore individual contributions to the scientific field
- Gather and summarize information
- Apply their understanding of databases
- Address the following National Educational Technology Standards (NETS) for Students Standards: 2—Social, ethical, and human issues; 3—Technology productivity tools; 4—Technology communications tools; and 5—Technology research tools

Description.   Students collect information about a scientist using different types of resources. Students use a database to store and organize information about scientists. Students share with peers their information by creating a multimedia presentation. Students discuss the relationships among scientists and illustrate these relationships by creating a concept map and time line.

Activity Preparation

- Students are familiar with basic operations of database software.
- Vocabulary terms that must be presented are *template, record, field,* and *key.*
- With younger students, teachers may want to design a template including fields such as
  - Name
  - Nationality
  - Science field
  - Born
  - Died
  - Contribution
- Older students can benefit from designing their own templates; this will give them experience in naming fields and designating keys.

Activity Procedure

1. Have students research the library and the Internet for biographies of scientists.
2. Students should keep note cards with pertinent information to be keyed in to the database later.
3. After records have been keyed in, students can access the database to share information they have uncovered or create trivia games.
4. Have students create brief multimedia presentations on the scientists they have researched.
5. As a class, discuss the relationships among scientists. Is there evidence that some of the scientists were influenced by others?
6. Using a concept-mapping tool such as Inspiration, create a concept map using terms from the contribution category.

Tools and Resources

SOFTWARE
- Database, presentation, graphics, concept mapping (Inspiration)

WEBSITES

■ Internet History of Science Sourcebook <http://www.fordham.edu/halsall/science/sciencesbook.html>

■ Women and Minorities in Science and Engineering <http://www.mills.edu/ACAD_INFO/MCS/SPERTUS/Gender/wom_and_min.html>

■ A Science Odyssey <http://www.pbs.org/wgbh/aso/> (especially the section on People <http://www.pbs.org/wgbh/aso/databank/bioindex.html>)

■ History of Science Link List <http://dbhs.wvusd.k12.ca.us/Chem-History/Hist-of-science.html>

OTHER

■ Presentation equipment to display students' spreadsheets to the whole class (large-screen monitor, LCD panel, or classroom television connected to a computer)

Assessment.   How many records are contained in the database? By which keys can records be retrieved? Do students understand the sorting capabilities of the database? Score the project with rubric. The rubric can reflect not only the multimedia presentation and database competency but also the research methods used to search, collect, and organize information.

Comments.   Students may wish to make use of the database to generate a time line that illustrates the scientists' contributions as well as other major events.

LEARNING ACTIVITIES FOR LANGUAGE ARTS

There may have been a time when teachers of language arts thought that the computer had nothing to offer their students. Fortunately, this is no longer the case. Many teachers and students have discovered that the computer is a wonderfully patient tutor of reading and writing skills. There is an abundance of word processing and desktop publishing software programs on the market for students of all ages. In addition, there are programs that assist with spelling, grammar, and word choice.

Activity Title: **Write a Story**

Grade-Level Range: PreK to 5

Purpose.   In this activity students

■ Work cooperatively with others to produce a storybook
■ Demonstrate their knowledge of short story elements
■ Express their ideas using a variety of media and technological tools
■ Address the following National Educational Technology Standards (NETS) for Students Standards: 1—Basic operations and concepts; 2—Social, ethical, and human issues; 3—Technology productivity tools; and 4—Technology communications tools

Description.   Students use basic functions of a word processing package or writing software program such as Pajama Sam's One-Stop Fun Shop to create a short story.

Activity Preparation

- Format a disk and create a document file with a story title.
- Students have had some practice with typing on a keyboard.
- Students understand the basic elements of a short story—plot, setting, and characters.

Activity Procedure

1. Introduce the activity by reading a short story aloud and reviewing its basic elements.
2. Explain the short story writing project to the class.
3. To demonstrate the process, write a class story. Begin the story by typing the first sentence or simply an introductory phrase such as "Once upon a time...."
4. After that, each student will add a sentence of his or her own.
5. Once all students have had an opportunity to add a sentence to the story, have everyone read aloud and in unison the finished story.
6. Students print the story (one to two sentences per page) and illustrate their sentence contribution. Have them take the story home to share with family members.
7. Discuss cooperating with others and sharing ideas.
8. Divide students into teams of three. Have them create a short story and illustrate it using a word processing, slide-show presentation, or story writing program.
9. Teams share their stories with the class.

Tools and Resources

SOFTWARE

- Word processing, graphics, presentation, Pajama Sam's One-Stop Fun Shop, Kid Pix Studio, Easy Book, Kid Works Deluxe

OTHER

- Presentation equipment to display students' stories to the whole class (large-screen monitor, LCD panel, or classroom television connected to a computer)

Assessment.   Were students able to formulate and type in original sentences? Were they interested in the story? Did the story have basic elements such as plot, setting, and characters? Assess students on their ability to work cooperatively with others and their contribution to the short story. Before the project, develop a rubric with the students that addresses state writing standards and short story elements.

Comments.   With very young children, it might be a good idea to provide illustrations that spark ideas and lend a coherent plot to the story. An interesting variation of this lesson is for the teacher to create a form in which students can fill in their own names and other information to create a story about themselves. Most major software companies have specific writing software programs that allow students to write and illustrate their own storybooks. The Key Caps accessory allows for foreign-language stories. Some programs are also available in a second language. Students should be encouraged to decorate their book covers further with their own artwork. This lends color and creativity to the book. Giant George and Ruby Robot, BIG and Little (Sunburst Communications) requires a Muppet Slate but also allows students to create and design various publications of differing sizes up to 5 feet tall. Clifford's Big Book Publisher (Scholastic New Media) provides graphics, clip art, and fonts for younger students to write their own big books. Other related programs are Print Shop Deluxe (Broderbund), Hyperstudio (Roger Wagner Publishing), Kids Works Deluxe (Davidson & Associates, Inc.), My Own Stories (The Learning Company), Children's Writing and Publishing Center (The Learning Company), and The Multimedia Workshop (Davidson & Associates, Inc.).

Activity Title: **Research Notes**

Grade-Level Range: 6 to 12

Purpose.   In this activity students

- Conduct research on a topic
- Demonstrate their knowledge of search strategies
- Apply their understanding of databases
- Address the following National Educational Technology Standards (NETS) for Students Standards: 1—Basic operations and concepts; 2—Social, ethical, and human issues; 3—Technology productivity tools; and 5—Technology research tools

Description.   Students use a database to store and organize research notes and format a bibliography.

Activity Preparation

- Students are familiar with basic operations and applications of databases.
- Students are familiar with the terms *template, record, field,* and *key.*
- Middle school teachers may want to design a database template including the following fields:
  - Author
  - Title
  - Publisher
  - City of publication
  - Year of publication
  - Topic(s)
  - Notes
- High school students may benefit from designing a template of their own and designating keys such as author, title, and topic.

Activity Procedure

1. Working with a common topic or with individual topics, students research the topics using library and Internet resources.
2. Students should keep note cards or word processing files with information to be keyed in to the database. After all the records are keyed in, students can retrieve information or print listings of it.
3. Depending on the report formatting capabilities of the database, students format bibliographies with correct placement and punctuation of information.
4. Students use a standard style sheet to format their bibliographies.

5. Have students work in small editing groups to proofread and revise their bibliographies.

6. Discuss other ways databases simplify the research process; for example, allowing direct access to up-to-the-minute information.

7. Explore ways in which the computer is likely to change the way we do research. Discuss the advantages of formatting various reports of the same data for different purposes.

Tools and Resources

SOFTWARE

- Database, presentation

WEBSITES

- Electronic Reference Formats Recommended by the American Psychological Association <http://www.apa.org/journals/webref.html>
- Guidelines for Evaluating Work with Digital Media in the Modern Languages <http://www.mla.org/reports/ccet/ccet_guidelines.htm>
- Modern Language Association <http://www.mla.org>
- A Guide for Writing Research Papers Based on Modern Language Association (MLA) Documentation <http://webster.commnet.edu/mla.htm>
- Using Modern Language Association (MLA) Format <http://owl.english.purdue.edu/handouts/research/r_mla.html>
- Research Papers <http://owl.english.purdue.edu/handouts/research/index.html>
- Network Bibliography (Example of database bibliography) <http://www.cs.columbia.edu/~hgs/netbib/>

OTHER

- Presentation equipment to display students' bibliographies to the whole class (large-screen monitor, LCD panel, or classroom television connected to a computer)
- Printer and bibliography style sheet such as the MLA's *Handbook for Writers of Theses and Dissertations*

Assessment.   Check the bibliographies for correctness and style. What have students learned about the process of research and the use of the computer to expedite research? How did students evaluate resources?

Comments.   This lesson can be used as an effective prelude to writing a research paper because students have created a working bibliography while completing the lesson. The WWW has access to most writing guidelines as well as step-by-step approaches for writing papers with projected time lines.

LEARNING ACTIVITIES FOR SOCIAL STUDIES

Disciplines within the social studies area have benefited greatly from computer applications such as database and spreadsheet. Especially in fields such as psychology and sociology, in which large bodies of statistical data contribute to a greater understanding of human behavior, the computer has made life easier for both teachers and students. Simulation programs can bring history to life by placing students in the midst of historical situations. Social studies teachers can choose from a wide range of computer applications to challenge their students.

Activity Title: **You Want to Sell Me What? The Many Forms of Advertising**

Grade-Level Range: 3 to 5

Purpose.   Through this learning activity, students

- Understand advertising and the role it plays in the marketplace
- Discover the ways in which the attributes of various media contribute to the effectiveness of advertising for a particular audience
- Become discriminating consumers of advertising strategies
- Address the following National Educational Technology Standards (NETS) for Students Standards: 3—Technology productivity tools; 4—Technology communication tools; 5—Technology research tools; and 6—Technology problem-solving and decision-making tools

Description.   This learning activity takes place over an extended period of time and explores the purpose of advertising media. As a class, students examine advertisements using focus questions to determine their attributes, audience, and influences. In small groups organized by media type, students use focus questions to research a specific media type. Groups then present their findings to the whole class using presentation software. Small groups meet again to design and produce an advertisement in their researched medium. They also conduct a market analysis, including the cost of placing their ads. Finally, they present their ad to the whole class using the focus questions for discussion.

Activity Preparation

- Gather samples of advertisements in various media forms: newspapers, magazines, radio and television recordings, and websites.
- Preview relevant media-related websites. Assemble and troubleshoot necessary technology tools (see Tools and Resources).
- Schedule a guest speaker who is either involved in advertising or uses advertising extensively to promote his or her business.
- Schedule adult helpers or cross-age tutors to assist younger children with group activities.

Activity Procedure

1. As a class, discuss the purposes of advertising.
    - How do advertisements influence the way you act on needs and wants?
    - How do fact and opinion play a part in advertising?
2. As a class, study one advertisement from at least three media types (choose from newspaper, magazine, radio, television, and the web). Discuss the following focus questions:
    - How does the ad make you feel?
    - Were you persuaded to buy the product?
    - What do you think the purpose of the ad is?
    - Who do you think is the target audience?
    - What ad components were effective?

- Was this a product that you need or that you want?
- Why is this medium effective for this particular ad?

3. In small groups, students research advertisements found in various types of media. Each group works with one of the following: newspaper, magazine, radio, television, or the web.

4. Each group chooses a representative advertisement in its medium and discusses the attributes of the ad, using the list of focus questions.

5. Using presentation software, each group presents the results of its analysis to the class. As a class, discuss the similarities and differences among the media types, and their perceived strengths and weaknesses. Determine why a particular media type was used for a particular target audience.

6. Small groups meet again to design advertisements for a product of their choice, for the media they have been working with. The group chooses a particular audience to which it will advertise the product, focusing on how consumers in this particular group can best be reached by the attributes of this media.

7. Small groups perform market research on their advertisements by soliciting opinions from their peers in a focus group setting. (Creating research questions that can be numerically analyzed is a valuable mathematics task.) How students ask questions about the product will define how the results are reported. (Use a rating scale? Comparison with other like products? Attributes of product? etc.) Market research begins by sharing ads with other groups in the class, other students at school, family members, or others in the local community. Students can then create graphs of their research results, using spreadsheet or graphing software.

8. After refining their advertisements, student groups use the web to find representative groups from their target audiences, experts in the advertising fields, and others with knowledge about their products. Students electronically send their advertisement to these groups for further comment.

9. Small groups investigate the cost of placing their advertisements in the media by contacting newspapers, magazines, and radio and television stations, or by researching the costs of advertising on the web. Discuss the impact of easy access to the web. Do a cost–benefit analysis comparing advertising costs with potential profits.

10. Small groups use electronic presentation software to present their final advertisements to the class, along with the results of their market research and cost–benefit analyses.

11. As a group, have the class reflect on the results of the small group work, discussing which media are most cost-effective for different audiences and purposes.

12. Further topics of discussion may include
    - Consumer spending habits of different population groups
    - How personal choices may affect the economy
    - How local advertisements compare with nationally run advertisements

Tools and Resources

SOFTWARE
- Word processing, presentation, spreadsheet or graphing, video editing

HARDWARE
- Audiotape player, video camcorder

WEBSITES

Newspapers

- <http://www.denverpost.com>
- <http://www.nytimes.com>
- <http://www.latimes.com>

Magazines

- <http://www.time.com>
- <http://www.usnews.com/usnews/home.htm>
- <http://pathfinder.com/people>
- <http://www.zdnet.com>

Radio stations

- <http://www.broadcast.com/radio>

TV commercials

- <http://www.malcolmdesigns.com/hwtvcom.html>
- <http://www.buckmans.com/tvcommercials.htm>
- <http://www.przyborski.com/com_list.html>

OTHER

- Newspapers, magazines, recordings of radio and television advertisements, World Wide Web advertisements (found on almost any commercial website)

Assessment.   Develop a scoring rubric to evaluate each group advertisement. As the assignment develops, share the rubric with the class. Be sure to adjust the rubric based on appropriate student suggestions. Students use the rubric to evaluate their group advertisements. Give samples of advertisements in various media and have students discuss the ad in terms of the beginning focus questions.

Comments.   Many teachers have found that the combination of group and individual work in this learning activity works well in meeting the needs of all students. This is especially true for classrooms in which there are second-language learners. Nuances in the words used in advertising can be deceiving to second-language learners. The group work helps take care of finding the many grammatical and spelling errors that used to show up in final projects. The use of the new technology has made this project much more successful than when conventional tools were used. Students are always pleased with the professional-looking results.

Activity Title: **Career Decisions**

Grade-Level Range: 8 to 12

Purpose.   Through this learning activity, students

- Access multiple sources to research topic
- Formulate a decision based on prioritizing strategies and data comparison
- Apply understanding of databases

- Address the following National Educational Technology Standards (NETS) for Students Standards: 3—Technology productivity tools; 4—Technology communication tools; 5—Technology research tools; and 6—Technology problem-solving and decision-making tools

Description.   Students make career decisions after researching several major U.S. cities.

Activity Preparation

- Students are familiar with basic database operations and terminology, particularly *template, record, field,* and *key.*
- Middle school teachers may want to design a template that includes fields such as
  - City
  - State
  - Population
  - Population under 35
  - Per capita income
  - Unemployment rate
  - Average temperature
  - Average rainfall
  - Number of colleges
  - Number of hospitals
  - Popular sports
  - Number of churches
- Older students can benefit from designing their own templates to include factors they consider important in making career decisions.

Activity Procedure

1. Tell the students to imagine that they have completed their education and are ready to enter their chosen career fields. They have received three job offers in three different cities. Before making decisions about which offers to accept, they are to conduct research about the three cities.
2. Either have the class choose three cities for research or have individual students select three cities that appeal to them.
3. Encourage students to select major cities so that current data will be readily available.
4. After students have conducted research on three cities, assist them in entering the data into the database. Students can then print a listing of their data for easy comparison.
5. After students have had an opportunity to review their listings, ask them to choose one of the job offers based on their findings.
6. Have them list the factors that most influenced their decisions and prepare brief presentations. Suggest that they use tables to show data comparisons.
7. Have students write essays explaining their decisions and the factors on which they are based.
8. Discuss the different factors people consider in relocating and how these factors are prioritized differently by different people.

Tools and Resources

SOFTWARE
- Database, presentation

WEBSITES
- USA City Information <http://www.pe.net/~rksnow/>
- The USA CityLink Project <http://www.usacitylink.com/>
- Maps <http://mapquest.com/>
- Weather Maps <http://www.weather.com/weather/maps/>
- The Travel Site <http://www.randmcnally.com/rmc/home.jsp>
- Understanding the USA <http://www.understandingusa.com/>
- Hoovers Online: The Business Network <http://www.hoovers.com/>

OTHER
- Presentation equipment to display students' spreadsheets to the whole class (large-screen monitor, LCD panel, or classroom television connected to a computer)

Assessment.   Were the students able to locate all of the information called for in the database? Did the students suggest additional characteristics that could be included? Were students able to reach decisions with which they felt comfortable?

Comments.   The Carmen Sandiego series by Broderbund may be used to build a classroom database on countries, states, and cities. Several commercial software programs and some WWW sites provide maps as well as related information.

LEARNING ACTIVITIES FOR SPECIAL EDUCATION

The computer is an extremely effective tool in the special education classroom because it is infinitely patient. Students can work at their own pace without feeling threatened or rushed. Also, the computer seems to motivate many students to repeat lessons and exercises, thereby reinforcing the knowledge they have gained. In effect, the computer provides the student with limitless individual attention that the special education teacher cannot always provide. Although there is limited educational software on the market that has been designed specifically for use in special education, most educational programs can be adapted to the unique needs of the special education classroom. It is especially easy to tailor educational software that includes authoring components so that the teacher may create questions or problems that relate specifically to the subject area under consideration. The lesson plans that follow present educational software that adapts well to use with exceptional students.

Activity Title: **Logic Builders**

Grade-Level Range: Because Logic Builders (Scholastic New Media) allows the student to choose from three levels of difficulty, the game can be adapted to a wide range of skill levels.

Purpose. Through this learning activity, students

- Improve their ability to follow directions by recreating spider webs according to computer-generated patterns.
- Address the following National Educational Technology Standards (NETS) for Students Standards: 1—Basic operations and concepts; 2—Social, ethical, and human issues; and 4—Technology communication tools

Description. Students use the software gaming program, Logic Builders, to create a graphic image.

Activity Preparation

- Students understand basic operations of the computer and have minimal typing skills.
- Teachers should be familiar with loading the programs and selecting the appropriate games from the main menu.

Activity Procedure

1. Students select DRAW A WEB from the main menu of Logic Builders. This game enables students to experiment with the process of drawing a spider web with the help of on-screen spiders.
2. Students play MATCH A WEB in which they are required to recreate a master design displayed on the right side of the screen.
3. Still more challenging is RECALL A WEB, which requires students to recreate the master web from memory. Students achieve high scores for recreating webs in as few moves as possible.
4. As students earn points, they receive promotions to the level of Big Boss.
5. Have students share their thoughts about the game using a synchronous communication tool (CHAT program).

Tools and Resources
  SOFTWARE
- Logic Builders (Scholastic New Media), synchronous communication tool

Assessment. The score maintained by the computer can be used as an indicator of student success in redrawing patterns. Do students select higher levels of challenge after gaining experience with the program? Do they demonstrate positive social and ethical behaviors when using technology?

Comments. Factory (Sunburst), The Oregon Trail 2 (The Learning Company), Lego TC Logo (LCSI), Carmen Sandiego series (Broderbund), and the Sim series (Maxis) of programs are alternative software approaches to this lesson. Students can do a screen capture to cut and paste their webs into a paint program to color them or even use them as screen savers.

Activity Title: **Recreation and Leisure**

Grade-Level Range: 8 to 12

Purpose.   Through this learning activity, students

- Locate and participate in recreational and leisure activities in the community.
- Address the following National Educational Technology Standards (NETS) for Students Standards: 1—Basic operations and concepts; 2—Social, ethical, and human issues; 3—Technology productivity tools; 4—Technology communication tools; and 5—Technology research tools.

Description.   Students use a database to store and organize their research findings.

Activity Preparation

- Students are familiar with databases and have minimal typing skills.
- Students are familiar with collecting data from the Internet.
- Design a template to include the following fields: Activity, Organization, Address, Cost, Services, Hours, and Eligibility.
- Develop a bookmark folder with local websites.
- Format a data disk in advance of the lesson.

Activity Procedure

1. Students create lists of recreational and leisure activities that they enjoy.
2. As a class, discuss what opportunities are available in the local community.
3. Students search online resources, contact public agencies, and conduct research to discover other leisure activities offered in the community.
4. After students have completed their research, have them key their data into the database. This is an excellent opportunity to teach students about retrieving and sorting records in the database.
5. Have students print a copy of their databases for a referral list.
6. Have students email friends, key pals, or relatives their listings of available community activities.

Tools and Resources
SOFTWARE
- Database (ClarisWorks, Filemaker, Inc.)

OTHER
- Reference materials on local recreational and leisure activities

Assessment.   Have students uncovered valuable information about leisure activities available to them? Are students able to enter and access their information quickly and easily? Do some of the students participate in any of the activities included in the database?

Comments.   As an ongoing class project, ask students to bring in information about new activities, schedule changes, and so forth to keep the database up-to-date. Students who participate in community activities can report their experiences to the class. Have students plan a class trip using their database information.

SUMMARY

Teachers of all content areas can incorporate technology-based learning activities into their traditional curricula. This increases the number of students who have experience with technology when they finish school. It also increases the amount of technology in use in the classroom and serves as a bridge to the future when technology-based learning activities will be the rule rather than the exception. The first step in incorporating technology into the curriculum is being able to develop effective technology-based learning activities.

In general, technology-based learning activities must account for the same factors that all learning activities depend on:

Grade-Level Range
Purpose
Description
Activity Preparation
Activity Procedure
Tools and Resources
Assessment

The learning activities presented in this chapter follow a format that includes all these features and may also include an activity description and comments.

With technology-based learning activities, additional factors must be taken into consideration. Most of these factors have to do with availability of software and hardware. Will students have unlimited access to several computers with network connectivity? This situation allows the teacher to plan more extensive use of technology than a situation in which students must go in pairs to a media center where they can use the computer for no more than half an hour. Are there programs available to handle the activities planned?

This chapter presented ten sample learning activities. There are two learning activities for each of the five content areas—mathematics, science, language arts, social studies, and special education. Under each content area, the first learning activity is for use by elementary teachers, the second by secondary teachers. It is the authors' hope that teachers will use these learning activities as a springboard for creating their own innovative and effective technology-based learning activities.

LEARNER ACTIVITIES

1. Present one of the activities in this chapter to your peers and report on the results.

2. Write a technology-based learning activity for your content area following the format suggested in this chapter.

3. Research the Internet, books, and periodicals that include technology-based learning activities. Develop a web-based bibliography of these resources.

4. Adapt one of the learning activities in this chapter for use with a specific software package.

5. Adapt one of the learning activities in this chapter for a higher or lower grade level.

6. Write a learning activity that develops a thematic learning environment and integrates several content areas.

7. Write a learning activity that includes the WWW for data collection.

8. Integrate cooperative learning into one of the learning activities. Try the activity with a class.

9. Modify one of the learning activities to include portfolio-assessment procedures.

BIBLIOGRAPHY

Allen, D. (1994a). A spring software sampler. Teaching with technology. *Teaching PreK–8, 24*(8), 20–22.

Allen, D. (1994b). Teaching with technology: Byte into math. *Teaching PreK–8, 24*(4), 22–27.

Allen, D. (1995). Teaching with technology. Software that's right for you. *Teaching PreK–8, 25*(8), 14–17.

Anderson-Inman, L. (1987). The reading–writing connection: Classroom applications for the computer, Part II. *The Computing Teacher, 14*(6), 15–18.

Anderson-Inman, L. (1990–1991). Enabling students with learning disabilities: Insights from research. *The Computing Teacher, 18*(4), 26–29.

Balajthy, E. (1988). Keyboarding, language arts, and the elementary school child. *The Computing Teacher, 15*(5), 40–43.

Barnes, S., & Michalowiczs, K. D. (1994). Now and then: From cashier to scan coordinator; from stones to bones to PC clones. *Mathematics Teaching in the Middle School, 1*(1), 59–65.

Bayliffe, J., et al. (1994). Tech time: Using technology to enhance "my travels with Gulliver." *Teaching Children Mathematics, 1*(3), 188–191.

Berlin, D. F., & White, A. L. (1995). Using technology in assessing integrated science and mathematics learning. *Journal of Science Education and Technology, 4*(1), 47–56.

Bitter, G. G., & Frederick, H. (1989). Techniques and technology in secondary school mathematics. *NASSP Bulletin, 73*(519), 22–28.

Braun, J. A., Jr., & Kuseske, T. (Eds.). (1994). A teacher's perspective on what's ahead for technology. Media corner. *Social Studies and the Young Learner, 6*(3), 26–28.

Bristor, V. J., & Drake, S. V. (1994). Linking the language arts and content areas through visual technology. *T.H.E. Journal, 22*(2), 74–77.

Browning, R., & Nave, G. (1983). Computer technology for the handicapped: A literature profile. *The Computing Teacher, 10*(6), 56–59.

Brush, T., & Bitter, G. G. (2000). An innovative approach to high-tech learning. *Learning and Leading with Technology, 28*(1), 23–30.

Cappo, M., & Osterman, G. (1991). Teach students to communicate mathematically. *The Computing Teacher, 18*(5), 34–39.

Collis, B. (1988). *Computers, curriculum, and whole-class instruction.* Belmont, CA: Wadsworth.

Connelly, M. G., & Wiebe, J. H. (1994). Teaching mathematics with technology: Mining mathematics on the Internet. *Arithmetic Teacher, 41*(5), 276–281.

Cuoco, A. A., et al. (Eds.). (1994). Technology tips: A potpourri. *Mathematics Teacher, 87*(7), 566–569.

Dickens, R. A. (1991–1992). Success with writing and the concept formation model. *The Computing Teacher, 19*(4), 27–29.

Faltis, C. J., & Devillar, R. A. (Eds.). (1990). *Language minority students and computers.* New York: Haworth Press.

Gagne, R. M. (1987). *Instructional technology: Foundations.* Hillsdale, NJ: Lawrence Erlbaum.

Gardner, H. (2000). The complete tutor. *TECHNOS, 9*(3), 10–13.

Glasser, L. (2000). Information technology in educational science: Chemistry teaching by computer. *South African Journal of Science, 96*(4), 155–160.

Goldberg, K. P. (1994). Applications: Using technology to understand the jury decision-making process. *Mathematics Teacher, 87*(2), 110–114.

Hardwick, S. W. (2000). Humanising the technology landscape through a collaborative pedagogy. *Journal of Geography in Higher Education, 24*(1), 123–130.

Harvey, J. G., et al. (1995). The influence of technology on the teaching and learning of algebra. *Journal of Mathematical Behavior, 14*(1), 75–109.

Heid, M. (1995). Impact of technology, mathematical modeling, and meaning on the content, learning, and teaching of secondary school algebra. *Journal of Mathematical Behavior, 14*(1), 121–137.

Hooper, S., & Rieber, L. P. (1995). Teaching with technology. In A. C. Ornstein (Ed.), *Teaching: Theory into practice* (pp. 154–170). Boston: Allyn & Bacon.

Hoyles, C., et al. (1994). Learning mathematics in groups with computers: Reflections on a research study. *British Educational Research Journal, 20*(4), 465–483.

Hunt, N., & Afford, L. (1991–1992). Involving students in computer-based cooperative lessons. *The Computing Teacher, 19*(4), 34–37.

Hussey, W. (2000). Technology and teaching music. *Computer Music Journal, 24*(2), 92–95.

Johnson, D. C., et al. (1994). Evaluating the impact of IT on pupils' achievements. *Journal of Computer Assisted Learning, 10*(3), 138–156.

Kader, G., & Perry, M. (1994). Power on! Learning statistics with technology. *Mathematics Teaching in the Middle School, 1*(2), 130–136.

Kapisosky, R. M. (1990). Math and science: Vitality through technology. *Media and Methods, 26*(4), 59–61.

Kaput, J. J., & Thompson, P. W. (1994). Technology in mathematics education research: The first 25 years in the JRME. *Journal for Research in Mathematics Education, 25*(6), 667–684.

Kelly, R. (2000). Working with WebQuests. *Teaching Exceptional Children, 32*(6), 4–13.

Kemp, J. E. (2000). John Dewey never said it would be easy: Designing education in the 21st century. *TECHNOS, 9*(3), 25–29.

Kuechle, N. (1990). Computers and first grade writing: A learning center approach. *The Computing Teacher, 18*(1), 39–41.

Lampert, M., et al. (1994). Using technology to support a new pedagogy of mathematics teacher education. *Journal of Special Education Technology, 12*(3), 276–289.

Layton, T. G. (2000). Why tomorrow's schools must learn to let go of the past. *Electronic School, 187*(9), 23–24.

Leu, D. J., Jr., & Kinzer, C. K. (2000). The convergence of literacy instruction with networked technologies for information and communication. *Reading Research Quarterly, 35*(1), 108–129.

MacArthur, C. A. (2000). New tools for writing: Assistive technology for students with writing difficulties. *Topics-in-Language-Disorders, 20*(4), 85–100.

Manes, M. A. (1994). Technology tips: A global electronic community. *Mathematics Teacher, 87*(8), 650–651.

McClain, K., Cobb, P., & Gravemeijer, K. (2000). Supporting students' ways of reasoning about data. In M. J. Burke & F. R. Curcio (Eds.), *Learning Mathematics for a New Century: 2000 Yearbook* (pp. 174–187). Reston, VA: National Council of Teachers of Mathematics.

Moni, K. B., & Jobling, A. (2000). LATCH-ON: A program to develop literacy in young adults with Down syndrome. *Journal of Adolescent and Adult Literacy, 44*(1), 40–50.

O'Connor, J., & Brie, R. (1994). The effects of technology infusion on the mathematics and science curriculum. *Journal of Computing in Teacher Education, 10*(4), 15–18.

Parr, J. M. (1999). Extending educational computing: A case of extensive teacher development and support. *Journal of Research on Computing in Education, 31*(3), 280–292.

Pert, T. (1990). Manipulatives and the computer: A powerful partnership for learners of all ages. *Classroom Computer Learning, 10*(6), 20–29.

Phelps, M. V. (1994). The federal role in educational technology. *Educational Media and Technology Yearbook, 20*, 142–150.

Phillips, R. J., et al. (1995). Evolving strategies for using interactive video resources in mathematics classrooms. *Educational Studies in Mathematics, 28*(2), 133–154.

Reinking, D., & Watkins, J. (2000). A formative experiment investigating the use of multimedia book reviews to increase elementary students' independent reading. *Reading Research Quarterly, 35*(3), 384–420.

Resources on computer-based reading and writing instruction. (1988). *The Computing Teacher, 16*(1), 24–27.

Riddle, B. (1988). Computer-based astronomy: The opposition of Mars. *The Computing Teacher, 16*(3), 20–23.

Risinger, C. F. (2000). Social Studies Portals: More than just a web page. *Social Education, 64*(3), 150–152.

Rowland, K. L., & Scott, D. (1992). Promoting language and literacy for young children through computers. *Journal of Computing in Childhood Education, 3*(1), 55–61.

Schack, M. B. (2000). The judicious use of instructional technology in science education. *Science Activities, 37*(1), 3–5.

Solomon, G. (1990). Learning social studies in a one-computer classroom. *Electronic Learning, 9*(7), 18–20.

Suddath, C., & Susnik, J. (1991). *Augmentative communication devices.* Reston, VA: Office for Special Education Technology.

Thomas, J., & Bitter, G. G. (2000). (Eds.). *National Educational Technology Standards for Students: Connecting Curriculum and Technology.* Eugene, OR: International Society for Technology in Education.

U.S. Department of Education. National Center for Education Statistics. (2000). *Teacher's tools for the 21st century: A report on teachers' use of technology.* NCES 2000–102 by Becky Smerdon, Stephanie Cronen, Lawrence Lanahan, Jennifer Anderson, Nichaolas Iannotti, and January Angeles. Washington, DC: Author.

Wicklein, R. C., & Schell, J. W. (1995). Case studies of multidisciplinary approaches to integrating mathematics, science and technology education. *Journal of Technology Education, 6*(2), 59–76.

Widmer, C. C., & Sheffield, L. (1998). Modeling mathematics concepts: Using physical, calculator, and computer models to teach area and perimeter. *Learning and Leading with Technology, 25*(5), 32–35.

Wilson, E. K., & Rice, M. L. (2000). Virtual field trips and newsrooms: Integrating technology into the classroom. *Social Education, 64*(3), 152–155.

Wissick, C. A., & Gardner, J. E. (2000). Multimedia or not to multimedia? That is the question for students with learning disabilities. *Teaching Exceptional Children, 32*(4), 34–44.

Wresch, W. (1990). Collaborative writing projects: Lesson plans for the computer age. *The Computing Teacher, 17*(8), 19–21.

Young, M. (1995). Assessment of situated learning using computer environments. *Journal of Science Education and Technology, 4*(1), 89–96.

Zola, J., & Ioannidou, A. (2000). Learning and teaching with interactive simulations. *Social Education, 64*(3), 142–146.

CHAPTER 12

TECHNOLOGY INTEGRATION IN MULTIDISCIPLINARY UNITS

FOCUS QUESTIONS

1. How can teachers use technology across disciplines?
2. What factors must a teacher consider when planning to integrate technology?
3. What are the benefits of using technology for learning across discipline areas?

Chapter 11 presented a number of suggestions for introducing students to common computer applications such as word processing, database, graphics, spreadsheet, as well as the Internet and educational software. Teachers can adapt learning technologies easily to fit into virtually all areas of the curriculum. This chapter will demonstrate how technology can be integrated into multidisciplinary units.

When creating multidisciplinary units that integrate technology, the teacher needs to consider the same factors discussed in Chapter 11. The availability and location of computer hardware certainly affect the way activities will be presented and whether students will work individually or in groups. When using educational software, read the product's suggestions for maximizing the learning experience. It is a good idea to review these suggestions carefully before presenting activities.

Teachers may also benefit from talking with other teachers about their technology integration experiences. For example, teachers who have used educational software before can judge how much knowledge—both of computer usage and of the subject being presented—is required for the student to operate the program effectively. Are there bugs in the program that may hinder learning? Are some activities in the program more interesting, more useful, or more challenging to students than others? Experienced software users can answer these and other questions that the new user may have. Schools could build a resource bank of technology-based learning activities that include teacher comments.

Planning is the key to integrating technology. For example, ordinary software may take several weeks to order and receive if it is not available at a local software or teaching supply store. Teachers may face limited choices if their districts have not set aside sufficient funds for the purchase of software. In some cases, it is possible to rent software for a short period of time at much less expense than the purchase price of the package. But rental also requires planning and lead time. Teachers are strongly urged to do some research of their own to see what other learning technologies are available for teaching all areas of the curriculum.

The sample multidisciplinary units follow the ISTE (Thomas & Bitter, 2000) *National Educational Technology Standards for Students: Connecting Curriculum and Technology* format for multidisciplinary resource units incorporating the following subheadings:

- Title of Unit
- Activities
- Tools and Resources

These units provide a powerful theme on which to build multidisciplinary learning activities. Each unit addresses content standards from two or more discipline areas as well as the National Educational Technology Standards for Students.

MULTIDISCIPLINARY UNIT FOR PRIMARY GRADES (PREK–2)

Title of Unit: Helping Hands

Helping Hands examines the theme of cooperation and community. This unit provides students with hands-on experience working with peers, family members, and other community members. Students learn how to work as a team and interact with others.

In this unit students address the following National Educational Technology Standards (NETS) for Students Standards: 1—Basic operations and concepts; 2—Social, ethical, and human issues; 3—Technology productivity tools; and 4—Technology communication tools.

Activities

1. Students use drawing or painting software to make a banner entitled Helping Hands. Assign each letter to a group of two or three students. Display the banner on a wall or bulletin board.
2. Have each student trace his or her hand on paper. Use a scanner to digitize the tracing. Use drawing or painting software to decorate the hand and use the text tool to write student's name anywhere on the hand. Print the hand pictures, cut them out, and decorate the banner with them.
3. Students use a digital camera to create group pictures (pictures of students working cooperatively).
4. Students use interactive CDs to explore and learn about community helpers.
5. Have students use Big Book software (e.g., Big Book, Scholastic SuperPrint Deluxe) to create and print a story based on a group picture.
6. Students use painting or drawing software to make a picture dictionary that describes and illustrates cooperation.
7. Use a video camera to document classroom activities. As a class, check the video for examples of cooperative and uncooperative behavior.
8. At the end of each day, determine the classroom cooperation level. Record cooperation levels on a large graph posted on a wall.

9. Have students use a spreadsheet program or graphing software to draw, tabulate, or graph the information for use in a class discussion.

10. Have students work with an adult family member to learn about neighborhood watches or other types of community activities designed to help neighbors meet each other and look out for each other. Use a digital camera to take pictures of your neighborhood. Use slide-show software such as Kid Pix Studio to create a neighborhood watch presentation.

11. Students visit Mr. Rogers' Neighborhood website to learn about families and their neighborhoods.

12. From a list of I-statements, have students select one to role-play cooperative behavior with a partner.

13. Go on a field trip to the local police station. Have students send the station a thank-you email.

14. Work with the local fire department to develop a home safety chart. Have students use the chart to investigate the safety level of their homes.

Tools and Resources

SOFTWARE

- Kid Pix Studio
- ClarisWorks for Kids
- Easy Book
- SuperPrint
- HyperStudio
- Kid Works Deluxe
- GraphPower
- Graph Club
- Richard Scarry's Busytown
- Multimedia encyclopedias

HARDWARE

- Color inkjet printer
- Video camcorder
- Digital camera
- Scanner
- Large-screen monitor, LCD panel, or classroom TV connected to a computer
- VCR

WEBSITE

- Mr. Rogers' Neighborhood <http://www.pbs.org/rogers>

MULTIDISCIPLINARY UNIT FOR INTERMEDIATE GRADES (3–5)

Title of Unit: Eco Busters

Eco Busters emphasizes the causal link between the United States' tremendous consumption of natural resources and the resulting effect of that consumption on the rest of the planet. Students will learn about the impact fossil fuels and other wastes have on Earth.

In this unit students address the following National Educational Technology Standards (NETS) for Students Standards: 1—Basic operations and concepts; 2—Social, ethical, and human issues; 3—Technology productivity tools; 4—Technology communication tools; 5—Technology research tools; and 6—Technology problem-solving and decision-making tools.

Activities

1. Students form small groups and list the items found in the garbage in their homes and in their classroom.
2. Have students research the impact unchecked consumerism has on the world's natural resources, as well as its effect on the rain forests, the coral reefs, and the Earth's atmosphere.
3. Students investigate means by which they can educate parents, relatives, and each other on how to reduce the damage done to our world.
4. Students publish their findings on a website as well as send an email or letter to all news media reporting their findings.
5. Go on a field trip to the sewage plant. Discuss modern technology's impact on waste disposal. Take digital pictures to record observations on how sewage is treated to become effluent. Working with an adult or older student, develop a small multimedia project that reports the observed water treatment processes. Send the sewage plant an email thanking the personnel there for the visit.
6. Go on a field trip to the recycling plant. Take digital pictures to record observations on the recycling process. Working with an adult or older student, develop a small multimedia project that reports the observed recycling processes. Send the plant an email thanking the personnel for the visit.
7. Students explore the environmental impact of landfills. Have students learn about landfills in their area, regulations imposed on them, and their expected ecological impact over time.
8. Have students create pieces of art constructed entirely of recyclable materials.
9. Students use the Internet to research different advocacy groups that campaign against vinyl plastics. Email one of these groups a question.
10. Have students chart statistics from the past ten years regarding recycling, landfill size, and monies involved in recycling.
11. Have small groups of students create charts examining the amount of time it takes for different products to biodegrade. Students share their findings by preparing a multimedia presentation.
12. Students working with a partner create recycling posters aimed toward motivating other students to recycle. Try to include statistics and other facts in each poster.
13. Working in small groups, students brainstorm solutions on how to make recycling a part of our daily life.
14. Have small groups of students develop a slide-show or multimedia presentation illustrating what happens to a plastic bottle or styrofoam cup sent to be recycled contrasted with one sent to the landfill, including the environmental effects of these processes and their results.

Tools and Resources

SOFTWARE
- Word processing

- Spreadsheet
- Graphics
- HyperStudio
- Presentation
- GraphPower
- Graph Club
- Web-page creation
- Multimedia encyclopedia

HARDWARE
- Color inkjet printer
- Video camcorder
- Digital camera
- Scanner
- Large-screen monitor, LCD panel, or classroom TV connected to a computer
- VCR

WEBSITES
- National Environmental Trust <http://www.igc.apc.org/eic/>
- Greenpeace <http://www.greenpeaceusa.org/>

EDUCATIONAL VIDEO
Available through Disney Educational Productions

- *Bill Nye the Science Guy* shows (Pollution Solutions, Garbage and the Water Cycle)
- *Recycle Rex* (stars animated recycling dinosaur)
- *The Energy Savers* (stars Donald Duck, Mickey Mouse, and Goofy)
- *Zort Sorts: A Story about Recycling*
- *The Great Search—Man's Need for Power and Energy*

MULTIDISCIPLINARY UNIT FOR MIDDLE GRADES (6–8)

Title of Unit: **Attitude Shapers**

Recognizing that "a picture is worth a thousand words," it is important that students understand how businesses and governments seek to shape our thoughts and opinions on everyday occurrences through the careful selection and dissemination of photographs and sound bites.

Students will analyze photographs, sound bites, advertisements, and any other media sources they encounter and investigate whether the published material accurately reflects the truth. Students will state whether the published material accurately reflects the actual events or advertised products, and they will state how the published material was used to shape the attitudes and opinions of a specified audience.

In this unit students address the following National Educational Technology Standards (NETS) for Students Standards: 1—Basic operations and concepts; 2—Social, ethical, and human issues; 3—Technology productivity tools; 4—Technology communication tools; 5—Technology research tools; and 6—Technology problem-solving and decision-making tools.

Activities

1. Students form small groups and select photographs, sound bites, advertisements, and any other media sources encountered that they believe misrepresent the truth.

2. Students investigate the selected media sources and research the background issues involved and compile their findings in a group multimedia presentation and written report.

3. Students explore Civil War–picture manipulations. As a class, discuss reasons for the inaccuracies and what benefits, if any, were obtained by the publisher of the inaccurate media.

4. Demonstrate various technologies showing how easily businesses and governments can manipulate media sources for their own purposes.

5. Working with a partner, have students select an inaccurate media source and compose a letter or email to the publisher of the information expressing their concerns about the inaccuracies found.

6. Have students write using a quote from George Orwell's *1984* as a prompt: "There were the huge printing shops with their sub-editors, their typography experts, and their elaborately equipped studios for the faking of photographs" (p. 43). Have students discuss their responses using a discussion board or classroom listserv.

7. Discuss the issue of responsible use of technology and information. Start the discussion by reading this statement by Hal Buell of the Associated Press: "I don't think your ethics can be any better or any worse using electronic methods than they are using the classical methods. Ethics is in the mind. It is not in the tools you use" (Bossea, 1985, p. 30).

8. In small groups, discuss whether computer manipulation should never be allowed or allowed for news/editorial purposes. Have each student write a position paper.

9. Have students investigate the economics of "sensational" journalism. Do publications that misrepresent the truth make a profit? Have students create charts demonstrating the differences in earnings for several types of publications and news shows.

10. Have students investigate how media shape our attitude about war. Divide students into small groups and have each group select a war. Groups create multimedia or slide-show presentations to report findings.

11. Discuss heroic qualities. Have students select one of the following heroes to investigate the qualities of heroism their selection represents and the historical circumstances in which their selection emerged. Students determine the historical accuracy or plausibility of the heroic action attributed to their selections. Class develops a website to publish findings.

    - Ellen Ripley/Sarah Connor
    - T. E. Lawrence (*Lawrence of Arabia*)
    - Joan of Arc
    - Ho Chi Minh
    - Luke Skywalker
    - David and Goliath
    - Homeric heroes—Achilles

12. Discuss Jean Bethke Elshtain's claim that our "attitudes to war are determined by the traditional stories and histories of war we hear and read" (see her book *Women and War,* p. 32).

Tools and Resources

SOFTWARE

- Word processing
- Presentation
- HyperStudio
- Spreadsheet
- Image-manipulating
- Web-page creation

HARDWARE

- Color inkjet printer
- Large-screen monitor, LCD panel, or classroom TV connected to a computer
- Scanner
- VCR
- Film projector

WEBSITES

- The ABCs of Web Site Evaluation: Teaching Media Literacy in the Age of the Internet <http://www.connectedteacher.com/newsletter/abcs.asp>
- Evaluation of World Wide Web Sites: An Annotated Bibliography <http://ericir.syr.edu/ithome/digests/edoir9802.html>
- Critical Evaluation Information by Kathy Schrock <http://school.discovery.com/schrockguide/eval.html>
- The Gallup Organization <http://www.gallup.com/index.html>
- Center for Media and Public Affairs <http://www.cmpa.com/>
- The Pew Research Center: For the People and the Press <http://www.people-press.org/index.htm>
- American Society of Newspaper Editors <http://www.asne.org/>
- On Shrinking Soundbites by Mitchell Stephens <http://www.cjr.org/year/96/5/soundbites.asp>
- Project for Excellence in Journalism <http://www.journalism.org/>
- American Memory Collection: Does the Camera Ever Lie <http://memory.loc.gov/ammem/cwpcam/cwcam1.html>
- Photojournalism Ethics: Chapter Six <http://commfaculty.fullerton.edu/lester/writings/chapter6.html>
- Visual Literacy Bibliography <http://ivla.org/news/rdocs/vlbib/>
- Photographic Evidence, Naked Children, and Dead Celebrities: Digital Forgery and the Law <http://www.thirdamendment.com/digital.html>
- DIGITAL PHOTOGRAPHY: A Question of Ethics by Bonnie Meltzer <http://www.fno.org/may97/digital.html>
- Computer Graphics Issues & Ethics <http://cg1.ccsn.nevada.edu/kanet/grc118_web%20page/lecture_notes/issues_ethics.htm>

BOOKS

- *The Eyes of Time: Photojournalism in America* by Estelle Jussim (Boston: Little Brown, 1989)

- *Photography and the American Scene* by Robert Taft (New York: The MacMillan Co., 1938)
- *Fallen Soldiers: Reshaping the Memory of the World Wars* by George L. Mosse (New York: Oxford University Press, 1990)
- *Women and War* by Jean Bethke Elshtain (New York: Basic Books, 1987)
- *1984* by George Orwell (New York: Harcourt, Brace, 1949)

FILM
- Thomas Doherty, *Projections of War: Hollywood, American Culture, and World War Two* (New York: Columbia University Press, 1993)

MULTIDISCIPLINARY UNIT FOR SECONDARY GRADES (9–12)

Title of Unit: **Know Your Propositions**

Every year people seek to place new laws on election ballots. The need for new laws arises from concerns, political agendas, mistakes, and historical events. Using a current local proposition, students examine the arguments for and against the proposition and consequences if enacted or not enacted. Students take a position for or against the proposition, supporting their decision with arguments and facts. Students predict the proposition outcomes and follow the election returns.

No specific websites are provided for several reasons. First, searching for information about propositions is considered a valuable part of the learning process. Second, new-proposition websites arise and fall with each new election. Hence, any suggested site will likely be defunct by the time this reaches publication. Third, Internet searches can be tailored to fit any political region around the world.

In this unit students address the following National Educational Technology Standards (NETS) for Students Standards: 1—Basic operations and concepts; 2—Social, ethical, and human issues; 3—Technology productivity tools; 4—Technology communication tools; 5—Technology research tools; and 6—Technology problem-solving and decision-making tools.

Activities

1. Students research pending ballot propositions on the Internet and through other sources and list them according to election date and topic.
2. Working in small groups, have students investigate the sponsors of the propositions, specific interests of the sponsors, and the potential benefits to the sponsors should the propositions be enacted into law. Create a database to store this information.
3. Have students collect copies of the official propositions, along with the official position statements, including officially published arguments for and against the propositions.
4. Working with a partner, have students research the published arguments.
5. Have a chat session with government officials and interest groups about their positions on a proposition.
6. Students take a position, supporting their decision with arguments and facts, and present their findings using a slide show.

7. Discuss the language selected by the government to describe the propositions to see if there exists an attempt to conceal the true effect of a vote, for or against the propositions.
8. Students draft separate reports of their findings that will be incorporated into a single group report, which will be delivered to the news media for publication.
9. In small groups, students calculate the amount of money, both public and private, expended by both proponents and opponents of the various propositions. Have students write their own proposition listing better uses for the funds spent on the propositions. Create a website to publish the student-generated proposition.
10. Publish class findings and conclusions on a website. Suggested format for displaying database information of the proposition's analysis follows.

Proposition Number
    Title:
    Sponsor:
    Major Provisions:
    Background:
    Policy Considerations:
    Fiscal Impact:
    State Government:
    Local Government:
    Taxpayers:
    Support Arguments:
    Opposition Arguments:

- Have students email the media, interested businesses, and government officials a summary of their findings plus a request to visit their website.
- Working in small groups, have students create a WebQuest for another grade level.
- Have students predict proposition outcomes and follow election returns. Discuss prediction reasoning. Have them calculate the accuracy of their prediction.

Tools and Resources

SOFTWARE
- HyperStudio
- Presentation
- Database
- Spreadsheet
- Web-page creation

HARDWARE
- Color inkjet printer
- Large-screen monitor, LCD panel, or classroom TV connected to a computer
- Scanner

SUMMARY

This chapter presented four multidisciplinary units based on a powerful theme. Learning through the use of multidisciplinary, student-centered activities has been shown to be effective. The multidisciplinary units follow a format similar to ISTE's publication *National Educational Technology Standards for Students: Connecting Curriculum and Technology* (Thomas & Bitter, 2000). The format design facilitates teachers in planning, carrying out, and evaluating units effectively. Teachers are encouraged to discuss with other teachers their technology integration experiences.

These units are intended to serve as guidelines for the teacher who is in the process of integrating technology. Each unit provides a variety of activities, related technology, thematically relevant information, tools, and resources. In addition, each unit addresses content standards from two or more discipline areas while also addressing the National Educational Technology Standards for Students. When designing multidisciplinary units, and lesson activities as presented in Chapter 11, teachers should reflect on how technology enables them to teach content at greater depth and how their use of technology enhances instruction.

LEARNER ACTIVITIES

1. Compare and contrast the following terms: *interdisciplinary, multidisciplinary,* and *transdisciplinary.* Share your findings with the class by creating a multimedia presentation.

2. Prepare a multidisciplinary unit for a grade-level range following the sample format.

3. Develop a plan for storing software, manuals, and student diskettes in the classroom.

4. Connect to the EDUCAST site at <http://www.educast.com> and research the resources available through this website. Download several lesson plans for class discussion.

5. Adapt one of the multidisciplinary units in this chapter for a higher or lower grade level.

6. Create a new lesson plan for software not included in this chapter. Follow the same format as the lessons in this chapter do.

7. The National Council of Teachers of Mathematics (<http://www.nctm.org>), the Academy of Sciences (<http://www.nap.edu/readingroom/books/nses.html/>), the National Council for the Social Studies (<http://www.socialstudies.org/standards/>), and the National Council of Teachers of English and the International Reading Association (<http://www.ncte.org/standards/index.shtml>) have established curriculum standards. Develop a multidisciplinary unit addressing these curriculum standards and integrating appropriate technology.

8. Select a multidisciplinary unit from this chapter and integrate new methods of assessment such as portfolios.

BIBLIOGRAPHY

Albrecht, B., & Davis, P. (2000). Measurement and modeling. *Learning and Leading with Technology, 28*(2), 32–35, 39–41.

Bossen, H. (1985, Summer). Zone V: Photojournalism, ethics, and the electronic age. *Studies in Visual Communication, 30*(3), 27–33.

Cerrito, P. B. (1994). Writing, technology, and experimentation to explore the concepts of elementary statistics. *Mathematics and Computer Education, 28*(2), 141–153.

Cuoco, A. A., et al. (1995). Technology tips: Technology and the mathematics curriculum: Some new initiatives. *Mathematics Teacher, 88*(3), 236–240.

Cuoco, A. A., et al. (Eds.). (1994). Technology tips: Technology in perspective. *Mathematics Teacher, 87*(6), 450–452.

Educational Software Evaluation Consortium. (1998). *The 1998 educational software preview guide.* Eugene, OR: International Society for Technology in Education.

Frederick, B., & Frederick, H. (1988). What's in it for me? An in-service approach to help integrate computers. *SIOCC Bulletin, 4*(3–4), 16–17.

Gerber, M. M., et al. (1994). Computer-based dynamic assessment of multidigit multiplication. *Exceptional Children, 61*(2), 114–125.

Hoyles, C., & Noss, R. (1994). Technology tips: Dynamic geometry environments: What's the point? *Mathematics Teacher, 87*(9), 716–717.

Hsu, L., & Lee, G. D. (1991–1992). Providing access for students who are visually impaired. *The Computing Teacher, 19*(4), 8–9.

International Society for Technology in Education. (1998, June). *National educational technology standards for students.* Eugene, OR: Author.

James, R. K., & Lamb, C. E. (2000). Integrating science, mathematics, and technology in middle school technology-rich environments: A study of implementation and change. *School Science and Mathematics, 100*(1), 27–35.

Johnson, D. L., Maddux, C. D., & Candler, A. C. (Eds.). (1986). *Computers in the special education classroom.* New York: Haworth Press.

Johnson, J. M. (1998a). New software releases. *Learning and Leading with Technology, 25*(5), 42–44.

Johnson, J. M. (1998b). Software reviews. *Learning and Leading with Technology, 25*(5), 45–51.

Lehman, J. R. (1994). Technology use in the teaching of mathematics and science in elementary schools. *School Science and Mathematics, 94*(4), 194–202.

Mason, M. (1983). Special education: A time of opportunity. *Electronic Learning, 2*(8), 54–55.

Milone, M. N., Jr. (1990). Painless grammar: Revising with the help of a grammar checker. *Classroom Computer Learning, 10*(6), 18–23.

Nelson, T. B., & Rogel, J. (1995). Operation Sluggie and other software products from the fourth grade. *The Computing Teacher, 22*(5), 39–41.

O'Connor, J., & Brie, R. (1994). Mathematics and science partnerships: Products, people, performance, and multimedia. *The Computing Teacher, 22*(1), 27–30.

Only the best. (1997–1998). Alexandria, VA: Association for Supervision and Curriculum Development.

Orwell, G. (1949). *1984.* New York: Harcourt Brace.

Pastorek, M. J., & Craig, L. (2000). Technical frience: Integrating science, foreign language, and social studies. *Learning and Leading with Technology, 28*(2), 18–21.

Phillips, R. J., & Pead, D. (1994). Multimedia resources in the mathematics classroom. *Journal of Computer Assisted Learning, 10*(4), 216–228.

Rice, M. (1995). Issues surrounding the integration of technology into the K–12 classroom. *Interpersonal Computing and Technology Journal, 3*(1), 67–81.

Schipper, D. (1991). Practical ideas: Literature, computers, and students with special needs. *The Computing Teacher, 19*(2), 33–37.

Selby, L., et al. (1994). Teachers' perceptions of learning with information technology in mathematics and science education: A report on Project Prometheus. *Journal of Computing in Teacher Education, 10*(3), 24–30.

Solomon, G. (1989). Computers help students see art in a different hue. *Electronic Learning, 9*(2), 16–18.

Stahl, G., et al. (1995). Share globally, adapt locally: Software assistance to locate and tailor curriculum posted to the Internet. *Computers and Education, 24*(3), 237–246.

Thomas, J., & Bitter, G. G. (2000). (Eds.). *National educational technology standards for students: Connecting curriculum and technology.* Eugene, OR: International Society for Technology in Education.

Thompson, E. O. (1989). Using the geometric supposer: Triangles. *The Computing Teacher, 17*(1), 30–34.

Vernot, D. (1987). New power in social studies software. *Electronic Technology, 6*(8), 36–37.

Waring, B. (1998). The 1998 New Media Hyper Awards. *New Media, 8*(3), 36–49.

Watkins, M. W., & Abran, S. (1985). Reading CAI with first grade students. *The Computing Teacher, 12*(7), 43–45.

Wepner, S. B. (1990). Computers and whole language: A "novel" frontier. *The Computing Teacher, 17*(5), 24–28.

Widmer, C. C., & Sheffield, L. J. (1994). Putting the fun into functions through the use of manip·, computers, and calculators. *School Science and Mathematics, 94*(7), 350–355.

CHAPTER 13

DATA ANALYSIS
AND SIMULATIONS

FOCUS QUESTIONS

1. How can teachers develop data analysis skills in their students?
2. What factors must teachers consider when planning data analysis activities?
3. What are the benefits of using simulations?

Chapters 11 and 12 presented several learning activities involving data analysis. With the influx of information, skill development in using data to reason and to make statistical-based decisions is necessary for students to become informed citizens and intelligent consumers (NCTM, 2000). However, teachers are reluctant to teach data analysis for several reasons: lack of time, skill, and motivation (Goodman Research Group, 1998; Russell, 1990). Employing the use of simulations may help reduce this reluctance. Simulations facilitate exploring and understanding problem solving, especially in the field of mathematics. As far back as 1972, cognitive scientists used simulations to help develop and validate learning theories (Newell & Simon, 1972). This chapter takes a closer look at data analysis and simulations, and offers suggestions and resources to support teachers' integration of these technology-based inquiry and problem-solving approaches.

DATA ANALYSIS

The technological discipline of *data analysis* emerged from the union of statistics, computer science, pattern recognition, artificial intelligence, and machine learning. Data analysis is the process of transforming data into information. Similarly, information evolves from data in the process of answering a question. Therefore, the question is the key part of the process. Computers have made it possible to aggregate several data sets into huge databases. Although problems arise—for instance, storage—when attempting to manage and make sense of large data sets, the time invested leads to the development of new software tools, with the expectation that the mined data will lead to better decision making.

In 1970 statisticians began to question the traditional paradigm of data analysis. The traditional process began by formulating a hypothesis, followed by collecting data, and ended by testing the hypothesis. To address their questioning of the traditional data analysis process, statisticians began to use open-ended data exploration methods. John W. Tukey of Princeton University and AT&T Bell Labs established a new approach called "exploratory data analysis." Tukey (1977) suggested investigating data as a detective investigates a crime scene with an open mind and few, if any, assumptions. Tukey saw data analysis as a mixture of science and art. The process of analyzing data includes the creative search for meaning as well as a systematic method for guiding the search. The goal of exploratory data analysis (EDA) is quite different from the traditional paradigm of hypothesis testing also known as confirmatory data analysis. EDA seeks to find "patterns in data for hypothesis generation and refinement" (Behrens & Smith, 1996, p. 952).

Computers are problem-solving tools that help implement a systematic method of exploration. Certain valuable cognitive skills warrant special emphasis for PreK–12 students;

- The ability to analyze a variety of problems and understand how to select and use productivity tools to find solutions
- The ability to understand the theoretical background to use software programs to solve different types of problems encountered in both personal and professional activities

Problem-solving activities help students learn how to collect, interpret, and represent data. In the long run, these computer-assisted activities help students deepen their understanding of using data analysis to answer questions, solve problems, and make decisions in business, politics, and research.

The National Council of Teachers of Mathematics (NCTM) advocates having students generate questions that require collecting and exploring data. The NCTM Data Analysis and Probability Standard (2000) for PreK–12 students has four goals:

1. Formulate questions that can be addressed with data; and collect, organize, and display relevant data to answer them.
2. Select and use appropriate statistical methods to analyze data.
3. Develop and evaluate inferences and predictions that are based on data.
4. Understand and apply basic concepts of probability.

The NCTM recommends a strong emphasis on developing data analysis skills in all grades as well as progressively increasing the sophistication of the concepts and procedures. This ensures that by the end of high school students have a strong statistical background and knowledge of using computers as a problem-solving tool.

SIMULATIONS

A *simulation* is the process of imitating a real situation or object with a set of mathematical formulae. Computer simulations can imitate weather conditions, chemical reactions, nuclear accidents, medical techniques, costs required to produce a particular design, biological processes, cockpit and spacecraft systems, and product safety testing to name just a few. Some situations or objects are more problematic to create than others relative to their ability to be reduced to mathematical data and equations. An important factor when creating simulations is to clearly define the situation or object and determine the most important factors. Simulations are used to test theories of causal relationships.

How can teachers effectively incorporate simulations into the curriculum? The critical task is to coherently integrate the simulation software as a vital part of the curriculum, not as an add-on. This means students use the simulation for an extended time period and should be engaged in extension activities based on the thinking skills embedded in the simulation (Henderson, Klemes, & Eshet, 2000). Computer simulations can be used but are not limited to

1. Visualize the invisible
2. Manipulate variables, observe results, and draw conclusions
3. Facilitate role playing

Simulations can be created with web pages (HTML), the scripting language of Javascript, authoring environments such as Director, animation environments such as Flash, and the programming language of Java. Commercial software programs such as KidSim and Microworlds allow students to create their own simulations. The simulated worlds students create have characters, who have rules, appearances, and properties.

STATISTICS

Simulation software and data analysis activities help develop the central elements of statistics. *Statistics* is defined as a set of methods used to collect, analyze, present, and interpret data. Whereas a computer assists in summarizing data, statistical methods focus on the interpretation of the output in order to make inferences and predictions. Young students start off working with simple classroom census data. At this age, the teacher may elect to generate the question at first. For example, the problem of deciding on a breakfast menu for an elementary school could begin with the question "What do kids like to eat for breakfast?" Students collect data to answer the question. The notion of sampling is difficult to develop. However, upper elementary and middle school students start to acquire an understanding about statistical inference. Before students leave high school, they should know that statistical techniques are used daily in work settings to solve problems and make informed decisions (NCTM, 2000).

Use of software programs as well as the websites that follow may be used as resources for the creation of curriculum units, educational resources, and learning activities. Yeo and Tan (1999) recommend designing simulations to "provide dynamic problem situations for learners," which foster a "theoretical understanding of the interactions in the simulated environment through direct feedback from their actions" (p. 70). This can be done by encouraging three types of feedback: self, peer, and teacher. Time should be provided for students to (1) reflect and write about their simulated experience and (2) share their reactions (Tomlinson, 2000). Students need to understand that computer systems and software programs are designed to perform specific jobs. This helps them acquire the skill and knowledge of selecting the best tools to accomplish a task, solve a problem, and/or make a decision based on available data.

When using simulations and other problem-solving programs, remember never to rely on the software to teach higher-order thinking skills. Students need teachers to help them make connections. Encourage students to explain their thinking frequently when working collaboratively. Brainstorming tools such as Inspiration help students structure a strategy needed to solve a problem by flowcharting or explore the problem domain by creating concept maps.

SIMULATION WEBSITES AND DATA RESOURCES

Free Simulations

BUSINESS SIMULATION–LEMONADE STAND
<http://www.littlejason.com/lemonade/index.html>
An online game that teaches the basics of supply and demand

CHEMISTRY SIMULATIONS <http://ir.chem.cmu.edu/irProject/>
The Ir Ydium Project at Carnegie Mellon University funded by the National Science Foundation to create simulation-based chemistry learning environments

COMPUTER TRAFFIC SIMULATION: GRAPHICAL VERSION
< http://www.math.toronto.edu/mathnet/carcompet/simulation.html>
Provides a simple model of traffic flow

PHYSICS JAVA APPLETS <http://home.a-city.de/walter.fendt/phe/phe.htm>
38 applets available for download covering buoyancy, optics, and the theory of relativity to name just a few

SIM SCIENCE <http://www.simscience.org/>
Devoted to areas of science in which computer simulations are at the forefront of discovery; provides access to four simulations: membranes, fluid flow, cracking dams, and crackling noise

SIMSURFACE <http://storm.shodor.org/simsurf/simsurfinfo.html/>
A simulation designed to solve the problem of minimization of potential energy using the computational technique of simulated annealing and the relaxation method

STOCK MARKET SIMULATION—TAKING STOCK
< http://www.santacruz.k12.ca.us/~jpost/projects/TS/TS.html>
An online interactive telecommunications project based on the inner workings of the stock market

THINKQUEST <http://www.thinkquest.org/library/>
Archived site of student-generated ThinkQuest Contest entries. Enter "simulation" in the search box to locate simulation entries

UNITED NATIONS SIMULATION—THE ELECTRONIC UNITED NATIONS
<http://www.simulations.com/eun/>
A United Nations simulation where classrooms become "classroom countries" and interact with other "classroom countries"

Activity Examples

NCTM SIMULATION EXAMPLE
<http://standards.nctm.org/document/eexamples/chap5/5.2/index.htm>
Grades 3–5 understanding distance, speed, and time relationships using simulation software

NCTM ELECTRONIC EXAMPLE OF USING DATA SETS AVAILABLE ON THE INTERNET
<http://standards.nctm.org/document/eexamples/chap5/5.4/index.htm>

THE CHAOS GAME <http://math.bu.edu./DYSYS/applets/chaos-game.html>
An online game designed to improve students' geometric intuition and algorithmic thinking

EASY FIBONACCI PUZZLES
<http://www.mcs.surrey.ac.uk/Personal/R.Knott/Fibonacci/fibpuzzles.html>
Provides puzzles that have Fibonacci numbers as their answers

STATISTICAL TEACHING ACTIVITIES <http://www.statcan.ca/english/kits/teach.htm>
Categorized by grade bands; provides interactive exercises focusing on data analysis and survey skills maintained and developed by Statistics Canada

STATISCOPE BY MIKAEL BONNIER
<http://www.df.lth.se/~mikaelb/statiscope/statiscope.shtml>
Interactive environment (Java applet) for summarizing data and descriptive statistical charts

THE WEBWINDS <http://webwinds.jpl.nasa.gov/>
An interactive data system for collecting, representing, and analyzing data, and statistical decision making

Other Online Resources and Data Sets

MATHEMATICS ARCHIVES <http://archives.math.utk.edu/software.html>
A collection of software, abstracts, and reviews

BUREAU OF CENSUS DATA—POPULATION DATA SET
<http://factfinder.census.gov/servlet/BasicFactsServlet> <http://www.census.gov/main/www/access.html>
A comprehensive site to locate population, housing, economic, and geographic data

NATIONAL CENTER FOR HEALTH STATISTICS <http://www.cdc.gov/nchs/>
Federal government agency provides statistical information to guide actions and policies for the purpose of improving the health of the American people; see its data warehouse at <http://www.cdc.gov/nchs/datawh.htm>

DR. B'S WIDE WORLD OF WEB DATA <http://research.ed.asu.edu/siip/webdata/>
Archive of data sets organized into topics areas; for example, education, crime and law, economics, and medicine and health

FORBES.COM <http://www.forbes.com/>
Source for business data; for example, a comparison of health benefits and 401(k) plans

LIBERTY LIBRARY OF CONSTITUTIONAL CLASSICS
<http://www.constitution.org/liberlib.htm>
Online collection of classic books and other works on constitutional governments ranging from antiquity to the present

U.S. FEDERAL ELECTION COMMISSION <http://www.fec.gov>
Comprehensive information on the voting process

Problem Activity 1: Business

This activity gives students experience in real-world business operations. Students develop decision-making skills by scaling up a simulated business.

Have students use the Lemonade Stand simulation at <http://www.littlejason.com/lemonade/index.html>. Provide students sufficient time to interact with the simulation and reflect on their experiences. Then ask them to conceptualize and define a problem resulting from the experience that they would like to analyze. Help them, if necessary, to formulate a question based on their problem spaces. Have them explore the solution by increasing the size and scope of their lemonade businesses. Challenge students to increase business profits and incorporate standard business operations, including inventory, sales, marketing, taxes, payroll, employee benefits, and personnel issues such as training. Have students explore purchasing and labor expenditures, and analyze consumer behavior and economic trends to assist their decision making about operational procedures and policies. Compare results and discuss their solution strategies. Determine which practices result in higher profits and why. Challenge students to form corporations and stage hostile takeovers. Have them work through the stock market simulation at <http://www.santacruz.k12.ca.us/~jpost/projects/TS/TS.html> in small groups (perhaps the corporate groups they formed). Challenge student corporations to offer stock options to their employees. Have them appoint board members and hold board meetings to discuss business operations. Plan a field trip to visit a local hospital or utility holding company's board meeting. Have students create a profit-and-loss statement as a culminating activity. For closure, discuss their responses to the experience.

Problem Activity 2: Politics

This activity gives students experience in real-world sampling and polling situations. Students develop skills in techniques of sampling and predicting from a sample as well as developing strategies for organizing and managing the data.

Create an election simulation based upon Kids Voting results based on either the last general election or any current issue before the U.S. Senate or other legislative body. Have pairs of students use the simulation for a designated period of time. Students should reflect on their experience and identify a problem to investigate, for instance, voter irregularity. They formulate questions such as "Does ballot design affect voting patterns?" Students divide according to the current U.S. registration ratios between the two major parties and any third-party "wannabes." Students campaign for their candidates and/or issues for a specified period of time and create supporting propaganda, which will be displayed in the classroom. Throughout the specified period, selected students in support of each candidate or issue will make speeches and hold press conferences. At the end of the selected time, an election will occur. If students are voting for candidates only, students will vote only to elect "electors," who will then gather later to actually elect the candidates of their choice. Students create their own ballot box and secure the ballots. Students create a program to automate the voting process on a computer. Following the voting students will compare, contrast, and critique results and procedures. The teacher or elected committee will rule upon challenges to any requested procedure. Students learn about issues relevant to any modern election, the effect of third-party vote dilution, as well as the need for coalitions to further their parties' interests.

SUMMARY

This chapter took a closer look at data analysis and simulations with suggested resources to support teachers' integration of these technology-based inquiry and problem solving approaches. Skill development in using data to reason and to make statistical-based decisions is necessary for students to become informed citizens and intelligent consumers (NCTM, 2000). A brief history of data analysis highlighted a new approach called "exploratory data analysis." The next section introduced the use of computers as problem solving tools, the NCTM Data Analysis and Probability Standard, and NCTM recommendation to develop data analysis skills in all grades. To help teachers teach data analysis, the use of simulations is recommended.

A stimulation is the process of imitating a real situation or object with a set of mathematical formulae. Simulations should be integrated as a vital part of the curriculum rather than an add-on. Simulations can be used, but are not limited, to:

1. Visualize the invisible
2. Manipulate variables, observing results, and drawing conclusions
3. Facilitate role-playing

Simulations software and data analysis activities help develop the central elements of statistics. Statistics is a set of methods used to collect, analyze, present, and interpret data. Two problem activities were provided as examples of using simulations and data analysis. A listing of free web-based simulations and data sets will help teachers develop learning activities and materials for classroom use.

LEARNER ACTIVITIES

1. Use the Lemonade Stand simulation. Create activities that extend the simulation and deepen students' understanding of data analysis. Reflect on how the computer simulation will influence students' thinking and behavior. Describe in detail how you plan to scaffold their learning.

2. Go to the NCTM site at <http://standards.nctm.org/document/eexamples/chap5/5.2/index.htm>. Complete the task as directed. Scroll down the page to the section entitled **Additional Tasks and Questions.** Select one of the three tasks to complete as directed. As

suggested, reflect on this question: What important ideas about functions and representing change over time can students learn while working on this activity?

3. Incorporate a data analysis activity into a unit or learning activity for your content area.

4. Integrate collaborative learning into one of the exploration activities. Try the activity with and without collaboration. Determine the best practice providing details on the context, grade level, and other relevant variables.

5. Create a web-based simulation to explore a problem in your content domain. Field-test your simulation. Use appropriate data analytic tools and statistical methods to formatively evaluate your simulation and refine the process based on your results.

6. After a thorough exploration of the simulation and data resources, post a question on your class discussion board or appropriate listserv to prompt a discussion of the theoretical principles underlying software programs and computer systems.

BIBLIOGRAPHY

Behrens, J. T., & Smith, M. L. (1996). Data and data analysis. In D. C. Berliner & R. C. Calfee (Eds.), *Handbook of educational psychology* (pp. 945–989). New York: Simon & Schuster Macmillan.

Goodman Research Group, Inc. (1998). *An evaluation of the testbed for telecollaboration.* Cambridge, MA: Author.

Hartley, K. (2000). Online simulations: Tools for inquiry-based science classrooms. *Learning and Leading with Technology, 28*(3), 32–35.

Henderson, L., Klemes, J., & Eshet, Y. (2000). Just playing a game? Educational simulation software and cognitive outcomes. *Journal of Educational Computing Research, 22*(1), 105–129.

Konold, C., Coulter, B., & Feldman, A. (2000). Engaging students with data. *Learning and Leading with Technology, 28*(3), 50–55.

National Council of Teachers of Mathematics. (2000). *Principles and standards for school mathematics.* Reston, VA: Author.

Newell, A., & Simon, H. (1972). *Human problem-solving.* Englewood Cliffs, NJ: Prentice-Hall.

Russell, S. J. (1990). Issues in training teachers to teach statistics in the elementary school: A world of uncertainty. In A. Hawkins (Ed.), *Training teachers to teach statistics.* Proceedings of the International Statistical Institute Round Table Conference (pp. 59–71). Voorburg, The Netherlands: International Statistical Institute.

Russell, S. J., Schifter, D., & Bastable, V. (2001). *Developing mathematical ideas: Collecting, representing and analyzing data.* Parsippany, NJ: Dale Seymour Publications.

Tomlinson, B. (2000). Using simulations on materials development courses. *Simulation and Gaming, 31*(2), 152–170.

Tukey, J. W. (1977). *Exploratory data analysis.* Reading, MA: Addison-Wesley.

Yeo, G. K., & Tan, S. T. (1999). Toward a multilingual, experiential environment for learning decision technology. *Simulation and Gaming, 30*(1), 70–82.

CHAPTER 14

MATHEMATICAL MODELING

FOCUS QUESTIONS

1. How are simulation and modeling activities different? Under what conditions is one approach more effective than the other?
2. How should a spreadsheet activity be structured?
3. What are the benefits to using modeling activities?

This chapter extends the introduction to data analysis and problem solving in Chapter 13 by discussing the use of mathematical modeling, spreadsheets, and a programming language. With the emergence of new data analysis tools and new types of data problems, novel types of models are consequently required to deal with them. Examples of these models include rule-based knowledge representations as used in expert systems, neural networks, genetic algorithms, multivariate adaptive regression splines, computer-intensive estimation methods such as the Markov chain, Monte Carlo methods, and statistical databases, which need operations such as datacube.

The modeling process is evolutionary. There are always other influences or factors, not anticipated in the first model or prototype, that interfere with prediction accuracy. Re-iterating steps in the modeling process, making improvements to define the problem, constructing the model, and improving data collection techniques improve not only the product but also the conceptualizing process. The refinement of a model may progress ad infinitum if using a trial-and-error approach and still achieve only an arbitrary degree of accuracy. However, in the context of data analysis, an extremely sophisticated data analytic technique can data mine the information and achieve more predictive power.

A strategy for data analysis descriptively plans the steps, decisions, and procedures to follow when analyzing data to build a model or answer a question. Generally stated, the steps are

1. Define the problem.
2. Extract and identify the most important factors.
3. Construct a model to describe the shape of the reduced data.

Effective procedures are called algorithms. Flowcharts are used to graphically represent algorithms, which are detailed sequences of simple steps needed to solve a problem. A problem is unsolvable if no algorithm can solve it and, if a decision problem, undecidable if no algorithm can decide it.

MATHEMATICAL MODELING

There are different types of models. For instance, a miniature replica of a spacecraft used to study design features is a *physical model*. Examples of this model type can be found at science fair exhibits in which students represent the solar system using a box with balls of various colors and sizes hanging from strings. Another, and perhaps the most useful, type is a *conceptual model*. For instance, a diagram of the water cycle is used to describe the behavior of the system, in this case water. When the language of mathematics is utilized to describe the system's behavior, a *mathematical model* is created. For example, representing the shape of the Earth as a sphere provides a mathematical model. In this case, elementary geometry is used to describe the system.

Models, both physical and conceptual, are problem-solving tools because they are easily manipulated and changed as needed. Models assist experimentation, which aims to achieve an understanding and generate new information about the modeled system. Some systems may be too complex or too inaccessible to explore in their original setting. In many business and scientific situations, the design and use of models in planning and production processes are critical. The process of modeling follows these steps:

1. Observing a system or problem
2. Constructing a mental image or model
3. Identifying important variables and constants (parameters)
4. Determining relationships
5. Developing equation(s) to express relationships
6. Testing
7. Revising

Modeling is used when simulations are not a feasible approach. Modeling activities can be used to demonstrate change. Additionally, modeling is a technique of expression and explanation. For an excellent learning activity for the secondary grade level, see ISTE's *National Educational Technology Standards for Students: Connecting Curriculum and Technology's* (2000) Chaos and Beyond (pp. 122–129 or search their website at <http://cnets.iste.org/index2ns.html>). Another source for a learning activity is Road Maps, which teaches the reader how to identify different kinds of systems and how to model these systems using a computer (see <http://sysdyn.mit.edu/road-maps/home.html>).

Problem Activity 1

Mathematical modeling can occur in nonmathematical contexts. Develop a mathematical model of how you plan to read this textbook. Share your model in a small group (no more than four). Work together to create a group model. Diagram or make a flowchart of your group process. How did your group achieve consensus?

Problem Activity 2

Consider the following real-world problem:

> What is the cost of illiteracy to a community? In groups of three or four, brainstorm the possible cost areas using a brainstorming tool such as Inspiration to develop a concept map. Identify the important variables and parameters. Decide on a data collection plan. After the data are collected and graphically represented, construct a mathematical model by developing an equation representing the relationships between variables and parameters. Test using what-if questions and refine your model. Would using a different definition of illiteracy change your model?

Mathematical modeling can be applied to additional real-world problems. Some examples are predicting wildlife populations, costs of long-distance phone calls, irrigation flow rates, and deciding on the fastest checkout line at a grocery store.

Modeling is effective in education. Due to changes and shifts in population, it is important for educational institutions to assess their immediate future needs, as well as long-term ones. By asking what-if questions based on census information and other known statistics, school districts, colleges, and universities can be better prepared to offer quality education. In the classroom, probability situations can be modeled with a computerized framework such as a spreadsheet. A spreadsheet model is created and its figure displayed; the user then asks the computer "what if" a specific value were to be changed. The value can be a change in actual numbers or an increase or decrease by a specified percentage rate. By experimenting with various probabilities, students can examine the basic theory of probability.

SPREADSHEETS

Spreadsheets are very useful for modeling activities (Scaife & Wellington, 1993) and are fast becoming programming environments (Carson, 1997). As explained earlier in Chapter 2, the spreadsheet's array of rows and columns may be organized in such a way as to be easily understandable to the reader. Because each piece of datum entered into the spreadsheet is considered as it relates to the other data, any change made in one part affects the whole spreadsheet. Subsequently, information can be manipulated to reflect potential change or what-if questions in any or all sections of the spreadsheet. This capability makes spreadsheets a useful tool to detect mathematical change. Having students graph and chart using spreadsheets helps them visualize change and learn the advantages and disadvantages of different graphical representations.

More on Spreadsheets: Their History and Use

The electronic spreadsheet made its debut in 1979, a creation of two Harvard Business School graduate students, Daniel Bricklin and Robert Frankston. They named their program VisiCalc, and it became the prototype for many other software programs that formed the first generation of electronic spreadsheets.

The second generation came on the scene with the introduction of Lotus 1-2-3 in 1982. This program was unique in being the first integrated software program. An integrated software program blends several different programs so that information can be presented in various forms. For example, a graphics option allows the user to create visual aids, such as line graphs, vertical and horizontal bar graphs, and pie charts. In this way, the figures from the spreadsheet can be converted into graphs that show at a glance what the user wishes to communicate about the financial picture.

Another option contained in Lotus 1-2-3 is database management. A database is an electronic filing system in which large volumes of data (information) can be stored and organized. For instance, names, addresses, phone numbers, and account numbers entered into a database that can then be sorted alphabetically, numerically, or in any other way that will be helpful to the user. In an integrated program, any of the needed stored information can be retrieved from the database and inserted into the spreadsheet. The time saved in locating and adding data to a spreadsheet made this new generation of software a welcome addition to the electronic spreadsheet family.

The most recent addition to this family, and the beginning of the third generation, is the integrated software program with extended capabilities. It adds word processing, expanded spreadsheet size, and communications between computers. Word processing allows text to be added to the report. In this way, an explanation of the spreadsheet figures or the graphic pictures can complete a financial report.

Another improvement is the potential size of spreadsheets. Spreadsheet programs vary in the numbers of rows and columns available, but average size is much larger now than what was originally offered. Any number of these columns and rows may be used, depending on the needs of the user and the memory capacity of the computer. Although only a small portion of this total picture appears on the computer screen at one time, the user may move around within the spreadsheet to display any part of it.

Yet another improvement in this latest generation of spreadsheet programs is the ability of computers to communicate with each other. Through the new technology of telecommunications, computers in different locations can communicate by telephone lines and exchange data as needed. Examples of programs combining all of the preceding options are AppleWorks and Microsoft Office 2000. Chapter 2 discussed the use of spreadsheets in education. The following section presents additional practical applications related to problem solving and data analysis.

Analysis and Projection

Spreadsheet information is essential in analyzing the financial condition of any organization. Spreadsheets also make analysis of statistical information more manageable and much faster. Analysis, then, is one of the more important uses of electronic spreadsheets. A natural outcome of analysis is projection for the future. Let's look now at the value of spreadsheets in these two areas.

In business and other organizations, analysis is the examination and evaluation of data to measure their impact on the particular organization for which it is being performed. Spreadsheets are an excellent way to compare data. To accomplish this, spreadsheets can be combined, both in part and in total. By defining a range of cells, rows, or columns, any part of a spreadsheet may be retrieved and made a part of others. In this way, very complicated data can be displayed for comparison. Windowing, discussed earlier, is most helpful for these operations.

As in education, planning for other public and social programs is dependent upon knowing what will happen if certain changes take place within society. Changes in the political climate, for instance, have an impact on almost every area of life. The educational community will obviously benefit quite as much as private business and industry by using the analytic properties of electronic spreadsheets.

By combining the information gained from analysis of a spreadsheet with expectations for the future, it is possible to project what may happen. Projection is the predicting, or forecasting, of what may be logically expected to occur in the future based on what we know about the past. There are three basic types of planning for the future: *operational, tactical,* and *strategic.* There are also two basic areas where planning is necessary—expense and income.

In the area of expense, operational planning is the simplest and covers a period of only a few months at a time. It deals with day-to-day operations. Usually done by lower-level managers, this type of planning obviously is short-term and therefore requires less complex spreadsheet information than do other types. An example of operational planning is the adjustment of teaching staff and classroom space.

Tactical planning is for an intermediate period, perhaps covering a time span of one to three years. This includes planned stages of development working toward long-term goals. An example of this type of planning is the revision of school budgets in response to projected increased enrollment.

Strategic planning occurs at the highest level of management and addresses the overall long-range welfare of the organization. Examples of this level of planning are direction of growth, curriculum development, and expansion of school districts.

Future income also requires planning and projection on the part of school administrators. For instance, expected changes in income due to school bond issues can be included in planning.

For higher-level educational institutions, administrators must predict potential changes in student population and project income based on tuition and fees. For instance, funds allotted from other agencies may change from time to time. For this and other reasons, planning for the future is essential to a smooth operation.

Government agencies have a similar need to make projections based on changes in population, income, and societal needs. One of the most obvious areas of public service is transportation. How many freeways to build? What is the projected need for public transportation? This is only one of many services provided by local, state, and national government agencies that may be better analyzed through the use of electronic spreadsheets.

Problem Activity 3

In small groups look at census data from your state. (Visit <http://factfinder.census.gov/java_prod/dads.ui.homePage.HomePage> for Bureau of Census data or <http://www.census.gov/main/www/access.html> for data sets.) Look at the available spreadsheet data files from the Crime & Justice Electronic Data Abstracts' website (<http://www.ojp.usdoj.gov/bjs/dtdata.htm#index>). Select a data set to download. Create a spreadsheet to compare the downloaded files. Look for a mathematical change to detect a pattern. Try out different types of representations such as maps or graphs. Based on exploratory data analysis, develop a question to explore using this sentence stem: Is there a relationship between xxx and yyy? Write a formula that represents the relationship. Test the formula. What happens numerically? Graph the change. Create what-if questions to further explore the changes. Present your findings to the class and discuss the results.

LOGO AS A LEARNING TOOL

As noted earlier, an important part of computer literacy is to familiarize students with the process of programming computers to perform specific functions. With the advent of languages such as Logo, programming skills can be taught to even the youngest students. The use of computer programming need no longer be limited to specialized secondary courses.

Many people have found that they can learn a great deal about programming by simply typing into the computer a Logo program that has been written by another person. This technique can be quite effective in the classroom. The student gains a sense of control over the computer by entering a set of program instructions and then observing the computer carrying out the instructions. Students come to understand some of the fundamentals in this manner. For example, they see that the computer can do only that which it has been programmed to do. They see the need for very accurate and concise instructions to avoid errors. They begin to understand that the computer can work for them once they learn to communicate with it.

For this reason, it is a good idea to begin exploring programming with user-friendly languages such as Logo. Students need to see that the computer can understand commands in plain English and that programming languages are not overwhelmingly complicated sets of numbers and esoteric symbols. Designing activities using Logo as the programming language is a good starting place because Logo is relatively accessible and understandable to students. Other options are Microworlds or Geo Logo.

A number of books have been published with public domain programs that students can key into the computer for practice. Some perform basic calculations to solve problems or track numerical data and others play games. The programs range from very simple to very complex, providing practice for students of all grade and skill levels. A word of caution is necessary, however. Not all the programs to be found have been debugged carefully. Students may be frustrated if they spend hours typing and correcting their typed instructions only to find that the program does not work as promised even when the instructions are typed correctly. Teachers who possess strong programming skills can help their students out of such difficulties. Teachers with less experience in this area may do well to read reviews of the materials before using them in the classroom.

Another good source of programs for students to use is popular Logo computer periodicals. Some of these periodicals feature program instructions (also called code) and documentation on a regular basis. Many school libraries subscribe to these periodicals, so the materials are often readily available to teachers and students.

The following Logo activity focuses on the area of mathematics. Gifted or highly motivated students can be encouraged to venture out on their own by tailoring the programs to perform additional functions as well. The activity focuses on using the computer as a tool for problem solving, which is really the forte of the computer. The authors suggest that teachers introduce programming early and in a nonthreatening way by integrating programming skills into subject areas across the curriculum. Specifically, because the computer is an excellent mathematical tool, it makes good sense to integrate the use of Logo to teach and explore mathematics. Students can learn programming skills with relative ease while they are mastering mathematical concepts. Teachers who want to introduce Logo to explore mathematics in their classrooms can use the following activity.

Teachers should use their own judgment in adapting the activity for their grade levels and use with their own students. How well students perform in programming depends on a number of factors, including previous experience, attitudes toward computers, and perceived value of programming skills. Class discussions conducted before programming activities are presented can aid the teacher in discovering and exploring these crucial factors.

Activity Title: **Problem Solving with Logo**

Grade-Level Range: 4 to 6

Purpose.   In this activity students

- Use Logo to solve mathematical and geometrical problems
- Explore the concept of symmetry
- Address the following National Educational Technology Standards (NETS) for Students Standards: 3—Technology productivity tools and 6—Technology problem-solving and decision-making tools

Activity Preparation

- Students need to be familiar with Logo commands used to draw shapes.
- Prepare and copy activity sheets.
- Draw several simple shapes on paper. Then using the mirror, introduce the students to the concept of mirror images.

Activity Procedures

1. Have students write Logo programs that will produce mirror images of the shapes displayed on the activity sheet.
2. Students test their programs to see how well they run.
3. Assist students in performing any debugging that may be required in order for the programs to recreate the shapes accurately.

Tools and Resources

- computer
- compatible Logo software
- activity sheet
- mirror

Assessment.   Do the students' programs draw mirror images of the shapes on the activity sheet? Have students been successful in locating and correcting errors in their programs?

Comments.   Another interesting experience would be to give students only one half of a shape so that the mirror images they create would complete the picture. Simple shapes such as houses or faces can be used effectively.

SUMMARY

Computers have been used by business, education, government, and individuals to organize and analyze all kinds of information. Mathematical modeling is an effective problem-solving approach used to represent systems. The spreadsheet is a useful tool for managing financial and statistical information in data analysis contexts. Called an electronic spreadsheet when done by a computer, this technique has become one of the most effective time-savers of our new technology.

From the prototype created by two Harvard students in 1979, to the latest sophisticated integrated software packages, electronic spreadsheets have grown from a useful tool to an indispensable fact of life. All areas of daily existence have been influenced by this development.

In education, spreadsheets are used in various ways. These include teaching (e.g., accounting, math, and science classes), maintaining student records, budgeting for both the entire school and various groups within it, and management of data by research groups.

Government agencies are also big users of electronic spreadsheets. They manage and manipulate vast amounts of data, analyze changes in all areas of society, and plan for the future needs of communities and the nation.

We as individuals benefit from this new tool as well. We use electronic spreadsheets for personal banking, household management, tax records, and budgeting.

Each of us is influenced either directly or indirectly by the widespread use of spreadsheets in the real world. For this reason, the practical application of spreadsheets has been stressed in this chapter. To implement a spreadsheet, a user must be familiar with the terms, modes, commands, formulas, and functions presented here.

Once a spreadsheet has been created and data entered, it may be used to analyze the data it contains and to make projections for the future based on that data and other knowledge and expectations. What-if statements may be used to set up theoretical conditions; the spreadsheet then calculates the potential results. The instant answers given by this method save many hours of tedious labor, without mathematical error.

Spreadsheets serve us all in many ways. In some cases, we use them to make our individual tasks easier. In other instances, we benefit from their use in business, government, and education.

This chapter presented two problem activities and one learning activity to assist teachers in using the computer to teach mathematical skills. As has been noted, even the youngest students can begin acquiring skills that are necessary in writing instructions for computers to follow.

The activities can be adapted to the various grade levels with minor modifications. All of the activities are aimed to develop problem-solving and data analysis skills. Numerous resources are available to teachers of all subject areas who want to use modeling, spreadsheets, or Logo in their learning activities. Students can learn a great deal about programming by typing into the computer the programs found in these resources and experimenting with them. Students also learn by modifying simple Logo programs to fit their own needs. Teachers should check their school media centers as well as local libraries for availability of computer periodicals that feature Logo activities.

Using modeling, spreadsheets, and Logo as problem-solving–decision-making tools prompts class discussions or avenues for further research. Students are also a valuable source of inspiration in the use of Logo. It is a good idea to encourage students to look for ways of enhancing programs or expanding applications of programs. After all, the more creative our future programmers are, the brighter the future for all of us.

LEARNER ACTIVITIES

1. Interview a student taking a computer programming class in a local high school or college. Write a summary about his or her experiences and expectations.

2. Present one of the activities in this chapter to your class and write a report on the results, include appropriate data analysis.

3. Locate a spreadsheet tutorial and follow several lessons. Evaluate its effectiveness in terms of utility, ease of use, time, and achievement.

4. Create a poster showing common commands in Logo.

5. Select one of the exercises from the Math Modeling Exercise website at <http://ais.coffee-hs. coffee.k12.tn.us/textbook/unit2/mathmodel.html. Work with a partner to complete the exercise and present your model to the class. Adapt one of the exercises for your content area.

6. Locate a data analysis activity using spreadsheets from an online resource. Write a review of the activity outlining its strengths and weaknesses and provide empirical support.

7. Create a learning activity using Logo to teach geometry concepts.

8. Plan a sequence of activities utilizing mathematical modeling, spreadsheets, or Logo to teach mathematical concepts aligned with the National Council of Teachers of Mathematics Standards.

9. Does Logo have a future use in education? Why or why not? Support your position with classroom scenarios.

BIBLIOGRAPHY

Branzburg, J. (2000). Spreadsheets. *Technology and Learning, 21*(3), 67.

Carson, S. R. (1997). The use of spreadsheets in science—an overview. *School Science Review, 79*(287), 69–80.

Drier, H. S. (1999). Do vampires exist: Using spreadsheets to investigate a common folktale. *Learning and Leading with Technology 27*(1), 22–25.

Golshan, B. (1997). *Problem solving with Microsoft Excel.* Williamsport, PA: Lycoming College.

Kosko, T. (1985). Some projects for your programming classes. *The Computing Teacher, 12*(6), 24.

Maddux, C. D. (1985). *Logo in the schools.* New York: Haworth Press.

Maddux, C. D., & Johnson, D. L. (1988). *Logo: Methods and curriculum for teachers.* New York: Haworth Press.

Ostler, E., & Grandgenett, N. (1999). *Mathematical modeling activities: A primer for grades 5–12.* Omaha, NE: Midwest Educational Technology Services.

Papert, S. (1980). *Mindstorms: Children, computers and powerful ideas.* New York: Basic Books.

Resnick, M. (1994). *Turtles, termites and traffic jams.* Cambridge, MA: The MIT Press.

Scaife, J., & Wellington, J. (1993). *Information technology in science and technology education.* Buckingham, UK: Open University Press.

Shimabukuro, G. (1989). A class act: Junior high students, Lego and Logo. *The Computing Teacher, 17*(5), 37–39.

Smith, D. N. (1997). Independent mathematical modeling. *Teaching Mathematics and Its Applications, 16*(3), 101–106.

Watt, D. (1989). Research on Logo learning as a path to professional teacher development. *Electronic Learning, 8*(5), 22–24.

Wiburg, K. M. (1989). Does programming deserve a place in the school curriculum? *The Computing Teacher, 17*(1), 8–11.

WEBSITES

Activities Using Formulas in Spreadsheets <http://www.cyberschool.k12.or.us/~thomas/mathontheweb/ss/activities.html>

Bureau of Justice—Crime & Justice Electronic Data Abstracts <http://www.ojp.usdoj.gov/bjs/dtdata.htm>

Fractal Modeling Tools <http://scan.shodor.org/master/fractal/>

Grade 9: The Learning Equation Math: Mathematical Modeling <http://dev1.epsb.edmonton.ab.ca/math14_Jim/math9/strand2/2102.htm>

Instructional Resources <http://scan.shodor.org/master/fractal/curriculum/>

Live Access to Pacific Marine Environmental Laboratory Data <http://ferret.wrc.noaa.gov/las/main.html>

Logo Programming in Theory <http://www.rdg.ac.uk/~ems97pc/logo.html>

Mathematical Modeling in a Real and Complex World <http://www.math.montana.edu/frankw/ccp/modeling/topic.htm#contents>

Mathematical Modeling of Evolution <http://pespmc1.vub.ac.be/:/MATHME.html>

Mathematical Models of a Falling Rock <http://excalibur.onate.nmhs.edu/textbook/unit2/rock.html>

Mathematics: Modeling Our World—Teacher Support Web Site <http://www.comap.com/highschool/projects/mmow/>

Math Modeling Exercises <http://ais.coffee-hs.coffee.k12.tn.us/textbook/unit2/mathmodel.html>

MathsNet Downloads <http://www.anglia.co.uk/education/mathsnet/software.html#MswLogo>

MathsNet Logo Page <http://www.anglia.co.uk/education/mathsnet/logo.html#ideas>

MSWLogo—free download <http://www.softronix.com/logo.html>

Some Simple Population Models <http://ais.coffee-hs.coffee.k12.tn.us/textbook/unit2/pop.html>

Spreadsheet Lesson Plan for Eighth-graders <http://www.dpi.state.nc.us/Curriculum/Computer.skills/lssnplns/SSlesson.G8.3.2.1.html>

CHAPTER 15

ORGANIZING AND MANAGING

1. What are some considerations behind the choice to group computers together into labs versus putting them into individual classrooms?
2. How can collaboration with colleagues lead to more student opportunities to use technology?
3. How might the physical conditions of a classroom and educational philosophy of a teacher affect how computers are placed?

Some would say that in a perfect world, every student would have his or her own computer. Students could work whenever they wanted or needed, they could gather together to learn collaboratively, and they could use computers as easily as they now use other learning tools, such as pencils or books. Because this dream is not yet a reality for the majority of schools, the question of how student learning can be organized in any given technology situation needs to be addressed. How can teachers make the most of what they have available, ensuring that students get experience with the types of skills that will be indispensable in their future academic and professional pursuits? Unfortunately, the simple logistics that are explained in teacher in-service trainings or in professional journals and books do not always prove simple when put into practical use.

CLASSROOM COMPUTERS VERSUS COMPUTER LABS

In order to devise a workable plan for both student and teacher computer use, you need to begin with an understanding of how computers are distributed in your school. There is an ongoing debate among educators as to how computers can best be arranged to offer students the most equitable and effective access to technology. One school of thought values a distributed model that breaks apart the traditional computer labs and distributes the machines out among the classrooms. It stresses that in order for technology to be truly integrated into the learning process, it must be immediately accessible to learners. If computers are located in a lab, that may mean that students place their hands on the equipment only once a week and then in only an artificial, disconnected way. Having a set "computer time" gives the impression that computers are some separate entity, a "field trip" on which students get to embark just once each week. This contrasts with the idea that the machines are viable learning tools that can provide endless research and production possibilities each day.

Educators on the other side of the debate see advantages in placing all of the computers into one computer lab, generally located in an extra classroom or other free space at the school (see Figure 15.1). This layout was the common practice during the early years when computers were still gaining an accepted place in our schools. It still makes the most sense to many technology planners today. It is cost-effective in that it gives all students in all grade levels a chance to use the machines, and it means that the expensive machines are used virtually all day. Each class typically schedules a weekly computer time when students can go to the lab together to work. If a school is fortunate, it may have a full- or part-time computer teacher to instruct with or about technology or to assist the classroom teacher with ideas and technical support.

Of course, lab advocates are quick to point out that a plan that involves sending all of the computers into the classrooms creates problems of its own. Although a small group of students can work on a timely activity in the classroom, the whole class cannot learn the same thing at the same time. Teachers may be forced to explain the same concept a number of times, as each group gets an opportunity to come to the class computer. Not having computers in one location also may preclude a designated technology teacher from presenting lessons. It instead might require the classroom teachers to assume the majority of technology instruction.

There are countless variations of computer distributions that fall somewhere in between these two extremes. Sometimes new computers are arranged together into labs so that all students have access to them, and the older computers are doled out to individual classrooms. Many schools are now experimenting with distributed computers in classrooms with the addition of "minilabs" of a small number of computers located in groupings around the school, possibly shared by two or three grade levels. Understanding the issues, and then considering which path your school has chosen to take and the thinking that went into making that choice, will help you plan for the smartest computer use possible for your class.

FIGURE 15.1   A school computer lab.

ORGANIZING LEARNING IN A CLASSROOM SETTING

A great deal of thought must go into how you plan on utilizing your classroom computers, whether you have one or are fortunate enough to have several. The use of the computer in your classroom should reflect your personal style and educational philosophies just as the use of any other learning tools do. Your very attitude about the computer's place in your instructional plan goes a long way in determining how your students will view its usefulness. If the computer sits in the corner under an inch of dust or if computer time is spent only "playing" games, students will naturally fail to see its potential importance in their learning. If, on the other hand, students see your enthusiasm for technology, if they see you using it as a tool to accomplish real goals despite your fear of learning something new, they will be drawn to learn and experiment with skills they must have to be successful in the future. For simplicity's sake, these recommendations will be directed primarily to the multiple-computer classroom, but they can be easily modified to fit the technology available to you as well as to fit the particular needs of your students.

Room Arrangement

How you arrange your classroom is an expression of the way you view the learning process, and how you integrate technical equipment into the physical space of your classrooms is an extension of these beliefs. Instead of pushing your classroom computers into the nearest corner, thoughtfully consider how they will be used by you and your students.

If you plan to have individuals or partners use computers while the rest of the class engages in other activities, you may want to put the computers off to one side of the room. Because what is seen on a computer monitor can be distracting to students working elsewhere, resist pushing the computers up against the wall, and instead turn them so that the monitors face away from the majority of the class. Bookshelves or other furniture can also be moved to create a more private computer area if desired. This, of course, makes it more difficult for you to view the computer screens to see how students are progressing, so be prepared to adjust your supervision habits.

If small groups will be using the computers, be sure there is enough room for several chairs to be pulled up and that there is easy access to other group work areas. If you plan to use the computer as one station in a series of learning centers to which students will be rotating, plan ahead for traffic patterns. Be sure students can easily get around the work area, even if others are sitting at the computer.

You might like to try using your classroom computer as a presentation aid for the whole class (see Chapter 16 for more information on presenting and producing with your classroom computer). In that case, you will want to be sure the computer is located so that it is easy to connect to a projection device or can be easily moved.

As important as the learning purpose is to deciding how to arrange computers, what also must be considered is the reality of the physical situation of your classroom. Computers must be within reach of electrical outlets, for example. Care should be taken so that the glare from windows does not make seeing the screen impossible. The actual furniture on which the computer is placed should also be given some thought. Some schools purchase specially designed computer furniture. Others have gone as far as to ingeniously build the computer monitor right into the desk itself, allowing students to see it through a sturdy, waterproof glass top, but leaving a flat work space across which students can easily see and be seen (Bozzone, 1997). If your school has not acquired any special furniture, you may be forced to creatively craft a computer workstation by pushing together existing desks and tables. Take the time to make this workstation as ergonomically appropriate for your students as possible, such as by raising or lowering the table legs. These preparations will make for a more functional technology classroom (see Figure 15.2).

Technical Procedures

When computers are distributed into classrooms, teachers must assume much of the responsibility for the day-to-day technical operation of the equipment. There may be a school or district technology specialist available, but you will want to be familiar with enough of the basic troubleshooting strategies to prevent long interruptions of student productivity. You will want to take time to study how the wires are connected to the computer and to other peripherals, such as a monitor and a printer. Organize software on the desktop with icons so that students will be able to quickly and easily find applications they need without disturbing other directories or programs.

Model appropriate care and use of the machine and software to prevent some potential problems. Dust the computer and the monitor weekly, for example. Keep floppy disks away from magnetic devices and excess heat or cold. Depending on students' ages or capabilities, they can be taught to handle many common operational and maintenance procedures, such as loading a new CD-ROM or replacing paper into the printer. When technical or other problems arise, think aloud to students as you consider your options, and demonstrate how you would solve them, thus providing a real problem-solving model. The more independently students can operate classroom computers, the more confident they will be in using them.

Scheduling Computer Use

Students should be made aware of the expectations you have for their computer use just as they are aware of expectations for other academic and behavioral habits. Make it clear when it is appropriate to go to the computer and when other work should be focused on.

FIGURE 15.2   A classroom computer workstation.

This will prevent congregation around a computer every time a new sound is heard or when your students enter the room at the beginning of the period.

Whether you have six or thirty computers in your classroom, you can design efficient use strategies by scheduling time for students to work on the computers. Your students will need time to use the computers in two different ways. It is first essential to provide time for students to explore and learn how to use computer hardware and software. This may be an informal discovery time or may be structured so that students work with one particular skill or program. Students also must have time to use what they have learned for productive purposes. These personal work times should allow students to use technology to work on class assignments or to pursue individual projects, but should be organized around an ultimate goal of a finished product.

A number of different strategies can be used to introduce new computer skills. To demonstrate some basic operational skills, such as manipulating text in a word processor or saving files to the school network, you may choose to show the entire class at once using a projection device. If you have received new software, you might decide to show it to a couple of students, and let them teach the next couple of students, and so on. You can also write some simple, developmentally appropriate directions and let students discover how to use a graphics program on their own using the directions as a guide. With any method, students must be allowed time to practice these ideas before they are required to use them for real purposes. Once students are confident with the basics, they can apply what they know to achieving other academic goals.

A signup sheet for computer time is one way teachers organize student computer use. Unfortunately, if students can sign up for time only when they have finished their other work, only a select few students will ever get regular computer experience. Creating a set weekly schedule for computer use can help to ensure equity in opportunities for students in a high student–computer ratio classroom. Look at all of the available time when your students are in the room, and divide this time into workable blocks of perhaps thirty minutes each. Slot in students' names so that each has time for both practicing new skills and authentic technology use, ideally scheduled in two separate work times to give them the best chance for quality learning. Schedule students for times during the day when they can work on the computers without missing instruction that they need. Depending on your students' experience levels and specific needs, having them work in pairs could be more beneficial than working by themselves. Post the schedule so that students know when their weekly times are and when there are open slots (see Figure 15.3). This allows them to plan when they will be working on the computers, and also shows open times that are available for spontaneous technology use. Students must feel that they have opportunity to word process a story or create graphics when they need to without necessarily having to wait for their slot once or twice a week. The posted schedule also encourages student monitoring of computer use. When a student's computer time is over, he or she can alert the next person on the list, relieving you to work with students in other capacities.

Assistance

Successful facilitation of a technology-rich classroom requires the coordination of help from a number of sources. Parent volunteers with computer experience can provide needed technical support, and those who are computer novices can encourage and supervise as they learn along with the students. Older students who are able to donate time can teach

	Monday	Tuesday	Wednesday	Thursday	Friday
8:00-8:30	Raymond	Jenny	Maura	Mary	Donna
8:30-9:00	Jonathon			Gene	Jeffrey
9:00-9:30		Ally	Tonya	Winston	
9:30-10:00	Rachel	John	Robin		
10:00-10:30		David			
10:30-11:00	Alex	Elaine		Harmony	Vonny
11:00-11:30			LUNCH		
11:30-12:00			RECESS		
12:00-12:30	Tricia	Joshua		Greg	Tommy
12:30-1:00			Gina	James	Shawna
1:00-1:30			Troy		
1:30-2:00	Marisa	Gwen		Jimmy	
2:00-2:30	Whitney		Travis		
2:30-3:00					

FIGURE 15.3   Weekly schedule of classroom computer use.

younger students the finer points of a new piece of software or can help with some of the manual work that sometimes slows down little hands, such as typing text into a word processor. Peers can also serve as teachers to one another, sharing special skills or teaming to work out a problem. They often can fill in where teachers may lack the technical expertise.

Make your students aware of their options for assistance so that they learn not to depend on you alone. This is a difficult lesson, especially considering the inherent technical problems that come with regular use of computers. A simple paper jam in the printer or a malfunctioning CD-ROM can bring to a standstill the immediate continued use of the computer. Students' first reaction is to think that you alone will be able to remedy the situation, and, indeed, many teachers new to using technology fall into the trap of running to solve every technical glitch that springs up. If this habit continues, being the sole technical problem solver will monopolize your time. An independent, problem-solving atmosphere established in your classroom will help students to troubleshoot technical problems themselves and with those who are there for them.

Teamwork

As talented at scheduling the use of limited computers as a teacher may be, there remain considerable limitations to having only a few machines. This is an excellent time when teamwork among your colleagues can be invaluable to your students. One easy way to make the most of the computers in classrooms is to work out a schedule with other teachers so that your students can go to use the computers when their students are not using them and vice versa. When schools have such a low ratio of computers to students, the time computer keys are sitting idle should be minimized.

ORGANIZING LEARNING IN A SINGLE COMPUTER SETTING

A single computer setting is not the ideal situation. However, with careful planning and a pioneering, creative spirit, the recommendations discussed can be modified to fit the one-computer classroom. If you plan on having students use the computer regularly, avoid the temptation of placing the computer on your desk. This location gives the impression that it is your computer and students are merely borrowing time on it.

A more drastic, yet potentially more beneficial, act is to consider teaming with other teachers to pool your single computers together to create a minilab. One teacher can volunteer to house the lab in a corner of the classroom, and a schedule can be worked out so that small groups of students from all the classes involved can come together to work on projects or content software. As teachers everywhere strive to effectively integrate technology into everyday learning experiences, they must all be open to the creative possibilities that happen when they work together.

ORGANIZING LEARNING IN A LAB SETTING

If the majority of your students' time with computers will be spent in a computer lab setting, some forethought and well-planned procedures can make for successful utilization of the technology. Many of the planning and operational procedures parallel those that have been discussed for classroom use, but the differences lie with the decreased freedom you have in room arrangement and scheduling. Trooping your entire class down to the computer lab without any plan as to what will happen there will only waste your students' valuable time with computers and cause undue frustration for everyone involved. Consider each of the following areas as they relate to the real situation at your school.

Equipment

Being prepared is a motto teachers live by, but when it comes to technology, that motto becomes a rule that simply cannot be broken. You need to be familiar with the equipment your students will be using so that you will be able to effectively facilitate their learning. Although this does not mean you need to be a technology expert, you must be at least familiar enough with the operation to facilitate your students' learning experiences.

Skill with computers is a unique area that is leading teachers to reconsider the notion that they must be knowledgeable about everything that they teach in the classroom. Students may in fact know more about a particular piece of software or hardware, and may have less fear of exploring the unknown, than many of their teachers. Although there are a multitude of ways teachers can encourage and capitalize on these individual strengths and desires to experiment, they should at the same time be making an effort to acquire a personal level of familiarity with the present technology. A learning experience in the computer lab will be more closely integrated into the ongoing curriculum and be therefore of greater educational benefit to students if you have taken the time to walk down to the computer lab to become comfortable with how the computers are configured prior to bringing your entire class down for a lesson.

Preplanning and Preinstructing

To make the most out of a brief weekly computer lab experience, students must be primed for what they will be doing and what will be expected of them. Valuable time will be wasted if the class must wait until they are seated in the lab to receive instructions for how their time will be spent. A lesson that fits well into a curriculum sequence will be planned in advance. Any materials students will need should be brought along with them. If groups will need to do any note taking, for example, they should have paper and pencils available. If students will be using a productivity tool to finish a piece of work, such as a word processor to type stories they have written, that work should be out and ready to go when you leave for the lab. If possible and appropriate, instructions can be given and work strategies discussed prior to arrival in the lab. This not only will maximize available lab time and prepare students with a productive mind-set for the work period but also will stress to students the continuity between what they learn in the computer lab and what they are learning in class. This strategy reflects the view that technology is just another tool in your instructional arsenal, rather than a special, disconnected activity.

Assistance

One important consideration when planning class use of a computer lab is the extent to which you can depend on supplemental assistance. If your school or district employs a designated technology teacher, find out how often this teacher is available to help you. Depending on other responsibilities, some technology specialists may offer to plan with you for technology integration, may co-teach an activity with you, or may even teach entire technology-rich lessons. Sometimes several schools are forced to share a technology teacher, meaning that the teacher's time available for each individual teacher is limited. Unfortunately, other districts, whether due to lack of funds or insufficient teacher interest, do not have additional technology help available. A situation like this puts the onus on teachers to plan and implement lessons with technology on their own. An enormous number of educational journals now address technology issues, providing current and very practical suggestions for lessons and projects. Subscriptions to a few of these will encourage meaningful discussion about effective technology integration within the school. In any case, knowing what type of assistance you can expect will allow you to plan accordingly (see Figure 15.4).

FIGURE 15.4   A parent assisting students with work on computers.

Teamwork and Creative Scheduling

In the absence of additional assistance, or with the intention of capitalizing on the benefits of collaboration, teachers must seek out opportunities to team with colleagues at their school. Collaborating with peers leads to the expansion of ideas and more concise use of time with any teaching endeavor, but even more so with the new and potentially time-consuming possibilities presented by technology. There is no need to "reinvent the wheel" each time you plan a lesson that takes advantage of a computer. Talking about successes and challenges with other teachers will motivate you to grow and explore more than you might be moved to on your own.

Working closely with peer teachers also allows for creative scheduling of time in the computer lab. If each class is allotted only one time slot per week, two classes working together could conceivably get twice as much time in the lab. Working with a partner on the computer is often a great way to learn, and at the same time students benefit from having the combined teaching expertise of two teachers. If just one or two students are not able to go to the lab with the rest of your class, or if they require more time to work on a project, a cooperative plan with another teacher could allow them to join the other class during its time. The newness of technology in the school setting has the potential to prove the many benefits of collaboration to teachers who would not otherwise consider opening themselves to the idea.

Basic Lab Procedures

Just as your class lives by a set of basic classroom rules, so should students have some key understandings to help their time in the computer lab operate smoothly. Although most of your regular classroom procedures will apply, teaching in a computer lab is unique because of the sheer addition of a room full of machines. Depending on how the furniture in the lab is arranged, moving around the room might be challenging and even potentially dangerous, with the multitude of connection cables and power cords protruding from the backs of computers. Many labs push the computer tables around the perimeter walls of the room, meaning students can see and talk to other students sitting directly on either side of them, but must get up to speak to others. Labs with tables arranged in long rows may make it difficult to get from one point in the room to another just a few rows back. Small groupings of four computers pushed together have been shown to allow for good student communication and room navigation. Unfortunately, although the "best" arrangement might depend on your students' needs and your own teaching philosophy, these types of room arrangement decisions will likely not be left up to you. Teachers using a communal school lab are generally at the mercy of those who originally set up the lab.

Large monitors sitting on top of the tables tend to hide students' faces, making it difficult to make eye contact with a student or gain the attention of the whole group when you need to make a general announcement. The quiet hum of one computer does not seem at all intrusive to normal conversation, but an entire room full of computers can sound something like a roar when trying to get the attention of someone across the room. In addition, many educational software programs rely heavily on auditory effects, which can turn the room into a circus of beeps and bells. Finally, students simply might just be so intensely engaged in the interactive work they are doing that they may not even be paying attention to what is going on around them. The introduction of a number of simple behavior habits adjusted to fit the students you teach and your own personal management style can facilitate a more productive atmosphere in the computer lab. Explaining and modeling these habits to students before the computers are even turned on will encourage their adoption and continued use.

Traffic and Communication Patterns.   Establish clear traffic and communication patterns with students. Consider the layout of the room, including where wires are located and the amount of space surrounding student work areas. You want students to be able to move through the lab safely and with a minimum of distraction to others who are working. Decide if it is best to have students be able to get up and move freely around the room when needed or if they need to speak only with those sitting directly next to them. Have a plan for where students can go during class to help ensure both their safety and the order of the classroom.

Help Signals.   It is sometimes difficult to see a small hand raised for help between all of the computer monitors, so another way for students to attract attention is needed. Some labs have signs or other objects that students can place on top of their monitors so that you can see at a distance when someone needs help. Reminding students to use this method rather than raising their hands sometimes seems to counteract the hand-raising habit they have in the regular classroom, but it generally works better than having them yell out when they need you. In addition, it allows other helpers, such as parents or older students, to respond to the request for help.

Group Attention Signals.   Because of the difficulty in attracting student attention in the lab setting, it is vital to have a highly visual signal to let students know you need their attention. Flickering the lights on and off works well. Having a set place for students to look to find you once you have given the attention signal can also help you focus their attention more quickly.

Time to Exit.   The time spent in the lab often seems to pass very quickly, but the time needed to prepare to leave can be great. Students not only need to reach a good stopping point in their work, but they need to save their files, close the programs they were using, and possibly shut down the systems. Give students ample warning before it is time to leave so that they will have time to prepare. This will save the rest of the class from waiting too long at the door and prevent conflicts when the next scheduled class enters the lab.

Volunteer Helpers.   To give your students the best chance for success while using the computer lab and to decrease the time they have to sit idly waiting for you to help them, solicit extra help during lab time. In addition to content instruction, students will need help operating new software programs and assistance with the ever-present technical problems. Many parents have experience with computers or are willing to volunteer despite their lack of computer knowledge. They can gain some computer familiarity of their own and at the same time can offer another set of hands to help students. Other invaluable help can come from older students who have some time between their own classes or can arrange to get away from class during your lab time. These students can reinforce their own skills and confidence by helping those younger than them. You might even have students in your own class take turns serving in the role of technical monitor, collaborating with peers on some problems and alerting you when your help is needed. Make sure that whoever is helping is introduced to the class so students know who is available to assist them. If you normally do not utilize outside helpers in your class, your students may need to develop a trust in the helpers before they stop waiting for help only from you. The combination of assistance can create a productive atmosphere in the computer lab.

File Storage

Encouraging students to use technology for authentic productive purposes often requires giving them the means to work on one project over the course of several class periods. Students therefore will need the ability to save their work for the next time through a number of storage methods.

If students will be sitting at the same computer each time they are in the lab, one storage solution is to have them save their work to a designated directory on that particular computer's hard drive. In this case, all teachers with students using the lab throughout the day would need to agree on a common directory structure. Directories can be made for each student on the machines they use, meaning directories for students in many classes could be found on any one computer. Students would need instruction on exactly where and how to save their work so as not to damage anyone else's files or any other application programs on the hard drive.

If a school is wired for a local area network, student work may be saved into the network drive, making it accessible from other school computers. Students would then be able to sit in a different location each time in the lab or could also edit their work from a computer elsewhere on campus. An organized directory structure should be planned for a network, such as making directories for all students in one class under their teacher's name.

If no network exists or if saving work to the hard drive of a computer in the lab restricts future work on projects, students can also save work on disks. Each student should be taught how to insert and remove disks, how to save to them, and how best to care for them. Because of the somewhat fragile nature of disks, you may want to develop a system for group storage of the disks, such as keeping all students' labeled disks in one basket that can be brought to the lab each time. Older students may be able to keep and care for their own disks, but should be introduced to the concept of always saving a backup copy of any important files (see Figure 15.5).

THE ROLE OF THE LIBRARY MEDIA CENTER

Becoming information managers and assisting students in becoming knowledge workers are new roles for teachers and media specialists. Learning with multimedia technology maximizes the time available for discussion, thinking, and creating knowledgeable responses to the data, issues, and problems.

Storytelling as an instructional strategy is both timeless and effective. Elementary school library media centers often take full advantage of this strategy and offer special areas for book talks, dramatic productions, story time, student-authored works, and independent free browsing, viewing, and reading. Electronic storybooks on CD-ROM, books on tape, videotaped readings of popular big books, books and stories presented in other languages, pop-ups, and flip animations may all be available for enjoyment.

Living in a global village has diminished the distance between the world's countries, while simultaneously illuminating the differences among cultures. Library media centers

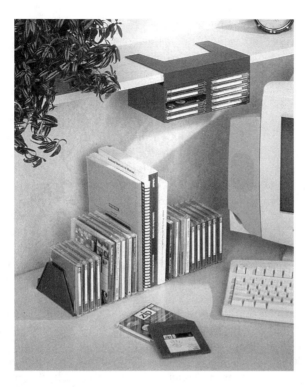

FIGURE 15.5   Student disks organized together.

may provide materials and resources in a variety of formats that learners may access. General reference material such as an encyclopedia (e.g., *The New Grolier Multimedia Encyclopedia* by Grolier Electronic Publishing), almanac, dictionary, thesaurus, maps, globes, and charts are all available in the digital formats of CD-ROMs and DVDs or accessible through CD-ROM networks, proprietary Internet indices, and web servers. A library management system of digital and traditional resources may also include posters, multimedia kits, audiocassette recordings, films, videotapes, models, and microforms.

Having a shared production area available within the library media center allows both faculty and students to create and publish instructional and learning materials. Ideally, there might be two or three production areas for students, faculty, and the library media specialists. A production area might provide a scanner, digitizer, copier, printer, project templates that integrate the Internet, website creation tools, VCR, video and digital cameras, audio equipment, CD burners, web server, and computers. Software would include desktop publishing; spelling and grammar editing programs; clip art; font, graphics, and art programs; and multimedia and publishing tools such as Multimedia and Publishing and Teacher Productivity Tools (Teacher Street), HyperStudio (Knowledge Adventure), and mPower (Tom Snyder Productions). Fully outfitted production areas might also include a darkroom facility, a multistation computer lab, and a video/audio studio with editing equipment.

The reference area should include both CD-ROM and DVD players to facilitate the many informational resources available in these formats. It should be a large, flexible space to accommodate both large- and small-group presentations and for individual research. Online electronic networks and database services might be available as well as videoconferencing capabilities. A computer with large-screen display capabilities using media source switching should be available for instructional presentations. Some reference areas include display space for student-produced work as well as realia. In addition to CD-ROM–DVD players, the reference area might contain equipment that facilitates video and screen capture, scanning, and viewing as well as docking stations for hand-held devices.

Many new library media centers are being built to include either an adjacent computer laboratory and/or an area within the center for hands-on mathematics and science activities. Within these areas, introductory robotics might be available such as Robolab, which is software that allows you to control a Lego programmable brick; computer-based microscopes might be available using the Intel Play QX3 Computer; bar-code weather-gathering equipment that may include an online database and simulation materials; and software such as Virtual Labs: Light (Edmark), Music Ace 2 (Harmonic Vision), Micoworlds Pro (LCSI), Survivors: Testimonies of the Holocaust (The Shoah Foundation), PC Globe (Broderbund), Health: Understanding Ourselves (ABC News Interactive), Science ToolKit (Broderbund), Visual Almanac (Optical Data), and SimCity (Broderbund). Technological equipment might include computers, printers, and graphing calculators with display capabilities. The instructional practice of using real-life models, patterns, data, and problems as the basis for learning activities is catching hold. Programs such as Conserving Earth's Biodiversity (Island Press) capture the interest of learners through interactive multimedia, engaging activities, and projects while integrating technology. Software that allows students the opportunity to study high-interest content while practicing skills is popular.

Simulation and data manipulation software that provides students with graphic displays such as histograms, bar graphs, and scatter plots are also available. Some schools have answers, decisions, and opinions that may be electronically polled and graphed by computer. The teacher may use the resulting information to make instructional decisions and to determine skill and concept attainment.

Having the library center's collection available through media management systems and computer terminals, which may be housed in other parts of the school as well as on site, provides faculty and learners with immediate means and the capability of enhancing and/or remediating the instruction through the availability of other resources and materials. If the school library media center is a participant in a resource-sharing project with other libraries, the quantity of resources is even greater.

Flexible use of space and the ability to electronically access information outside the center and school are the two key factors when designing or recreating school library media centers. The library media center must house, circulate, and distribute information in all formats to hundreds of users on a daily, hourly, and minute-by-minute basis. Reading, viewing, accessing information, and learning are all encouraged to become pleasurable lifelong activities within the library media center of the twenty-first century. The dust on the old library warehouse of books has been swept away!

SUMMARY

Because budget shortages in school districts preclude the purchase of a computer for each and every child, choices must be made regarding the best placement of the available machines. Schools can opt for distributing them to individual classrooms, grouping them

CLASSROOM VIGNETTE

Charonda and Adam sat together in front of the computer by the door in their classroom. This was their "Exploration Time" for the week, and this week's assignment was to explore the new software Mrs. Jaworska had shown them last week, PowerPoint (Microsoft Corporation). She had said that they could use PowerPoint to make presentations, possibly for their history projects that were coming up.

Charonda took the laminated page of activities called "Try This" that Mrs. Jaworska had left next to the computer for them to work with during their thirty minutes. She read the first activity out loud to Adam: "Make a new slide."

The two continued working through the page of activities, creating a sample slide show. They reminded each other of how Mrs. Jaworska had demonstrated the program and worked together to figure out how to do the couple of things she had not shown. The last item on the Try This page required them to think of ways that they might be able to use this program in a real way.

"I think we could make some slides to show what we learned in history," began Adam. "Maybe we could put the words we want to say on the screen and then we could just read the screen when we are talking in front of the parents. Then if we forget what to say, we could just look up there at the screen."

"Yeah," said Charonda. "And maybe we could put some pictures in so it looks good. My project is on the Colonists, so maybe I could find some picture of the *Mayflower* or of what the people looked like then. But I don't want to wait that long to try it. I think I'm going to make a slide show tomorrow during my 'Production Time' or maybe when we're in the computer lab."

The two practiced showing their sample slide show for the rest of their time, trying to speak without looking at the screen just as Mrs. Jaworska had shown them.

together into a computer lab, or some variation between those two extremes. The debate between supporters of each end of the spectrum wages on, but teachers must be prepared with some strategies for teaching with technology no matter where it is located.

With computers distributed in the classroom or only a single computer in a classroom, students use the electronic tool in a spontaneous, integrated manner. With a single computer, though, only small groups of students can work at any one time. Teachers may be forced to reteach a concept a number of times so that everyone gets a chance to learn. With computers installed in a lab, students can all work on the same thing at the same time, and all students in a school can get their hands on a computer every week. The drawback to the lab setting, however, is that each student in the school might get a chance to use a computer only once a week, turning technology into a special activity disconnected from other learning.

Educators must have strategies in place to make the most of teaching with either several or only one computer in their classrooms or in a computer lab away from their classrooms. Teachers with classroom computers should plan the machines' location carefully to reflect its intended uses. A schedule can ensure equity in student access to computers. Modeling of basic technical procedures can make it possible for students to solve many simple technical problems.

To keep work in a lab relevant and efficient, teachers need to be prepared and informed. Giving students the information they need on what the goal is for a lab session prior to setting foot in the lab allows them to have a proper mind-set. It emphasizes the connectivity between what they work on in the lab with other learning processes. The unique attributes of working in a room with multiple computers humming away demand that students be taught specific procedures for getting help, giving their attention, moving safely around the room, and storing their work files.

Soliciting help from parents or older students provides for smoothly operating computer work in either setting. Creative collaboration with colleagues can create even more opportunities for students to use computers as a tool in authentic learning endeavors.

LEARNER ACTIVITIES

1. Visit several elementary, middle, or secondary schools, or speak with several teachers. How are the computers at these schools organized? How successful do the teachers appear to be at making the arrangement into an effective learning environment?

2. Using a weekly teaching schedule from an actual classroom as a guide, create a weekly computer use schedule for students at your intended level. Without having any student miss a required activity, how much time per week can each use one classroom computer? How much free space in the schedule is there available for spontaneous use?

3. List the pros and cons of both lab and classroom placement of computers.

4. Prepare a budget proposal for purchasing a computer for every student at a school near you. Include in your plan the number of students, the approximate price of computers based on current retail prices, and any furniture that would be necessary.

5. Write a lesson plan that effectively incorporates a trip to the computer lab. Include related preparation ahead of time and follow-up work afterward, so that the uses of the technology tools are framed in context.

6. Write a letter to convince parents to volunteer their time to help students with using technology.

7. Visit a computer lab at a local school. Based on the specifics of the room layout, make a list of procedures you think would be necessary for safe and organized use of the lab. How does your list compare with any procedures that are actually used in the lab?

8. Design a floor plan that would facilitate effective computer use in a one-computer or six-computer classroom.

9. Write a unit of practice that effectively incorporates computer use in either a one- or six-computer classroom. Include related preparation ahead of time and follow-up work afterward, so that the uses of the technology tools are framed in context.

10. What are ways to propose team collaboration on computer use? How can cooperation be encouraged among new teams?

11. How do you envision classrooms of the future? How many of these procedures will still apply?

BIBLIOGRAPHY

Anderson, G. (1996). Setting up computer workstations in classrooms and libraries. *Media and Methods, 32*(5), 14–16.

Banaszerski, R. (1997). Strategies for the one computer classroom. *Learning and Leading with Technology, 25*(1), 32–33.

Bozzone, M. A. (1997). Technology for kids' desktops. *Electronic Learning, 16*(5), 47–49.

Buchanan, L. (1996). Planning the multimedia classroom. *MultiMedia Schools, 3*(4), 16–21.

Ekhaml, L. (2000). Virtually yours. *School Library Media Activities Monthly, 16*(9), 37–40.

Federico, C. (1995). In defense of dabbling: The case for drop-in sessions. *Technology Connection, 2*(7), 13–16.

Ferguson, D. B. (2000). Change is good: The new face of the library media center. *Curriculum Administrator, 36* (1), 30–37.

Fraundorf, M. C. (1997). Distributed computers and labs: The best of both worlds. *Learning and Leading with Technology, 24*(7), 50–53.

Green, E. E. (1996). Fitting new technologies into traditional classrooms: Two case studies in the design of improved learning facilities. *Educational Technology, 36*(4), 27–38.

Keller, J. (2000). Learning from our mistakes. *Technology and Learning, 20*(11), 60–66.

Maxwell, D. J. (2000). Making libraries mobile: Innovative means to give information services. *Education, 120*(4), 722–732.

McKenzie, J. (2000). Winning with information literacy. *Technos, 9*(1), 28–32.

Pasnik, S. (2000). What technology can do: Research and resources. *Technology and Learning, 20*(11), 50–58.

Schulz, C. D. (1997). Today's school library media center: Technology is key. *Educational Horizons, 75,* 78–82.

Scott, R. (1995). How to get your own computer lab in your classroom. *English Journal, 84*(6), 62–64.

Sills-Briegel, T. M. (1996). Teacher–student proximity and interactions in a computer laboratory and classroom. *Clearing House, 70,* 21–23.

Waddick, J. (1997). Physical considerations in the development of a computer learning environment. *British Journal of Educational Technology, 28,* 69–71.

Wright, D. (1997). Successful furniture solutions. *School Planning and Management, 36*(2), 34, 36, 38, 40.

Zeitz, L. (1995). Troubleshooting computer problems: A teachers' guide. *Learning and Leading with Technology, 23*(1), 16, 32–33.

CHAPTER 16

PRODUCING AND PRESENTING

1. In what ways might the specific purpose for a multimedia production guide the planning?
2. What forms of media can be used to enhance instructional presentations?
3. What preparations must be made in advance of giving a technology-aided presentation?

As current educational research lauds the advantages of authentic, project-based instruction and assessment, it becomes apparent that educators and students alike can use the capabilities of technology to make these new goals a practical reality. Technology presents some amazing opportunities to compile varied, quality informational products and effectively present those products to groups of people in meaningful ways.

Multimedia productions are so named because they are designed by integrating different media of information, such as text, graphics, video, audio, and animation elements. As opposed to a traditional lesson or presentation, in which the user sits passively and receives the information in only the one way it is presented, multimedia can cater to a whole range of learning and teaching styles. At one end of the spectrum, multimedia can enhance somewhat traditional presentations in which the control for the sequence of the presentation of information lies primarily with the presenter. On the opposite end of the range, multimedia can form hypermedia environments, whereby the user has the freedom to make decisions as to how or in which direction to explore. A hypermedia structure creates an environment without the linear restrictions associated with many paper-based learning materials. These hypermedia environments let the user access information in any order he or she wishes. This access simulates the natural, nonlinear ways in which humans learn and allows for individual construction of knowledge. The flexibility and interactivity that can be achieved by synthesizing information with these multimedia elements can create a sensory experience that matches individual thinking patterns of both presenters and learners.

The process of creating multimedia products ideally reflects the philosophy that teachers and students are at times both the experts and the learners in the classroom. Both groups can use technology to prepare and present cohesive lessons or to demonstrate what has been learned in a unit of study. As with any use of technology, multimedia projects should be seen as a natural part of the teaching, learning, and evaluating processes that occur regularly in classrooms, rather than as some separate, added-on requirement. This chapter will outline a practical process both teachers and students can follow when using technology to author informative products and present them to others.

PLANNING AND RESEARCH PREPARATION

Defining the Purpose

Creating a multimedia production can provide not only for real acquisition and use of technology skills but also for the practice of visioning, planning, and making purposeful choices. Just as with any lesson, you and your students can make the most of the preparation process and the unique attributes of the technology if you understand the distinctive purpose of each project from the beginning. For what audience will it be prepared? To what extent will technology play a role in the creation and presentation of the production? Putting together a quick lesson for your class on the differences between warm- and cold-blooded animals in your area of the country will require different preparation than a research project undertaken to convince the school board to purchase new, safer playground equipment. The following is a sample of types of multimedia projects teachers and students can design:

Lessons. Whether taught by teachers or peer students, new concepts can be presented to others with the variety of media required to ensure all learners have the chance to learn in ways that make sense to them. Lessons can be prepared for whole groups to view at once, for small groups, or even for individual tutorial purposes.

Research projects or book reports. Resources can be collected and reports written as usual, but they can then be compiled with relevant media about the topic or author. These projects can be used as the sole form of holistic evaluation or as a comprehensive review for another, more traditional assessment.

Stories or games. A simple story written by a student can be transformed into an interactive project by infusing media elements and giving the user some decision-making ability. This gives an alternative to simply word processing a story and drawing pictures to accompany it.

Parent or community informational works. Both text and media elements can cooperate nicely to inform others of rules, current events, and policy. This type of project could be realized as continuously running slide shows as participants enter a room or even stand-alone, kiosk-type, self-guided tours.

Electronic portfolios. Just as artists collect samples of what they have produced, students can bring together choice bits of written work, scanned images, photos and videos of events and explain the importance of each in their own voice by recording a voice-over narration. Students can choose work they most want to include and may even be required to defend their choices in front of a group of teachers, parents, and peers. Electronic portfolios reflect the current educational philosophy that places value on what students can actively do rather than relying only on static scores they receive on a test to tell the story of what they have learned. Teachers might also maintain portfolios, documenting instructional and professional growth and providing some proof of accountability. (See Chapter 17 for more on portfolio assessment.)

Background Research

Multimedia projects, like traditional projects, require strong, accurate content. Students and teachers should never make the mistake of thinking that audio clips and pretty pictures can make up for flimsy descriptions or missing facts. If you are teaching a lesson to students, make sure you have solid objectives and examples. Students should follow whatever research techniques and writing processes they normally do, making use of both text-based and electronic resources. Notes and other text can be word-processed during this stage or simply handwritten. It is helpful for later procedures if this text is proofread and ready to be made into a final draft form.

Storyboarding

The importance of visually planning for the organization of a project was stressed in Chapter 10 with regard to the design of websites, but it is as equally vital to the successful creation of other electronic projects. You and your students should list the titles of the final drafts of the written forms of projects and transfer them to storyboard form, such as onto 5" × 7" index cards. These cards can be easily arranged and rearranged in order to arrive at a visual, logical flow of information. Storyboards can be created with varying amounts of detail, from sketches only to full graphic plans. This detail will be determined, again, by your purpose, time constraints, and the developmental levels of the audience.

Screen Design

Considering some basic design features at this stage in the planning will help ensure clear presentations. Model examples and nonexamples of these recommendations to even very young students so they can make personal judgments about what guidelines would make for the clearest presentations. Always temper each of these general recommendations with an understanding of the audience for the presentation or instruction. If an instructional presentation would benefit from an unorthodox use of text or color, make the best call for the purpose. Whatever design choices you make, remember that consistency is key. Random design features will make for a busy, distracting presentation. (See Table 16.1 for additional design tips.)

PRODUCING MULTIMEDIA ELEMENTS

Once the content of the presentation is mapped out, you and your students can begin to consider what media elements might lend themselves to creating a complete learning experience. Inclusion of these elements will depend on the extent and quality of the equipment available to you at your school, but as with any teaching endeavor, resourcefulness and creativity will take you past many of the technical limitations.

TABLE 16.1   Multimedia Design Issues

1. Limit the amount of text on each screen. Different audiences of students can handle varying amounts of text, but leave some space around the text or use graphics to break up large text pieces.

2. Choose a font that will be legible to learners. Some fonts prove easier to read when viewed on a computer screen or when projected up on the wall. A sans serif font, one without any decorative letter features, in a size of between 18 to 24 points is the easiest to read from a distance.

3. Use phrases or just keywords rather than complete statements.

4. Words written in all capital letters are difficult to read. Underlined text should be reserved for hypertext links only.

5. Use colors appropriate for the topic and audience. Be sure text color contrasts with the background color, such as light text on a dark background or dark text on a light background.

6. Use graphics or other media elements for a real purpose rather than for mere decoration.

Text

Text can include multimedia menus, navigation elements such as site maps, and content. Text files are prepared using a word processing program such as Corel WordPerfect or Microsoft Word. When creating text for multimedia, determine how much information will appear on one screen and how the related pages or links will fit together. Text in presentations, such as a slide show using Corel Presentations or Microsoft PowerPoint, should be key phrases and limited to small chunks of information. To format information effectively, keep the following techniques in mind:

Place text next to a graphic.
Convert sentences with serial items to lists.
Use white space to separate points.
Use headings as content summarizers.
Place complex information into tables.

Fonts. Millions of fonts are available from free shareware, CD-ROMs, and application software such as Corel DRAW. There are five basic font styles:

Serif. Small points called serifs cap the ends of most strokes. Times New Roman is the most common serif font.

Sans serif. Sans means "without," so no points cap the strokes. Helvetica and Arial are the most common sans serif fonts.

Script. Fonts that mimic handwriting. Kaufman and Lucida Handwriting are examples.

Novelty. Fun and frivolous fonts not designed for large amounts of text. This type of font is used for logos and commonly appears in advertisements, especially billboards. Font collections offer many novelty fonts, especially ones for the holidays such as Bones or Snowcaps.

Special purpose. Fonts that fill a specific need, such as the set of numbers printed at the bottom of your bank checks. They are primarily used for technical purposes.

When selecting a font color make sure there is a high contrast between text and the background. For example, use dark text on a light background or light text on a dark background. If the presentation will be projected, use light text and dark background. Projected colors tend to wash out.

Selecting a font size also depends on viewing distance. For individuals viewing a desktop monitor, use a font size of 12 or 14, but for younger children use a larger font size. For a group viewing a large screen from a distance, use font size 22 or 28, depending on the distance.

Graphics

Graphics can include any visual component, even the artful representation of text. Graphics in a presentation should serve an instructional purpose rather than merely providing aesthetic decoration or clutter. A picture can show concepts that words can only hint at, illustrating relationships that might remain unclear with mere descriptions. Graphics can come from a number of sources and can include drawings, paintings, graphs, and photographs.

Clipping.   Premade clip art graphics can be "clipped" from a CD collection or a sample from another program and placed into your program. Although clip art is often a good place to start, especially for those who are hesitant to try their hand at creating their own artwork, clip art can provide only a generic illustrative component. When using clip art read the copyright information. If using a CD collection, this information appears in the front of the image catalog. Some collections are copyright-free without restrictions and others state restrictions and prohibitions.

Drawing and Painting.   Most integrated software suites contain some sort of a graphics program that allows you to create your own graphics. Painting programs provide a selection of tools that allow you to create pictures by assigning color attributes to the actual pixels that comprise the screen, similar to how you would use paint to create a picture on a canvas. Drawing tools allow you to create illustrations by combining different line-based objects. These objects can be selected individually and moved around to be placed in any desired position (see Figure 16.1).

More advanced computer-aided design (CAD) software has carried the design of jet engines, automobile parts, circuit boards, tools, bridges, and homes to new heights of sophistication. Three-dimensional (3-D) graphics programs allow you to create 3-D images. Many 3-D tools are available that will create 3-D text and animate the image as well. 3-D modeling tools allow you to place two-dimensional (2-D) objects into a "virtual" scene. Mathematica is an integrated technical computing system, which combines interactive calculation (both numeric and symbolic), visualization tools, and a complete programming environment. Mathematica allows you to create 2-D and 3-D graphics.

Screen Capture.   Screen capture programs are utility tools. They allow you to capture any text or picture you see on a screen and save it as another file format. The captured image can very easily be cropped and edited. Some capture programs let you edit the image in various ways. You can add drop shadows, create a button, and even feather the edges.

Scanning.   Scanning allows project designers to customize their presentation with a range of graphical elements. By using a flatbed scanner, you can convert any graphic into

FIGURE 16.1   Paint, available with Microsoft Windows.

digital form that can be added to a multimedia presentation (see Figure 16.2). Traditional artwork, such as sketches and paintings, paper creations, magazine pictures, and even photographs, can be scanned in. If copyrighted graphics are used for a student learning opportunity, proper credit should be given to the original source, and if your presentation will have a potentially wide audience, obtain permission to use copyrighted material first.

Taking Digital Pictures.   Digital cameras can be used to take pictures just like traditional cameras, but instead of recording the image on film, they save the image electronically (see Figure 16.3). These cameras can then be plugged directly into a computer and the images can be downloaded right onto the hard drive. Some cameras store the images on a removable disk. Pictures can be taken of students, families, surroundings, special events, or anything else of particular interest. An excellent digital photography resource is located at <http://www.shortcourses.com>. This website offers tutorials and accurate information on selecting and using digital cameras.

FIGURE 16.2   Viviscan DeskSaver Scanner.

Samsung SSC-410N
Digital Still Camera

(a)   **(b)**

FIGURE 16.3   (a) **Samsung's digital still camera. (b) Casio QV-300 digital camera.**

Video

The proliferation of camcorders has made novice video producers out of many families. Video segments can illustrate an event or a procedure so that learners feel as though they were actually there. With the help of some special equipment, videos can easily be inserted into multimedia presentations.

Using Video Clips.   Like clip art in still graphics, prerecorded video is available for purchase on disk or CD-ROM. In addition, search portals at <http://Realguide.real.com>, <http://windowsmedia.com>, and <http://broadcast.com> help you find videos on the web. The quality of these clips is often high because they are professionally produced. They are often copyright-free and so can be used for educational purposes. These types of premade clips are ideal for presentations on topics that you would have no way of viewing personally, such as of exotic wildlife or historical events.

Digitizing Prerecorded Video.   Once a video clip is chosen from a videotape using a standard VCR or a camcorder, it must be transformed into digital form in order to be incorporated into a multimedia program. Digitizing applications can be used to perform this process and to produce as a result a movie in one of several formats, including QuickTime movies and AVI files (see Figure 16.4). The platform operating system you have will dictate what movie format is required. Once the video is digitized, it can be edited and saved using digital video editing equipment. The ability to digitize video allows personal experiences, such as a family trip or a school event, to become part of a presentation.

Recording Digitally.   Digital video cameras record directly into digital form. Although these cameras remain relatively expensive, they allow the video segments to be dropped directly into a multimedia presentation without the need for other preparation.

Audio

From voice-overs to sound effects to background music, the addition of audio elements has the potential to create any learning atmosphere you or your students can imagine.

FIGURE 16.4   Computer Eyes frame grabber.

Using Sound Effects and Music.   Digitally recorded sound effects, such as nature or other environmental sounds, are readily available on CD-ROM or as part of many authoring programs. Regular music that is digitally recorded on CD can also be used. Simple sound-mixing programs, some that come packaged on computers and others available as part of CD-ROM sound effects packages, allow you to easily record and edit clips of the music as you play it through the computer's CD-ROM drive. Experimenting with the combinations of lifelike sounds can help ensure a learner-friendly environment.

Recording Sounds.   Simple recording applications let you use a microphone to record voice-over narration or the reading of a favorite story. What is recorded can be saved and then manipulated using a sound-mixing program (see Figure 16.5). Adding your own voice to a presentation personalizes it as well as allows complete customization of what is being said.

Creating Sounds.   Computer music synthesizers combine a pianolike keyboard with a music synthesizer and computer software. When using a synthesizer to create music, musical issues such as pitch, amplitude, special effects, tempo, note sequence and duration, and other important elements of music can be considered. During and after the composition process, music can be played back through the computer and, in some cases, through stereo speakers. Compositions can be stored on diskettes and played and retrieved at any time.

FIGURE 16.5   Sound Recorder recording application, available with Microsoft Windows.

Animation

Animation shows a series of slightly different still graphics in quick succession to give the impression of action and movement, similar to the idea of flipping the pages of a pad of paper quickly to see the sketched figures appear to move. Animation can illustrate something happening that video may not be able to ideally portray, such as the completion of the water cycle or the activity of the inside of a volcano.

Using Premade Animations.   Like the other media mentioned, collections of premade animations are available on CD-ROM that can be dropped right into a multimedia presentation. Animations can be extremely time-consuming to create because of the many numbers of drawings it might take to effectively simulate an action. Therefore, finding a ready-made animation that illustrates a desired effect will save time and allow those with little experience with the animation process to benefit from the usage of this medium.

Animating.   Many sophisticated authoring and presentation programs now offer tools to facilitate animation. Flash by Macromedia is a very popular animation program. Still images can be made to appear to move without requiring the user to have extensive animation skills. Still images can easily be animated with simple animated GIF programs. Many of these programs are available free from the WWW (see websites at <http://www.tucows.com> or <http://download.cnet>).

  The capabilities of these programs can only be expected to improve, allowing novice multimedia designers to incorporate quality effects with minimal effort.

AUTHORING MULTIMEDIA PRODUCTIONS

With the content planned and the media elements selected and prepared, the next step in the production process is actually to drop the text and media into a program that serves as a "shell" that comprises the final product. Although some programs work best in creating multimedia-enhanced presentations and others result in full nonlinear hypermedia programs, all share some basic properties that are important to understand. The procedures outlined here are general but are applicable to whatever software tools to which you will have access.

Building Blocks

What we are capable of doing with technology is often difficult for us to comprehend, so analogies to other things with which we are familiar are frequently used as a way of explanation. Multimedia programs are often built on basic units called "cards" or "slides" (see Figure 16.6). The analogy to index cards or transparency slides is deliberate. You can write pieces of information or notes for a presentation on index cards and put all the cards together into a stack. These index cards can then be moved around, arranged in any order, and rearranged as needed to fit the purpose of the presentation and the meaningful flow of the content. So, too, can the electronic cards and slides be ordered and reordered within the electronic "stack," thus providing a very editable presentation format.

  Each card or slide has a background, which can be made to be a color or a design. Authoring and presentation programs offer a selection of premade backgrounds or you can use

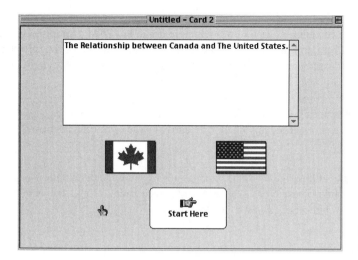

FIGURE 16.6   A card in a Hyperstudio stack.

one of your own graphics. These backgrounds are generally designed to remain constant throughout the presentation, although the designer may choose to change the background color or graphic to fit the purpose of the content of each card. Any text that needs to be seen on every card or slide, such as the date or a school logo, can be placed on the background.

Objects

Onto each card or slide can be placed any number of objects. Objects can be text fields, graphics, or other media items in the form of buttons. Placing these objects on the cards or slides is like writing information on traditional index cards, except that the objects on these cards can be moved around easily to make for effortless layout editing. When the card or slide appears in the presentation, those objects appear superimposed on the background (see Figure 16.7).

FIGURE 16.7   Objects inserted onto a PowerPoint slide.

Text Fields.   In order to place text onto a card or slide, you must first create a text field. A text field is a rectangular tablet onto which text can be typed or imported from a word processing program and then edited as needed. The field can be moved anywhere on the card or slide and can be resized and reformatted. Text can be arranged within multiple text fields on each card or slide.

Graphics.   Prepared graphic items, including clip art, scanned images, and digitally produced pictures, can be placed anywhere on a card or slide. They can be moved, resized, and overlapped.

Media Buttons.   Other media items, such as audio, video, and animations, can be placed on any card or slide. These types of objects can be accessed during a presentation by clicking on an icon or button or can even be set to play automatically.

Transitions

The way in which a user moves from one card or slide to another in a multimedia program is the defining difference between presentation slide programs and hypermedia programs and is one reason why an author might choose one type of production software over the other. Presentation programs that are composed of a series of slides are typically intended for the sequential presentation of information. The presenter or user can view slides in ascending order by clicking the mouse button or can view the slides in order passively by using an automatic timed advance feature. A previous slide can be reviewed, and particular slides can be brought up by number from a navigational menu. You and your students may choose to use a slide program when designing an information product or a more traditional instructional lesson.

Hypermedia authoring programs capitalize on the concept of nonlinear movement among slides. Just as buttons can be added to a slide in order to utilize media elements, buttons can also be used to offer the user options for movement to other information. The project author adds a button to a card and assigns an action to the button. Some actions define media usage and others function as transitions to other specific cards. Rather than require a user to know a specific slide number in order to go directly to that slide, the author can make the button a direct avenue to any card in the stack. Depending on the complexity of the authoring program and the sophistication of the author, these buttons can be chosen from a selection of predefined actions or can be customized with special scripting languages. Hypermedia authoring programs offer unlimited interactive design for any type of research project, story, or portfolio. Table 16.2 lists several popular presentation and hypermedia programs.

TABLE 16.2   Example Presentation and Hypermedia Software Tools

PRESENTATION/SLIDE SOFTWARE	HYPERMEDIA AUTHORING SYSTEMS
KidPix (Learning Co.)	HyperStudio (Knowledge Adventure)
PowerPoint (Microsoft Corporation)	Digital Chisel (Pierian Spring Software)
AppleWorks (Apple Computer, Inc.)	Authorware (Macromedia)

PRESENTING WITH MULTIMEDIA TECHNOLOGY

Regardless of whether your audience of learners fills an auditorium or fills one chair, or whether your presentation is intended to prompt a live presenter or is meant to function as a stand-alone product, computer hardware and software facilitate clear, effective presentation of ideas. Understanding the differences in possibilities technology presents over traditional presentation methods will make you and your students confident presenters of all types of information.

Hardware

The hardware that is needed to present information using a computer depends on the purpose of the presentation. If an individual or small group of students will be working through a hypermedia lesson, a standard computer monitor may be sufficient for all to see. Make sure the computer is located in an area with room to pull up enough chairs for all learners and other aspects of the setting, such as lighting, are such that everything on the screen can be seen without problem.

   If your audience, however, is an entire class or even a larger crowd, you will need a compatible projection device. Some rooms are equipped with television monitors that can be interfaced with a computer so that the screen display can be displayed on the monitors. An AverKey (<http://www.avermedia.com>) is an inexpensive and durable projection device that attaches between the computer and television monitor to display the computer screen. Liquid crystal display (LCD) panels are lightweight, flat devices that can be placed onto an overhead projector and attached to a computer to project an image of the computer screen. The clearest images are produced with projection devices that connect to a computer and shine the display directly up onto a wall screen in either a small room or a large auditorium. Become familiar with what is available to you at your school or district. Practice connecting the computer with the projection devices, becoming familiar with the physical layout of the cables and adapters. Note any adjustments that are needed to the screen resolution to make the image viewable on the larger screen. Connect and disconnect the peripherals several times with your students, if appropriate, so that they see what kind of preparation is necessary to pull off a successful presentation. Many preferences need to be set correctly for a computer to cooperate with a projection device to project its image onto a larger screen, so do not leave these types of preparations to the last minute (see Figure 16.8).

Software

Each presentation or hypermedia program has specific procedures for showing the final product. Become familiar with these procedures, and use them to do a "dry run," advancing through every card or slide in a presentation using the mouse or keyboard as will be required in actual usage. When giving a lesson or presentation in front of a group, rehearse what you will say to accompany the program content. When students are using a program to learn independently, check all buttons to make sure they perform the planned action.

Preparation

The best advice you and your students could follow when planning to use your computers for presentations is always to have a backup plan. Even a thoroughly planned presentation

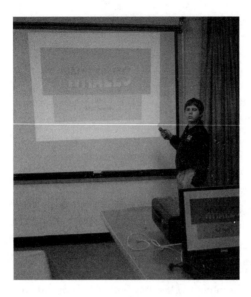

FIGURE 16.8   Practice connecting and adjusting to pull off a successful presentation.

can be thwarted by unforeseen technical problems. Something as simple as a missing cable adapter or an incompatible version of software can stand in your way of making a successful presentation. If it is essential that the instruction be carried off at a certain time, make transparencies of the slides so that you can make do with an overhead projector if necessary. If the instruction can be handled in another method or at another time, be ready to make an instructional switch at the last minute. Although we always hope our plans can be carried out smoothly, modeling this kind of quick thinking will teach your students invaluable, real-world problem-solving skills.

SUMMARY

The capabilities of technology can be used to support authentic instruction and assessment by both teachers and students. Presentations for a variety of purposes can be created by combining different media with instructional or informational ideas.

A quality multimedia production must first begin with careful background research and planning. Consideration of details such as consistent screen layout and design will contribute to ease of learning. Accurate, comprehensive facts and examples will complete the presentation.

Text, graphics, video, audio, and animation are multimedia elements that can be used to frame the learning environment. There are a range of file formats that are acceptable for use in multimedia design. Any of these files can be adopted from premade media collections or originally created using a number of methods.

These media elements are then placed, along with any text, into an authoring or presentation program. Presentation applications are comprised of individual slides that can be shown in order, whereas authoring applications let the author create nonlinear productions of information and media placed on individual cards. Choosing which type of production is most appropriate requires considering both the intended purpose and the needs of the audience.

CLASSROOM VIGNETTE

Tyler and Ashley's kindergarten class has just finished learning about dinosaurs, but none of them is going to be sitting down to take a test to assess what they have learned. Instead, each student will design one slide in a class multimedia presentation, highlighting facts and illustrations about his or her favorite dinosaur. The slide show will be presented to students' parents at this semester's Open House, so everyone wants to do his or her best.

Tyler chooses to draw a picture of a Stegosaurus. He uses the drawing program to outline the dinosaur from a picture in a book his teacher had read to them. He has trouble drawing the tail, so he erases it and redraws it. When the picture is complete, he adds a text field to type in all the dinosaur words he knows. He finds the microphone on the computer shelf above the monitor, plugs it into the computer, and records his slide narration: "This is my Stegosaurus. He's as big as the whole page and he just stepped on a little tree." When he is done with his slide, he saves it to his personal folder because his teacher said she would put all the slides together when everyone was done.

That afternoon, Ashley starts her dinosaur slide. She has trouble deciding which dinosaur to choose, so she decides to split her slide in half and show the differences and similarities between carnivores and herbivores. She draws a detailed illustration of two dinosaurs she remembers from a CD-ROM her class used last week. She finds a book that tells about carnivores and herbivores, and because she does not know all the words herself, she slowly copies some of the sentences into two text boxes. When she hears that it is time to go to lunch, and she still has not finished the slide to her liking, she saves it to her folder so that she can complete it tomorrow.

When the night of the Open House comes, Tyler and Ashley walk excitedly through the door of the classroom, knowing that right inside is the computer on which the slide show is playing over and over, or "looping" as their teacher had called it. She had put all of the students' slides into one show and programmed it with an automatic timing option so that when parents entered, they could watch the entire show at their leisure. Parents commented on how good all of the slides looked. When Mrs. Guidiá, the principal, looked in to check on the progress of Open House, she was able to see very quickly what students had learned and how technology was facilitating the instruction and assessment of students at all levels.

Either type of production can be presented in a number of ways using technology, from using a regular computer screen for teaching to a small group to projecting the program images onto a larger screen for many to see at once. Computers must be configured to work with projection devices. Checking connections and setting preferences ahead of the scheduled time for a class or presentation will help ensure a working presentation system. Being prepared with a backup plan, such as skipping ahead to another lesson or using transparencies of the slides to give the presentation, is vital to establishing the flexibility necessary to be proficient in the skills of technology-enhanced presentations.

LEARNER ACTIVITIES

1. Find out what authoring applications are available on your school's computer systems. Familiarize yourself with one of the programs by creating a sample multimedia production.

2. Write simple directions for creating a production using the authoring software. Include specific references that would be appropriate for students who are new to the concept of authoring.

3. Use a presentation slide application to create a simple slide show. Experiment with the colors and transition effects to arrive at an effective presentation environment.

4. Make a list of instructional or informational situations that would require a nonlinear presentation and those that would best be accomplished using a slide-type presentation.

5. How might a multimedia project be used to assess a student's understanding of a concept in your area of interest? Give specific examples and criteria that could be used in making a judgment of understanding.

6. A series of steps necessary to creating a multimedia product are outlined in this chapter. Adapt this list to a more specific step-by-step plan that could be followed with students at the level you are interested in teaching.

7. Design three example screen layouts for presentations with three very different end purposes. Include color, font size and placement, and graphics that would be appropriate for both the topics and the audiences.

8. Find a commercial collection of clip art or video segments. How extensive is the collection? When would it be appropriate to use these premade media elements and when would original creations be more suitable?

9. Borrow a digital camera or digital video camera. Record an event using the equipment and choose several pictures or video segments that would be useful in illustrating an informative presentation on the event. How does having the pictures or video already in digital form affect the job of compiling the product? What types of considerations would need to be made when using such equipment with students at the level you plan to teach?

10. Obtain a projection device that is compatible with an available computer. Learn how to connect the cables and configure the computer preferences in order to make it work. Practice projecting in different-sized rooms and in various conditions. How long does it take you to set up in preparation for a presentation? Make a list of the types of technical problems you think you could possibly run into.

BIBLIOGRAPHY

Allen, D. (1995). Teaching with technology: Enhancing student projects. *Teaching PreK–8, 26*(30), 20–23.

Barron, T. (1996). Getting friendly with authoring tools. *Training and Development, 50*(5), 36–46.

Clark, J. H. (1996). Bells and whistles…but where are the references? Setting standards for hypermedia projects. *Learning and Leading with Technology, 23*(5), 22–24.

Cross, L. (1995). Preparing students for the future with project presentations. *Learning and Leading with Technology, 23*(2), 24–26.

D'Ignazio, F. (1996). A multimedia publishing center from scratch (and scavenge). *Book Report, 15*(3), 19–22.

Downs, E., & Clark, K. (1997). Guidelines for effective multimedia design. *Technology Connection, 4*(1), 8–9.

Dunham, K. (1995). Helping students design hypercard stacks. *Learning and Leading with Technology, 23*(2), 6–7, 61.

Elin, L. (2001). *Designing and developing multimedia: A practical guide for the producer, director, and writer.* Boston: Allyn & Bacon.

Ennis, W., & Ennis, D. (1996). Ten tips to aid teachers creating multimedia presentations. *Journal of Computing in Teacher Education, 13*(1), 16–20.

Farmer, L. S. J. (1995). Multimedia: Multi-learning tool. *Technology Connection, 2*(3), 30–31.

Florio, C., & Murie, M. (1996). Authoritative authoring: Software that makes multimedia happen. *NewMedia, 6*(12), 67–70, 72–75.

Gribas, C. (1996). Creating great overheads with computers. *College Teaching, 44,* 66–68.

Jordahl, G. (1995). School-grown videos. *Technology and Learning, 15*(8), 26–27, 30, 32.

LeCrone, N. L. (1997). Integrating multimedia into the curriculum. *Technology Connection, 4*(1), 14–15.

Lewis, S. (1995). Student-created virtual tours. *Learning and Leading with Technology, 23*(2), 35–39.

Mauldin, M. (1996). The development of computer-based multimedia: Is a rain forest the same place as a jungle? *TechTrends, 41*(3), 15–19.

Milone, M. N., Jr. (1995). Electronic portfolios: Who's doing them and how? *Technology and Learning, 16*(2), 28–29, 32, 34, 36.

Milone, M. N., Jr. (1996). Kids as multimedia authors. *Technology and Learning, 16*(2), 22, 24, 27–28.

Milton, K., & Spradley, P. (1996). A renaissance of the Renaissance: Using HyperStudio for research projects. *Learning and Leading with Technology, 23*(6), 20–22.

Monahan, S., & Susong, D. (1996). Author slide shows and Texas wildlife: Thematic multimedia projects. *Learning and Leading with Technology, 24*(2), 6–11.

Reese, S. (1995). MIDI-assisted composing in your classroom. *Music Educators Journal, 81*(4), 37–40.

Reinking, D., and Watkins, J. (2000). A formative experiment investigating the use of multimedia book reviews to increase elementary students' independent reading. *Reading Research Quarterly, 35*(3), 384–419.

Roblyer, M. D. (1997). Videoconferencing. *Learning and Leading with Technology, 24*(5), 58–61.

Sammons, M. C. (1995). Using in-house CD-ROM publishing to store and present classroom materials. *Educational Technology Review, 4,* 26–32.

Stafford, D. J. (1997). PowerPointing the way. *Technology Connection, 4*(1), 16–17.

Strasser, D. (1996). Tips for good electronic presentations. *Online, 20*(1), 78–81.

Taylor, H. G., & Stuhlmann, J. M. (1995). Creating slide show book reports. *Learning and Leading with Technology, 23*(1), 8–10.

Thorp, C. (1995). Choices and consequences. *Teaching PreK–8, 26*(2), 58–60.

Troutner, J. (1996). Yes, they put on quite a show, but what did they learn? *Technology Connection, 3*(1), 15–17.

Troxclair, D. (1996). Teaching technology: Multimedia presentations in the classroom. *Gifted Child Today Magazine, 19*(5), 34–36, 47.

Tuttle, H. G. (1997). Electronic portfolios tell a personal story. *MultiMedia Schools, 4*(1), 32–37.

Welsh, T. (1997). From multimedia to multiple-media: Designing computer-based course materials for the Information Age. *TechTrends, 42*(1), 17–23.

Woodward, M. (1997). Developing a multimedia product. *English in Education, 31*(1), 48–54.

CHAPTER 17

ASSESSING AND EVALUATING

FOCUS QUESTIONS

1. What roles does technology play in the assessment of student learning?
2. How can technology resources assist with data collection and analysis?
3. What methods of assessment determine appropriate student use of technology?

Understanding your students' grasp of the content and their ability to apply what they have learned completes the instructional sequence of planning, teaching, and assessing. The power of technology can make the assessment process more efficient, but is most effective when the following questions are considered:

- Why and in what ways are you looking to make judgments about students' work?
- What skills and abilities are you attempting to measure?
- How might technology assist your efforts to collect, record, analyze, and communicate measurement data?

This chapter will begin by defining some basic assessment and evaluation terms. Then it will draw distinctions about the focus of measurement and finally will explore specific strategies for the use of technology for understanding the progress of students.

MEASUREMENT DEFINITIONS

To understand the role that technology might play in measuring student progress, it is first helpful to understand what types of measurement you would like to make. Although the terms *assessment* and *evaluation* are frequently used interchangeably, the two can be distinguished by the nature of the processes. *Assessments* are collections of written, oral, observational, and performance measures that provide information to determine student abilities and progress toward reaching intended objectives. Assessments can take the form of (1) quantitative, numerical measures, such as quiz scores, or (2) qualitative records, such as informal teacher observations, anecdotal notes, or reflective comments that recognize learning and performance in complex, authentic situations. *Evaluation* is the use of various assessments to make judgments about a student's ability and informed decisions about continued instruction.

Teachers make assessments and evaluations continuously and for various purposes. *Formative* evaluations are measurements made throughout the instructional sequence to attempt to answer the question "How are we doing?" The information gained through formative assessments is key to informing and redirecting the learning process. *Summative* assessments typically occur at the end of an instructional segment to answer the question "How have we done?" These measurements are intended to examine the outcomes of instruction by indicating an end mastery of objectives or demonstration of competency. The distinctions among these definitions will help you to consider the most effective ways in which technology can assist in understanding students' progress.

TECHNOLOGY AS THE FOCUS

Measurement choices regarding technology depend both on how the role of technology is perceived and on what types of assessment information are desired. The following section will deal with the prevailing opinion in the educational technology community that technology is an instructional and assessment tool with the focus of assessment on the content that students learn. First, however, teachers should be aware of other types of assessments of technology in educational settings that focus on technology itself. A brief introduction to these perspectives will help to clarify the participation of classroom teachers.

Technology is frequently the focus of assessment on the large national, state, or district scale to determine if the purchase of computers has been a good investment. To measure the effect technology has had on student learning, lawmakers, district administration, and taxpayers look to assessments that might include counting the number of computers in classrooms, the number of "contact hours" teachers and students spend using computers on a regular basis, the attitudes teachers and students have toward technology, teacher and student skill levels, and perhaps the contexts in which technology is being used. These assessments are most meaningful when school and community stakeholders determine the performance indicators necessary to define success (Sun, 2000) and when these indicators are built into a comprehensive technology plan. Findings of such evaluations are ultimately reported to the appropriate stakeholders and then ideally used to plan future goals, such as customizing professional development training to meet teachers' skill needs.

Data to answer these questions of technology use are often collected by surveying technology directors, principals, or teachers. Local assessments can be informed by nationally recognized assessment tools such as the CEO Forum's StaRChart (<http://www.ceoforum.org>) and by the Milken Exchange's Seven Dimensions for Gauging Progress of Technology (<http://www.mff.org/edtech/>). Other data collected from individual students may further describe technology use habits, such as from achievement tests or attendance records (Barnett, 2000). However, these individual data are generally used only to compile school or district profiles rather than to assess individual competence (Sun, 2000).

To measure a student's ability to operate a computer or use a software tool, teachers often use checklists based on national, state, and local standards of what students should be able to do with computers to efficiently note abilities and deficiencies. These assessments might be handled in an informal observational manner or in more deliberate performance tasks. Classroom teachers are closest to the learning contexts and understand best the abilities of students, meaning they are in the best position to report a true picture of classroom technology use.

CONTENT AS THE FOCUS

When technology is seen as the tool for instructional delivery, communication, or information seeking, student learning is measured on mastery of content objectives rather than on mastery of technology use. Strategies for assessing student learning through technology-assisted processes and technology-produced products should be consistent with strategies used for assessing learning through more traditional means. This is especially true if the existing strategies already address the student-centered, problem-based, interdisciplinary learning that is characteristic of constructivist learning environments. *Constructivist learning* integrates disciplines, skills, and strategies, challenging teachers to assess student learning in a format that most closely matches how the information was learned, as well as with formative methods that will provide students feedback with which to inform further learning.

Student learning through collaborative team projects, including those products that have been produced using technology tools such as multimedia presentations, cannot adequately be assessed using traditional methods. More appropriate strategies for assessing growth in content knowledge within project-based, integrated learning activities include conferences with students, anecdotal records, and observation (Kumar & Bristor, 1999). *Rubrics* can strengthen these assessments. Simkins (1999) defines rubrics as "sets of formal guidelines we use to rate examples of student work…usually presented in the form of a matrix with performance levels in the top row and performance dimensions along the left column" (p. 23).

Well-constructed rubrics assist teachers in making decisions about student skills, competencies, abilities, and attitudes within complex learning processes and products (see Table 17.1). Students also focus on learning when they know ahead of time what will be expected of them in an activity. Student teams can learn by assessing peer projects according to rubric criteria. Simkins (1999) provides these tips for constructing effective assessment rubrics:

- Construct rubrics that are not too task-specific—more general rubrics can be used again for other projects.
- Construct rubrics that are not too general because they will lack the specificity required to make appropriate distinctions.
- Avoid highly detailed criteria that become more of a checklist than a rubric.
- Use a limited number of dimensions, or main areas of focus, in order to decide where to look for the main learning priorities of the project.
- Use key criteria that matter the most about each dimension of the project.
- Use measurable criteria that can be counted or ranked.
- Select descriptors that clearly describe traits that should be present in work.
- Use four performance levels that make fine enough discrimination, yet are not too divisive.
- Maintain an equal interval distance between levels so that the highest and next highest are an equal distance to the lowest and next lowest.

TABLE 17.1   Assessment Rubric Example

	EXEMPLARY	EXPECTED	ADEQUATE	INADEQUATE
Content	Information is in a logical, intuitive sequence; information is clear, appropriate, and accurate.	Information is in a logical sequence; information is largely clear, appropriate, and accurate.	Information is in some logical sequence; some information is confusing, inappropriate, or inaccurate.	Information is not in a logical sequence and is confusing, inappropriate, or inaccurate.
Written work	Maintains clear focus and logical organization; establishes a tone appropriate to the intended audience; clearly conveys complex ideas with ample supportive details; has no misspellings or grammatical errors.	Maintains focus and displays organization; conveys complex ideas with supportive details; has fewer than two misspellings and/or grammatical errors.	Attempts to maintain focus and organization, but occasionally is not clear; simple ideas are conveyed well, but more complex notions are not developed and supported with details; has multiple misspellings and/or grammatical errors.	Frequently loses focus and organization; ideas are not conveyed clearly or supported with details; has significant spelling errors and/or grammatical errors.

■ Involve students in creating rubrics so they will clearly understand what the expectations are and "buy in" to using them.

Numerous rubric examples can also be found on the web (e.g., Kathy Schrock's Guide for Educators at <http://school.discovery.com/schrockguide/assess.html>). Practical assessment strategies using technology tools are described in the final section of this chapter.

TECHNOLOGY AS A DATA COLLECTION TOOL

The jury is still out on how two powerful educational trends—the rise of constructivist teaching practices and the increased demand for accountability as expressed through standardized testing—will find ways to coexist in education practice. For now, society still expects student progress to be translated into numerical form for easier understanding and comparison. Standardized tests are required not only of those students desiring to pursue postsecondary study but also of students every year in most K–12 classrooms. While we know that learner-centered and problem-solving activities help students to make sense of the world, local standards and curriculum still place great value on memorization of discrete data and demonstration of other lower-order skills. It is therefore important that educators comprehend how the power of technology can contribute to the organization and accuracy of test taking, from sophisticated college entrance exams to simpler tests and quizzes that teachers can create themselves and use in their classrooms with all ages of students.

Objective tests assess knowledge that can be responded to in right or wrong answers. Other assessment tasks, such as mathematical computational problems or longer written works, do not lend themselves as well to electronic tests. Using a computer to deliver a test offers testing on demand, the inclusion of multimedia elements to create real-life testing scenarios, and fast, accurate scoring and reporting of results (Straetmans & Eggen, 1998).

Teachers can use information to make immediate adjustments in instruction, and test questions can be edited and updated at any time to reflect instructional variation (Bushweller, 2000).

The most sophisticated computerized tests, *computer adaptive* tests, are "smart" enough to actually change their form in response to a test taker's responses. More traditional paper-and-pencil tests assess all students at the same level, meaning all students must take a longer test consisting of all levels of test items, some too difficult and some too easy. Computer adaptive tests attempt to mimic a human examiner by adjusting to a level of difficulty appropriate to each individual user (Straetmans & Eggen, 1998). During examination, the computer selects an item from a large item bank and presents it to the user. If the user responds correctly, a more difficult item will be presented next; if incorrectly, the computer presents an easier item. The goal is to assess student knowledge accurately in the quickest sequence of test items. Computer adaptive formats are now being offered for the Graduate Record Exam (see GRE at <http://www.gre.com>), and computerized versions of the SAT and ACT are being considered. Software is also available for districts to create computer adaptive exams based on local standards (e.g., Northwest Evaluation Association <http://www.nwea.org/cat-int.htm>).

Computer-based tests are direct electronic versions of their paper-and-pencil counterparts. The computerized format is attractive because of the ease and accuracy of scoring large quantities of tests, leaving teachers time for more academic tasks, such as planning and instruction. Students can take the tests when and where they want, feedback is individual and immediate, and students can return to previous answers for further deliberation.

Results on the effectiveness of computer-based tests are mixed, with some studies demonstrating increased student accuracy on computer-based exams than the same paper versions (e.g., Bocij & Greasley, 1999) and others showing computerized and standard formats to be correlated (e.g., Haaf, Duncan, Skarakis-Doyle, Carew, & Kapitan, 1999). Results for computerized assessment of more subjective responses, such as essay writing, are even more inconclusive. Essay grading software matches scores of human graders 50 percent of the time on the Graduate Management Admission Test (GMAT) (Bushweller, 2000). This type of software assesses items such as passage length, redundancy, and spelling, but is less effective at assessing cleverness or organization of a written piece (see, for example, the Intelligent Essay Assessor, <http://LSA.colorado.edu>).

Teachers also find computers a useful tool in creating their own informal electronic exams and quizzes, either for grading or review purposes in the classroom. Electronic tests can be created by entering questions and answers into test-creation software (e.g., HotPotatoes <http://web.uvic.ca/hrd/halfbaked>). Some websites (e.g., WebAssign <http://www.webassign.net/info>) allow teachers to take advantage of ready-made tests or to create exams based on item banks that can be given and scored online. Other sites give teachers freedom to easily create exams and quizzes in a variety of formats, such as multiple choice or essay, and have student results emailed directly to them (e.g., FunBrain's Quiz Lab, <http://www.funbrain.com> and Quia, <http://www.quia.com>). These sites also feature databases of ready-made quizzes searchable by content area or grade level (see Figure 17.1).

TECHNOLOGY AS A RECORDING, ANALYSIS, AND COMMUNICATION TOOL

Any instructional effort is undertaken by both the instructor and the learner with the hope that the learning of something new will be the end result. Almost continuously, teachers

FIGURE 17.1   FunBrain.com.

arrive at various forms of evaluative conclusions that shape and guide plans for future instruction. The recorded products of evaluative activity can take a number of forms, but can
generally be discussed in two chief categories: quantitative and qualitative records. Classroom technology can assist teachers with both types of record keeping, making the tedious,
potentially error-prone activities easy and accurate, thus facilitating the straightforward
report of progress to parents. Further, technology tools can be invaluable in the ongoing
presentation of student learning.

Quantitative Record Keeping

Traditionally, students have been assessed according to standard, established criteria. Their
achievement has been compared either to each other as in *norm-referenced* assessments or
according to their mastery of the objectives themselves as is the case with *criteria-referenced*
conclusions. In either case, scores received on assessments must be recorded and compiled
so that a longer-term evaluation of an individual can be accomplished. A teacher's grade
book has always been thought to hold all the answers regarding a child's progress. The story
was told in the neat columns and rows of handwritten names and numbers.

The way in which records can be kept has received a helping hand from spreadsheet
software. Now, instead of entering student names by hand, names can be easily typed in.
Records for new students can be inserted into the alphabetically correct position, rather
than being tacked on to the bottom of the list out of order. Grades that are entered can be
modified if assignments are resubmitted without creating a mess of erasings and blobs of
correction fluid (see Figure 17.2).

Mr. Brooks 8th Grade English 3rd Hour	Assignment 9/14	Assignment 9/16	Assignment 9/18	Assignment 9/20	Assignment 9/24	quiz #1	quiz #2	quiz #3	quiz #4		Total	%	
Total Points	**20**	**20**	**20**	**20**	**20**	**5**	**5**	**5**	**5**		**120**	**100%**	
Berland, C.	20	17	17	20	18	5	5	5	5		112	93%	
Booth, D.	19	19	19	19	18	5	4	4	5		112	93%	
Chambers, A.	17	16	19	20	18	5	5	5	5		110	92%	
Davis, M.	17	17	19	20	18	5	5	4	3		108	90%	
Gillis, L.	20	18	19	20	18	4	5	5	5		114	95%	
Goetz, M.	20	18	19	12	18	3	5	4	3		102	85%	
Hatten, A.	20	18	19	20	18	3	5	5	5		113	94%	
Kinney, R.	19	18	20	20	15	4	0	4	4		104	87%	
Landers, M.	20	20	20	20	20	3	1	3	5		112	93%	
Levy, D.	17	19	17	20	19	4	2	2	5		105	88%	
Livingston, P.	14	19	14	20	19	2	2	3	5		98	82%	
Marshall, J.	10	19	20	19	19	5	4	2	5		103	86%	
Nedley, H.	18	18	20	19	14	5	4	3	5		106	88%	
O'Connor, M.	20	20	20	19	20	5	3	4	4		115	96%	
Quesada, S.	12	14	20	19	20	2	3	5	5		100	83%	
Scott, T.	17	19	20	19	20	2	3	5	5		110	92%	
Steele, R.	13	5	20	19	20	2	5	5	5		94	78%	
Tencer, J.	15	19	19	19	20	1	4	3	5		105	88%	
Vanderpool, V.	20	20	20	20	20	5	5	5	5		120	100%	
Wyatt, K.	20	19	19	19	20	5	5	1	5		113	94%	

FIGURE 17.2   A gradebook created using spreadsheet software.

The most powerful advantage of using a spreadsheet to keep track of student grades is the software's ability to perform computational functions on numbers. No longer does a teacher need to take time to enter each grade for a student into a calculator to calculate an average grade. With a drag to highlight a row of grades, and a click on a shortcut button, a simple average computation can be placed into a target spreadsheet cell. Formulas can also be easily written to perform more complicated calculations, such as applying different weights to the scores received on different assignments. Keeping grades using spreadsheet software allows teachers to represent scores graphically, as most programs will produce any number of graphs and charts to present student achievement in ways that are readily understandable and comparable. Visually tracking student performance is an ideal way to involve students in assessing and understanding their own progress.

Numerous programs are designed expressly for the purposes of recording and calculating grades, planning seating charts, and keeping attendance (e.g., 1st Class Gradebook, Chancery Software's Grade Machine, and Jay Klein Productions' Making the Grade). Formulas most useful in calculating grades are already written and made easily accessible in these programs, and graphical outputs are created especially for student progress reporting purposes. Web-based grade book management systems allow teachers to manage grades from any computer connected to the Internet and email students when grades are updated (see, for example, Excelsior Pinnacle at <http://www.gradebook.com/> and the free-of-charge mygradebook at <http://mygradebook.com>). Parents can input their child's student identification number and a PIN code to access real-time progress, grade, and attendance reports. Despite these features, though, many teachers prefer the flexibility and customizability that a generic spreadsheet program gives them in creating their own system over these purpose-specific products (see Figure 17.3).

Qualitative Record Keeping

As educational philosophy demands that students have authentic opportunities to demonstrate their unique understandings and capabilities, views of what type of information provides adequate indication of learning are changing. The steadfast belief that numbers can tell the complete story of a learner is giving way to a recognition that what a teacher observes in daily interactions with students is in fact very telling of the growth of those students. Indeed, as educators embrace this new anecdotal method of assessment, at the same time they scramble to find ways to consistently and comparably report student progress in words instead of numbers. This challenge can be made more manageable, and perhaps more meaningful, with the help of classroom technology.

By creating or adding to an existing database (e.g., Microsoft Access) record for each child, teachers can record observations in a central, organized location (see Figure 17.4).

Student	CURRENT STUDENT TOTALS
1 Archer, Dennis E.	76.4=C
2 Bowles, Charles A.	61.5=D
3 Chancellor, James L.	86.0=B
4 Dickerson Michael R.	82.6=B
5 Garcia, Eugene F.	75.7=C
6 Glenn, Helen B.	90.9=A
7 Gray, Kathleen R.	70.5=C-
8 Howard, Stacey E.	79.5=C+
9 Huntington, Susan L.	92.1=A
10 Huston, Stephen B.	88.1=B
11 Ingram, Thomas L.	69.8=C-
12 Jansen, Beverly H.	88.4=B
13 Jenkins, Lynn T.	63.1=D
14 Knight, Rebecca J.	46.1=F-
15 Kosterman, Jason D.	78.7=C+
16 Lee, Tamara C.	73.1=C
17 Lewis, Jeffrey P.	56.8=F
18 Mc_Cann, Molly M.	78.7=C+
19 Morgan, Donald T.	81.8=B
20 Nuss, Timothy A.	76.6=C
21 Ogden, Kristi A.	64.4=D
22 O'Grady, Shelli N.	80.7=B-
23 Powell_Jr, John C.	81.2=B-
24 Raymond, Carle S.	71.6=C
25 Rutledge, Michael S.	77.0=C
26 Sampson, Eugene J.	74.5=C
27 Smith, Vickie R.	93.2=A
28 St._James, Lester L.	73.5=C
29 Torrence, Jeremy D.	84.5=B
30 Winston, Kristin R.	80.3=B-
31 Yoder, Jeremy D.	71.1=C-

ASSIGNMENT TITLES	POINTS	ITEMS	X-FACTORS
34 COMPOSITION 1: The Nature of Man [10/28]	100	100	1.000
35 QUARTER I: Spelling Final Test [10/28]	200	100	2.000
36			

FIGURE 17.3   Making the Grade gradebook software.

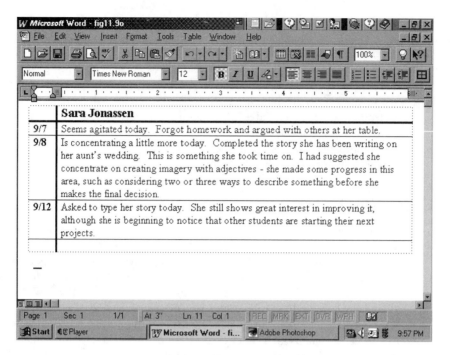

FIGURE 17.4 Anecdotal records kept on a word processor.

Even word-processed notes can provide handy reminders of progress when reporting to parents. Both options allow a teacher opportunity to scroll back up through a student's record to track patterns or make predictions. Although this type of recording could, in essence, be done with paper and pencil, handwritten notes are static documents. The text of anecdotal records recorded in a database can be searched by keywords to see, for example, how frequently a student has offered an answer in class or has had a problem behaving with another student. These records can additionally be merged into word-processed documents to create instant parent reports of student progress.

Because it is not practical to run over to the computer to access the database whenever a student says or does something of note, teachers can develop note-taking practices that work with the technology-based record keeping. Keeping a notepad handy allows teachers to quickly jot down the names of the students and what indication of progress they notice. At a later time, just as a teacher would need to take time to record quantitative grades, a teacher can sit with the database application open and enter in the observations. Voice recognition technology holds promise in the future of simplifying this observation process by allowing teachers to record their verbal comments and translate them automatically into digitized text format.

Portfolio Assessment

Portfolios are alternative assessment forms that have been described frequently as the intersection between instruction and assessment. The Northwest Regional Educational Laboratory defines a portfolio as "a purposeful collection of student work that tells the story of student achievement or growth" (Arter, 1995). Barrett (2000) adds the concept of the portfolio as a "reflective tool." Whereas answers given on tests can indicate only a student's response to a given stimulus (Kennedy, 1999), a portfolio can function as a window into that student's head, as well as a broad time line of learning. A powerful portfolio should do the following:

- Demonstrate that a student has engaged in self-reflection so that he may learn about and assume ownership for his own learning.
- Involve the student in the selection of the pieces to be included in the portfolio.
- Convey the rationale, intents, contents, standards, and judgments of the student's work.
- Show growth.
- May serve a different purpose in progress than it serves at the end (Paulson, Paulson, & Meyer, 1991).

The distinct advantage of portfolio assessment is that the ownership of learning and product production shifts away from the teacher (Wiggins, 1989). Instead, portfolio development reflects a jointly negotiated process, reached by the teacher and the student, which entails detailed discussions and customized evaluation of learning. Educators should strive for a balance between student-centered portfolios and teacher-centered portfolios. In the former, students collect, select, and compile items to illustrate personal learning. In the latter, portfolios are created and maintained by teachers with items that demonstrate learning in accordance with program goals (Barrett, 1998). Students must be carefully introduced to the concept of portfolios and to the methods of selecting items and reflecting on learning relevance (Stone, 1998). However, prescribing too structured of a portfolio format eliminates student creativity (Mills, 1997).

Traditional educational portfolios are collected in notebooks, binders, and even boxes, filling shelves and file cabinets. As artifacts of learning are increasingly represented with digital products, electronic portfolios provide a natural solution to representing student learning. Electronic portfolios can include word-processed writing examples, spreadsheets, scanned writing or drawing, digital photos, videos of performances or actions, audiotaped narration reading, or multimedia projects. Years' worth of work can be efficiently stored on disk or CD-ROM, making work much more portable than large binders of pages.

Educational portfolios serve purposes distinct from other professional portfolios, not a collection of every single item, as is the case with stock portfolios, yet not solely the best of the best examples that constitute artistic portfolios. Carlson (1998) suggests two distinct types of portfolios: *process* and *product*. Process portfolios collect students' work throughout a period of time in order to show growth in ability and attitude. Product portfolios exhibit a selection of a student's best work.

Niguidula (1997) suggests that all stakeholders ask a series of questions to guide the creation of a portfolio-based assessment system:

1. *Vision.* What should a student know and be able to do?
2. *Assessment.* How can students demonstrate the school vision? Why do we collect student work? What audiences are most important to us? How do we know what's good?
3. *Technology.* What hardware, software, and networking will we need? Who are the primary users of the equipment? Who will support the system?

4. *Logistics.* When will information be digitized? Who will do it? Who will select the work? Who will reflect on the work?

5. *Culture.* Is the school used to discussing student work? (pp. 27–28).

Once these areas have been considered, Barrett (2000) identifies the following stages of electronic portfolio development.

Stage 1: Defining the Portfolio Context and Goals.   Educators should consider why the assessment is occurring, what standards students should be able to meet, what resources are available, what skill levels teachers and students possess, and who the audiences for the portfolios are.

Stage 2: The Working Portfolio.   The main concerns of this stage are the types of items to select for the portfolio, determined by the goals set in the first stage. Storage and software options should also be considered as work is collected.

Stage 3: The Reflective Portfolio.   Criteria for selecting and judging learning artifacts can be managed with a rubric. Student self-reflections on artifacts and goals for future learning are key to determining the quality of the portfolio.

Stage 4: The Connected Portfolio.   Learning artifacts can be organized and linked so that they can be navigated to demonstrate that the learner has met the learning goals. Such connecting also aids evaluation and planning for future instruction.

Stage 5: The Presentation Portfolio.   Final storage options must be considered here so that work can be preserved, and students will share their portfolios in some manner, as in student-led conferences.

Electronic Portfolio Formats.   Electronic portfolios might take a number of formats depending on available technology and skill levels. The most basic collections can be created with slide-show software (e.g., PowerPoint), which is primarily linear in structure but can incorporate some hyperlinks. Easy-to-use multimedia software (e.g., HyperStudio) can allow for the linking and presentation of work samples, and more advanced authoring software (e.g., Macromedia Authorware) allows for the creation of more sophisticated portfolio interfaces. Electronic portfolios can also involve the use of relational databases (e.g., Access) to organize student work samples so that they can be sorted, clustered, and compared over time.

Web-based portfolio formats further encourage individuality by allowing students to demonstrate creativity in presentation and organization, to create multiple design formats for multiple audiences (Watkins, 1996), and to establish connections easily among related portfolio components (McKinney, 1998). The web, as both a technology and an interface, enables students ultimate control in assembling and ease of reorganizing, as well as the ability to integrate narrative captions among the learning evidence to emphasize the interrelated nature of the learning (Watkins, 1996). The web environment permits students the flexibility to maintain their portfolios in either a protected intranet environment or on a web space that can be remotely accessed from anywhere at any time, by the student, faculty, peers, scholarship review committees, and potential employers. Finally, web-based portfolios promote seamless access to student work by eliminating software and platform incompatibilities encountered when viewing electronic portfolios created with multiple authoring tools (Mills, 1997). As a caveat, online web-based portfolios will require password protection to protect student privacy on the Internet. They will further necessitate some local consideration of the types of photos or videos of students that are appropriate to post. Other drawbacks of using portfolio assessment on a large scale: Portfolios are less efficient than numerical scores, more difficult to administer, more time-consuming, not as easily standardized, and ultimately, more costly (Madaus & O'Dwyer, 1999).

SUMMARY

Technology can make the assessment process more efficient if the role of technology and the types of assessment information desired is considered. Technology can be either (1) the focus of assessment on large scales to justify the purchase of computers or (2) the tool for instructional delivery, communication, or information finding, basing student learning on mastery of content rather than technology use. Learning through integrated activities is best assessed using alternative methods such as student conferences, anecdotal records, and observation, guided by rubrics.

Educators should understand how the power of technology could contribute to the organization and accuracy of test taking. Computerized formats make scoring large quantities easier and more accurate so that teachers can attend to academic tasks. Sophisticated computer adaptive tests change form in response to a test taker's responses. Other computer-based tests directly mimic their paper-and-pencil counterparts.

■ ■ ■ ■ ■

CLASSROOM VIGNETTE

The French culture multimedia projects were nearly finished. Some students in Cassie Lichtner's eleventh-grade French class were putting in a last few minutes of rehearsal before the parent presentations that evening. Others were completing the Project Reflections necessary to submit with their projects to their electronic portfolios.

Students write reflections to accompany all major projects, listing strengths they perceive of the assignments, as well as those aspects they would do differently next time. This was a difficult process for many students at the beginning of the year, because they had never been asked to think about their own learning before. At first, some students only described the assignment, rather than considering their own effort and learning. Ms. Lichtner often meets with students individually to ask them questions before they write their reflections so students will better be able to elicit thought and self-reflection.

Ms. Lichtner reads her students' reflections for a better understanding of each one's learning habits, but does not grade them. The purpose of the reflections is to record personal understandings at the time of the assignments. At the end of each nine weeks, students will spend extensive time reviewing their entire portfolios to assess their learning and set goals for the next quarter. If students waited several weeks to look back at each assignment, they would not recall the detail and relevance.

Quantitative record keeping can be more efficient with the use of spreadsheet software and qualitative anecdotal assessment methods are made more manageable through the use of database records or word-processed notes. Electronic portfolios can incorporate various electronic learning formats and can be stored easily on disk or CD-ROM. Web portfolios enable students control in assembling, reorganizing, narrating, and maintaining learning artifacts, while also allowing remote access and viewing by multiple audiences.

LEARNER ACTIVITIES

1. Research your state or district's technology resources.

2. Search the web using such keywords as *portfolios* and *technology.* What types of portfolio examples do you find?

3. Design a four-level rubric for a course activity you have recently been asked to complete. How might your grade on that assignment have changed with a rubric-driven assessment?

4. How can a classroom that already uses portfolios transition toward using electronic portfolios? Write a short plan consisting of easy to more advanced strategies.

5. Rate your school's technology preparedness using the CEO Forum's StaRChart (<http://www.ceoforum.org>).

6. Research technology skills checklists for students found online. Are there other skills that should be included? How do you imagine using such a checklist to assess your students' technology proficiency?

7. Using a spreadsheet application, design a simple grade book for a fictitious class. Include scores for several assignments and formulas to calculate the final grades.

8. What does the research say about the use of anecdotal records? What are some methods that experienced teachers use to keep track of these types of observations?

9. Design an electronic form on which to record qualitative, anecdotal records on individual students. What will be the best way to keep these records updated?

10. Design an online quiz using FunBrain's Quiz Lab (<http://www.funbrain.com>). Have three friends take the quiz and email the results to you. How long does this whole process take from start to finish?

BIBLIOGRAPHY

Arter, J. A. (1995). *Portfolios for assessment and instruction.* ERIC Clearinghouse on Counseling and Student Services (Report No. EDO-CG-95-10). Greensboro, NC: ERIC Clearinghouse on Counseling and Student Services. (ERIC Document Reproduction Service No. ED 388890.)

Barnett, H. (2000). Assessing the effects of technology. *Learning and Leading with Technology, 27*(7), 28–31, 63.

Barrett, H. C. (1998). Strategic questions: What to consider when planning for electronic portfolios. *Learning and Leading with Technology, 26*(2), 6–13.

Barrett, H. C. (2000). Create your own electronic portfolio: Using off-the-shelf software to showcase your own or student work. *Learning and Leading with Technology, 27*(7), 15–21.

Bocij, P., & Greasley, A. (1999). Can computer-based testing achieve quality and efficiency in assessment? *International Journal of Educational Technology, 1*(1). [Online]. Available: <http://www.out-reach.uiuc.edu/ijet/v1n1/bocij/index.html> [2000, June].

Bushweller, K. (2000). Electronic exams. *Electronic School* [Online]. Retrieved 6/20/00 from <http://www.electonic-school.com>.

Carlson, R. D. (1998). Portfolio assessment of instructional technology. *Journal of Educational Technology Systems, 27*(1), 81–92.

Haaf, R., Duncan, B., Skarakis-Doyle, E., Carew, M., & Kapitan, P. (1999). Computer-based language assessment software: The effects of presentation and response format. *Language, Speech, and Hearing Services in Schools, 30*(1), 68–74.

Kennedy, D. (1999). Assessing true academic success: The next frontier of reform. *The Mathematics Teacher, 92*(6), 462–466.

Kumar, D., & Bristor, V. J. (1999). Integrating science and language arts through technology-based macro-contexts. *Educational Review, 51*(1), 41–53.

Madaus, G. F., & O'Dwyer, L. M. (1999). A short history of performance assessment: Lessons learned. *Phi Delta Kappan, 80*(9), 688–695.

McKinney, M. (1998). Preservice teachers' electronic portfolios: Integrating technology, self-assessment, and reflection. *Teacher Education Quarterly, 25*(1), 85–103.

Mills, E. (1997). Portfolios: A challenge for technology. *International Journal of Instructional Media, 24*(1), 23–29.

Niguidula, D. (1997). Picturing performance with digital portfolios. *Educational Leadership, 55*(3), 26–29.

Painter, D. D. (2000). Teacher as researcher: A means to assess the effectiveness of technology in the classroom. *Learning and Leading with Technology, 27*(7), 10–13, 27.

Paulson, F. L., Paulson, P. R., & Meyer, C. A. (1991). What makes a portfolio a portfolio? *Educational Leadership, 48*(5), 60–63.

Simkins, M. (1999). Designing great rubrics. *Technology and Learning, 20*(1), 23–24, 28–29.

Stone, B. A. (1998). Problems, pitfalls, and benefits of portfolios. *Teacher Education Quarterly, 25*(1), 105–114.

Straetmans, G. J. J. M., & Eggen, T. J. H. M. (1998). Computerized adaptive testing: What it is and how it works. *Educational Technology, 38*(1), 45–52.

Sun, J. (2000). How do we know it's working? *Learning and Leading with Technology, 27*(7), 32–35, 41, 49.

Watkins, S. (1996). World Wide Web authoring in the portfolio-assessed, (inter)networked composition course. *Computers and Composition, 13*(2), 219–230.

Wiggins, G. (1989). A true test: Toward more authentic and equitable assessment. *Phi Delta Kappan,* 703–713.

CHAPTER 18

PRODUCTIVITY AND CLASSROOM ADMINISTRATION

FOCUS QUESTIONS

1. How can basic software tools be used to facilitate print-based communication?
2. What types of planning and scheduling can be aided with the use of technology?
3. What specific-purpose software aids teacher productivity?

The one aspect of a teacher's job description that rarely makes it into most discussions in college teacher preparation programs is that of being a classroom administrator. Many new teachers arrive in their first classrooms ready to get on with the job of "teaching" and instead discover that they are poorly prepared to manage the day-to-day operation that a bustling classroom community requires. It is unrealistic to see modern teachers solely in the role of instructors. In fact, their necessary administrative duties require them to wear many of the hats that most leaders in the professional world must also don. Noninstructional activities make up a large segment of a teacher's typical day, and those daily responsibilities could easily infringe on the time allocated for actual instruction. Although teachers are often ready to consider ways in which students can benefit from technology, they sometimes are not aware of how technology can help them in accomplishing administrative duties (Office of Technology Assessment, 1995). Technology can aid greatly in making time spent in these routine administrative tasks effective and efficient, and this undoubtedly can lead to more minutes available for meaningful contact with an educator's clients, the young learners.

Because computerizing these basic administrative affairs can make for more consistent and accurate management systems as compared to the handwritten and figured approach, more democratic leadership patterns can emerge in the classroom. Teachers are finding that students of all ages are capable of some degree of responsibility for the routine tasks that surround and make possible the learning environment of the classroom. This shift in policy necessarily accompanies the general shift from teacher-directed learning situations to productive, child-centered learning contexts. Technology facilitates greater student participation by providing safe, predictable organizational systems.

By reflecting and modeling this shift in pedagogical and organizational focus, this chapter will serve to provoke thought and experimentation on the part of teachers in how they might best use technology to ensure their daily efforts are faster and more efficient. The ideas here should not be construed as comprehensive nor should every idea be assumed to be vital to successful classroom management in the Information Age. A teacher's individual management style and the unique composition of each individual class will determine the extent to which technology might streamline administrative tasks.

Step-by-step instructions will not be given in this chapter on the operation of software tools, such as how to create a document using a word processor or how to write a formula in a spreadsheet; proficiency with common productivity tools has begun to be considered a baseline skill for employment in any professional field. (See Chapter 2 for an overview on using word processors, spreadsheets, and databases.) The purpose of this chapter, rather, is to suggest beginning points for implementing a technologically-organized plan of action. The chapter is arranged according to administrative purpose, with ideas for those software choices that might best be used for each task. Uses for productivity software tools that come packaged on most computers are primarily discussed because teachers are more likely to have access to these basic programs in their classroom computers. Features of some specific-purpose tools that are applicable to particular administrative responsibilities are also described.

COMMUNICATING

Inherent to the role of a classroom teacher is the need to act as a liaison among many groups of people: parents, administrators, students, other teachers, students from other classes, and community members. Strong, organized strategies are a must to pull off communication that often rivals corporate public relations campaigns. The Information Age has brought with it the ability to communicate electronically, such as through email, as discussed in Chapter 3. However, paper-based communication forms remain a necessary component to a teacher's communication arsenal. Many of the stakeholders that make up a classroom community do not have the capabilities to communicate electronically, and many items, such as those giving parent permission, require handwritten signatures. Basic productivity tools to which most teachers have access can prevent the job from becoming a correspondence nightmare. The suggestions that follow may seem like obvious uses of computer technology, but will serve as basics on which to build a strong communication platform.

Student Contact Information

Keeping in touch with your students' families is made easier by keeping up-to-date student records. Schools often provide teachers with printed lists of student information, but these pages represent a static form of keeping this information. If a family changes phone numbers, or a parent gets a new job with different hours, a printed list can be modified only by hand, leaving a messy record-keeping system.

Creating a database record for each student in class allows for a neat, easy-to-update filing system. The fields in a database can be customized to allow for information specific to particular students and situations. A database for a class in which most students ride the school bus may need to include a field identifying the bus number in order to be complete. A database on secondary students might include students' after-school work numbers. Larger text fields can be used to add anecdotal comments. Databases not only provide for a convenient, consistent compilation of information about students, but that information can also be searched and sorted. If, for example, all of the students who have other siblings attending the same school need to be contacted, students with completed "sibling" fields can be sorted and printed out. Student information can be entered into a database by teachers, or the task can be shared. Having the database open on the computer screen, along with an example of a student record, as parents come in for a "Meet-Your-Teacher" night at the beginning of the school year can serve as an invitation for parents to fill in their own child's data. Not only does this spread the workload, but it also introduces parents to some of the many ways technology is being used in the classroom.

Letters

Whether it is a lengthy summary of a semester's work or a brief response acknowledging a note received, writing letters to parents is a requirement of most teachers' jobs at the K–12 level. With teachers having little time in the daily routine to sit and compose an intelligible letter, a word processor can prove invaluable. Letters can be generally typed faster than they can be handwritten, especially if a computer is available in the classroom. Time can further be saved by beginning with a previously written letter as a template and modifying it to fit the current purpose. Most word processing programs include ready-made templates or wizards to assist with composing letters.

Letters that are sent home can be saved in case a parent does not receive it or there are questions regarding what was said (see Figure 18.1). Spelling and grammar can be checked, formatting adjusted, and personal touches, such as a class or school logo, can be inserted to design a professional-looking letter. Parents will appreciate the legibility of a typed letter and therefore may actually be more likely to respond to it. As with any typed

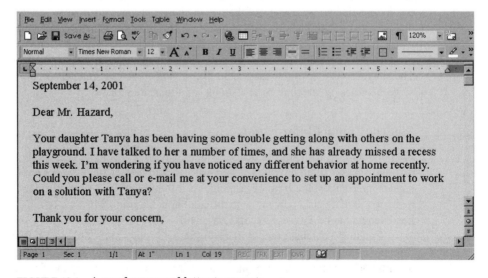

FIGURE 18.1   A word-processed letter to parents.

letter, always be sure to sign it by hand. A letter with a typed signature implies that little care was taken to elevate it past the status of a mere form letter, lowering the letter's importance in parents' eyes to that of junk mail. Word processors can also be used to create thank-you notes and solicitations for help or information to other teachers, community members, and content experts.

The merge function greatly streamlines the process of sending out letters to multiple families. First, you begin with a word-processed letter. In places that require personal information, such as names or specific comments, you insert a field name. This field name corresponds to a field in another program, such as your student contacts database. The *merge* function allows you to insert information automatically from this other document into the letter, creating a letter customized with names and other information for each family in the time it takes to write one letter. The merge function can also be used to print address labels to further assist the process.

Newsletters

Keeping parents up-to-date on classroom and school occurrences is vital to the maintenance of a strong parent–school network, and the job can easily be done by publishing a weekly newsletter. Publishing a professional-looking newspaper-type document right on the classroom computer is possible with most word processors. Parents can be notified of class study topics, upcoming events, and new policies.

Depending on the ages and abilities of students, class "reporters" can actually write much of the text of the newsletter. This gives students an authentic writing purpose with a real audience, and the student participation guarantees a newsletter with the appeal of personality and variety. Many classrooms come up with a catchy title for their weekly publication and find or create relevant graphics with which to personalize the final product. The basic layout can be saved as a template to be used week after week, minimizing time spent to simplify what it takes to insert the new information each week. Many schools where teachers do have convenient access to word processors now require teachers to produce a newsletter of some sort to send home on a regular basis.

Official Correspondence

Parent permission is frequently required for participation in anything from field trips to Internet usage. Creating, printing, and copying these types of releases to send home makes for consistent, professional-looking records of parent responses. Although most schools, or even districts, have standard forms for these purposes, occasions may arise for which there is no set form in place, such as requesting permission to take home a class pet, for example, or notifying families of an end-of-semester recital. Teachers should make sure any forms that are sent home are easy to understand and provide ample writing space for parents.

PLANNING

Regardless of the personal teaching style and philosophy of each teacher, most create some sort of plans to reach both long- and short-term objectives. Plans that are sketched out on paper may grow messy and unreadable through subsequent modifications. Productivity software can aid in planning activities by saving teachers' time and making quality, functional, final products.

Lesson Plans

When a newly certified teacher heads to the teaching supply store, the first item placed in the shopping cart is usually a "Teacher's Plan Book." These books contain blank weekly calendars, with the days identified down the left side of the page and half-hour increments clearly marked across the top. As schedules of special activities and class times are mapped out, changed, and finalized throughout the weeks before the start of the school year, and sometimes well into the first days of school, the neat order of most plan books begins to suffer. Handwritten schedules get crossed out, erased, and modified. Even when weekly plans do settle down into routine schedules, daily activities must still be handwritten into the book. Regularly scheduled activities must be repeatedly entered week after week. Many times activities take longer than the time planned and must be carried over into other time slots. All in all, handwritten plan books are messy, redundant, and generally not an effective utilization of a teacher's time.

Productivity software, such as word processing or spreadsheet software, can make some of this hassle more manageable. Using a spreadsheet, teachers can easily map out a generic weekly schedule (see Figure 18.2). If activities change, they can simply be deleted or moved. Classes that occur predictably at the same time every day or week can easily be copied over to the next cells. Teachers who require more space to plan for lessons can format their planning pages to allow for large blocks of planning space. Tentative plans can be printed out on a daily, weekly, or longer basis, or plan templates, with recurring activities blocked in but learning time left blank, can be printed out to allow for handwritten adjustments.

Planning for days when a guest teacher will be in is also simplified. Typed plans supply the guest teacher with accurate information on all necessary special student and schedule considerations and can be prepared ahead of time to lessen the busy work of preparing to be absent for a day. The planning options are as endless as the variety of teaching styles and circumstances.

Longer-term planning can be accomplished using software tools as well. Monthly calendars can be created manually using a spreadsheet, with help from templates or Wizards that come packaged with most word processing software or even by using software especially intended to create calendars. An entire school year can be mapped out ahead of time, making it possible to see how thematic units might interrelate or how required curriculum elements can be coordinated into the allotted school days. As plans change, calendars can be easily modified accordingly.

Visually aided planning can also be facilitated with the use of technology. It is common for teachers to plan for various related curriculum areas at the same time often with student input, using a web-type graphical representation so connections between topics or activities can easily be seen. Using a simple drawing program, teachers can map out thematic units or entire semester plans, making it possible with one glance to see how learning might be structured. Specific concept-mapping software (e.g., Inspiration at <http://www.inspiration.com/>) can simplify the planning process with premade symbols and relational indicators.

New lesson plan software that is now available is designed to assist educators of all teaching levels in planning, editing, and organizing lessons for multiple classes (e.g.,

	Monday
8:00-8:15	Opening (Attendance, Lunch Count, Calendar)
8:15-9:30	Language (Literature, Writing)
9:30-10:00	Music
10:00-11:30	Math
11:30-12:15	Lunch
12:15-1:30	Science/Social Studies
1:30-1:50	Recess
1:50-2:30	Group Work
2:30-3:00	Journals, Storytime

FIGURE 18.2   A simple, word-processed lesson-planning page.

Lesson Manager Professional at <http://www.isdsoftwaredesign.com/edu.htm>). Such software provides word processing and database tools, standardized lesson formats, drag-and-drop capabilities among lessons and units, project time lines for a graphical overview of a lesson, and calendar and agenda tools (see Figure 18.3).

Planning for Individual Student Needs

As teachers make plans for reaching both long- and short-term goals, customizing those plans to meet the educational needs of individual students can be facilitated by referring to a database of individual student concerns. Whether added to a main database of student information, or created as a separate file of learning characteristics, comments on everything from student learning modalities to special classes required can be recorded, making planning to meet the needs of students easy. If, for instance, three students leave to go to work with a speech pathologist every Tuesday at 1:00, a guest speaker can be scheduled around that time so that the students would still be able to participate. Whereas scheduling around one or two students' special schedules or planning for ways in which they will learn best might be possible without any help from a computer, effectively planning based on the

FIGURE 18.3   Lesson Manager Professional.

needs of 30 students or close to 200 teachers who see a series of different classes throughout the day could become problematic. A database created for this purpose will maximize planning and teaching time by helping to manage the specific characteristics a teacher must remember about every student.

Designing a Classroom Layout

How the furniture in a classroom is physically arranged reflects both the personal style and the teaching style of a teacher. Not only does the placement of desks or bookshelves contribute to the aesthetic atmosphere, but it determines the functional traffic patterns of the room. Desks pushed into groups are more conducive to different learning experiences than are desks organized into measured rows. Regardless of the desired learning atmosphere, graphics software can be of great assistance. Available furniture can be mapped out and moved. Student names can be assigned to desks or tables and shuffled to achieve a workable mix of personalities and learning styles. These types of modifiable seating charts are especially helpful for guest teachers to become familiar with students (see Figure 18.4).

SCHEDULING

Along with the educational planning necessary in quality learning environments, much attention must also be paid to the fundamental scheduling of activities and other arrangements. Budgeting money, booking guest speakers, and making arrangements for field trips can all be simplified with the use of classroom technology.

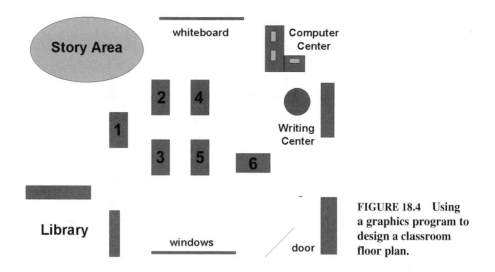

FIGURE 18.4   Using a graphics program to design a classroom floor plan.

Budgeting Money

Operating a classroom frequently involves the planning, collecting, accounting, and distributing of money. Money might be collected to pay for a field trip, raised by having a school candy sale or saved to reach a class goal. When students begin bringing in wrinkled dollar bills and handfuls of coins, an orderly system of money management is vital. The features of a spreadsheet are best designed for the purpose of budgeting money. Columns can be organized to account for who has brought in what amount, and functions can calculate the total amounts. Time estimated to reach monetary goals can be planned, relying on calculations based on an anticipated income from a money-raising event. A legible spreadsheet accounting for every penny is a much superior method of tracking classroom expenses than a handwritten list of names and amounts scrawled on the back of an envelope full of dollars and change (see Figure 18.5).

Total Cost for Field Trip to Mexico			
Cost per student X	**# of Students =**		**Total Cost**
$900.00	27		$24,300.00
Candy Sale			$14,000.00
Car Washes			$2,500.00
Bake Sales			$800.00
Remaining Personal Contributions			$7,000.00

FIGURE 18.5   Budgeting classroom expenses with a spreadsheet.

Booking Classroom Guests

Despite the perception of isolation that four walls give to most classrooms, there are, in reality, often enough visitors moving in and out of classrooms to give teachers plenty of practice in the role of talent-booking agents. Guests may range from parent helpers to community experts, but the appearances of all visitors must be carefully choreographed to fit in seamlessly with the natural flow of classroom learning. Teachers and students can use word processors to compose initial letters inviting guests to come to the class. These letters might even be based on generic letter templates written to include all of the basic information about the class that a visitor might need to know. Scheduling visitors can be done with either a spreadsheet or a calendar program, making accurate work of keeping track of who can be expected each day of school. Consulting online schedules regularly will remind teachers of upcoming visits so that if any unexpected schedule changes occur, guests can be contacted and rescheduled in a timely manner. Guest contact information should be carefully recorded into a database, so that it can be quickly accessed. Finally, word processors and possibly even graphics programs can be utilized to write thank-you notes easily.

GENERATING

Teachers generate learning documents every day, no matter the subject or age of students taught. Even teachers who adhere closely to a packaged curricula have frequent cause to supplement commercial materials with those that are teacher-made. Working from what is known about individual and collective abilities of students, as well as on the pace and climate of learning, workpages, recording sheets, quizzes, tests, dictated stories, and an unlimited number of other materials need to be created. Many teachers have scribbled down a handwritten quiz at the last minute only to have students run into problems trying to read the handwriting; the variable widths of handwriting make for poor-quality copies. When students are faced with a handwritten page with which to work, they may not put forth their best effort because it does not appear as though a great effort was shown in the creation of the assignment itself. Word-processed documents are professional, neat, and customizable (see Figure 18.6). Topics that come up on the spur of the moment can be quickly added to an existing document, and an appropriate amount of space on the page can be left for students to write depending on the size handwriting with which students of that particular age are capable. Any special grading practices employed by a class can be accommodated by creating custom documents.

The web now offers teachers a great number of easy ways to generate fun, appropriate, and free activities to use with all ages of students. For example, Lightspan (<http://www.lightspan.com/teacher>) lets teachers make customized certificates with Award Maker and flashcards with Printable Flashcard Maker. Quia (<http://www.quia.com/>) has online game creation with a seemingly limitless selection that includes matching, flashcard, concentration, word search, pop-ups, jumbled words, hangman, and scavenger hunt games. Microsoft in Education (<http://www.microsoft.com/education/lesson/monthCert.asp>) offers the Certificate of the Month Club with printable certificates according to monthly and current events. As with anything on the web, these offerings tend to change frequently. Teachers can quickly locate other learning tools, already made and ready to use, with a web search.

Another strength of using technology in generating learning materials for the classroom is that it facilitates sharing of ideas among teachers. So often, a teacher who wants to use a page that another teacher has created is left to merely copying the document, making do with

Quiz

1. What was the main point our speaker was making
   today?

   _____

   _____

   _____

   _____

2. How will this message help you in your life?

   _____

   _____

   _____

   _____

   _____

3. How might you find out more about this topic?

   _____

   _____

   _____

   _____   **FIGURE 18.6   A teacher-made quiz
   generated using a word processor.**

   _____

any portions that do not directly pertain to the class, or attempting to cut and paste to customize it to fit a unique purpose. Word-processed documents are superior because they can be shared either on disk or through a network and can be easily modified to reflect class needs.

CONCLUSION

The few ideas presented here are only beginning thoughts of how technology can aid in the administrative duties of a teacher. Once teachers conquer initial fears that technology will only give them more work to do, they can start to understand how truly liberating technology tools can be (Sandholtz, Ringstaff, & Dwyer, 1997). Software is continually being improved, adding automatic features that perform functions that now must be done manually. Teachers should be aware of what software is available to them through their schools and must always be ready to consider new ways that technology can make their jobs easier and more organized.

SUMMARY

Along with their instructing responsibilities, teachers must serve as administrators of the day-to-day operations of their classrooms. Basic software tools can make it easy for teachers to create consistent, professional, and accurate products for communicating, planning, scheduling, and generating management tasks.

In addition to electronic communication like email, teachers still have many occasions when print-based communication is necessary. Word processing applications can be used to quickly send all kinds of letters, from newsletters to thank-you notes. Teachers can begin with a template form and can then save finished products for future use. Contact information on students' families and other community members with whom teachers and students need to communicate can be stored and organized in a database application.

CLASSROOM VIGNETTE

Margaret Anderson unlocked the door to the sixth-grade class in which she would be substitute teaching today. As a regular substitute teacher for the district, she had seen all types of teaching situations, and worked with all levels of preparation left by the classroom teacher. It was always a mystery as to how much information would be given to her when she walked into each new day of substituting.

Margaret could see that the day's plans, as usual, were left on the teacher's desk. Right away, she knew the outlook for a successful day was good. The plans were word-processed and very explicit. It appeared as though these were the regular teacher's plans, but they had been modified to include notes especially for someone not familiar with the regular class routine. For example, typed next to where the day's plan listed the day's starting time as 8:00 A.M. was "You will find students lined up outside next to the large tree."

Such helpful details were sprinkled throughout the plans:

- "Remember to send Jason to speech class at 10:35."
- "Pick up students from lunch at the west side of the cafeteria."
- "A guest speaker, Mrs. Hernandez, will be coming at 2:10 to speak about her job at the county courthouse. She is aware that you will be here, and she will bring everything she needs."

Margaret got the impression not only that this teacher was organized but also that she was smart. Keeping her lesson plans electronically made it easy to make changes. Rather than having to handwrite directions thorough enough for a stranger to keep the class moving throughout the day, she had had to modify her existing plans with only a few pertinent notes. It left Margaret feeling confident that she had enough information to make the day a good experience for both the students and herself.

Her impression of this teacher's ability to use technology to keep a well-managed classroom was furthered when the students entered the classroom. The first girl to walk in turned on the computer by the doorway and launched a database application. She found her name, signed herself in, and entered her lunch order. One by one these jostling, active sixth-graders made their way through the door and independently used the computer to take their own attendance and lunch count. All that was left for Margaret to do was glance at the list to make sure it was complete and send it to the office via email. It appeared that more teachers than just this one were using technology to their advantage to make this school run more smoothly and efficiently.

Planning for both short-term lessons and longer-term curriculum maps can be done by using a word processor or a spreadsheet. Regular, predictable activities can be automatically scheduled, and individual student schedules can be planned. Seating charts designed with a graphic program can keep the classroom layout functional and can serve to inform guest teachers.

Teachers have a need to schedule a number of different items, and a spreadsheet application is ideal for keeping accurate records. Money for special activities or trips must be counted and accounted for. Classroom guests and helpers must be booked into the set schedule and then planned around it.

Regardless of the topic being taught, there are frequently teacher-made materials, including practice pages and quizzes, that are required. Word processing programs and graphics applications allow for nearly spontaneous generation of all types of professional-looking print materials. Documents are easy to share among colleagues and to modify to fit individual needs.

LEARNER ACTIVITIES

1. Look for the templates that are included in the word processing software you generally use. What possibilities does the program present for the administrative tasks of teachers?

2. Locate a website that offers printable teaching tools, such as flashcards or games. Customize and print a learning tool that corresponds to a topic with which you have experience. How long does it take and how does the quality compare with something you could have created yourself without the tool?

3. Make a list of ways in which the students you plan to teach can participate in administrative duties of their classroom.

4. Open a database program and experiment with creating a student database of information. What types of categories might be required to keep complete records of your students?

5. Using a template or beginning with a blank page, design a weekly newsletter for your class. Include a catchy title, any necessary graphics, and all formatting to create a finished product. What types of information will you include on a regular basis? How much of the writing and compilation of the letter can realistically be done by your students?

6. Obtain a teacher's plan book after it has been used for several months. Study the types of activities that are written, as well as how much space is used and how many lessons appear to be moved around or otherwise altered after being planned. Based on this teacher's planning habits, how would you design a custom lesson-planning page using a software application?

7. Create a calendar for scheduling classroom guests and other long-term special activities. Brainstorm a list of all possible visitors to your classroom, including those who will help on a regular basis as well as the types of people who might come only once.

8. Use a graphics program to design a classroom floor plan. Visit a classroom at the level you will teach to see the type of furniture that is used and in what ways it can be organized. Plan for smooth traffic patterns and varying size group work areas.

9. Create a small contacts file with a database, and write a form letter to parents. Use the mail merge function of your word processor to create custom letters.

10. Download a trial version of concept-mapping software and use it to plan a content-based curriculum project.

BIBLIOGRAPHY

Office of Technology Assessment. (1995). *Teachers and technology: Making the connection.* OTA-CHR-616. Washington, DC: U.S. Government Printing Office.

Sandholtz, J. H., Ringstaff, C., & Dwyer, D. C. (1997). *Teaching with technology: Creating student-centered classrooms.* New York: Teachers College Press.

■ ■ ■ ■ ■

CHAPTER 19

THE PROFESSIONAL EDUCATOR

FOCUS QUESTIONS

1. How can teachers use technology to develop and maintain collegial relationships from a distance?
2. What information about funding opportunities is available online?
3. In what ways can technology assist teachers to remain lifelong learners?

The notorious image of the teachers' lounge brings to mind educators escaping for brief minutes between responsibilities to vent frustrations about students, parents, and administrators. In the old model of teacher communication, these stolen moments were often the only adult contact during otherwise isolated days within the four walls of the classroom. This isolation perpetuated stagnant teaching models, as teachers did not have consistent opportunities to share with and learn from each other.

Technology allows teachers to break that mold by giving them convenient access to remote resources, colleagues, and experts not previously as available. Teachers can access on the web everything from traditional resources, such as information on print-based journal subscriptions, to entirely electronic resources, such as listservs. And at the same time that this professional information is so widely available, a concerted effort is being made to develop and maintain teachers' professional skills. Ongoing training in both content and pedagogy is advocated by professional organizations, school districts, and society, as more than ever, teachers are being perceived as professionals who must be lifelong learners.

This chapter will introduce the broad categories of web-based professional information for teachers. It begins with a discussion of the resources and strategies for online collegial communication, followed by information about contacting national professional organizations. An overview is given of the types of online funding sources for the support of classroom projects, and the chapter concludes with online professional development sources.

COLLEGIAL COMMUNICATION

The most prominent professional education websites now offer virtual communication areas whereby teachers can discuss educational trends, share innovations in specialty fields, and get advice for challenging situations (see Table 19.1 for example sites). Teachers can post favorite lesson plans or air frustrations they have with students or colleagues. Some websites match teachers with partner classrooms for email collaborations, whereas others invite experts to participate through "guest appearances." "Host" teachers, representative of a particular content area or grade level, moderate some of these online conversations, whereas other dialogues are open for free discussion. Teachers can communicate about both traditional and technology-assisted activities, so those "tried-and-true" strategies that prior to the Internet lived only in the minds of our expert teachers can now be widely shared with others for the ultimate benefit of students.

Electronic discussion areas offer a convenient avenue for collegial sharing, allowing teachers access to colleagues any time of the day or night. A teacher might need to post an online query during his only planning break at 2:45 in the afternoon to see if there is anyone else experiencing the same behavior issue. Or another might want to log on late at night after a school board meeting to see if others are facing similar challenges with administrative relations. Some sites offer conversation threads for first-year teachers to seek advice from the more seasoned, as well as to commiserate with others at their own level during that frequently overwhelming initial year of teaching.

The power of these electronic conversations can be found at opposite ends of the spectrum. From the global perspective, the advice and viewpoints reflect teaching traditions around the country and even the world. No longer do teachers have only the individuals in their own school to rely on for advice. On the other hand, teachers are often surprised to find colleagues who actually live quite near to them, in their own state or even district. These local perspectives are insightful in sorting through new state standards or regional events. The ease and flexibility with which teachers can access these electronic forums match the professional needs of classroom teachers while catering to the unique nature of teaching.

PROFESSIONAL ASSOCIATIONS

Professional associations provide the glue that binds a whole range of diverse educators who share very important common interests, and the web provides the ideal communication medium to bring those educators together at any time from any location. With a by-the-people, for-the-people purpose, professional associations introduce like minds, from experts to novices, and prolific scholars to reluctant observers. Educators at all levels, from

TABLE 19.1   Online Teacher Collaboration Sites

After School Online <http://www.tappedin.org>
Classroom Connect's Connected Teacher <http://connectedteacher.classroom.com/home.asp>
"Conversations" at Discoveryschool.com <http://school.discovery.com/quizcenter/info/userguide.html>
Education World <http://www.education-world.com/boards/wwwthreads.pl>
Lightspan.com <http://www.lightspan.com/teacher/pages/communication/>
Microsoft Classroom Teacher Network <http://www.microsoft.com/education/mctn/default.asp>
Milken Educator Virtual Workspace <http://www.mevw.org>
Teachervision.com <http://www.teachervision.com/>

early childhood to secondary, from researcher to practitioner, join in the conversations. Teachers who work in relative isolation among their immediate peers, such as the one German teacher in the foreign-language department or the only reading specialist in the school, can find solace with colleagues with similar concerns in professional associations. Teachers negotiating the practical day-to-day activities can learn of theoretical advances and research connections that complement their individual endeavors, while at the same time helping researchers stay in touch with the reality of classrooms. Even if teachers cannot personally attend the national conferences sponsored by their professional associations, concerns and common interests shared online help them to experience virtually these face-to-face gatherings. New teachers are encouraged to participate in their professional associations from the beginning of their careers; the satisfaction from contributing to a growing body of professional knowledge sustains a career. See Table 19.2 for example professional association websites, and conduct a web search for new sites not listed.

EDUCATIONAL FUNDING OPPORTUNITIES

The financial hardships of school districts are well documented. Teachers are often motivated to spend their own money to provide the supplies they feel are necessary for their students' learning. Many teachers go through their entire teaching careers without recognizing that there are a great number of organizations, foundations, and agencies that aim to fund exceptional and innovative education programs. Thus, the web serves as a vital information source. Federal programs set aside funds to provide assistance on a broad national scale. Professional associations finance projects related to their missions and goals. Private foundations give to district and classroom projects in accordance with stated objectives and beliefs. In addition, both national and local corporate donors sponsor educational initiatives. Along with good teaching, good teachers must now also take an active role in seeking a share of these outside financial resources for their students.

Most money available for education is awarded in the form of competitive grants, and it is in this area that web-based information can be the most helpful. The writing of grant proposals is both a time- and resource-intensive process. Websites for granting orga-

TABLE 19.2   Professional Association Websites

American Association for the Advancement of Science (AAAS) <http://www.aaas.org/>
International Reading Association (IRA) <http://www.reading.org/>
International Society for Technology in Education (ISTE) <http://www.iste.org>
National Association for Bilingual Education (NABE) <http://www.nabe.org/>
National Council for Teachers of English (NCTE) <http://www.ncte.org/>
National Council of Social Studies (NCSS) <http://www.ncss.org/>
National Council of Teachers of Mathematics (NCTM) <http://www.nctm.org/>
National Council on Economic Education (NCEE) <http://www.ncee.org/>
National Endowment for the Humanities (NEH) <http://www.neh.gov>
National School Boards Association (NSBA) <http://www.nsba.org/>
National Science Teacher Association (NSTA) <http://www.nsta.org/>

nizations give proposal writers easy access to announcements of new grants, proposal guidelines, application forms, and information for new grantees. Table 19.3 lists a small selection of web-based fund-raising resources. Others are announced daily.

Recent web-based innovations offer new ways for educators to raise much-needed funds. One group of e-commerce websites designates a percentage of all sales to selected schools. (See, for example, FundingFactory.com at <http://www.fundingfactory.com> and Schoolcash.com at <http://schoolcash.com>). Another family of online resources facilitates the often bewildering purchasing process for school districts, including budgeting, managing bids, negotiating contracts, finalizing payments, and tracking shipping (e.g., Simplexis at <http://www.simplexis.com> or eschoolmall.com at <http://www.eschoolmall.com>). It seems that the public's interest in seeing education succeed matches its love affair with the web; expect such innovative corporate–educational alliances to continue.

PROFESSIONAL DEVELOPMENT

School districts make substantial ongoing commitments to develop and maintain their teachers' professional skills and inspire fresh and innovative teaching practice. Good professional development transcends the "one-shot" standard to include continuous practice, reflection, and classroom application based on individual goals and prior experience. The difficulty with providing effective professional development lies with individualizing training to meet the needs of teachers. Should beginners be exposed to advanced procedures? Should more experienced teachers be forced to sit through the basics? With traditional training methods, the answer to both questions is yes. However, web-based training offers teachers who are open to the unique online learning format up-to-date instructional options that can be customized to fit their needs.

A number of districts are experimenting with developing their own online workshops and training modules for their teachers and staff, on topics from content standards to cafeteria training. Some districts that have been early leaders in this professional development process have packaged their efforts for other districts to purchase. For-profit professional development sites provide a wider range of specialized instruction at a greater number of proficiency levels. The realization that educators need to continually improve their abilities makes even fee-based web training appealing. In addition to these commercial sites, most universities are offering courses, certificate programs, and even full advanced degrees online. Table 19.4 lists a sample of web-based professional development choices, although, as with all web resources, this selection will constantly change. A simple web search will turn up both local and distant colleges and universities with online offerings.

TABLE 19.3   Educational Fund-Raising Resources

The Foundation Center Grantmaker Information <http://fdncenter.org/grantmaker/index.html>
National Educational Association's Foundation for Educational Improvement <http://www.nfie.org/>
National Endowment for the Humanities <http://www.neh.gov>
Scholastic Awards and Grants <http://www.scholastic.com/aboutscholastic/programs/awards.htm>
U.S. Department of Education Grants Information <http://ocfo.ed.gov/grntinfo.htm >

TABLE 19.4   Online Professional Development Sites

Apple Learning Interchange <http://ali.apple.com>
Connected University from Classroom Connect <http://cu.classroom.com/info.asp>
Disney Learning Partnership <http://disney.go.com/disneylearning>
Skylight Professional Development <http://www.skylightedu.com/>
Teach.com <http://www.teach.com>
Teacher Universe <http://www.teacheruniverse.com>
T.H.E. Institute <http://www.thejournal.com/institute>

SUMMARY

Technology provides teachers with convenient access to remote professional resources, colleagues, and experts not readily accessible otherwise. Professional education websites offer virtual communication areas wherein teachers can discuss educational trends, share innovations, and get advice for challenging situations at any time of the day or night. The advice and viewpoints reflect teaching traditions around the world or around the state. Professional associations bring together diverse educators who share common interests, and most now have a web presence. As professional educators' responsibilities expand to include financial procurement duties, web-based information and tools for competitive grants for education can be invaluable. Finally, web-based training offers teachers up-to-date instructional options that fit their individual needs.

LEARNER ACTIVITIES

1. Inquire into the interest groups available in your district. If there is not a group that matches your interests, research the possibilities of starting a listserv for other teachers in the district with the same interests.

2. Scan the communication areas of at least two of the websites listed in this chapter. Which do you find easier to use?

3. Visit the website of a professional association in your content or interest area. Subscribe either for online access or for print publications, or see if your school has money available for a school subscription.

4. Obtain an online application and guidelines for a local or national grant for which a project you are involved with or want to develop would qualify.

5. Gather a team of colleagues who are interested in writing a grant proposal. Find an online tutorial on writing grant proposals, and work through it together, perhaps collaborating via email.

6. Investigate whether your district has any existing funding relationships with local corporations. Then, use company websites to learn about the company, its mission, and its corporate giving policies. Locate contact information and see if sources will consider funding a class project.

7. Compare the prospect of taking a course from a local university with an online course. How do the price, selection of courses, and overall quality seem to compare?

8. How does your district or a district in which you are interested in teaching offer professional development? Are there online training opportunities?

9. Explore the U.S. Department of Education website for funding opportunities. Bookmark the pages that show promise for future grants.

10. Use one of the websites listed in this chapter to find another class across the country that your students can be keypals with.

CHAPTER 20

SOCIAL, ETHICAL, LEGAL, AND HUMAN ISSUES

FOCUS QUESTIONS

1. What are the social issues of technology in society?
2. What are the ethical concerns of technology in education?
3. What are the policies for software use?
4. What are the equity issues of technology in education?
5. In what ways can education overcome the ethical, equity, and social concerns about technology in the schools?

We have only to look around to see the myriad of daily applications of computers in our lives. Computers are now so pervasive in our society that the question of how they can be used most wisely, efficiently, and ethically is no longer academic. Instead, it is a human issue that demands the attention of anyone interested in computer use. Although many of the purposes for which computers are used are extremely beneficial to the individual and to society, there is a wide range of misuse as well. For the past several decades, science fiction writers, philosophers, educators, and many others have been warning us about dramatic changes that computers will cause in our lives. What will these changes be? How will we adapt to such drastic reorganization of our routines?

Implementation of these changes and adaptations requires that we act responsibly with our new technologies. How do we, as pioneers and educators, encourage ethical behavior on the technological frontier? Current research offers more questions than answers. We must grapple with these issues now if we are to shape a productive and humane future. Computer fraud, invasion of individual privacy, and freedom of speech are issues impacting our lives. They are immediate concerns to be addressed. This chapter will examine the contemporary social and human issues of computer crimes, security, privacy, and the ethical, legal, and equity concerns in education.

COMPUTER FRAUD AND MISUSE

Hundreds of thousands of large mainframe computers are used in the United States. People involved with these systems number in the millions. Many others have access to mainframes through microcomputers. These figures add up to an alarming increase in the incidents of computer abuse, especially computer-related crime, a trend that will likely continue into the future. Let's look briefly at two examples of computer fraud before examining some ingenious thefts.

Theft of Money

A computer analyst at a Wall Street brokerage house programmed a computer to sell nonexistent securities through fictitious accounts. The analyst pocketed $832,000 before the fraud was discovered.

A computer security consultant defrauded a Los Angeles bank of $10.2 million by requesting a funds transfer to an account in a Soviet bank in Switzerland through a computerized system.

What is the cost of this type of theft? Estimates are billions of dollars annually, and this may be conservative. Computer crime is big business.

One ingenious case of computer-related theft involved a bank employee whose only computer training was operating a terminal. The employee selected accounts with large amounts of money and few transactions and used a computer to change the balance figures. Pocketing the difference, he then made sure that the computer quickly "corrected" the error. Using his position as a chief teller to receive advance notice of audits and inspections, he was able to prevent the bank and the customers from becoming suspicious. During a period of three years, he transferred $1.5 million, enabling him to spend up to $30,000 per day to support his gambling habit.

In another case, the perpetrator never even touched a computer, although he apparently understood the computer system. After being granted a 12-month installment loan, he noted the codes on the installment payment forms he received from the bank. Instead of including the top form with his first payment, he sent the bottom form. The bank's computer generated a form thanking him for paying off the loan so promptly. He did not literally steal the money and when the error was finally discovered, he was not prosecuted because he claimed that he had simply made a mistake by sending in the wrong form.

Other cases involve indirect interaction with the computer as well. Several crimes have been committed by using the magnetic or specially shaped character codes placed on checks and deposit slips. In one such case, a man opened an account in the usual fashion and deposited several thousand dollars. After receiving his personalized checks and deposit slips on which his account number was printed, he obtained the blank courtesy deposit slips that are left on the bank's counters. Then he had his magnetic ink code printed on these deposit slips and returned them to the counters in the bank. A number of depositors unwittingly used these fraudulently imprinted deposit slips, expecting the money to be credited to their own accounts. The computer read the fraudulent coding and the money was sent to the thief's account instead. The error was noticed when customers complained their checks were bouncing after they made deposits to their accounts. By this time, $250,000 had been diverted and $100,000 had disappeared.

Rounding is another technique for diverting funds from one account to another. Banks routinely round interest amounts up or down. Dishonest programmers can instruct the computer to place the rounded-down amounts into a separate account that they created for this purpose. If there are discrepancies, depositors often blame their own mathematical errors and do not complain to the bank.

Theft of Goods

Not only money but also goods are stolen via the computer. Often, goods are ordered in some way through the computer and are sent to a pickup point. For example, one case involved 217 railroad boxcars owned by a bankrupt railroad. Federal agents investigating the case found that a computer program had been altered to show that these cars had been sold to a fictitious company. This company would later "resell" or rent the cars, returning the profit to the owners of the bankrupt company.

Another story of computer-stolen goods began on a young man's way home from school. While rummaging through various trash cans owned by the telephone company, he acquired a library of operating manuals for telephone equipment. He also obtained discarded telephone equipment as well as the instructions for ordering new equipment. Through various ruses, he succeeded in getting the codes to access the ordering system. He then set up the telephone equipment in his home, in conjunction with an automatic remote dialer and his own terminal and began ordering new equipment for resale. This project increased to such a grandiose scale that he hired several employees and organized a company to sell the equipment to private suppliers and users before he was caught.

Private industry and individuals are not the only victims of computer-related crime. There are numerous cases on record involving theft of government goods. It is a relatively simple matter for dishonest personnel to adjust computerized supply records so that huge quantities of food, vehicles, parts, fuel, and clothing are delivered to the wrong hands for later resale. Items less tangible than money and goods are also stolen or tampered with.

Theft of Information

Stealing information from a computer and using a computer to market stolen information illegally are not uncommon practices. Many private companies and government agencies maintain computerized lists of their customers and clients. Once unauthorized personnel access these lists, the information can be sold to others for various uses. For example, a Department of Motor Vehicles employee was charged with adding more than a thousand names to a computerized list of approved applicants for driver's licenses. The employee then sold the licenses to unqualified drivers for a profit of more than $300,000.

Police personnel have been known to sell computerized lists of criminal records to be used as bribery or for blackmail. Tax calculation methods have been sold to those in high tax brackets that benefit from legally claiming deductions. Even health records have been sold. Some information has been held for ransom. The list goes on and on.

Theft of information is a serious concern to school personnel who store student records on computers. With access to a computer and the determination to break into confidential records, students have been known to alter the grades of their friends and enemies. Also, students or others can destroy data that are critical to school administrators. Even if the data can be recovered, school personnel must spend a great deal of time and money recreating lost records.

Theft of Time

The theft of computer time is another computer-related crime on the increase. In one case, a high school student who was an electronics enthusiast gained access to a company's computer system to play computer games. People who invade computer systems without authorization are called hackers, and their escapades are not always innocent. In another case, a man used secret passwords to gain access to the computer owned by his former employer. Over long-distance phone lines, he used the computer to direct the operation of machines owned by his present employer. The total commercial value of the time consumed was $15,000. Another case of time theft involved an illegal bookmaker who used a university computer to make his betting calculations.

We have seen how computers can be used to commit crimes against individuals, banks, industries, and government agencies. Computers can also be used to commit crimes against other computer companies. This includes getting access to new computer specifications, future product details, customer lists, and marketing information.

Because computers can be very expensive to buy, rent, operate, and maintain, some users share computers to reduce cost. However, once users gain access to a computer, they have the potential to raid the computer's memory. Some cases on record involve millions of dollars in business and information stolen in this manner.

Theft of Programs

Software piracy, another very serious problem, is the theft of computer programs. Software piracy occurs whenever a person purchases a computer program and then copies it for friends or resale. This type of theft is known as bootlegging software. This is a violation of state and federal law, and those engaged in the practice are criminals.

Software theft occurs on such a large scale that it costs an estimated $2.5 million each month—$1.0 million in actual losses and $1.5 million in lost sales opportunities. Because of the wear and tear on program storage devices (e.g., CD-ROMs and disks), most computer programs are written with the capability to make backup copies. It is easy to copy computer programs, and for that reason the victimless practice may appear harmless and practical.

Bootlegging has spread to Internet-based companies and individuals who maintain libraries of programs available over the Internet. Their computers distribute software over millions of networked computers. Anyone can download these programs for free. Although some distribution facilitators claim the contrary, their distribution programs facilitate copyright infringement. Organizations such as the Software and Information Industry Association (SIIA) are initiating criminal investigations and filing actions against Internet software pirates. FBI investigations of software pirates have skyrocketed in recent years.

Unfortunately, piracy also occurs in the classroom. Many teachers are caught in a bind: They have a class full of students who want to use the same software at the same time, but there's not enough software to go around (usually because of budget limitations). Given the ease with which software can be pirated, it is tempting to make unauthorized copies. Although the act of piracy takes only a few minutes, the ramifications are long-term. First, piracy sets a poor example for students, who are, after all, the computer users of the future. Second, it ultimately results in higher software prices because publishers must raise prices to compensate for losses through piracy. See <http://www.spa.org> for copying guidelines and other policies on software use.

COMPUTER SOFTWARE: COPYRIGHT ISSUES

Have you ever "borrowed" a computer program from a friend or coworker? Are copyrighted computer programs currently installed on your home or office computer? If so, do you know whether those programs were borrowed or installed with the permission of the copyright owner? Federal copyright law gives the copyright owner the exclusive right to determine who can install or borrow copyrighted computer software. If you or an authorized University representative purchased software from a reputable vendor, then that purchase probably included the purchase of a licensee for the purchaser of the software. Before you use, share, or distribute the software, you should understand the terms of the license. If the software was purchased "off the shelf" or prepackaged, then the packaging will include the license terms. This method of disclosing the license terms is sometimes referred to as "shrink wrap" licensing, because the language often provides that by opening the (shrink wrap) packaging, the purchaser agrees to be bound by the terms of the licensee. If the software was developed or customized for a particular purpose, an underlying written agreement may contain the terms of the license. If University employees developed the software in the course—of or as part of their employment—then the copyright in the software will belong to the Arizona Board of Regents. This means that no one can distribute the software or license or allow others to use it without the express, written authorization of someone authorized to contract on behalf of the board. Agreement to licensee software created by ASU employees should be reviewed by the Technology Collaboration and Licensing Office or the Office of General Counsel. If the University hired a consultant or independent contractor to develop the software, the agreement with the consultant or contractor should either assign ownership of the copyright in the resulting software to the University or should contain the license terms governing the use and distribution of the software. All agreements with third parties (including students) for the purchase, lease, creation, or adaptation of software or other copyrighted materials for use by the University should be reviewed by Purchasing and Business Services or the Office of General Council. License terms may restrict the individuals or sites that are authorized to use the software. The term of the use, the purpose of the use, and the ability to distribute and copy the software may also be limited by license terms. The license may describe penalties for violation of its terms. Unauthorized copying or distribution of software may also result in civil criminal liability under federal and state laws. The University and the individuals involved in the unauthorized copying may be liable even if the software was copied for an educational or a nonprofit use.

Software publishers have taken aggressive steps to protect against infringement of their copyrighted software. These steps may include an audit of University computers to search for software being used without authorization. The presence of unlicensed software may result in considerable liability for the University and for individuals involved in unauthorized copying. In other words, unless you are an authorized user, that "free" copy of a copyrighted software program may not be free at all.

Source: Arizona State University Office of General Counsel, 1997.

Software developers must divide the cost of writing, packaging, and marketing software among the many potential buyers of prepackaged software. Piracy results in fewer legitimate customers and, consequently, higher-priced software packages. Thus, software piracy affects all computer users.

Theft of Identity

Theft of identity is the fastest-growing white-collar crime. Using a variety of methods, criminals assume another person's identity. Victims' identities are assumed through stolen social security numbers, drivers' licenses, ATM cards, and credit cards. While impersonating their victims, criminals quickly spend as much money as possible before moving on to another stolen identity. Common means of accessing identity information result from employee data theft, benefits fraud, stolen credit cards, and computer hacking.

Thieves use computer databases and the Internet to access large amounts of personal data. They steal passwords, social security numbers, and banking information from websites and employer databases. With this information, identity thieves apply for loans and make purchases over the Internet. Sometimes thieves "spam" or send unsolicited email offers requesting identification data. Naïve email recipients provide the requested information, unaware of the fraud. Other thieves contact victims by representing themselves as Internet service providers (ISPs) or website employees. Identity thieves create websites with links to legitimate sites to acquire passwords and credit card numbers. Some websites display forms and run scripts that provide unscrupulous webmasters with any information a person is foolish enough to post on an online form. Other information is directly mined from website visitors' computers while they browse a site.

Increasingly, theft of identity cases are the result of employee theft. Workers with access to company data steal employee and customer information for unlawful purposes. Employees either use the stolen information themselves or sell it to others for fraudulent purposes. Today the social security and drivers' license numbers of others, as well as any public record, can be purchased or obtained over the Internet. They can also be readily obtained at neighborhood swap meets. Business credit reports, individual credit reports, criminal records, civil records, bankruptcies, license verifications, marriage licenses, divorce records, death records, driving records, property records, utility records, and social security number verifications can all be accessed online (see <http://www.infoseekers. com> and <http://www.fastbreakbail.com>). Consequently, the Internet is a valuable resource for identity thieves. Self-policing by the information broker industry has not restricted the sale of sensitive personal information to the general public.

Identity theft increased alarmingly in recent years, and with the explosive growth of the Internet, the trend will undoubtedly continue. The Financial Crimes Division of the United States Secret Service investigated 9,455 identity theft cases in 1997. Losses that year totaled $745,000,000. In addition, the Secret Service investigated 1,153 cases of Social Security fraud. Trans Union, a credit reporting bureau, estimated it received 522,922 inquiries from consumers in 1997, which was an increase from 35,235 inquiries in 1992. Trans Union estimated two thirds of the inquiries were related to identity theft (GAO, 1998). The federal government estimated 500,000 to 700,000 persons were victims of theft of identity in 2000. On average, victims of identity theft believe it took an average of 175 hours to remedy the theft of their identities. Average out-of-pocket expenses were $808 per victim (Benner, Givens, & Mierzwinski, 2000).

The IRS reported that in 1992 about $1.4 billion was lost due to identity theft, and the numbers are increasing. There were 2,270 identity schemes reported in 1999. The rise is attributed to the electronic filing of tax returns. The popularity of electronic tax return filing guarantees this fraud will continue. Victims are more likely to be online tax return filers, rather than those who file paper returns.

Identities are also being compromised to facilitate crime in general. The increase in online criminal behavior is directly related to identity theft. The spread of computer viruses is, in part, an attempted theft of identification data. In 2000, the Melissa Virus assumed control of users' accounts and gave intruders access to private data. At the same time, other computer hackers created viruses to seek out users' passwords, and they used the combined computers of others to overwhelm Internet traffic to businesses. Internet fraud is and will remain a major contributor to international crime.

To reduce these crimes, biometric manufacturers developed devices to ensure privacy, protect assets, confirm identity, and guard against unauthorized access. Biometric devices scan body parts such as fingerprints or retinas. The devices compare a "live" image with a stored digital template to verify identity. Biometric technologies and smart cards are replacing the antiquated method of using passwords or PIN numbers. A smart card is a plastic credit card type device with an embedded integrated circuit for storing information.

A smart card was used to sign into law the Electronic Signatures in Global and National Commerce Act (ESA) in 2000. Electronic signatures, or *e-signatures,* represent a new form of technology used to verify a party's identity so as to certify contracts that are agreed to over the Internet. Wills, eviction notices, late-fee penalties, and real estate transactions are excluded from the legislation. The new law defines an electronic signature as an electronic sound, symbol, or process attached to or logically associated with a contract or other record, and executed or adopted by a person with the intent to sign the record. In theory, these new forms of secure technologies should minimize the risks of stealing an identity.

Now let's look at crimes in which the computer itself is a victim. We examine some of the reasons behind these attacks and then explore some of the methods of abuse.

PHYSICAL ABUSE OF COMPUTERS

Recently, several books and articles have attempted to explain the motivation behind physical abuse of computers. Many attacks result from persons who view the computer as a destroyer of personal identity. Some people regard the computer as a detested symbol of corporate capitalism. Computer users commit other acts in moments of frustrated, irrational outbursts. Sometimes attacks are planned for political reasons.

Computer equipment can be damaged in many ways. Instruments used to damage computers include guns, pointed objects, fire, and magnets. In 1986, students at a high school in Sacramento, California, fired numerous shots into a computer used to notify parents of student absences. Radical and revolutionary groups have also used computer sabotage. During the war in Vietnam, a number of computers at American universities were targets of abuse, especially those thought to be connected with Defense Department research. Many examples have been cited. In 1970, in a bombing at the University of Wisconsin, one person was fatally injured; damage to the computer was estimated at more that $500,000. During the same year, a Molotov cocktail damaged a computer at Fresno State University in California, costing the school $1 million. In 1973, in Melbourne, Australia, antiwar demonstrators used a double-barreled shotgun to extensively damage a computer in the offices of an American computer manufacturer.

Demagnetization is another commonly used method of destroying data stored magnetically, as on magnetic tape and floppy and hard disks. By passing any magnetic material near the storage medium, the data will be erased. In 1970, an antiwar group attacked data-processing facilities, destroying equipment, punch cards, and magnetic tape. Several magnets were found in the rubble, and because some of the tapes had been erased by demagnetization, it is safe to assume that these magnets were used to destroy the data. Reconstructing the lost information cost more than $100,000.

Viruses also attack computers. Viruses are destructive programs that wreak havoc on computer data. Saboteur computer hackers bury virus programs within other harmless data. The delivery method evolves daily. No longer are viruses confined to executable files. Viruses can now invade all forms of media and data. Only through constant upgrades of antivirus programs can users be relatively safe from infection.

Computer viruses might not be immediately noticed. Some are designed to lie dormant until triggered by a sequence of keystrokes or a date. On November 1, 1988, a person entered a virus that was intended to live innocently and undetected in ARPANET, a U.S. Department of Defense computer network, the original "Internet." A design error in the virus caused it to replicate out of control. It jammed more than 6,000 computers nationwide, including computers at the Rand Corporation, SRI International, Lawrence Livermore Laboratories, the Massachusetts Institute of Technology, and military bases all over the United States. The virus spread by "mailing" itself to other computers under the auspices of a legitimate user. Because it continued to replicate, all infected computers slowed down and eventually shut down. Computer viruses are no laughing matter.

To combat viruses, antivirus programs detect and eradicate known viruses. To be effective, antivirus programs must be updated weekly. (See the Antivirus Research Center for more information at <http://www.symantec.com/avcenter/>.)

MAINTAINING SECURITY

There is a definite need for security of computer equipment and computer data. This is true for a computer system of any size, from a large mainframe system with extensive peripheral equipment to a computer on a student's desk. Whereas it is reasonable in large organizations to allow only authorized personnel to enter the computer room, in most schools such a security measure would be unrealistic. However, access to the administrative computer containing confidential records should be limited. Security measures in the computer lab and in individual classes should be necessarily broader.

Security measures are actions taken to prevent the fraudulent use or destruction of computer equipment. These measures include something a person has (a key or badge), something a person knows (a password), or something about a person (a fingerprint, a voiceprint, a facial feature).

Most large companies have security systems that one must pass through to gain access to the computer room. These systems may use special cards to insert or buttons to press on the outer door of the computer room.

However, according to many computer security experts, security needs to be even tighter. They advocate the use of many logical but frequently overlooked security measures.

One measure allows only the personnel necessary to perform certain functions to be in a certain place, for instance, in the computer room. Therefore, once programs are written and in place, computer programmers should not be allowed to go into the computer room and should never be allowed to run their programs. Another measure requires the investigation of staff and security clearances for those who work with confidential information. A third measure establishes a system for efficiently investigating suspected breaches of security.

No system is ever foolproof, but every effort should be made to ensure the security of both computer and data. Setting up controls helps to prevent unauthorized and fraudulent modification of data during processing. It also ensures the validity, integrity, and accuracy of applications and system software during design, programming, testing, and implementation.

Computer centers commonly use another popular measure—the password, which is usually a coded sequence. Passwords are frequently used to gain access to the computer via a computer terminal or a telephone hookup. Most users have limited access to perform specific functions. Other users require more flexible access. Authorization is granted to particular users at different levels, ranging from a specific group of items in the database to an entire data file, database, or program.

For example, student files set up for the teacher's use should not be accessible to students. Similarly, the teacher should not be able to access the personnel files available to the principal.

One effective security measure organizations can use to minimize the possibility of computer crime is to screen potential employees carefully during the hiring process. Many private detective agencies have investigators who specialize in this area.

Although the security risks covered here threaten large computer systems, microcomputers are also at risk. These systems are even more vulnerable because they are transportable and more easily hidden. For instance, data files and programs can be stolen by simply slipping a disk into a coat pocket or a briefcase. In addition, disks can be destroyed easily by magnets or fire.

An effective security system drastically reduces computer crime. But, as we have seen in the beginning of this chapter, it is not always easy to eliminate fraud. Computer crimes have been discovered in a number of ways, including accidental exposure, careful audits, inside informants, and unfortunate circumstances (unfortunate, that is, for the perpetrator). Detection of crime is one matter; reporting crime is often quite another.

Teaching and regulating ethics are extremely difficult. Once breaks in security are discovered, many organizations become very reluctant to admit to them. Consider what happens when a company reveals a fraud scheme involving its computer.

First, if customers see how easy it is to tap the company's records and accounts, the trust and integrity of the company might easily be undermined. Large amounts of business could be lost, costing the company more than the original theft. Second, the case would be reported in newspapers. The company executives would be embarrassed and seem foolish; they might even lose their jobs. Third, losses not covered by insurance would have to be made up from company profits, which would certainly displease stockholders and owners. Therefore, the reasons for keeping computer crimes secret are easy to understand. Fortunately, many industries, especially the banking industry, have federal controls that encourage reporting of such crimes.

Other factors cause businesses to hide computer crimes. Proving that someone has stolen materials or money using the computer is often difficult and, consequently, costly. It is sometimes cheaper to write off losses and then work to prevent such situations from occurring again. Indeed, it may even be cheaper to keep the crime a secret than to prosecute.

The problem associated with computer crime stems from the relative newness of handling large amounts of data by computer. In the past, data were handled in ways that provided physical evidence. Nowadays, experts must authenticate computer-generated physical evidence—printouts. Sometimes the originals must be located. The legal system is currently wrestling with this and other evidential issues.

INDIVIDUAL PRIVACY

Thus far, we have discussed crimes and abuses committed by individuals for their own personal gain. Some of these crimes affect us only indirectly, through increased prices and lowered standards of quality. However, another computer crime, related to identity theft, may have an impact on each and every one of us: invasion of privacy resulting from improper use of databases or data warehouses. A data warehouse is a collection of data from a variety of sources, which is analyzed for patterns and trends to support decisions. Although data warehouses provide a highly effective problem-solving environment for research (i.e., the Environmental Protection Agency's Envirofacts Warehouse at <http://www.epa.gov/enviro>), the potential for abuse exists.

Our digital identities are being stored in databases of companies we've never heard of. Private information is not just being captured online via the Internet; it's being collected in our offline world as well. Buying patterns are data mined from point-of-sale terminals via your supermarket club card. Advancements in biometric scanning technologies warrant a closer examination of our networked world of private information.

Until 1974, there was little concern about privacy with regard to databases. Few databases shared their information, because access was slow and inefficient. However, as technology advanced and databases evolved into data warehouses, so concern for individual privacy increased. In 1974, President Gerald Ford signed the Privacy Act into law. Its purpose was to protect confidentiality of files generated by the federal government. Its principles are paraphrased as follows:

- There must be no personal data record-keeping systems whose very existence is secret.
- There must be a way for individuals to find out what information about them is in a record and how it is used.
- There must be a way for individuals to prevent information about them obtained for one purpose from being used or made available for other purposes without their consent.
- There must be a way for individuals to correct or amend records of identifiable information about them.
- Organizations creating, maintaining, using, or disseminating records of identifiable personal data must assure the reliability of the data for their intended use and must take reasonable precautions to prevent misuse of the data.

Let's examine the privacy issue with regard to several situations. First, consider credit checks. Today, we are a nation of borrowers. In fact, we have become so dependent upon credit that business probably could not exist without it. Cars are bought on time payments, merchandise is charged to credit cards, and homes are mortgaged. All these items are bought on deferred payment plans requiring the establishment of credit.

Problems always arise whenever there is access to credit information. Questions range from who is authorized to access the information to how much information that person is entitled to know. In addition, the information available may or may not be accurate. For example, data might have been entered incorrectly, resulting in denial of credit purchases. Often, information is entered into a system but is never removed. A record of an arrest in a law enforcement database may be entered without indication of whether the person was acquitted of the charge. This same information may result in a university refusing an applicant admission. Another problem results from the unrestricted use of data. The large amounts of data available today often become accessible to more people than originally intended. The growth of government obviously increases the amount of data collected. In addition, data collected by one agency is often shared and used by other agencies for other purposes.

Tax forms are submitted to the Internal Revenue Service each year. The Census Bureau gathers information while law enforcement databases compile criminal records. Motor vehicle departments annually update data on registered car owners and licensed drivers, and voter registration lists abound. With this wide range of available information, these databases could be merged into data warehouses. These mergers could produce a detailed picture of an individual, threatening the individual's right to privacy. Many doctors and other professionals are reluctant to store client information in computer systems because of such a threat.

The shift to networked information environments challenges privacy in additional ways. Some popular email systems allow senders of bulk commercial email to track email recipients' web browsing behavior. Web browser cookies help companies match website visitors with their email addresses. When you receive an email message containing a graphic from a website, an email security loophole allows you to be assigned a unique serial number in a cookie, which is a text file stored in your hard drive and readable by other computers. This serial number or cookie is stealthily transmitted as you browse the web.

Technological advances are increasingly undermining privacy. Safeguarding our privacy is therefore a major issue requiring a thorough understanding of who is warehousing data, for what purpose, and how personal information is collected without our consent. The computer is invaluable in the management and distribution of information. However, it is up to those with access to this information to use it legally, wisely, and ethically. A strong need exists for improved oversight and stricter enforcement of current laws. To ensure that legal protections are not ignored, a public research center, the Electronic Privacy Information Center (EPIC), established a website at <http://www.epic.org> to disseminate information on emerging civil liberties issues including privacy and First Amendment concerns.

Privacy issues are increasingly a concern for educators as well. The handling of student information is protected under the Family Educational Rights and Privacy Act (FERPA) of 1974. This federal law provides parents and students with the right to see their school records and to request corrections to records believed to be inaccurate or misleading. Schools must have written consent from parents or eligible student (18 years or older) before releasing any information on a student. However, exceptions exist for certain entities, for instance, school employees or a contract agency conducting a study.

Referred to earlier in Chapter 5, the Children's Online Privacy Protection Act (COPPA) of 1998 protects the privacy of children using the Internet. Before collecting, using, or disclosing personal information from children under 13, websites or online services must obtain parental consent. Compliance with COPPA requires websites or online services to provide a prominent link to a notice disclosing how personal information is collected, used, and/or disclosed. Passive collection through techniques such as cookies must be disclosed. To find this information look for a link entitled Privacy Policy (see the bottom of Yahooligans! homepage <http://www.yahooligans.com/> for an example).

So far our discussion of computer crimes and threats to privacy illustrate some of the drastic changes computers are causing in our society. Another key set of issues, ethics and equity, impacts new responsibilities facing educators. The next two sections explore these concerns in education.

ETHICAL AND LEGAL CONCERNS IN EDUCATION

Educators share with parents and society the task of teaching ethical use of computers and the Internet. To help teachers develop a set of ethics applicable to computer and Internet use, schools create and implement an *Acceptable Use Policy (AUP)*. The AUP is a critical part of the school's technology plan and states the rules governing computer and Internet use and the consequences for violations. Parents and their children are held responsible to adhere to this policy. Many schools install filtering software to monitor and block access to questionable materials. The use of filtering software is itself controversial. Filtering software constitutes a prior restraint of the First Amendment's protection of freedom of speech. For example, forcing adult library patrons to use filtering software in public libraries is unconstitutional. (See <http://www.aclu.org/issues/cyber/hmcl.html> for a discussion of the issue.) Notwithstanding the filtering issues, students need to acquire technology skills, and we need to help students learn to act ethically and responsibly.

Teachers are role models. Therefore, there is no substitute for ethical teacher behavior and proper supervision of students. Teachers must set an example of ethical behavior whenever using or discussing computers. A lecture on the evils of software piracy becomes meaningless if the teacher practices piracy. Understanding current copyright issues and the term *educational fair use* are paramount to teachers' ethical behavior.

The federal agency charged with administering the law is the Copyright Office of the Library of Congress. (Visit its site at <http://lcweb.loc.gov/copyright/title17/> to review the law or <http://www.loc.gov/copyright/circs/circ1.html> to review the basics.) A copyright gives the creator the exclusive right to reproduce, distribute, perform, display, or license her or his work. When the original work is "fixed" in a "tangible medium of expression," copyright is automatic and notice is not necessary. For example, the email you write is copyrighted. Copyright protection lasts the lifetime of the creator plus 70 years; however, limited exceptions exist for types of "fair use."

Fair use is defined in Section 107 of the 1976 Copyright Act (see <http://www.loc.gov/copyright/title17/92chap1.html#107>). Use for criticism, comment, news reporting, teaching (including multiple copies for classroom use), scholarship, or research is not an infringement of copyright. To determine if a use is "fair" under the above law, the following factors must be considered but are not limited to:

- "The purpose and character of the use, including whether such use is of a commercial nature or is for nonprofit educational purposes;
- The nature of the copyrighted work;

- The amount and substantiality of the portion used in relation to the copyrighted work as a whole; and
- The effect of the use upon the potential market for or value of the copyrighted work."

In 1998 the Digital Millennium Copyright Act (DMCA) was signed into law. The DMCA's purpose is to update our copyright law for the digital age. The Association of Research Libraries' website <http://www.arl.org/info/frn/copy/copytoc.html> is a good source to acquire current and accurate information on copyright issues.

Teachers can spend class time discussing ethical issues with students. There are many role-playing models that cast students as software pirates, software publishers, and so on. One very important topic for discussion is plagiarism. Finding information on the Internet makes verbatim text very convenient to cut and paste into student papers. Even entire essays can be downloaded and passed off as original works. Entrepreneurs can acquire a repository of essays and research papers for resale. In less than a second after entering the search word *essays* into Yahooligans!, you can find a website listing more than thirty student essays. Giving students opportunities to role-play and discuss these issues helps them develop and clarify their own ethical codes.

EQUITY IN EDUCATION

Equity issues are a major concern of educators utilizing technology. Gender and equal availability of technology for everyone are the main issues. Research has documented that boys are more interested and involved with technology than are girls. Software generally tends to emphasize male-dominated activities. Games often include violence and competition as motivation. These software characteristics tend to attract males. Therefore, careful student software selection is essential for addressing gender in the classroom.

Student access to technology is dependent on the financial capabilities of a school or school district. Although student-to-computer ratios are steadily improving, many low socioeconomic schools have limited access to computers and the World Wide Web, especially classroom access. The Universal Service Fund for Schools and Libraries, referred to as the "E-Rate" was created in 1996 to provide discounts on the cost of telecommunication services and equipment to public and private schools and libraries. The E-Rate program has connected over a million classrooms to the Internet. Although Congress and state governments have taken steps to increase access through the E-Rate as well as other technology grant programs, the gap is still significant. A new type of poverty—information poverty—has emerged from this gap or *digital divide.*

Educators are concerned that this digital divide will create a form of technological elitism. In a technologically oriented economy, people with more computer experience will obtain higher salaries. On the other hand, those with little or no computer experience will be disadvantaged. The U.S. Department of Commerce (1999) documents the digital divide and reports a 25 to 30 percent increase in the gap since 1994. Educators have a responsibility to ensure that all students have sufficient access to computers and the Internet, regardless of gender, ethnicity, socioeconomic background, and disability.

Although the U.S. Department of Commerce (2000) documents slight increases in minority access to technology, people with disabilities are only half as likely (based on the national average) to have Internet access. Only 25 percent of the population without disabilities have never used a computer, while close to 60 percent of the population with disabilities have never used a computer. Only 20 percent of the people who are blind or vision-impaired have Internet access. When selecting computer hardware and software applications for classroom use, educators need to evaluate the hardware and software to determine their accessibility by students with disabilities. Techniques for ensuring accessibility to a website are documented by the Web Access Initiative of the World Wide Web Consortium (<http://www.w3.org/wai/>).

Vision-impaired students may use screen access software, which translates information on the screen into synthesized speech or Braille. If a site does not offer a text-only version, comprehension problems may occur when the screen access software reads the available text. For instance, when a graphic is a navigational element such as a button or arrow and the image label reads 009.gif or the button's text is labeled "click," the screen access software reads 009.gif or click. Vision-impaired students may not understand the decontextualized text and become disoriented. Even with assistive computer technology installed for students with disabilities, Internet research is not possible with inaccessible web-page design. The Center for Applied Special Technology (CAST) is a nonprofit organization dedicated to expanding educational opportunities for individuals with disabilities through the development and innovative uses of technology (see its website at <http://www.cast.org/index.cfm>). CAST developed a web-based program that identifies a website's accessibility problems and suggests solutions. The Equal Access to Software and Information (EASI) website at <http://www.rit.edu/~easi/> provides invaluable resources for teachers using technology as a tool toward inclusion and curriculum integration for students with disabilities.

Teachers must take advantage of technology so all students can be involved in more than drill-and-practice activities, often common in lower socioeconomic schools. Teachers need to be aware of web designs that do not take cultural connotations and disabilities into consideration. Access to technology is more importantly about the effective use and careful integration of technology into the curriculum than simply providing access or the acquisition of hardware and software.

How can we ensure adequate and equal access to technology? Two strategies are critical: funding and teacher professional development (Kuperstein & Gentile, 1998). Parent groups, fund-raising, industry partnerships, and careful budgeting in schools can help improve access to technology. Interest groups such as the National Coalition for Equity in Education (<http://www.math.ucsb.edu/NCEE/>) disseminate information. Similarly, the Digital Divide Network <http://www.digitaldividenetwork.org> is an online resource connecting communities with resources needed to address the current inequalities. Ongoing professional development and technical assistance support teachers' efforts to transform their practice. Teachers must strive to arrange equitable access and facilitate students' use of technology that addresses their individual needs, including their cultural identity, and promotes interaction with the global community.

SUMMARY

We have only begun to experience the radical changes that computers will make on society, as we know it. Computer scientists and sociologists differ in their estimates of our technological future: Some foresee a stark "1984"-type world; others, Toffler among them, predict a bright future in which humans, aided by advanced technology, function with greater freedom than ever before. Who is right remains to be seen, but this much is certain: Computers are bound to change our lives and our society in dramatic and irrevocable ways.

Computer fraud and abuse take many forms: theft of money, goods and identity; unlawful use of information stored in computers' memories; and unauthorized use of computer time. Sometimes computers themselves are victims of sabotage. Hackers enter computer systems without authorization. Software piracy, which is the theft of computer programs, can cause software prices to increase. (The software license is an incentive to discourage piracy.) The computer virus is another major concern of computer security. The entry of a virus can destroy or damage records and shut down computers. Generally, viruses are difficult to detect, but vaccines are available to overcome them.

Computer crimes are on the increase partly because of the increasing number of computers in society. Computers affect more and more lives every day in many ways. Some people feel intimidated by a machine with so much influence. Perhaps with the advent of microcomputers, more people will see that the computer is a beneficial tool that can be controlled. There are various methods of maintaining security in the computer room, primarily by limiting access to the room to authorized personnel. The password is the traditional method of controlling entry into a computer system and limiting access to records. Biometric technology is increasingly being used to maintain security. In addition, many organizations screen potential employees in the hiring process. However, computer crime is often difficult to detect. In many instances, the crime is not reported to law enforcement agencies for fear of losing customer confidence in the company and its services.

In addition to concerns for the security of organizations, there is concern for the rights of individuals. The Federal Privacy Act of 1974 was enacted to protect the confidentiality of files generated by federal government computers. Several state governments have passed laws to further protect the average citizen from illegal use of computer information.

Besides computer crime, the issue of change in the labor force is another major concern.

Teachers face new challenges in technology-based education. First, they must strive to provide equal access to computers for all students, regardless of gender, ethnicity, socioeconomic background, and disability. Second, they must promote computer ethics in their classrooms. They can do this by setting an example of ethical computer use and by using tools such as role playing and simulations to examine ethical questions. Educators and parents are concerned about student privacy and access to inappropriate sites. In addition, plagiarism concerns on student assignments utilizing the World Wide Web are becoming a major concern. Technology provides opportunities but also provides concerns to teachers and parents. All must work together to take advantage of this powerful tool!

LEARNER ACTIVITIES

1. List the major educational issues and concerns for the Internet and WWW.

2. Do the principles of fair information in this chapter seem reasonable?

3. List the major classroom ethical and equity issues.

4. List ethical and equity issues related to the Internet and WWW.

5. Discuss the gender-related differences in attitudes toward computers.

6. What are the dangers of technological elitism?

7. Describe recent cases of fraudulent uses of computers.

8. Discuss security measures necessary for a computer center.

9. Research violations of individual rights to privacy through unauthorized access to records.

10. Research the problem of training displaced industrial workers and suggest several methods of accomplishing such training.

11. Visit a local credit bureau and list the steps necessary for accessing your personal credit information.

12. List several recent cases of computer viruses and what was done to remove them.

13. Describe how the U.S. government maintains security on all records pertaining to individuals.

14. List all the local, state, and national government databases that contain data about you. Be as specific as possible.

15. Summarize the research on girls and attitudes toward computers.

16. Summarize the research on low-income technology access.

17. Review a popular educational software package and check for male-dominated roles in the software.

18. Review the methods of blocking pornographic websites for eliminating student access in schools.

19. What dangers do you foresee in new technology? Will new technology render life more impersonal or threaten our privacy?

20. Compare the privacy policy of Yahoo.com <http://www.yahoo.com> to the privacy notice of Amazon.com <http://www.amazon.com>. (Look at the bottom of the main page for the link to privacy information.) Take note of the "cookies" and personal information sections.

BIBLIOGRAPHY

Apple, M. W. (2000).The hidden costs of reforms. *Educational Policy, 14*(3), 429–436.

Atwater, M. (1998). Science literacy through the lens of critical feminist interpretive frameworks. *Journal of Research in Science Teaching, 35*(4), 375–377.

Au, K. H., & Raphael, T. E. (2000). Equity and literacy in the next millennium. *Reading Research Quarterly, 35*(1), 170–188.

Becker, G. H. (2000). Copyright in a digital age. *Electronic School, 187*(6), 26–31.

Benner, J., Givens, B., & Mierzwinski, E. (2000). *Nowhere to turn; Victims speakout on identity theft.* Sacramento, CA: CALPRIG's Consumer Program.

Brown, M. R. (2000). Access, instruction, and barriers technology issues facing students at risk. *Remedial and Special Education, 21*(3), 182–193.

Cruz, J. M. (2000). A closer look: Teaching SMART and beyond point and click. *Equity and Excellence in Education, 33*(1), 91–94.

Dietz, L. D. (1982). Computer security: Not just for mainframes. *Mini-Micro Systems, 15*(6), 251–256.

Eline, L. (1992). Safeguarding online systems. *Technical Training, 9*(2), 24–31.

Emmans, C. (2000). Internet Ethics. *TECHNOS, 9*(1), 34–36.

Engler, P. (1992). Equity issues and computers. In Gary Bitter (Ed.), *Macmillan encyclopedia of computers* (pp. 359–367). New York: Macmillan.

Fleming, P. M. (2000). Three decades of educational progress (and continuing barriers) for women and girls. *Equity and Excellence in Education, 33*(1), 74–80.

Gardiner, C. S. (2000). The search for bias-free educational software. *ENC Focus, 7*(4), 45–46.

Gordon, A. (1988). Viruses pose tricky threat to computers. *The Arizona Republic,* p. AA1.

Hannah, L. S., & Matus, C. B. (1984). A question of ethics. *The Computing Teacher, 12*(1): 11–14.

Keyboard bandits who steal your money. (1982, December 27–1983, January 3). *U.S. News and World Report, 92,* 68–69.

Koski, W. S., & Levin, H. M. (2000). Twenty-five years after Rodriguez: What have we learned? *Teachers College Record, 102*(3), 480–514.

Kuperstein, J., & Gentile, C. (1998). *The connected learning community technology roadmap.* Redmond, WA: Microsoft Corporation.

Lee, J. (1992). Hacking. In Gary Bitter (Ed.), *Macmillan encyclopedia of computers* (pp. 425–434). New York: Macmillan.

Legal bulletin. (1997). Tempe: Arizona State University Office of the General Council.

Lockheed, M. E., & Frant, S. B. (1983). Sex equity: Increasing girls' use of computers. *The Computing Teacher, 11*(8), 16–18.

Luft, J. A., Bragg, J., & Peters, C. (1999). Learning to teach in a diverse setting: A case study of a multicultural science education enthusiast. *Science Education, 83*(1), 100.

Markoff, J. (1988). Computer "virus" linked to "bored students." *The Arizona Republic, 99*(171), 1–2.

McAdoo, M. (1994). Equity: Has technology bridged the gap? *Electronic Learning, 13*(7), 24–34.

Nieto, S. (2000). Placing equity front and center. *Journal of Teacher Education, 51*(3), 180–188.

Parker, D. B. (1981). *Computer security management.* Reston, VA: Reston.

Perez, C. (2000). Equity in the standards-based elementary mathematics classroom. *ENC Focus, 7*(4), 28–31.

Perryess, C. S. (2000). Reality Check. *Educational Leadership, 57*(8), 78–80.

Puma, M. J., Chaplin, D. D., & Pape, A. D. (2000). *E-Rate and the digital divide: A preliminary analysis from the Integrated Studies of Educational Technology.* Washington, DC: The Urban Institute.

Revenaugh, M. (2000). Beyond the digital divide: Pathways to equity. *Technology and Learning, 20*(10), 38–50.

Robyler, M., Dozier-Henry, O., & Burnette, A. (1996). Technology and multicultural education: The "uneasy alliance." *Educational Technology, 35*(3), 5–12.

Roth-Vinson, C. (2000). Cybersisters jumpstart girls' interest in math, science, and technology. *ENC Focus, 7*(4), 23–27.

Toffler, A. (1981). *The third wave.* New York: Bantam Books.

U.S. General Accounting Office. (1998). *Identity fraud: Information on prevalence, cost, and internet impact is limited.* (GAO/GGD-98-100BR). Washington, DC: Author.

U.S. Department of Commerce. (1999). *Falling through the net: Defining the digital divide.* Washington, DC: National Telecommunications and Information Administration.

U.S. Department of Commerce. (2000). *Falling through the net: Toward a digital inclusion.* Washington, DC: National Telecommunications and Information Administration.

Weissglass, J. (1997). Deepening our dialogue about equity. *Educational Leadership, 54*(7), 78–81.

WEBSITES

10 Big Myths about copyright explained <http://www.templetons.com/brad/copymyths.html>

American with Disabilities Act (ADA) <http:www.usdoj.gov/crt/ada/adahom1.htm>

Antivirus Research Center <http://www.symantec.com/avcenter/>

Copyright and Multimedia Law for Webbuilders and Multimedia Authors <http://bailiwick.lib.uiowa.edu/webbuilder/copyright.html>

Equal Access to Software and Information <http://www.rit.edu/~easi/>

E-Rate and the Digital Divide: A preliminary analysis from the Integrated Studies of Educational Technology <http://www.ed.gov/offices/OUS/eval/erate_fr.pdf>

Fair Use Documents for multimedia and distance learning <http://www.libraries.psu.edu/mtss/fairuse/default.html>

Fair Use of Copyrighted Works <http://www.cetus.org/fairindex.html>

The International Publication on Computer Virus Prevention, Recognition, and Removal <http://www.virusbtn.com/>

ISTE guidelines and related information <http://www.iste.org>

Milken Family Foundation <http://www.mff.org/edtech/>

National Telecommunication and Information Administration <http://www.ntia.doc.gov/ntiahome/digitaldivide/>

SPA copying guidelines and related information <http://www.spa.org/>

Security Web Portal <http://www.alw.nih.gov/Security/security-www.html>

The Software and Information Association <http://www.siia.net>

Tool (Bobby) to analyze a URL's web accessibility <http://www.cast.org/bobby/>

Tools to detect plagiarism <http://www.plagiarism.org/>

University of Maryland University College—Center for Intellectual Property and Copyright in the Digital Environment <http://www.umuc.edu/distance/odell/cip>

U.S. Copyright Office <http://www.loc.gov/copyright/>

Web Accessibility Initiative (WAI) <http://www.w3.org/WAI/>

Web Content Accessibility Guidelines 1.0 <http://www.w3.org/TR/1999/WAI-WEBCONTENT-19990505/#themes>

Women in Technology <http://www.ability.org.uk/womentec.html>

ADDITIONAL READING

Business Week
Communications of the *ACM*
Computerworld
DC Week
eMediaweekly
Information Week
InfoWorld
Interactive
Network World
NewMedia
Newsweek
Time
U.S. News and World Report
U.S. Today
Wall Street Journal

SOFTWARE PUBLISHER CONTACT INFORMATION

ABC News Interactive
Order from Optical Data Corp.

A.D.A.M. Software
1600 RiverEdge Pkwy., Suite 800
Atlanta, GA 30328
770-980-0888
800-755-2326
Fax: 770-955-3088
<http://www.adam.com>

Adobe Systems, Inc.
Contact Douglas Stewart for reseller
referrals.
800-765-0062
Fax: 608-221-5217
<http://www.adobe.com>

Against All Odds
P.O. Box 1189
Sausalito, CA 94966
415-460-9801
<http://www.digiville.com>

**Aladdin Books/Children's Division
of Simon & Schuster**
1230 Avenue of the Americas
New York, NY 10020
800-223-2348
<http://www.simonsays.com>

Aladdin Systems, Inc.
45 Westridge Dr.
Watsonville, CA 95076
831-761-6200
Fax: 831-761-6206
<http://www.aladdinsys.com>

Alfred Publishing
Visit your local music store or check
its website.
818-891-5999
800-625-3733
Fax: 818-892-9239
<http://www.alfredpub.com>

Annenberg/CPB
401 9th St., NW
Washington, DC 20004
800-532-7637
Fax: 802-864-9846
<http://www.learner.org>

Anywhere Technology Distribution
17837 Rowland St.
City of Industry, CA 91748
888-383-7178
Fax: 415-647-6633
<http://www.anywaretechnology.
com>

Apple Computer, Inc.
1 Infinite Loop
Cupertino, CA 95014
408-996-1010
<http://www.apple.com>

Apple Education
408-987-3022
800-747-7483
Fax: 408-987-7105

Arch Publisher's Group
Order from Educorp.

Arizona State University
Attn: Gary Bitter
Technology Based Learning
and Research
Tempe, AZ 85287-0111
480-965-3322
Email: bitter@aus.edu

ARS NOVA Software
P.O. Box 637
Kirkland, WA 98083
425-889-0927
800-445-4866
Fax: 425-889-8699
<http://www.ars-nova.com>

Attica Cybernetics, Inc.
8936 Nestle Ave.
Northridge, CA 91325
818-882-9184
Fax: 818-882-9185

Aurbach & Assoc.
9378 Olive Street Rd.,
Suite 102
St. Louis, MO 63132-3222
314-432-7577
800-774-7239
Fax: 314-432-7072
<http://www.aurbach.com>

Autodesk, Inc.
Order from an authorized
distributor.
<http://www.autodesk.com>

BareBones
P.O. Box 1048
Bedford, MA 01730
781-687-0700
Fax: 781-687-0711
<http://www.barebones.com>

Big Top Productions
548 4th St.
San Francisco, CA 94107
415-978-5363
Fax: 415-978-5353
<http://www.bigtop.com>

BMG Interactive
Order from a national educational
software distributor.
<http://www.bmg.com>

Bogas Productions
751 Laurel St., Suite 213
San Carlos, CA 94070
415-592-5129
Fax: 415-592-5196

Borland Inprise Corporation
100 Enterprise Way
Scotts Valley, CA 95066
831-431-1000
800-331-0877
Fax: 831-431-4122
<http://www.borland.com>

Boxer Learning
105 West Main St.
Charlottesville, VA 22902
804-817-5900
800-736-2824
Fax: 804-817-5910
<http://www.boxerlearning.com>

Brooks/Cole Publishing
511 Forest Lodge Rd.
Pacific Grove, CA 93950
408-373-0728
800-354-9706
Fax: 408-375-6414
<http://www.brookscole.com>

Bytes of Learning
60 Renfrew Dr., Suite 210
Markham, ON L3K OE1
905-907-4646
800-465-6428
Fax: 905-475-8650
<http://www.bytesoflearning.com>

Bytes of Learning
150 Consumers Rd., Suite 203
Willowdale, ON M2J 1P9
Canada
416-495-9913
800-465-6428
Fax: 416-495-9548
<http://www.bytesoflearning.com>

Caere Corp.
100 Cooper Ct.
Los Gatos, CA 95030
408-395-4874
800-654-1187
Fax: 408-395-1994
<http://www.caere.com>

Calliope Media
Order from Sumeria Inc.
<http://www.calliope.com>

Cambrix Publishing
6269 Variel Ave., Suite B
Woodland Hills, CA 91367
818-992-8484
800-992-8781
Fax: 818-993-6201
<http://www.nowwhat.com>

Cascade International
Order from a national educational
  software distributor or through
  its website.
<http://www.cascade-int.com>

CE Software
P.O. Box 65580
West Des Moines, IA 50265
515-221-1801
800-523-7638
Fax: 515-221-2258
<http://www.cesoft.com>

Cendant Software
19840 Pioneer Ave.
Torrance, CA 90503
310-793-0600
800-556-6141
Fax: 310-793-0601
<http://www.education.com>

**Center for Image Processing
  in Education**
P.O. Box 13750
Tucson, AZ 85732-3750
520-322-0118
800-322-9884
Fax: 520-327-0175
<http://www.cipe.com>

Chancery Software
3001 Wayburne Dr., Suite 275
Burnaby, BC V5G 4W3
800-999-9931
Fax: 604-294-2225
<http://www.chancery.com>

Chancery Software
275-3001 Wayburne Dr.
Burnaby, BC V5G 4W1
Canada
604-294-1233
800-999-9931
Fax: 604-294-2225
<http://www.chancery.com>

Chariot Software Group
123 Camino De La Reina
San Diego, CA 92108
619-298-0202
800-242-7468
Fax: 619-491-0021
<http://www.chariot.com>

Coda Music Software
Order from a national educational
  software distributor.
<http://www.codamusic.com>

**Cognitive Technologies
  Corporation**
4884 Cloister Dr.
Rockville, MD 20852
301-581-9652
800-335-0781
<http://www.cogtech.com>

Corbis
Order from Forest Technologies.
<http://www.corbis.com>

**CORD Communications/
  CCI Publishing**
324 Kelly Dr.
Waco, TX 76710
254-776-1822
800-231-3015

Creative Multimedia
1869 NE 15th Ave.
Fort Lauderdale, FL 33305
877-823-5730
954-767-9610
Fax: 954-767-9626
<http://www.createmultimedia.
  com>

Creative Wonders
Order from The Learning Company.

**Critical Thinking Books
  and Software**
P.O. Box 448
Pacific Grove, CA 93950-0448
831-393-3288
800-458-4849
Fax: 831-393-3277
<http://www.criticalthinking.com>

Cultural Resources
30 Iroquois Rd.
Cranford, NJ 07016
908-709-1574
Fax: 908-709-1590

CyberPuppy
Download from the Internet.
<http://www.cyberpuppy.com>

Davidson & Associates
Order from Cendant Software.

Delorme Mapping
P.O. Box 298
Yarmouth, ME 04096
207-846-7000
800-511-2459
Fax: 800-575-2244
<http://www.delorme.com>

DeltaPoint
22 Lower Ragsdale
Monterey, CA 93940
408-648-4000
800-446-6955 and 800-367-4334
Fax: 408-648-4020
<http://www.sitetech.com>

DEMCO, Inc.
P.O. Box 14260
Madison, WI 53714
608-241-1201
800-448-8939
Fax: 800-828-0401
<http://www.demcomedia.com>

Deneba Software
1150 NW 72nd Ave.
Miami, FL 33126
305-596-5644
Fax: 305-273-9069
<http://www.deneba.com>

Design Science, Inc.
4028 Broadway
Long Beach, CA 90803
562-433-0685
800-827-0685
Fax: 562-433-6969
<http://www.mathtype.com>

Discis
Order from Harmony Interactive.

DK Multimedia
3817 Sharpsburg Dr.
Modesto, CA 95357-1562
209-529-0368
800-903-5040
Fax: 209-549-0464
<http://www.dkonline.com>

Don Johnston, Inc.
1000 N. Rand Rd., Bldg. 115
P.O. Box 639
Wauconda, IL 60084-0639
800-999-4660
Fax: 847-526-4177

Dragon Systems
320 Nevada St.
Newton, MA 02460
617-965-5200
800-825-5897
Fax: 617-965-2374
<http://www.naturalspeech.com>

Eastgate Systems
134 Main St.
Watertown, MA 02472
617-924-9044
800-562-1638

Fax: 617-924-9051
<http://www.eastgate.com>

Edmark
P.O. Box 97021
Redmond, WA 98073-9721
425-556-8400
800-691-2986
Fax: 425-556-8430
<http://www.edmark.com>

Educational Activities
P.O. Box 392
Freeport, NY 11520
800-645-3739
Fax: 516-623-9282
<http://www.edact.com>

Educorp
12 B West Main St.
Elmsford, NY 10523
914-347-2464
800-843-9497
Fax: 914-347-0217
<http://www.educorp.com>

Electronic Bookshelf
5276 S. County Rd., 700 West
Frankfort, IN 46041
765-324-2182
800-327-7323 (EBS-READ)
Fax: 765-324-2183
<http://www.ebsread.com>

**Emerging Technology
    Consultants, Inc.**
216 Heritage Ln.
St. Paul, MN 55712
651-639-3973
800-395-3973
Fax: 651-639-0110
<http://www.emergingtechnology.
    com>

Encyclopedia Britannica Ed. Corp.
310 S. Michigan Ave.
Chicago, IL 60604
312-347-6900
800-554-9862 and 800-668-1644
    (Canada)
Fax: 312-347-7903
<http://www.ebec.com>

Equilibrium
1101 Fifth Ave., Suite 200
San Rafael, CA 94901
415-453-4427
866-554-4445
Fax: 415-259-0726
<http://www.equilibrium.com>

Fairfield Language Technologies
165 South Main St.
Harrisonburg, VA 22801
540-432-6166
800-788-0822
Fax: 540-432-0953
<http://www.trstone.com>

Falcon Software, Inc.
One Hollis St.
Wellesley, MA 02482
781-235-1767
Fax: 781-235-7026
<http://www.falconsoftware.com>

FileMaker, Inc.
5201 Patrick Henry Dr.
Santa Clara, CA 95054-1171
408-987-7000
800-325-2747
Fax: 408-987-7563
<http://www.filemaker.com>

Follett Software Company
2233 West St.
River Grove, IL 60171-1895
708-583-2000
800-621-4345
Fax: 708-452-9347
<http://www.follett.com>

Forefront Group
Order from Forest Technologies.

Forest Technologies
765 Industrial Dr.
Cary, IL 60013
847-516-8280
800-544-3356
Fax: 847-516-8210
<http://www.foresttech.com>

Fractal Design
Order from Ray Dream, Inc.

FreeSoft Company
150 Hickory Dr.
Beaver Falls, PA 15010
412-846-2700
Fax: 412-847-4436

Gale Group
27500 Drake Rd.
Farmington Hills, MI 48331
800-877-4253
248-699-4253
Fax: 800-414-5043
<http://www.gale.com>

Gessler Q
10 East Church Ave.
Roanoke, VA 24011

540-456-5825
800-456-5825
Fax: 540-342-7172
<http://www.gessler.com>

Great Wave Software
5353 Scotts Valley Dr.
Scotts Valley, CA 95066
408-438-1990
800-423-1144
Fax: 408-438-7171
<http://www.greatwave.com>

Grolier Education
90 Sherman Turnpike
Danbury, CT 06816
203-797-3500
800-353-3140
Fax: 203-797-3197
<http://www.grolier.com>

Group Logic
4350 North Fairfax Dr., Suite 900
Arlington, VA 22203
703-528-1555
800-476-8781
Fax: 703-528-3296
<http://www.grouplogic.com>

H. W. Wilson & Co.
950 University Ave.
Bronx, NY 10452
718-588-8400
800-367-6770
Fax: 718-590-1617

Harmony Interactive
4936 Yonge St., Suite 702
North York, ON M2N 6S3
Canada
416-225-6771
Fax: 416-221-8631
<http://www.discis.com>

Harvard Associates Inc.
10 Holworthy St.
Cambridge, MA 02138
617-547-5646
800-774-5646
Fax: 617-492-4610
<http://www.harvassoc.com>

Hasbro Interactive
50 Dunham Rd.
Beverly, MA 01915-1844
508-921-3700
Fax: 508-921-3704
<http://www.hasbro.com>

Hi Tech Expressions
1800 NW 65th Ave.

Plantation, FL 33313
800-447-6543

Hi Tech of Santa Cruz
202 Pelton Ave.
Santa Cruz, CA 95060
800-336-2558
831-425-5654
Fax: 831-425-8041
<http://www.teachertools.com>

Houghton Mifflin Interactive
222 Berkeley St.
Boston, MA 02116
617-351-5000
800-733-2828
Fax: 800-733-2098
<http://www.hmco.com>

Humanities Software
Order from Sunburst Communications.

Humongous Entertainment
Order from Infogrames, Inc.
<http://www.humongous.com>

IBM K–12 Education
<http://www.solutions.ibm.com/k12/
    welcome.html>

Infogrames, Inc.
3855 Monte Villa Pkwy.
Bothell, WA 98021
425-486-9258
<http://www.humongous.com>

Insignia Solutions, Inc.
41300 Christy St.
Fremont, CA 94538
510-360-3700
800-848-7677
Fax: 510-360-3701
<http://www.insignia.com>

Inspiration Software, Inc.
7412 SW Beaverton Hillsdale Hwy.,
    Suite 102
Portland, OR 97225-2167
503-297-3004
800-877-4292
Fax: 503-297-4676
<http://www.inspiration.com>

Intellimation
P.O. Box 1922
Santa Barbara, CA 93116
805-968-2291
800-346-8355
Fax: 805-968-9899
<http://www.abc-clio.com>

International Thomson Publishing
5101 Madison Rd.
Cincinnati, OH 45227

513-527-6159 and 513-271-8811
Fax: 513-527-6951
<http://www.thomson.com>

Interplay Productions
16815 Von Karman Ave.
Irvine, CA 92606
949-553-6655
800-INTERPLAY
Fax: 949-252-2820
<http://www.interplay.com>

Intuit
2535 Garcia Ave.
Mountain View, CA 94043
650-944-6000
800-624-8742
Fax: 619-784-1070 and 888-241-0502
<http://www.intuit.com>

**Jostens Learning Corp./
    CompassLearning**
9920 Pacific Heights, Suite 500
San Diego, CA 92121
619-587-0087
800-247-1380 and 800-244-0575
Fax: 619-622-7873
<http://www.compasslearning.com>

Jump! Music
201 San Antonio Circle, Suite 172
Mountain View, CA 94040
415-917-7460
800-289-5867
Fax: 415-917-7475

Key Curriculum Press, Inc.
1150 65th St.
Emeryville, CA 94608
510-595-7000
800-995-6284
Fax: 800-541-2442 and 510-595-7040
<http://www.keypress.com>

Knowledge Adventure
Order from Cendant Software.

Laureate Learning Systems, Inc.
110 East Spring St.
Winooski, VT 05404-1837
802-655-4755
800-562-6801
Fax: 802-655-4757
<http://www.llsys.com>

Lawrence Productions
P.O. Box 458, 1800 S. 35th St.
Galesburg, MI 49053
616-665-7075
800-421-4157
Fax: 616-665-7060
<http://www.lpi.com>

LCSI
P.O. Box 162
Highgate Springs, VT 05460
514-331-7090
800-321-5646
Fax: 514-331-1380
<http://www.lcsi.ca>

LCSI
3300 Cote Vertu Rd., Suite 201
Montreal, QC H4R 2B7
Canada
514-331-7090
800-321-5646
Fax: 514-331-1380
<http://www.lcsi.ca>

Learn Technologies Interactive
361 Broadway, Suite 600
New York, NY 10013
212-334-2225
Fax: 212-334-1211
<http://www.learntech.com>

Learning Company, The
319-247-3325
800-395-0277
<http://www.learningco.com>

Learning in Motion
500 Seabright Ave., Suite 105
Santa Cruz, CA 95062-3481
831-457-5600
800-560-5670
Fax: 831-459-6876
<http://www.learn.motion.com>

Legacy Interactive, Inc.
6834 Hollywood Blvd., Suite 400
Los Angeles, CA 90028
323-463-0300
888-708-8715
Fax: 323-463-1300
<http://www.legacysoft.com>

LEGO DACTA
550 Taylor Rd.
Enfield, CT 06082
860-749-2291
800-527-8339
Fax: 860-763-2466

Little Planet Publishing, Inc.
5045 Hillsboro Rd.
Nashville, TN 37215-3745
615-386-0058
888-974-2248
Fax: 615-385-9496
<http://www.littleplanet.com>

LivingSoft, Inc.
P.O. Box 819

Susanville, CA 96130
530-257-1100
800-626-1262
Fax: 530-257-1111
<http://www.livingsoft.com>

Logos Research System, Inc.
715 SE Fidalgo Ave.
Oak Harbor, WA 98277
360-679-6575
800-875-6467
Fax: 360-675-8169
<http://www.logos.com>

Lotus Development Corporation
400 Riverpark Dr.
North Reading, MA 01864
800-465-6887
Fax: 617-693-3899
<http://www.lotus.com>

Macmillan/McGraw-Hill
195 Scott Swamp Rd.
Farmington, CT 06032
860-678-1212
Fax: 860-677-5405
<http://www.mmhschool.com>

Macromedia, Inc.
600 Townsend St.
San Francisco, CA 94103
800-457-1774
Fax: 415-626-0554
<http://www.macromedia.com>

Mark of the Unicorn
1280 Massachusetts Ave.
Cambridge, MA 02138
617-576-2760
Fax: 617-576-3609
<http://www.motu.com>

MathResource
5516 Spring Garden Rd., Suite 203
Halifax, NS B3J 1G6
Canada
902-429-1323
800-720-1323
Fax: 902-492-7101
<http://www.mathresources.com>

Mattel Interactive
6493 Kaiser Dr.
Fremont, CA 94555
510-792-2101
Fax: 510-713-6072

Maxis
2121 N. California Blvd. #600
Walnut Creek, CA 94596
510-933-5630
800-336-2947

Fax: 510-927-3581
<http://www.maxis.com>

McGraw-Hill
P.O. Box 182604
Columbus, OH 43292
877-833-5324
Fax: 614-759-3759
<http://www.mheducation.com>

MECC
Order from Mattel Interactive.
<http://www.mattelinteractive.com>

MediAlive
19160 Cozetti
Cupertino, CA 95014
408-863-4800
Fax: 408-863-4801
<http://www.cdtechnology.com>

Meridian Creative Group
1762 Norcross Rd.
Erie, PA 16510
814-824-6365
800-530-2355
Fax: 814-824-6377
<http://www.meridiancg.com>

MetaTools
Order from a national educational
    software distributor.
<http://www.metacreations.com>

Microsoft Corporation
Order from a national educational
    software distributor.
<http://www.microsoft.com>

Microspot Software
Order from a national educational
    software distributor.

Mindplay
160 W. Fort Lowell Rd.
Tucson, AZ 85705
520-888-1800
800-221-7911
Fax: 520-888-7904
<http://www.mindplay.com>

Mindscape
88 Roland Way
Novato, CA 94945
415-895-2000
Fax: 415-895-2102
<http://www.mindscape.com>

Miracle Software
64 Riverside Dr.
P.O. Box 296
Colton, NY 13625
801-681-0348

Fax: 315-262-2959
<http://www.miracleinc.com>

Misty City Software
3400 188th St., SW, #695
Lynnwood, WA 98037
425-820-2219
800-795-0049
Fax: 425-820-4298
<http://www.mistycity.com>

MSC Working Knowledge
66 Bovet Rd., Suite 200
San Mateo, CA 94402
650-574-7777
800-766-6615
Fax: 650-574-7541
<http://www.krev.com>

**National Geographic
    Educational Services**
P.O. Box 98018
Washington, DC 20090-8018
202-828-6605
800-368-2728
Fax: 301-921-1575

Netscape Communications
Download from website.
<http://www.netscape.com>

New Media
P.O. Box 390
Pound Ridge, NY 10576-0390
914-764-4104
800-672-6002
Fax: 914-764-0104

Newsbank
P.O. Box 219
Chester, VT 05143
800-243-7694
Fax: 802-875-2904
<http://www.newsbank.com>

Nordic Software
P.O. Box 6007
Lincoln, NE 68506
402-475-5300
800-306-6502
Fax: 402-488-2914
<http://www.nordicsoftware.com>

Optical Data Corp.
512 Means St. NW, Suite 100
Atlanta, GA 30318
800-524-2481
Fax: 844-221-4520
<http://www.opticaldata.com>

Optimum Resource, Inc.
18 Hunter Rd.
Hilton Head, SC 29926

803-689-8000
888-784-2592
Fax: 843-689-8008
<http://www.stickybear.com>

ORBIS Software
P.O. Box 73745
Puyallup, WA 98373
253-848-6899
Fax: 253-848-6505

Paramount
Order from a national educational
    software distributor.

PC Direct
800-426-7235
<http://www.pc.ibm.com>

Peter Norton Computing
Order from a national educational
    software distributor.

Physics Academic Software
Dept. of Physics
North Carolina State University
Raleigh, NC 27695-8202
919-515-2524
Fax: 919-515-2682

Pierian Spring Software
5200 SW Macadam Ave., Suite 570
Portland, OR 97201
503-222-2044
800-213-5054
Fax: 503-222-0771
<http://www.pierian.com>

Piranha Interactive Publishing
1839 West Drake, Suite B
Tempe, AZ 85283
602-491-0500
Fax: 602-491-8990
<http://www.piranhainteractive.com>

Qualcomm Incorporated
5775 Morehouse Dr.
San Diego, CA 92121
858-587-1121
Fax: 858-658-2100
<http://www.qualcomm.com>

Quark
307-772-7100
800-676-4575
Fax: 307-772-7123
<http://www.quark.com>

Queue
338 Commerce Dr.
Fairfield, CT 06432
203-335-0906

800-232-2224
Fax: 203-336-2481
<http://www.queueinc.com>

Quiltsoft
P.O. Box 19946
San Diego, CA 92159-0946
619-583-2970
Fax: 619-583-2682
<http://www.quiltsoft.com>

Rand McNally
P.O. Box 1906
Skokie, IL 60076-9714
800-678-7263
Fax: 800-934-3479

Ray Dream, Inc.
Contact Douglas Stewart for retailer
    referrals.
800-279-2795
Fax: 608-221-5217
<http://www.dstewart.com>

RES Software
Professional Plaza Suite 215
3155 Route 10
Denville, NJ 07834
973-328-8088
800-969-9673
Fax: 973-328-2893
<http://www.wowwords.com>

Roger Wagner Publishing
1050 Pioneer Way, Suite P
El Cajon, CA 92020
619-442-0522
800-497-3778
Fax: 619-442-0525
<http://www.hyperstudio.com>

Sanctuary Woods Multimedia, Inc.
Order from Theatrix Interactive.
<http://www.theatrix.com>

Scantron Quality Computers
20200 Nine Mile Rd.
P.O. Box 665
St. Clair Shores, MI 48080
810-774-7200
800-777-3642
Fax: 810-774-2698
<http://www.thelinq.net>

Scholastic New Media
P.O. Box 7502
Jefferson City, MO 65102
800-541-5513
Fax: 314-635-5881
<http://www.scholastic.com>

School Zone Publishing Co.
1819 Industrial Dr.
Grand Haven, Ml 49417
616-846-5030
800-253-0564
<http://www.schoolzone.com>

Sierra On-Line, Inc.
Order from Cendant Software.

Simon & Schuster
1230 Avenue of the Americas
New York, NY 10020
212-373-8500
800-223-2348
Fax: 212-373-8192
<http://www.simonsays.com>

SIRS, Inc.
P.O. Box 272348
Boca Raton, FL 33427-2348
561-994-0079
800-232-7477
Fax: 561-994-4704
<http://www.sirs.com>

SmartStuff Software
P.O. Box 82284
Portland, OR 97282
503-231-4300
800-671-3999
Fax: 503-231-4334
<http://www.smartstuff.com>

Softkey School
Order from Mattel Interactive.
<http://www.mattelinteractive.com>

Soleil Software, Inc.
3853 Grove Ct.
Palo Alto, CA 94303
650-494-0114
800-501-0110
Fax: 650-493-6416
<http://www.soleil.com>

Steck-Vaughn Company
P.O. Box 690789
Orlando, FL 32819-9998
800-531-5015
<http://www.steck-vaughn.com>

Strata
Order from a national educational
    software distributor.

Sumeria Inc.
100 Eucalyptus Dr.
San Francisco, CA 94132
415-586-3820
Fax: 415-586-3941

<http://www.sumeria.com>

Sunburst Communications
101 Castleton St.
Pleasantville, NY 10570
914-747-3310
800-321-7511
Fax: 914-747-4109
<http://www.sunburstonline.com>

SurfWatch Software, Inc.
175 South San Antonio Rd.
Los Altos, CA 94022
831-431-1300
800-368-3366
Fax: 831-431-1800
<http://www.surfwatch.com>

Symantec Corporation
800-441-7234
Fax: 541-984-8020
<http://www.symantec.com>

Tanager Software
1933 Davis St., Suite 208
San Leandro, CA 94577
510-430-0900
800-841-2020
Fax: 510-430-0917

Teacher Support Software
3542 NW 97th Blvd.
Gainesville, FL 32606
352-332-6404
800-228-2871
Fax: 352-332-6779
<http://www.tssoftware.com>

Tenth Planet
Order from Sunburst
    Communications.

Terrapin Software
Order from Harvard Associates Inc.
<http://www.harvassoc.com>

Texas Caviar
3933 Steck Ave., Suite B115
Austin, TX 78759
512-346-7887
800-648-1719
Fax: 512-346-1393

Texas Instruments
7800 Banner Dr.
Dallas, TX 75251
<http://www.ti.com>

Texas School for the Deaf
P.O. Box 3538
Austin, TX 78764-3538

<http://www.tsd.state.tx.us>

Theatrix Interactive
1250 45th St., Suite 350
Emeryville, CA 94608-2924
510-658-2800
800-795-8749
Fax: 510-658-2827
<http://www.theatrix.com>

Thynx
141 New Rd.
Parsippany, NJ 07054
201-808-2700
Fax: 408-655-6071

Tom Snyder Productions
80 Coolidge Hill Rd.
Watertown, MA 02472
617-926-6000
800-342-0236
Fax: 800-304-1254
<http://www.teachtsp.com>

True BASIC
P.O. Box 5428
West Lebanon, NH 03784-5428
802-296-2711
800-436-2111
Fax: 802-296-2715
<http://www.truebasic.com>

Turner Educational Services, Inc.
One CNN Center, Box 105366
Atlanta, GA 30348
404-827-3149
800-344-6219
Fax: 404-827-3954
<http://www.turner.com>

Turner Multimedia
105 Terry Dr., Suite 120
Newtown, PA 18940
800-344-6219 and 800-563-4422
    (Canada)
Fax: 215-579-8589
<http://learning.turner.com>

Ventura Educational Systems
P.O. Box 425
Grover Beach, CA 93483
805-473-7380
800-336-1022
Fax: 800-493-7380
<http://www.venturaes.com>

Vicarious Entertainment
3 Lagoon Dr., Suite 300
Redwood City, CA 94065
415-610-8300
800-465-6543

Fax: 415-610-8302
<http://www.vicarious.com>

Videodiscovery
800-548-3472
<http://www.videodiscovery.com>

Virgin Sound and Vision
122 South Robertson Blvd.
Los Angeles, CA 90048
310-246-4666
800-814-3530
Fax: 310-246-9999
<http://www.vsv.com>

Vividus Corp.
378 Cambridge Ave., Suite I
Palo Alto, CA 94306
415-321-2221
Fax: 415-321-2282

Voyager Company
Order from Learn Technologies
   Interactive.
<http://www.learntech.com>

VR Didatech
720 Olive Way, Suite 930

Seattle, WA 98101-3874

VR Didatech
4250 Dawson St., Suite 200
Burnaby, BC V5C 4B1
Canada
604-299-4435
800-665-0667
Fax: 604-299-2428

Waterloo Maple Inc.
57 Enlo St., W
Waterloo, ON N2L 6C2
Canada
519-747-2373
800-267-6583 (U.S. and Canada)
Fax: 519-747-5284
<http://www.maplesoft.com>

**White Pine Software, Inc./
   CUseeMe Networks**
542 Amherst St.
Nashua, NH 03063
603-886-9050
800-241-7463
Fax: 603-886-9051
<http://www.cuseeme.com>

William K. Bradford Publishing
16 Craig Rd.
Acton, MA 01720
508-263-6996
800-421-2009
Fax: 508-263-9375

Wolfram Research, Inc.
100 Trade Center Dr.
Champaign, IL 61820-7237
217-398-0700
800-965-3726
Fax: 217-398-0747
<http://www.wolfram.com>

World Book Educational Products
Order from Edmark or PC Direct.
<http://www.worldbook.com>

World Game Institute
3215 Race St.
Philadelphia, PA 19104-2597
215-387-0220
Fax: 215-387-3009
<http://www.worldgame.org>

INDEX

CREDITS

19, 102 (left), courtesy of Wolfram Research; 20, 21, courtesy of New York Public Library; 25 (top left), courtesy of Texas Instruments; 25 (left), courtesy of Hewlett-Packard; 26, courtesy of Apple Computer, Inc.; 27, courtesy of Cray Research, a Silicon Graphics Company; 29, 37, 92 (top left), courtesy of Sharp Electronics; 29, courtesy of Compaq; 31, courtesy of Interlink Electronics; 31, courtesy of FastPoint Technologies; 32, courtesy of IBM; 35 (top left, bottom left, middle right), courtesy of Panasonic; 35 (bottom right), 36 (bottom right), 93 (bottom), 270 (left), courtesy of Samsung Electronics America, Inc.; 35 (top right), courtesy of LG Electronics; 36, courtesy of Plustek; 36 (bottom left), courtesy of SMILE International, Inc.; 38 (left), courtesy of Fargo Electronics, Inc.; 38 (right), courtesy of Mita; 41 (top), courtesy of FTG Data Systems; 41 (bottom left), courtesy of TDK Systems; 41 (bottom right), 91, 99 (bottom right), courtesy of Mitsubishi; 63 (top), 75, 76, 77, 80, 186, 188, Netscape Communicator browser window © 1999 Netscape Communications Corporation. Used with permission. Netscape Communications has not authorized, sponsored, endorsed, or approved this publication and is not responsible for its content; 63 (bottom), 269 (top), 271 (bottom), 273 (bottom), 288, screen shot reprinted by permission from Microsoft Corporation.; 66, courtesy of Liszt; 80, Digital, Alta Vista, and the Alta Vista logo are trademarks or service marks of Digital Equipment Corporation. Used with permission.; 82 (top), courtesy of WS-FTP; 82 (bottom), courtesy of Fetch; 90, 99 (top), 102 (right), courtesy of Philips; 92 (top right), courtesy of Franklin Electronic Publishers; 92 (middle left), courtesy of Geofax, Inc.; 92 (middle right), 270 (right), courtesy of Casio, Inc.; 92 (bottom), courtesy of Brother; 93 (top left), courtesy of Texas Microsystems, Inc.; 93 (top right), courtesy of Minstrel; 94, courtesy of NTT Soft; 95, courtesy of Virtual i-O, Inc.; 97, courtesy of Pctel; 99 (bottom left), 269 (bottom), courtesy of Vivitar; 100, courtesy of Bausch and Lomb; 101 (top), courtesy of Wizzard Software; 101 (bottom), courtesy of Hunter Digital; 133, SuperKids Education Software Review, http://www.superkids.com; 149, courtesy of Davidson & Associates; 150, 153, courtesy of Tom Snyder Productions; 152, courtesy of DK Multimedia; 156, image courtesy of CLEARVUE/eav, Inc. © 1999 CLEARVUE/eav, Inc. and Zane Publishing, Inc.; 165, © 2001 Education World, Inc.; 169, Volcano World—University of North Dakota; 168, courtesy The Franklin Institute; 170, courtesy of Capitol Advantage, McLean, VA; 171 (top), xpeditions@nationalgeographic.com; 171 (bottom), ArtsEdge: The National Arts & Education Information Network; 173 (top), http://www.goals.com/; 173 (bottom), AskERIC Homepage; 174 (bottom), The Kidlink Network; 222 (top), courtesy of Digital Vision, Inc.; 259, courtesy of Curtis Computer Products; 273 (top), Hyperstudio ® is a registered trademark of Roger Wagner Publishing, Inc. This Hyperstudio screen image is used with permission of Roger Wagner Publishing, Inc.; 285, courtesy of FunBrain.com, part of Learning Network; 287, used by permission, Jay Klein Productions, Inc.; 300, © 1992–2000 ISD Software Design http://www.isdsoftwaredesign.com.